FREEDOM AND INDIGENOUS CONSTITUTIONALISM

Indigenous traditions can be uplifting, positive, and liberating forces when they are connected to living systems of thought and practice. Problems arise when they are treated as timeless models of unchanging truth that require unwavering deference and unquestioning obedience. *Freedom and Indigenous Constitutionalism* celebrates the emancipatory potential of Indigenous traditions, considers their value as the basis for good laws and good lives, and critiques the failure of Canadian constitutional traditions to recognize their significance.

Demonstrating how Canada's constitutional structures marginalize Indigenous peoples' ability to exercise power in the real world, John Borrows uses Ojibwe law, stories, and principles to suggest alternative ways in which Indigenous peoples can work to enhance freedom. Among the stimulating issues he approaches are the democratic potential of civil disobedience, the hazards of applying originalism rather than living-tree jurisprudence in the interpretation of Aboriginal and treaty rights, American legislative actions that could also animate Indigenous self-determination in Canada, and the opportunity for Indigenous governmental action to address violence against women.

JOHN BORROWS is the Canada Research Chair in Indigenous Law in the Faculty of Law at the University of Victoria and is the winner of both the Canadian Political Science Association's Donald Smiley Prize (for *Recovering Canada*) and the Canadian Law and Society Association Book Prize (for *Canada's Indigenous Constitution*).

Freedom and Indigenous Constitutionalism

JOHN BORROWS

UNIVERSITY OF TORONTO PRESS
Toronto Buffalo London

© University of Toronto Press 2016
Toronto Buffalo London
www.utppublishing.com
Printed in Canada

ISBN 978-1-4426-3093-2 (cloth)   ISBN 978-1-4426-2923-3 (paper)

♾ Printed on acid-free, 100% post-consumer recycled paper
with vegetable-based inks.

Library and Archives Canada Cataloguing in Publication

Borrows, John, 1963–, author
Freedom and indigenous constitutionalism / John Borrows.

Includes bibliographical references and index.
ISBN 978-1-4426-3093-2 (cloth). – ISBN 978-1-4426-2923-3 (paper)

1. Native peoples – Legal status, laws, etc. – Canada.   2. Native peoples –
Canada – Politics and government.   3. Native peoples – Civil rights –
Canada.   4. Ojibwa law.   I. Title.

KE7709.B6738 2016   342.7108'72   C2016-900084-2
KF8205.B6738 2016

University of Toronto Press acknowledges the financial assistance to its
publishing program of the Canada Council for the Arts and the Ontario Arts
Council, an agency of the Government of Ontario.

Canada Council   Conseil des Arts
for the Arts   du Canada

ONTARIO ARTS COUNCIL
CONSEIL DES ARTS DE L'ONTARIO
an Ontario government agency
un organisme du gouvernement de l'Ontario

Funded by the   Financé par le
Government   gouvernement
of Canada   du Canada

Contents

Miigwech

This book was crafted in stages. The first phase was written in response to invitations for contributions to the literature, and these texts were published through edited academic collections and government inquiries.[1] The next phase of writing occurred as I began teaching as a law professor at the University of Minnesota.[2] These works were also published as separate pieces. During each phase, I planned many trips home to speak with my family and friends. At these times, I read large portions of this manuscript to my mother, father, sister, and daughter. My purpose was to seek a synthesis of these various ideas. While encouraging me, they also identified major weaknesses in my arguments.

The next stages of my preparation took me to a remote cabin at Neyaashiinigmiing, on the Cape Croker Indian Reserve in Southern Ontario. The cabin in which I worked was solar powered. I was 'off the grid.' There was no phone, Internet, or television. These distractions were a world away. In the peace of that setting I rewrote, amended, and substantially added to my earlier materials while weaving an overall thematic structure through them. It was a productive time. Outside my door, the snow melted in the deep bush. Small rivers soon flowed across the land. When the thaw abated, it wasn't long before three-flower trilliums blanketed the forest floor. In turn, the air quickly filled with music. Birds returned from their southern journeys, and insects emerged from their sleep. Skunks, raccoons, and porcupines wandered past my door, peering through the screens, curious about their visitor. Chipmunks chastised me for my presence. Bears awoke from their long hibernation, making their appearance along the shore. It was an inspiring time. Through the sun's power and my cabin's solar panels my computer kept working, and so did I.

When I returned from the reserve, I put the book aside. I wanted to see if it would pass a small test of time. I taught at Victoria, Minnesota, and Princeton and gave speeches on parts of the book at Dalhousie, Concordia, Osgoode Hall Law School, Simon Fraser University, and the Universities of Toronto, Manitoba, Chicago-Kent, Calgary, British Columbia, Ottawa, and Western Ontario. I am grateful for the comments I received in these venues. They revealed further gaps in my thinking, which I have tried to address in this version of my work.

Over ten years have passed since this project began. While the errors are all mine, I have many people to thank for their help in this book's preparation, including Hannah Askew, Ben Berger, Jean Borrows, Jennifer Borrows, Joseph Borrows, Lindsay Borrows, Gillian Calder, Jamie Cameron, Brenda Child, Gordon Christie, Hamar Foster, Hadley Friedland, Robert Gibbs, Shin Imai, Darlene Johnston, Rebecca Johnston, Sonia Lawrence, Johnny Mack, Patrick Macklem, Kent McNeil, J.R. Miller, Aaron Mills, Val Napoleon, Kent Roach, Douglas Sanderson, Kerry Sloan, Emily Snyder, Richard Spearman, Heidi Stark, James Tully, Mark Walters, and David Wilkins. I have also greatly benefited from supportive colleagues at the Law Schools of the University of Victoria and University of Minnesota. Dean Andrew Petter, Dean Donna Greschner, Dean Jeremy Webber, and Dean David Wippman all encouraged me as a writer, and ensured that I had sufficient support to complete this book. Lastly, I thank my wife, Kim, for her unfailing encouragement and support. She lives the themes discussed in this book: freedom, goodness, mobility, civility, acceptance, and constructive critique. She is my best friend, and this work would not be possible without her.

FREEDOM AND INDIGENOUS CONSTITUTIONALISM

Introduction

In my view, there is no timeless trait, characteristic, custom, or idea that is categorically fundamental to being Indigenous. The categories of Mi'kmaq, Abenaki, Cree, Haudenosaunee, Anishinaabe, Assiniboine, Dakota, Secwepmec, Salish, Nuu-Chah-Nuulth, Gitksan, Tlingit, Haida, Dene, Metis, Inuit, etc., are all context-dependent classifications. They are political, social, legal, linguistic, and/or cultural facts that are fluid and subject to change through time.[1] Indigeneity does not *necessarily* reside in any particular blood, language, land, culture, clan, family grouping, spiritual practice, economic activity, story, teaching, song, relationship, etc. – though these criteria are very important components of belonging in particular contexts. It is misleading to claim that Indigenous societies possess an unalterable central essence or core. This is what I label false tradition. While each category looks and feels relatively stable from the inside, if measured by short-term (centuries-long) metrics, changes in society, which may be gradual, can produce dramatic shifts over the longer term. This book considers conceptions of tradition rooted in fundamentalist views about the immutable nature of Indigenous people and their societies. False notions of traditions can be held by anyone. While national governments, courts, and the media often characterize Indigenous peoples by reference to conceptual cores and integral characteristics, Indigenous peoples can also fall into this trap. The challenges such views present to freedom and a good life, especially as they are deployed in the law, is a major focus of this work.

This book does not deny the profound importance of traditions; it merely attempts to distinguish those which inhibit Indigenous peoples' freedom from those which can be emancipatory. In fact, this book argues that traditions can be uplifting, positive, and liberating forces within communities if they are connected to living and applied systems of thought and practice. They can provide deep meaning for many people. Their reproduction and transmission can present powerful justifications and alternatives for resisting domination and structuring good lives. They offer resources and repertoire for constructive confrontation and engagement. Traditions can provide important context for taking action. They can embody time-tested wisdom drawn from past experience, which can be extremely valuable in making contemporary decisions. Furthermore, the contrast that traditions provide can highlight the broad range of choices Indigenous peoples possess when they interact with others. Thus, traditions can be a valuable source of inspiration, guidance, and encouragement if they are seen as resources for thought and action. They can make life worth living. However, problems arise when traditions are treated as timeless models of unchanging truths that require unwavering deference and unquestioning obedience. This book seeks to celebrate and cultivate the emancipatory potential of Indigenous traditions, even as I am critical of how they can be falsely conceptualized and used in many contexts, both Indigenous and non-Indigenous.

One powerful source of false tradition scrutinized throughout this book is found within Canadian constitutionalism. While Canada's constitutional traditions exhibit many of the strengths identified above, they can be problematically rooted in abstract reasoning disconnected from social, political, and other real-life experience. This book demonstrates that Canada's constitutional traditions are particularly specious when Aboriginal and treaty rights are at issue. They simultaneously universalize and marginalize Indigenous peoples' ability to exercise power in the real world. This book analyses and deconstructs how, based on these false constitutional traditions, power is unjustly distributed in Canada. It challenges categorical rationalizations that destroy Indigenous peoples' territorial and bodily freedoms. The application of conceptual hypotheses that are essentialized without regard to context is a widespread challenge in political life. Thus, this book's discussion of law, freedom, and a good life has significant implications for Canada's constitutional traditions more generally, even as Indigenous traditions are also focus of this work.

Alongside constitutional law, the traditions most frequently cited in this book emanate from the Anishinaabe nation. I am a citizen of the Chippewas of the Nawash First Nation at Neyaashiinigmiing on the Saugeen Peninsula shores of Georgian Bay in Southern Ontario, and thus am most familiar with this group. Anishinaabe or Ojibwe people are the fourth-largest Native American group in the United States, after the Navajo, Cherokee, and Lakota Nations.[2] They are the second-largest Indigenous group in Canada, after the Cree.[3] Anishinaabe people live within the Great Lakes watershed,[4] and they surround large parts of Lakes Superior, Huron, and Michigan. They also occupy the farmlands and woodlands north of Lake Ontario and Lake Erie and have reservations in the forests and prairies of northern Minnesota and North Dakota, Wisconsin, Michigan, Ontario, Manitoba, and Saskatchewan.[5] Historically, the Anishinaabe were organized as clans in a loose confederacy more recently called the Council of the Three Fires.[6] Many still live in mixed 'Three Fires' communities in their ancient homelands, while others have spread throughout the continent and live in cities, towns, and villages throughout the United States and Canada.[7] Anishinaabe traditions, like all others in the world, are capable of diminishing or enhancing peoples' freedom to live a good life. It all depends on how we envision and apply them.[8]

While some approaches to Anishinaabe tradition are problematic, Anishinaabe people have many rich traditions which facilitate freedom by encouraging people to live a good life.[9] I was reminded of the importance of these traditions during a recent visit back home. Each season, I travel back to the Cape Croker Indian Reserve (Neyaashiinigmiing). I visit with family and catch up with friends in many settings – in living rooms, on roadsides and shorelines, and at funerals, feasts, and other informal gatherings. We talk about the weather, work, politics, sports, and our extended families – the stuff of everyday life. Sometimes the conversations are more serious and deep, but most are quite unremarkable. Of course, they are coloured by cultural traits that make them somewhat distinctive. They are inflected by Anishinaabemowin words and syntax. We have our own turns of phrases and a distinctive humour. Like most people, we have our 'in-jokes' and code words that would be disorienting or confusing to others.[10] However, most exchanges are common and ordinary and would be intelligible to most Canadians.

For example, teasing is an important part of life in many communities, and Indian reserves are no exception.[11] Teasing helps us explore the bounds of appropriate behaviour, and it is alive and well at Cape Croker. During a recent powwow back home, I felt its gentle sting. As I visited with some former students, they asked where I was currently teaching. When they found out I had moved cities many times since they had graduated, they wondered aloud if I had trouble holding a job. They speculated about the laws I had broken and my possible secret vices. These barbs were pointed but offered in good-natured fun. As I was receiving some well-deserved torment, the conversation quickly shifted when an Elder joined our group. Dr. Basil Johnston, an author and family friend, quietly smiled as he listened to our verbal volleys. After a few moments, our attention swung to him. He briefly acknowledged my frequent moves and then said something like, 'Don't worry about it, John. We are born to be free. That is who we are as a people – free to come and go as we please. That is how the old people lived. That's a good way to live today.'[12] I was happy to hear Basil's words. Not only did he forestall the teasing, I found deeper wisdom in his observation. His counsel has great significance as an introduction to this book: *We are born to be free. That is who we are as a people – free to come and go as we please. That is how the old people lived. That's a good way to live today.*

In Anishinaabe tradition, freedom can be characterized by healthy interdependencies, with the sun, moon, stars, winds, waters, rocks, plants, insects, animals and human beings.[13] Freedom is holistic and does not just exist in an individual's mind. It is much more than a product of an individual's will; it is lived. In Anishinaabemowin the word for living a good life is *mino-bimaadiziwin*.[14]

While its practices and meanings can be contested this word can be roughly translated as 'living well in this world.'[15] Because freedom of choice is an important part of life, the pathways for pursuing *mino-bimaadiziwin* are many.[16] 'Ojibwe teachings say that we exist to live out and give expression to our vision, and that in so doing we find meaning and purpose in life. And because each of us has a different vision, it must be lived as we alone can understand it.'[17] Thus, *mino-bimaadiziwin* emphasizes an individual's 'power control' within a broader network of relationships as a physical and social fact.[18]

The philosopher Hannah Arendt once observed that 'the raison d'être of politics is freedom, and its field of experience is action.'[19] She said, 'To be free and to act are the same.'[20] I agree with her words because they correlate with what I have learned about the significance of freedom to live a good life within Anishinaabe constitutional traditions. Freedom is an embodied experience and is evidenced in public settings. It is relational. In Anishinaabemowin, such freedom can more particularly be described as *dibenindizowin*, which can mean a person possesses liberty within themselves and their relationships.[21] Freedom has, *sui generis*, property-like connotations in the Ojibwe language. It implies that a free person owns, is responsible for, and controls how they interact with others. The same root word can be used to describe a person who is a member of a group; thus the Anishinaabe term for citizen is *diben-jigaazowin*: he or she who owns or controls their associations.

When I think about examples of Anishinaabe freedom to live well, I am drawn to tales involving our trickster: Nanaboozhoo. His stories illustrate a tradition of action; they do not emphasize abstract principles or rigid behavioural codes. He is not an 'ideal' character and does not always model exemplary behaviour.[22] He can be unstable and erratic, like the humans he often represents. We learn as much from his flaws and imperfections as we do through his heroism and great deeds. Nanaboozhoo (or Nanabush as he is often called) constantly moves from place to place and encounters many beings who challenge his liberty. His life is fluid, and his actions and responses are varied and flexible, even unpredictable. In his earliest encounters, Nanaboozhoo escapes from a lodge to bring fire to his grandmother,[23] he persuades his grandmother to let him journey to the west where he fights his father,[24] and he frees himself from *michi-bizhew* and the rising waters during the great flood.[25] Nanaboozhoo subsequently names the rocks, plants, and animals and other living beings through collaboration and conflict as he travels throughout the world.[26] These encounters enhance knowledge and enlarge fields of possibility for future action. These stories illustrate the complex nature of *dibenindizowin* worked out through his relationships with other beings. Nanaboozhoo cannot do whatever he wants, because his actions are always constrained in some way. At the same time, he has a wide range of options for living a good life because of his ability to transform himself and those around him through their interactions. In other words, Nanaboozhoo is free, even as real-world relationships both facilitate and constrain the scope of his actions.

Remembering these stories, terms, and teachings, and Basil's encouragement to 'come and go as we please,' I recall other lessons about freedom found in Anishinaabe history. There is a tradition of relational mobility among the Anishinaabe, who would train 'runners' to connect communities over long distances. Runners from Neyaashiinigmiing on the shores of southern Georgian Bay could easily journey to Toronto in four days.[27] It took one day to travel from Toronto to Niagara. A trip from Niagara to Detroit took eight days, and was considered a short journey. Runners generally covered 80 kilometres a day, and they could easily travel over 1,500 kilometres in one month.[28]

My great-grandfather Charles Kegedonce Jones was a 'runner.' When he was quite young, he would travel throughout Ontario without constraint. He often took official messages from our Chief to Walpole Island, Toronto, Parry Island, Ottawa, and places in between.[29] To appreciate the scope of his freedom, we should remember that he knew which plants would sustain him along these journeys. He didn't have to carry much with him, because the fields, forests, rivers, and lakes of Ontario were his grocery store. His mother was a medicine woman who taught him which plants would help him through different seasons.[30] He also knew people throughout Anishinaabe-akiing and therefore would never be far from friends and relatives. His freedom to travel around the Great Lakes was facilitated by a relationally Indigenous infrastructure that gave him the capabilities to meet his community's needs. He thrived in this environment, even as the bounds of his reserve were increasingly contracted by a developing colonial state. My great-grandfather lived to be over 100 years old. He was a loving person and a respected *ogimaa* and Chief. He was the most important male figure in my own mother's young life because he lived a good life. *Mino-bimaadiziwin* and *dibenindizowin* were living, practical pursuits for him, as they have been for many Anishinaabe people throughout history.

Another example that reminds me of the physicality of freedom within Anishinaabe society comes from my experience learning Anishinaabemowin. It's a second language for me, and it's one that I have struggled with over the years. It is a notoriously hard language to learn. During my childhood I remember hearing Anishinaabemowin from my grandfather and his older siblings. My mother used Anishinaabe words throughout her life, but fluency was locked within her because of the trauma she witnessed in those who spoke the language in her school. Memories of the beatings children received for speaking Anishinaabemowin physically froze my mother's tongue.[31] So when I came to learn Anishinaabemowin, I found it was more than a memorization exercise. It was physical and public exercise; it was embodied and pursued in relation to others. It was relational, and as my skills developed it slowly became constitutional. First of all, I had to move to places where healthy speakers were willing to teach me. Second, I had to change my work, social, and family patterns to make time for daily classes, language tables, and ceremonies. Third, I had to learn how to manipulate my tongue in new ways and feel how Anishinaabemowin flowed differently through my throat, nose, lungs, and ears. Fourth, I experienced some physical anxiety when first learning Anishinaabemowin because of how the language connected to the trauma I saw in my mother. When I initially started using these words, my chest muscles would contract, my heart would race, and my skin would flush. It was as if I was pushing through hundreds of years of colonialism when I began regularly speaking Anishinaabemowin. It was exhausting, because so much seemed to be at stake. Fortunately, with the support of good teachers, family, and some hard work, I overcame these struggles and now enjoy speaking and teaching the language, though I am far from fluent at the present time. I get teased and frequently laugh at myself when I speak. While the language's construction lends itself to playfulness and humour, much of the laughter comes from my near-constant mistakes. This has made learning the language a lot easier. My mother says 'If you are not laughing when you speak Ojibwe you are not really learning the language.' While I still have much work ahead of me, I have been free to break down other barriers in my life because of my experiences learning Anishinaabemowin.[32] Anishinaabe traditions remind us that we do not have to accept the world as we find it; we can challenge and change how and where we live, think, and speak, at least to a degree. Freedom allows us to question the limits of our lives while at the same time helping us to reach beyond them.[33] But this is hard work, and there are limits to what we can accomplish. As will be explained, some of these limits may even be healthy and facilitate our happiness and well-being. When we understand such constraints, our search for freedom prompts the identification of ideas and practices that facilitate good lives,[34] while we simultaneously question universalized assumptions about 'traditional' requirements in this quest.[35] Seen in this light, Anishinaabe traditions help people live in ways that some may consider beyond question. We can live trickster-inspired, unpredictable, physically mobile, multivocal lives, if that is our goal. Or we can choose otherwise.

Thus, the quest for freedom and a good life within Anishinaabe tradition synchronously exalts and resists what we consider to be universally true. As noted, it requires appropriate submission to forces that are real 'limits' in an individual's and community's life. At the same time, these teachings can vigorously challenge and overturn ideas and practices that are not real 'limits.'[36] Traditions related to *mino-bimaadiziwn* and *dibenindizowin* are both deeply attentive to context, which is one key to teaching us how to live well in the world while resisting that which is not good for us.[37] In this respect, they are constitutional because they help us form a living relationship with the world around us.

This book contends that, as we make these decisions and distinguish between helpful and harmful traditions, our freedom is at its strongest when it is publicly interactive and aimed at good living. In a respectful relational context, the quest for freedom to live a good life becomes a self-governing activity, a simultaneously individual and collective practice. It embodies self-determination *and* individual self-examination, critique and deliberation. In this respect, freedom is pursued inter-subjectively, meaning that Indigenous peoples' identities are non-binary, and are continuously recreated in the context of their struggles against and alliances with one another,[38] occurring under the influence of competing and complementary traditions.[39] There is no relationship-free place for Indigenous or any other peoples, whether positively, negatively, or 'mixedly' construed.

Since this book does not examine Indigenous or other traditions from a metaphysically pure perspective, it grounds its analysis in the messy world of physical experience.[40] Thus, this book takes as its starting point the observation that Indigenous peoples' lives are 'shot through with relations of inequality, force and fraud, broken promises, failed accords, degrading stereotypes, misrecognition, paternalism, enmity and distrust.'[41] At the same time, this text also acknowledges that Indigenous lives are saturated with *nibwaakaawin* (wisdom), *zaagi'idiwin* (love), *mnaadendiwin* (respect), *aakwaadiziwin* (bravery), *dbaadendiziwin* (humility), *gwekwaadiziwin* (honesty), and *debwewin* (truth).[42] These practices, known as the *Niizhwaashiwaan Mishoomisinaan/Gookomisinaan Kinomaagewinaan*, or Seven Grandfather/Grandmother Teachings,[43] allow individuals to exercise significant 'power control' in structuring daily living. They help people live free and responsible lives. However, these teachings do not presume to provide precise answers to any given question. They are not universal categorical imperatives. Thus, what these teachings require in any particular context will often be contested. Furthermore these teachings also intermingle with more malignant forces, which also profoundly shape the field of action for freely pursuing a good life.[44]

Starting in the middle of the complex state in which we find ourselves, and working towards a better state, is what I term *akinoomaagewin*, or physical philosophy.[45] *Akinoomaagewin* is derived from observation and practice; learning in this way does not stem from identifying first principles and deducing conclusions from abstract propositions. The word *gikinawaabiwin* communicates this same point.[46] Anishinaabe physical philosophy is inductive and derives conclusions from experience, observation, and discussion. This approach does not claim to reveal uncontested or absolute truth. In line with the Anishinaabe term *debwewin*, it permits a person to 'tell what one knows according to his/ her fluency; to have the highest degree of accuracy; to be right; correct, to have truth.'[47] Nigikoonsminikaaning Elder Ogimaawigwanebiik puts it this way: 'Debwe, debwe iwe gaa-ikidod, gakina awiya debwe … Endanakiiyan, mii omaa gegiin ezhi-gikinoo'amaageyan, ingojiwang ingoji waasaa. Awiya bizindaman booshke ingoding gii-ikobiiyaat gichi-ayaa'aag gakina bebikaan ikidowag akina ge-wiinawaa ogik-endaanaawaa wa'-izhi-gikinoo'amaagewaat.' (The truth, he speaks the truth; everyone speaks his or her truth … When you live in your community that is how you pass on the teachings. They all have their own stories as to how they pass on their teachings.)[48] Anishinaabe 'truth' is understood in context. This is why this book highlights traditions as *practice*. It engages with the real world's constraints and opportunities which Indigenous peoples encounter, rather than attempting to answer questions by an *a priori* appeal to idealized forms and timeless traditions.

In their context, all traditions are 'invented traditions,' whether they are Indigenous or otherwise. They are continually subject to contestation and revision in practice. They are given meaning in particular places. There is no social or political space which is tradition-free. Traditions explicitly or implicitly colour our every thought and action in our political, social, scientific, religious, cultural, linguistic, and economic lives. Thus, while abstract metaphysical inquiries may shed some light on living a good life, I start from 'where I think we are' and then attempt to move in a better direction. Thus, my approach is comparative and probabilistic in terms of suggesting future action. It aims to diminish domination in real-world contexts by simultaneously working within and critiquing lived and idealized traditions, rather than claiming that subordination can be eliminated by following any one particular ideology or intellectual path.

Since my methodology makes contextually comparative rather than absolute claims, I hope that this book will build consensus, provoke critique, and foster positive reformulations. I would also insist that this book should be rejected if its leads people away from freedom and good living. This work would be particularly offensive to me if it categorically reified or rejected tradition in a way that diminished prospects for living free and good lives.[49] While disagreement must be treasured and appropriately encouraged, even as we value harmony,

I do not believe in or practise disagreement for its own sake.[50] Dissent is a very important practice that can lead towards freedom, if its strength is directed towards the pursuit of a good life, or *mino-bimaadiziwin*, with its many paths and meanings. However, unqualified dissent for its own sake, detached from context, and regarded as an absolute value, can ensnare people and nations in its conceptual grip.[51] This book explores avenues to freedom and a good life that are forged through both dissent *and* agreement.[52] It maintains that Indigenous and other traditions are best understood and practised if experienced in this broader light.

The intermingling of agreement and dissent makes living tradition a messy affair. As we will see, traditions can be both competing and complementary – sometimes at the same time. They must not be simplified for the sake of a singular conception of a good life, because this would diminish freedom for those pursuing varied paths. When traditions are regarded as being relationally formed through contending and comparative interpretations, no one individual or institution can as effectively control their meaning. This caution is particularly relevant in a Canadian context, where non-Indigenous traditions related to Indigenous traditions are often intensely oppressive. Non-Indigenous traditions receive much greater support in government, educational, and media circles. This presents enormous problems for Indigenous peoples in their attempts to create healthier relationships among themselves and their neighbours.

Canada has a long way to go in developing traditions that facilitate freedom in its relations with Indigenous peoples. It has not effectively embraced the constitutive character of Indigenous traditions. This is the case despite the fact that Canada is described as a 'free and democratic' society in section 1 of the Canadian Charter of Rights and Freedoms.[53] While freedom is paired with democracy in Canada's political order, the state has not created sufficient place or space for Indigenous peoples to pursue conceptions of a good life in reference to their own traditions and self-determining objectives. This has hurt Indigenous peoples, but it has also harmed Canadians more generally. They are cut off from Indigenous insights and practices that could also enhance their freedoms. Within Anishinaabe tradition, freedom is not just the absence of coercion or constraint,[54] it is the ability to work in cooperation with others to choose, create, resist, reject, and change laws and policies that affect your life.[55] These practices could greatly benefit Indigenous peoples and Canadians more generally. Ultimately, this book argues that Indigenous traditions, as fluid as they are, must resist, intermingle with, be separated from, and/or practically inform other traditions (and vice-versa) to structure a freer, better life.[56] Traditions must be drawn from living, complex relationships to be freely constitutive. Indigenous peoples must enjoy freedoms 'from,' freedoms 'to,' freedoms 'with,' and freedoms 'alongside' other people in order to responsibly own themselves and their relationships (*dibenindizowin*). They must be free to construct freedom inside and outside of a liberal, conservative, national, Marxist, or other categorical construct. Each chapter aims to demonstrate this point.

Thus, in pursuing this goal, the book unfolds as follows: The first chapter examines Indigenous and Canadian legal traditions by demonstrating how mobility is an important activity in Indigenous peoples' pursuit of freedom. Despite the prevalence of Indigenous intellectual and physical movement, legal stereotypes erect barriers to Indigenous peoples' fuller participation in the world around them. With these constraints, Indigenous peoples are characterized as 'once-upon-a-time' groups that can only occupy a very narrow space in contemporary democracies – if they are regarded as having any place at all. In response to this approach, I argue that Indigenous peoples must continue to freely move throughout our countries, and across the broad world of ideas. We should resist laws and policies that strip us of our freedom if we do not relate to land and ideas as others expect. In particular, I outline two steps that might be taken to facilitate Indigenous freedoms. First, I suggest that Indigenous peoples must be permitted to regulate and integrate others into their communities. Second, I discuss the importance of mutual harmonization of Indigenous and non-Indigenous laws and policies. In so doing, I explore the positive constraints that Indigenous autonomy would impose on Indigenous peoples and thus would be an important freedom-enhancing measure.

The second chapter discusses the relationship between civil (dis)obedience, freedom, and the pursuit of a good life. It identifies real and false limits in the practice of direct physical action. It suggests that civil (dis)obedience can be an important democratic practice, which facilitates freedom and builds good lives. I bracket the prefix *dis-* in *disobedience* to indicate that disobedience to one set of laws can be construed as obedience to another set of laws, or the product of different interpretations of the same law. Despite these variations, however, this chapter also suggests that direct action facilitates democratic self-determination only if it is genuinely constrained by respect for broader relational concerns. In fact, I will argue that civil (dis)obedience can be dangerous and deeply undemocratic if practised for its own sake, in the pursuit of abstract ideologies unrelated to the context in which it is deployed. Direct action can create false horizons that constrain freedom when conflict constructs essentialized and binary relationships between individuals and groups. After briefly discussing these points, this chapter focuses on ways in which civil (dis)obedience has worked in Canada. A short inventory of nine blockades set up by Indigenous peoples in Canada within the past forty years reveals that civil (dis)obedience can be consistent with democracy and freedom if such action connects Indigenous peoples with their neighbours.

Accordingly, the chapter challenges the false idea that civil (dis)obedience can never be democratic. At the same time, I argue that civil (dis)obedience should not be seen as a panacea for facilitating freedom, because in some contexts it is oppressive and anti-democratic. It can be based on essentialist patterns of thought, which ignore the deeply relational contexts that constitute Indigenous life. Freedom and the pursuit of a good life cannot simply rely on rebellion or resistance (as important as they may be); practices of cooperation and mutual aid are often (though not always) needed in the pursuit of these goals.

The third chapter examines Indigenous peoples' relationship to the ongoing formation of Canada's constitution. It reveals another path to freedom and a good life for Indigenous peoples – simultaneous resistance to and engagement with Canada's constitutional values, structures, and traditions. Indigenous people both reject the legitimacy of Canadian constitutionalism and simultaneously work with its more complementary elements – as the occasion requires. In so doing, Indigenous peoples demonstrate significant ambivalence towards Canada's formal constitution. There is a great deal of tension in how they relate to its structure and participate in its evolution. The idea of testing Aboriginal and treaty rights through Canadian political and legal institutions does not hold universal appeal for Indigenous peoples. In fact, this approach is deeply problematic and feeds the continued subjugation of Indigenous peoples in numerous ways. Historically, Indigenous resistance to a state-based recognition paradigm led to conflicting and complementary goals in the debates preceding the entrenchment of Aboriginal and treaty rights in the constitution's patriation in 1982, and this chapter will review these events, exploring Canada's recent legal history and outlining Indigenous peoples' constitutional suspicions. It chronicles their participation (or lack thereof) in Canada's unending constitutional formation as part of their quest for freedom.

The fourth chapter of this book turns from constitutional formation to constitutional interpretation to examine another dimension of freedom. This chapter attempts to place Canadian constitutional interpretation on non-discriminatory footings. Unfortunately, Canada's constitution contains a deep and distressing interpretive inconsistency. Most constitutional rights in Canada are interpreted in accordance with a living-tree approach. Living constitutionalism allows courts to look beyond frozen historical moments of a constitution's formation. Living-tree jurisprudence gives meaning to a constitutional provision in the light of contemporary circumstances. Regrettably, Canada's constitution does not generally apply living constitutional approaches when interpreting Aboriginal and treaty rights within Canada's constitution. Indigenous rights are largely interpreted through an originalist lens which relies on *a priori*, abstract, essentialized forms of reasoning. Originalism freezes Indigenous traditions. The Supreme Court requires Indigenous peoples to prove 'integral' practices prior to European arrival to claim Aboriginal rights. In the treaty context, the Court requires proof of common intent at the time agreements were signed, because originalism holds that such rights cannot advance beyond precise historical moments. This chapter explains the differences in living-tree and originalist approaches within Canadian constitutional interpretation. It highlights their adversely discriminatory effects for Indigenous peoples. As a potential antidote to these problems, this chapter outlines some non-discriminatory alternatives for interpreting Indigenous rights in Canada.

The fifth chapter of this book explores another path to freedom. It questions an article of faith in Indigenous political circles which has been around since Prime Minister Pierre Elliott Trudeau proposed repealing the *Indian Act* and assimilating Indigenous peoples. Indigenous peoples in Canada have been exceedingly reluctant to seek legislative recognition or protection of their rights through formal legislation – for very good reasons. Assimilation and off-loading of constitutional responsibilities to provincial authorities has characterized most formal legislative proposals emanating from Ottawa. The application of provincial legislative power through section 88 of the *Indian Act* and other means is one of the most problematic provisions of the *Indian Act*. Section 88 of the *Indian Act* largely strips Indigenous communities of their decision-making responsibilities. Most laws that apply to Indians on reserve are not of their making and, in fact, the province is generally prohibited from even considering their interests when it passes laws that apply to them. This is the disaster of section 88 of the *Indian Act*. The application of federal and provincial law to Indigenous peoples without their participation or consent has done more to deprive Indigenous peoples of their freedoms than any other action I can identify. Nevertheless, while this chapter recognizes the extremely problematic nature of working with Canadian governments, it also suggests that freedom and a good life could be enhanced *if* self-determination marked federal legislative initiatives related to Indigenous peoples. This chapter draws examples from the United States in chronicling areas of legislative action that could also animate Indigenous self-determination in Canada. Although U.S. examples are critically analysed for their problematic aspects (of which there are very many), U.S. experience also illustrates areas where Indigenous peoples could benefit from having legislation that advanced self-determination in Canada. This chapter's review of legislative initiatives falls into three categories: (1) Indigenous control over federal government services for Indigenous people, (2) the protection of Indigenous cultures and communities, and (3) Indigenous control in relation to natural resources and economic development. Being open to legislative possibilities even in the light of significant cautions and critiques demonstrates the challenges and possibilities of philosophical mobility for Indigenous peoples. Legislation presents potential paths to freedom in appropriately calibrated circumstances, even as this activity presents one of the greatest dangers Indigenous peoples encounter in living free and good lives.

The sixth chapter addresses violence against Indigenous women. I argue that most Indigenous people are not free because of how gender and governance are essentialized in political, social, and legal circles. Indigenous and non-Indigenous peoples often act as if violence against Indigenous women can only be formally addressed through federal or provincial power. I believe this occurs because most judges, lawyers and elected leaders incorrectly believe that Aboriginal and treaty rights relate only to land. I argue this is a false tradition. This chapter insists that Aboriginal and treaty rights also directly implicate the health, safety, and welfare of Indigenous peoples' bodies, including Indigenous women. One of the purposes of section 35(1) of the constitution is to protect physical survival.[57] Decisions concerning the health, safety and welfare of Indigenous women are obviously relevant to individual and community well-being. Therefore they must lie within an Indigenous constitutional sphere. Chapter 6 thus advances this proposition by deconstructing constitutional traditions, which marginalize

Indigenous women and Indigenous governments. In the process, I identify alternative jurisprudential approaches that could open space to more effectively facilitate freedom in addressing violence against women. In so doing, I make the point that Indigenous peoples' own law-making responsibilities could play an important role in this process, even as I am careful not to essentialize and overplay this activity.[58] Accordingly, this chapter continues to maintain that we must be open to 'in-the-alternative' approaches to ensure freedom and the pursuit of a good life are not diminished by single-sourced prescriptions about how we should be constituted as human beings.

Finally, this book's conclusion recounts an Anishinaabe story about a mother, a father, and their son to advance my themes. I do so to demonstrate how freedom must be a living tradition at many societal levels, including families and nations. Indigenous peoples must apply their own best legal practices across many scales to facilitate freedom. Freedom is not a licence to do anything we want or desire. The story attempts to show that the pursuit of a good life should discourage us from forcing others into our own preferred ways of living. For Anishinaabe people, this is an important constitutive tradition. We have learned that, like the trickster, freedom can wear many false faces. Some pursuits followed in freedom's name are deeply coercive and produce real limits in peoples' lives. Other practices of *dibenindizowin* actually allow people to experience liberty within themselves and in their relationships. Indigenous peoples and Canadians more generally could benefit from a greater infusion of agency-enhancing practices discussed in this story, particularly those linked to *nibwaakaawin* (wisdom), *zaagi'idiwin* (love), *mnaadendiwin* (respect), *aakwaadiziwin* (bravery), *dbaadendiziwin* (humility), *gwekwaadiziwin* (honesty), and *debwewin* (truth). They reflect a legal morality that places the everyday practice of constitutional law in a community, home, and individual's life. In this respect, these practices give focus to Hannah Arendt's words, 'to be free and to act are the same.'

As Indigenous peoples, we cannot just theorize our way to freedom – we must act well in the world. We must more fully and responsibily own, relate to, and control how we interact with others. *Dibenindizowin* and *mino-bimaadiziwin* are enhanced when this occurs. This is the reason this book examines freedom, law, and a quest for a good life.[59] It challenges philosophies that define us in accordance with pre-existing norms and fundamental characteristics. It argues that these views must give way to practices that treat us as contemporary, flexible, and fluid societies. It shows that we are capable of resisting and adapting to change according to our practical needs and desires. We must 'bob and weave' between what would appear to be inconsistent alternatives, if we measured life by essentialized 'truths.' We cannot afford to pour our futures into the mould of any one Western or Indigenous philosophy, theory, or approach. They may all be helpful. Likewise, each *a priori* view of the world may be just as likely to corrode our abilities to live well with all our relations (*mino-bimaadiziwin*). When we are free to act in complex, multifaceted, and variable ways, we more fully enrich our own and others' lives. When we break the bonds of false tradition, we are freer to pursue good lives in accordance with our wide-ranging and ever-changing circumstances. This is the sense of constitutionalism that guides the remainder of this book.

Chapter One

Physical Philosophy: Mobility and Indigenous Freedom

You might as well expect all the rivers to run backward as that any man who was born free should be contented penned up and denied liberty to go where he pleases.

Hin-hah-too-yah-lat-kekht (Chief Joseph), Nez Perce[1]

With freedom and a quest for a good life as a compass, this chapter explores the philosophical terrain occupied by Indigenous peoples in Canada. It seeks to chart practices located near the centre and edges of our social life. In taking our bearings we could focus on the familiar landmarks of Indigenous struggle, including land rights, governance, economic development, environment, citizenship, language, education and health care, and so forth. While these issues deserve close attention, our orientation could become clearer if we recognized that Indigenous peoples travel through political struggles 'in relation' to themselves and others. An intersectional approach to tradition reveals the complex pathways traversed by Indigenous peoples in the wider world.

In scanning Indigenous peoples' legal horizons, it is apparent that real and conjured limits lie before us. We see prominent, problematic borders, with signs marking Indigenous traditions as closed, static, and frozen, where only distinctive, authenticated, essentialized people can dwell.[2] These barriers seem firm, until you press closer and notice that they have little substance. They are abstractions. Like desert mirages they vanish when you move towards them or, even worse, they reveal themselves as perpetually receding.

Of course there are other views of Indigenous traditions that more accurately map onto real life, but they seem somewhat distant. While they do not loom large in law and policy, they mark Indigenous traditions as fluid, hybridized, contingent, contested, cross-cutting, and ever-changing.[3] Their composition also makes them difficult to grasp. Traditions combine differently in each person and group, thereby challenging simplistic categorizations. Nevertheless, when you approach these boundaries they are experienced as being genuinely substantial. They arise as real limits in Indigenous peoples' relationships because they are embedded within everyday practices; within their context, a tradition's limits are treated as necessary to live well within a community in any given moment of time.

When most Indigenous travellers describe their journeys through Canada, they acknowledge negotiating both terrains. While verifying the challenging limits imposed upon them by false horizons, they also confirm the social realities of these genuine, outer bounds. Indigenous peoples thus find themselves entangled by both constraints, though this is not always recognized. Some live as if abstract conceptions of Indigeneity were the final destination for themselves and other Indigenous peoples. They build Indigeneity on their own idealized view of 'the' truth. Others resist. They oppose these abstractions as a form of domination within and outside their communities; they do not see their societies as being built upon *a priori* ideas of 'Indianness' or other similar categorizations.[4] Seeing larger Indigenous realities, they recognize that traditions are built through inter-subjective practices and experiences that flow through time. There are many ways of being Indigenous in relation to the 'limits' described herein. Nevertheless, Indigenous travellers are often connected despite their differences because they desire greater freedom in moving towards destinations of their own choice.

For these reasons, I believe intellectual and physical *mobility* is a major issue that Indigenous peoples encounter in struggling for freedom and a good life. As such, this chapter explores the myriad ways that Indigenous mobility might be enhanced by simultaneously testing its real limits, *and* challenging limits that seem real, but which are the product of stereotyping and other essentialized subconscious forms of thought and practice. My approach illustrates a 'form of "possible crossing over (*franchissement*)" of one or the other of the boundaries' that constrain Indigenous freedom.[5] In taking this path, this chapter maps the borders of Indigenous traditions, and problematizes how we travel in relation to them.[6]

A. Methodologies of Mobility: Physical Philosophy

Mobility is a current Indigenous practice, but one that nation states manipulate or ignore because Indigenous mobility contests the limits of national law and politics. Mobility (or a perceived lack thereof) has often been used to undermine Indigenous peoples' freedom to pursue a good life because of stereotypical characterizations. Indigenous peoples are denied space in contemporary political life if they move too frequently. Conversely, freedom can also be diminished if they move too little. This result impedes advancement in other matters of crucial importance.

When Indigenous mobility is at issue it seems as though Indigenous peoples cannot win. In many systems of legal thought, Indigenous peoples are characterized as being either too nomadic or too static to protect their most significant relationships. Thus, mobility should be of special concern for Indigenous peoples.[7] Its negative characterization and consequence undermines Indigenous peoples' free, democratic, and self-determining engagement with others in the world.

Many Indigenous peoples have histories of cultural movement despite claims to the contrary. Notwithstanding our frequent moves, Indigenous peoples are not rootless. Our travels usually occur in relationship to territories with which we have long-standing associations. Indigenous peoples are constantly in states of settled flux. Our perpetual motion coexists with a persistent and enduring near-permanence. Ancient homelands remain a pivotal axis around which most Indigenous peoples' lives revolve. We may wander far and wide but our journeys generally take their orientation from an older sense of place in the world, even when such views are open to reinterpretation. Of course, there are some Indigenous peoples who move less than others due to group or individual pressures, preferences, personalities, and poverty. Yet even in these instances, mobility or the lack thereof is a substantial concern. Its practice shapes many of the most important issues Indigenous peoples encounter in the modern world.

Indigenous peoples not only move through physical space; we also move through time. Our traditions are not frozen in the past, as commentators too often assume.[8] We interact with other societies as we journey through the generations.[9] In the process, we accumulate insights from other traditions. In uneven steps we discard and retain old ways and adapt and resist new ones. This can lead to significant change as the past intermingles with the present and transforms our societies.

As noted, this view of Indigenous movement also challenges assumptions about Indigenous traditions. We are too often seen as intellectually stagnant, with unchanging, static views of life.[10] Some consider our ideas to be the product of another age that have little relevance to the contemporary world.[11] They see our philosophies as quaint anachronisms of another time. Others might regard our ideas as intellectually compelling, even correct, but too feeble to prevail in their encounter with the modern age.[12] Thus, Indigenous traditions are often seen as primitive or naive, and destined to vanish from the earth.[13] I do not accept these views. I believe Indigenous peoples renew, retain, and transform their traditions as they move through time. Unfortunately, these are difficult points for some to grasp because they defy deeply entrenched stereotypes concerning Indigenous peoples.[14] For those holding such views, understanding Indigenous peoples' travels through time can be even more challenging than comprehending the complexities of our physical movements through material space.

I can identify at least two prominent issues related to Indigenous mobility: physical and philosophical movement. As noted, Indigenous peoples' physical orientation to the world often occurs in relation to enduring patterns, despite the presence of significant flux. As with our physical travels, so it is with our ideological wanderings: we are not rootless. Our journeys through the world of ideas can take guidance from familiar, time-honoured patterns. For example, Anishinaabe people often try to understand the future by remembering the past. Insight can be derived from such reflection because we often regard time as being cyclical. While we also view and experience time as linear, many of our most important teachings orient us towards a life that stresses recurrence.[15] In this light, the present and the past can almost seem co-extensive. This is often the case when the layered repetitions of analogous events are brought into focus. These particular forms of tiered movement can help us holistically understand mobility. Spring turns into summer, fall gives way to winter, and the cycle begins over again. Babies grow into youth, youth mature and become adults, and adults persevere to become elders, before the circle repeats itself.[16] For Anishinaabe people, important elements of our cosmology are built on this pattern.[17] I have noticed that some other Indigenous peoples follow these cycles in understanding their world.[18] Thus, in exploring how domination can be diminished in the present day, I will examine how Indigenous peoples might confront present limits by also being critically mindful of the past.

B. Models of Mobility

When viewed in this broader context, Indigenous mobility is not just a future issue; it also has clear parallels to the past. In my own life, I have moved through many seasons and places. When I was four years old, we moved from my first house. This began a pattern that has followed me through life. While I did spend ten years of my youth living on the same farm, off the reserve, most of my experience has involved a near-constant roving of the earth. I never seem to be in the same place for more than a year or two. In my first quarter-century of marriage, we have happily lived in over twenty-five different places. I don't know what the future will bring, but I will be surprised if I really 'settle' anywhere outside of Anishinaabe territory. Physically, I seem to be constantly on the move.[19]

The same observations could be applied to my conceptual mobility. I have sampled and cycled through many ideas in my life. I feel like they have accumulated as layers in my soul as I have been exposed to different ways of thinking. For example, I first moved through understandings that framed the world through my mother's eyes. Her significant formative influence gave me a template to make sense of what I learned.[20] There was much that was Anishinaabe in her teachings because she judged the world in these terms. Then, as spring turned into the summer of my life, I travelled through universities, churches, popular culture, and self-directed study. Sometimes, in the moment of each experience, this movement seemed like a dramatic departure from the past. Fortunately, in time, I found many of the best ideas from these sources connected to the Anishinaabe teachings of my childhood. As I grew I tried to convey this perspective to my children. Now, with my daughters in their twenties, I have moved into the early fall of my life.[21] I continue to circle through ideas that come from many sources. I simultaneously compare and contrast, accept and reject what I am taught through many varied experiences. As with earlier stages in my life, I also try to learn more about what it means to be Anishinaabe.[22] I feel that I experience my most profound intellectual, physical, and spiritual journeys as an Anishinaabe person.

Despite these reflections, there are times when I wonder if I am out of step with my ancestors. Stereotypes cause me to ask myself: Do I move too frequently to be Indigenous? There are some who might tell me there is too much change in my life to claim Indigeneity.[23] They would say I have departed from my roots, that I have been physically dislocated and conceptually contaminated through so-called non-Indigenous experiences. It might be said I have crossed a 'real' boundary that takes me beyond the 'limits' of what it means to be Indigenous, or Anishinaabe. These arguments, of course, only make sense if we have an *a priori* idea of what it means to be Anishinaabe. Once I test the real world of grounded Indigenous practices against a notional universalized Indigenous person, I understand that a 'real limit' to Indigeneity has not been crossed at all. I am still Anishinaabe despite, and maybe even because of, my wandering ways. While there may be generally accepted understandings, there is no conceptual purity or abstract authenticity to be found in any Indigenous person or community.

Despite these observations, it is surprising how often courts and scholars express an almost universalized, essentialist view of Indigenous peoples and traditions.[24] These false limitations on Indigenous mobility disembody real people and perpetuate false stereotypes but they can be internalized and vocalized by Indigenous people. In fact, I have heard similar sentiments from my extended family. I have a cousin who says he does not read books, magazines, or newspapers because he wants to avoid becoming polluted by non-Indigenous ideas. He believes that a 'real' Anishinaabe person does not take ideas from other peoples.[25] He says he practises an uncorrupted form of self-conscious traditionalism. He embraces 'strategic essentialism.' I have known a few Indigenous law and graduate students who have expressed this same sentiment through the years.[26] After graduation, they have stopped reading and referencing non-Indigenous work because they say it colonizes and contaminates their thought and action. These are troubling views when they imply or lead to intellectual isolation and societal segregation. While I strive to enhance and sometimes even privilege Indigenous sources and world views in specific contexts, I worry about the exclusivity and ethno-nationalism that can attach to these views. Thankfully, when I give these approaches deeper thought, I am reminded of many stories that contest this view.[27] As noted in the introduction, the Anishinaabe creation story sees Nanaboozhoo, our trickster, travel through the four directions in bringing knowledge to the world. The first animals from whom we claim kinship radiated out from Michimakinakong to eventually surround the Great Lakes.[28] Their journeys eventually took them even further afield; they interacted with others. We have migration stories that recount the return to our Great Lakes homelands after time away across great waters. Through the past ten thousand years, the Anishinaabe have travelled among different First

Nations (and therefore different peoples) prior to the arrival of Europeans in our territories.[29]

My own great-great-great-grandparents followed this pattern of mobility. In this respect they were also free. Kegedonce and his widow, Sakeon, periodically moved between what is now known as Ohio, Michigan, and Ontario in the late 1700s.[30] My great-great-grandmother, Margret McCleod, moved from the Prairies to the north shore of Lake Huron, and then to our home reservation at Neyaashiinigmiing in what is now Southern Ontario in the mid-1800s.[31] My great-great-grandfather, Peter Kegedonce Jones, Margret's husband, moved between Neyaashiinigmiing to Lake Simcoe and places in between throughout his life.[32] My great-grandfather was born at Neyaashiinigmiing and spent much of his time there. He was the 'runner' of whom I spoke earlier. He also permanently hunted, fished, and lodged throughout what became Grey and Bruce Counties in Ontario during his 100-year lifespan. My Grandpa Josh roamed even further, from Neyaashiinigmiing and then through Michigan, Kentucky, Utah, and California for a twenty-year span before returning home to the reserve. He brought home a young American girl as his wife in the process.[33] My mother had similar experiences, venturing out from Neyaashiinigmiing as a young girl to escape residential school internment, only to return to the reserve when she was in the fifth decade of her life. She brought her Yorkshire-born husband home when she returned, and they live on the reserve to this day. This history helps me remember that the Anishinaabe have been highly mobile for a very long time, even as they have maintained an enduring relationship with a particular stretch of earth. They have also incorporated people from other nations into these relationships. If they married people from other communities their children could be regarded as Anishinaabe. All through this process, my ancestors also examined, rejected, and accepted ideas and traditions from other peoples. Physical and philosophical mobility seems to be the course of my life, too.

As noted, other Indigenous peoples have histories and traditions that address mobility. These journeys not only changed their territorial residences, but they also transformed beliefs and practices. Historically, the Maori tell of their journey from Hawaikii to Aoteoroa.[34] These voyages led to new understandings of themselves as people.[35] This occurred for other Polynesians, too, as they sailed thousands of miles around the Pacific to make their many homes.[36] Indigenous Australians speak of their movements through the Dream-time and the

Walk-about.[37] For millennia, the Sami continually moved through what became the countries of Norway, Finland, Sweden, and Russia, herding reindeer and teaching one another about what they learned in the process.[38] The Navajo chronicle their migrations around the deserts of the American Southwest, and others talk of their arrival from an indeterminate place in the north.[39] The Hopi relate their journey from inside the earth.[40] The Maya report that they moved through many cycles of creation and destruction to build their societies in Central America.[41] Each of these physical treks also gave rise to important ideological journeys, as new lessons were related to older teachings. Physical and intellectual mobility has long been a defining characteristic of many of our societies.

Indigenous mobility is also much in evidence in more recent times.[42] The peoples of the North American Pacific Northwest 'turned the 1600 kilometre stretch of coastline between Puget Sound and the Gulf of Alaska into a hotly-contested maritime region.'[43] The great North American Prairies hosted a constant flow of Lakota, Cheyenne, Cree, Crow, and other peoples following the great buffalo herds.[44] The Apaches of the American Southwest occupied territories that spanned the Sonoran and Chihuahuan deserts, and ranged over the intersections of the Sierra Madre and Rocky Mountains.[45] The Iroquois Confederacy could trade, travel, and raid from the Great Lakes to the Carolinas.[46] The Algonkian-speaking peoples of the east coast eventually paddled their way down the Mississippi and across the rivers of Canada to the Rocky Mountains when early European traders and missionaries arrived in their midst.[47] Once again, it needs to be emphasized that, in the process, their journeys also had significant spiritual and ideological dimensions.

Consistent with these experiences, Indigenous peoples are also highly mobile today – both in where they live and through the ideas that guide their lives. Over 50 per cent of First Nations people in Canada live off-reserve. Over 80 per cent of Maori live in New Zealand's urban centres. Australian Aborigines occupy both cities and wide stretches of traditional country, with 30 per cent living in the cities of that continent. Many Indigenous peoples in Mexico have relationships that reach back and forth between North American cities and historic homelands.[48] In the United States, the picture is similar; over 60 per cent of Native Americans live outside their reservations. It should also go without saying that these new living arrangements have led to a variety of patterns of learning, as time accumulates to produce new ways of

seeing the world in relation to past experiences.[49] Where we have sufficient resources, we increasingly go to universities, colleges, and trade
schools, while we simultaneously learn in ancient societies, lodges, and
longhouses. If we are not coerced to relocate or retrench against our
will, we take many healthy lessons from changes we encounter around
us. The intermingling of the past and present, as we move between
historic territories and other places, demonstrates the importance of
mobility in Indigenous peoples' lives.These practices contain great lessons in pursuing freedom and a good life.

These experiences are highlighted by one of the great insights found
in recent geographic and demographic analysis of Indigenous living
patterns in Canada. It has been shown that many First Nations peoples retain significant connections to their homelands, even as they
congregate in the cities in significant numbers.[50] Studies have shown
that permanent 'ghettos' of First Nations people in Canadian cities do
not exist, at least as we think of that phenomenon in relation to other
ethnic groups in the United States.[51] While there are identifiable neigh-
bourhoods of Indigenous people in western Canadian cities, the people
who live there continually move back and forth between the reserves
and cities.[52] Thus, while Canadian cities may have sections of town that
have been occupied by Indigenous people for generations, these sites
are not necessarily intergenerational. This means a person could search
for a long time to find a family living in the same neighbourhood as
their great-grandparents. There are huge flows of First Nations people,
resources, and ideas between cities and traditional territories.[53] These
circulations have great significance for how Indigenous peoples live
their lives. Unfortunately, the reality of Indigenous mobility and our
cyclical orientation to the earth is not being accurately reflected in most
nations' socio-political and legal regimes.[54] When this occurs we operate under false limits – we live under the influence of false traditions.
Even contemporary framings of Indigenous peoples' own law might
not properly take into account the energy found in our residential and
intellectual movements in the present day.[55]

C. Manipulating Mobility: Settled and Unsettled Law

Despite the reality of our near-constant motion, most legal systems
manipulate conceptions of mobility to deny or diminish Indigenous
freedom. Laws are devised to limit our movements and to foster confinement within ever-diminishing spaces. Such coercion can lead to

exceedingly concentrated living arrangements. This system creates perverse incentives. It promotes the mainstream idea that we have only one path to freedom – escape into the surrounding society through assimilation. Such abstractions, when embodied in law and policy, can contribute to our removal from wider territories and relationships. At the same time, these ideas promote the fiction that Indigenous peoples have similar limitations when it comes to their own intellectual horizons. As noted, having forcibly lived through this onslaught, some people have internalized the view that Indigenous peoples do not move. They have almost become strict isolationists, who view themselves as almost completely separated from the world. They regard traditions as being fundamentally fixed and essentially unalterable. If lived in for a generation or two, reservations and residential schools can make captivity appear natural to some caught in this web.

The law in every country with significant Indigenous populations is generally supportive of a narrow view of Indigenous mobility. This recruits Indigenous people in the state's troubling boundary patrol if we view ourselves through this lens. In these circumstances, command coincides with internalized control to sustain colonialism's forced confinements.[56] The injustice and intolerability of this situation promotes Indigenous assimilation because many people are forced or feel compelled to flee colonialism's firm grip, only to find that upon leaving the reserves they are under even greater colonial control. Alternatively, many nestle themselves ever more deeply in colonialism's grasp by being in a constantly reactive mode, setting their identity and traditions solely through oppositional politics. Non-recognition, resistance, and direct action (while extremely important when applied in proper contexts) are often endorsed to the exclusion of other forms of political and legal action. This gives nation states the power to define the scope of Indigenous peoples' struggles. In these circumstances, Indigenous limits are co-dependently defined as contrary to the state and, as a result, their further entanglement grows in step with their opposition. Struggles become defined in binary, oppositional terms, with little room for nuance, gradations, and finer distinctions within and between Indigenous or Canadian positions more generally. In making these observations, it is an understatement to say the law inappropriately stereotypes Indigenous residential and cultural patterns. The ideas encountered deny and diminish Indigenous freedoms because we cannot meet the artificial legal standards promoted by most nation states.

i) 'Damned if We Move': The Too Unsettled Thesis

When examining legal regimes, one finds that Indigenous rights are often premised on contradictory views concerning mobility. These manipulations generate an ironic injustice that works against Indigenous peoples from opposing directions. Manipulation is possible because Indigenous claims are judged through the metaphysical abstraction of rights. This conception of rights often exists in the realm of theory.[57] Under current rights conceptions, Indigenous peoples must prove their practices accord with a preconceived ideal form, or they will not receive constitutional protection.[58] When rights are measured by conceptual purities, this approach often prevents decision-makers from accurately mapping messy realities born of physical relationships in the real world. The space between the ideal represented by a right and an actual practice can be manipulated to deny freedom. When this framework is applied to Indigenous peoples, there are times when they are characterized as too physically and philosophically mobile to claim or prove rights. Conversely, there are moments when courts find we are too sedentary and unchanging to claim legal protections.

In the light of these conflicting manoeuvres, I conclude: We are damned if we move, and we are damned if we don't.[59] The court's inconsistent lurching between these two extremes takes place with too little notice or critique. This fosters false traditions within Canada's own legal system and prompts similar beliefs within Indigenous societies, too. When it comes to issues of mobility, rights are manipulated in ways that are the most detrimental to Indigenous freedoms.

For example, Indigenous peoples can face laws that imply we are too unsettled to claim homelands. In these circumstances, courts might find Indigenous peoples do not have rights if we move too much. The Supreme Court of Canada has held that, when present possession is relied upon to establish possession prior to the Crown's assertion of sovereignty, Aboriginal title cannot be proved without a 'substantial maintenance of the connection' between Indigenous people and their lands.[60] This connection requires sufficient occupation through regular use because 'not every passing traverse or use grounds title.'[61] The High Court of Australia counsels that the 'tide of history' can wash our rights away if we don't remain securely connected to the land through our laws.[62] The incorporation of practices from other communities can become a justification for finding we have abandoned our laws and lands.[63]

Throughout its history, the United States of America has implemented detailed displacement policies aimed at mobility, from the *Dawes Act* of 1887 to the *Termination Acts* of the 1960s. These acts were designed to get Indians to move from their territories and thereby facilitate their assimilation, as if this were the only road to freedom.[64] Similar attempts to get Indigenous peoples removed from their lands for assimilative purposes can be observed in places like New Zealand, Norway, Brazil, South Africa, Malaysia, Chile, and numerous other countries in the world.[65] In all these cases, legal interpretations of mobility can be fatal to Indigenous peoples. If we are forced or choose to leave, our reserves, homelands, our traditions and freedoms are legally attenuated. This creates the risk of being completely severed by the legal regimes of the surrounding nation states.

Even if we have lived in the same area for centuries, and do not leave our traditional territories, mobility can be manipulated by the law to diminish Indigenous rights. Our lives can be characterized as hyper-mobile within our homelands, thereby allowing others to lay superior claims. In such cases, freedom is presumptively reduced because we are labelled as nomadic.[66] The United States Supreme Court accepted this view in the *Tee Hit Ton* case, where they held that 'nomadic tribes of Indians' have a form of occupancy that does not amount to owner-ship.[67] The United States Supreme Court is not alone in diminishing Indigenous rights for this reason.[68] It has long been thought that so-called nomadic people do not sufficiently mix their labour with the soil to acquire its underlying benefits. For example, John Locke convinced others to believe this so-called limit – this fiction.[69]

In fact, Canada's Supreme Court seemingly accepted troubling implications that flow from this dubious line of argument. In *R. v. Marshall; R. v. Bernard*, the Court ruled that Mi'kmaq people had insufficient connections with specific sites to establish Aboriginal title, despite living in an area for thousands of years before any European ever set foot on their soil.[70] They wrote, 'The common law right to title is commensurate with exclusionary rights of control ... If the ancient aboriginal practices do not indicate that type of control, then title is not the appropriate right.'[71] These views demonstrate that the concept of physical mobility can be deployed to facilitate assimilation because past relationships with land are interpreted too narrowly.

Thus, the recognition and retention of Indigenous rights can sometimes depend too heavily on notions that we are too unsettled. I sometimes even sense this tendency among my own people. If you are away from the reserve for too long during one of your travels, your Indigenous identity can be questioned. While peer pressure in this context can be a good thing, if it causes you to remember your obligations to your land, family, and home, it can be negative when it is implied that 'real' Anishinaabe do not move too much. These views can tether us too tightly to *colonially constructed* reserves and thereby interfere with our freedom to live throughout our own territories, in accordance with our long-standing patterns of movement.

ii) '... and Damned if We Don't': The Too Settled Thesis

While Indigenous peoples are told we cannot have rights if we move too much, we are also informed we cannot possess rights because our societies move too little. Caught in these cross-currents, Indigenous peoples face contradictory doctrines that deny legal rights for reasons directly opposed to one another. While the last section noted how we can lose freedom by being characterized as too unsettled, judges can contribute to our domination by finding we are too settled, unmoving, intransient, and static in our cultural practices. This approach is best illustrated by understanding how courts treat Indigenous peoples as they move through time.

Judges have not generally been inclined to view us as contemporary peoples who retain or develop rights when we interact with other traditions. They often freeze our status, and pin it upon the date of non-Native contact or sovereign assertion. They entrench this approach in the law, thus making it difficult for us to travel beyond their abstracted assertions. These doctrines are widespread throughout the world. The courts' stereotypes imply that Indigenous political communities are inferior to those who arrived subsequently, because only non-Indigenous states and peoples are given the privilege of moving through time with unfettered power relative to pre-existent societies. Under this approach, Indigenous peoples' interaction with other societies is held to create assimilation and a loss of rights.

For example, if Indigenous peoples in Canada adopt new practices in response to colonial intrusions, these innovations are not protected as rights.[72] Developments that take place subsequent to colonial influence are regarded as not being 'integral to our distinctive cultures.'[73] We are not permitted to claim rights flowing from practices developed after Europeans arrived because they are regarded as developing *solely* though European influence (as if Indigenous development could be 'solely' tied to European influences).[74] Aboriginal title contains inherent limits that prevent us from using our territories in ways that the courts consider irreconcilable with our historically settled ways.[75] By these standards, the courts assume that European arrival initiated change that travelled beyond Indigenous peoples' previously inert, 'integral' state. In this light, we are regarded as being too culturally settled at the time of contact to expect new rights to develop from that point forward.

In Australia, even if we adapt or reactivate legal, cultural, and political traditions, they do not receive protection as Indigenous rights.[76] Once we 'abandon' old ways, we are told we cannot reactivate them. To allow Indigenous peoples to invent or revitalize tradition would seemingly shatter stereotypical views that imply we cannot be authentically Indigenous if we move beyond our so-called ancient culturally settled state. These views inappropriately depict Indigenous societies as stationary, non-dynamic, and invariable before others arrived in our lands. These stereotypes create a hierarchical caste system which places Indigenous societies lower on the scale of social order, relative to the creation of subsequent political groupings like nations, states, provinces, and municipalities. These are false traditions that structure how nations relate to Indigenous peoples in legal, political, and social terms.

This approach is echoed in the United States where courts have severely restricted the application of Indigenous jurisdiction over non-Indians because they have found this to be 'inconsistent with their status.' Like their Canadian and Australian counterparts, the United States Supreme Court subjectively patrols the borders of Indigenous domination through their ability to control the characterization of Indigenous traditions. In the U.S. context, the Court's touchstone for determining the so-called essence of Indian status is whether non-Indians are affected.[77] This interpretive approach has undermined Native American rights in cases involving zoning,[78] taxation,[79] and criminal and civil jurisdiction over non-Indians on reservations.[80] According to this definition, assimilation is appropriate, as long as it only runs in one direction – from the colonizing power to the Indigenous society. In this view, it is impermissible for Indigenous peoples to draw others into their cultures, traditions, and laws and expect the courts to protect these activities as rights. In this regard, we are not entitled to the same freedoms enjoyed by other peoples. Once again, *a priori* conceptions about Indigenous traditions stand in the way of freedom.

This troubling double standard prevents nation states from properly recognizing and affirming Indigenous peoples' ability to develop through time. Rights are terminated when Indigenous peoples' political journeys take them beyond the point of colonial contact or sovereign assertions of authority. Shutting the gate to these travels constrains Indigenous philosophical and cultural mobility. We are told 'you can't go there' when we want to trek beyond imposed ideological boundaries, which stereotype us as past-tense peoples. The same restrictions cannot be said to apply to non-Indigenous people. When they venture through land or time they are largely presumed to carry their rights and freedoms with them.[81]

The false limitations of this approach become further entrenched when judges do not acknowledge our knowledge as Indigenous if we have incorporated ideas from the surrounding society.[82] In Canada, many of our most respected Elders and chiefs have been discredited because they make claims by referencing events that occurred after European arrival. For example, in *Ontario (Attorney General) v. Bear Island Foundation*, the Supreme Court dismissed an Aboriginal title case arising from the Ontario High Court of Justice because the Temagami Anishinaabe understanding of history was 'influenced by a small, dedicated and well-meaning group of white people,' who pieced together 'limited pieces of oral tradition.'[83] This view echoes a discredited historiography that regards Indigenous aspirations as inappropriately influenced by outsiders, thus casting doubt on their authenticity as Indigenous.[84] While the Supreme Court of Canada questioned the trial judge's findings regarding historic occupation it did not explicitly rehabilitate Chief Potts status as a credible Indigenous oral historian.[85]

It seems that Chief Potts had four strikes against him, thereby making his testimony suspect as Indigenous knowledge.[86] First, he had a white mother and a father who was not of 'pure' Indian ancestry. Second, his family purportedly arrived in the territory after the disputed event had taken place. Third, he could not speak Anishinaabe (even though his Elders could speak English). Fourth, Chief Potts learned his oral history by reading a short academic memoir about the Temagami in his teenage years and, for the next twenty years, questioning other people about it, including his father. The trial judge said this was 'obviously not oral tradition in the normal sense.'[87]

It is important to underscore what the trial judge finds abnormal in Chief Potts' testimony as Indigenous traditional knowledge. He had seemingly travelled too far beyond what courts consider to be authentically Indigenous. The judge's conclusions illustrate how cultural stereotypes about Indigenous peoples' conceptual journeys are inappropriately limited. If one was being provocative, they might even label these views as racist.[88] It is wrongly thought that Indigenous peoples' ideas travel away from authenticity if their ancestry is not pure, if their ancestors were physically mobile, if Elders and youth communicated with one another in English, and if they learned oral tradition prompted by their own literacy and active inquiry about the world. This is another example of the courts inappropriately blocking our journeys through time. The manner in which the trial court depicted Chief Potts illustrates an exceedingly narrow view of who constitutes an authoritative Indigenous person, and thus what qualifies as Indigenous tradition. These conclusions constrain philosophical mobility. They constrain freedom.

Fortunately, the Supreme Court of Canada later chastised judges who undervalued Indigenous oral history and thereby narrowed its reach.[89] In *Delgamuukw v. British Columbia*, Chief Justice Lamer stated that treatment of evidence in Aboriginal rights cases must accord 'due weight to the perspective of aboriginal peoples.'[90] Thus, the courts must 'come to terms with the oral histories of aboriginal societies' by placing them on an 'equal footing with the types of historical evidence that courts are familiar within.'[91] Unfortunately, despite the Court's caution, and its potential to respect Indigenous knowledge,[92] Indigenous peoples still encounter stereotypes regarding their knowledge and mobility.

For example, in *R. v. Marshall; R. v. Bernard*, the Supreme Court of Canada affirmed conclusions that Chief Steven Augustine could not be trusted to properly recite oral tradition because of the so-called feedback affect from ideas generated outside his own culture and a product of his own literacy.[93] In *Mitchell v. M.N.R.*, the Court regarded Chief Mike Mitchell's evidence of Mohawk mobility and trade across the St. Lawrence River, which was accepted by the trial judge, to be 'sparse, doubtful and equivocal.'[94] Chief Mitchell's testimony, which was substantial during the hearing, largely disappeared from the Federal and Supreme Court's opinions.[95] The Supreme Court in particular was unwilling to draw inferences that Mohawk trade would accompany cross-river mobility, despite the finding of 'ample evidence ... that trade was a central, distinguishing feature of the Iroquois in general and the Mohawks in particular.'[96] It should be noted that Chiefs Potts, Augustine, and Mitchell are among the most prominent and well-respected Chiefs of their Nations. They also have significant reputations as strong First Nations leaders throughout Canada. If these people have trouble convincing courts of the authenticity or trustworthiness of Indigenous tradition, one can glimpse the difficulties other Indigenous peoples will encounter if they adopt insights from their conceptual travels through other cultures.

Furthermore, when Indigenous peoples enter the policy arena, outside of the courts, they also find that their philosophical mobility is manipulated by being construed as past-tense and backward-looking. For example, when Indigenous peoples look to the future, they often seek to secure their objectives through negotiation, agreement, and treaties. In this sense, they want to nest their freedoms in an ongoing democratic framework, which one might expect would be respected and applauded. Yet, when Indigenous peoples make these moves, it is revealing to observe how they are re-characterized by too many non-Indigenous politicians. These politicians often call for extinguishment, certainty, or finality regarding Indigenous rights, as if somehow Indigenous peoples and the conflict their ongoing presence generates will magically come to an end through a treaty process and settlement.[97] These views illuminate false assumptions that regard treaties as largely being about the past. As such, this interpretation stifles democratic engagement today.

Many non-Indigenous leaders believe that treaties are about concluding old, unfinished business. They do not generally see treaties as creating structures for present and future Indigenous growth and interaction with the nation state.[98] This leads to the presumption that once treaties are settled, Indigenous peoples will generally participate in political life much like other citizens. The Indian Claims Commission in the United States created a settlement process that focused on extinguishment.[99] The New Zealand government set 2020 as the date for a full and final settlement of Waitangi Treaty claims.[100] Maori people worry that the government's approach makes their political and philosophical aspirations appear anachronistic. Many iwi, hapu, and whanua wish to see the Treaty of Waitangi as an intergenerational agreement that guides political philosophies and relationships through time.[101] Unfortunately, many non-Indigenous politicians do not want to travel down this path, and thus impliedly seek to limit Indigenous peoples' ability to move their ideas and practices into the future.

D. Recognizing and Affirming Indigenous Physical Mobility

Inappropriate physical or philosophical conceptions of Indigenous mobility should not be used to deny or diminish freedom and a quest for a good life. Rights should not be used to alienate us from our lands, even if we 'stay put,' or are forcibly removed or constantly move within our territories. Our territorial relationships should not be conceptualized in the same manner as common-law property rights. In the last century, the Judicial Committee of the Privy Council advised that 'much caution is essential' when interpreting 'the various systems of native jurisprudence throughout the Empire.'[102] They noted that such caution is essential because judges are susceptible to the danger of only recognizing property law within Indigenous societies if they find analogies to concepts within English law. The court said 'this tendency has to be held in check' because it would prevent the recognition of beneficial rights that developed under Indigenous systems.[103] This caution is appropriate when considering issues of mobility. Legal traditions which manipulate rights to forcible removal or coercive confinement are wrong. Cases that remove Indigenous peoples from their territories on the basis of mobility must be overturned. They are inconsistent with emerging international legal norms, and do not represent the best in cutting-edge developments we see in comparative jurisprudence. If we are going to use rights to adjudicate Indigenous issues, which I question later in this book, we should at least take guidance from developing international standards because they are more attentive to the physical circumstances on-the-ground in these communities.

For example, the *Western Sahara* case from the International Court of Justice precludes a region from being termed uninhabited if so-called nomadic or resident tribes with a degree of social and political organization are present in the area.[104] The *Awas Tingni* case from the Inter-American Court of Human Rights found that traditional patterns of mobile use and occupation of territory by the Indigenous communities of the Atlantic coast of Nicaragua generated customary law property systems that should be protected as property rights in Nicaragua's constitution.[105] The *Dann* case from the Inter-American Commission on Human Rights held general principles of international law included 'the right of indigenous peoples to legal recognition of their varied and specific forms and modalities of their control, ownership, use, and enjoyment of territories and property.[106] This should be interpreted to encompass Indigenous usages that incorporate mobility. Article 14(1) of the International Labour Organization's Convention 169 also recognizes the importance of protecting Indigenous rights to land that arises from mobility. It states that 'the rights of ownership and possession of the peoples concerned over the lands which they traditionally occupy shall be recognized ... [and] particular attention shall be paid to the situation of nomadic peoples and shifting cultivators in this respect.'[107] Finally, Article 26(2) of the UN Declaration on the Rights of Indigenous Peoples proclaims that 'Indigenous peoples have the right to own, use, develop and control the lands, territories and resources that they possess by reason of traditional ownership or other traditional occupation or use, as well as those which they have otherwise acquired.' If Indigenous peoples traditionally used or owned land in a manner which incorporated elements of mobility, these principles should protect rather than eliminate Indigenous land rights.

In a domestic context, certain countries are beginning to apply these and similar principles to overturn traditions which denied Indigenous peoples land rights because of their rotational uses. The South African Constitutional Court held that 'racial discrimination lay in the failure to recognize and accord protection to indigenous law ownership while, on the other hand, according protection to registered [non-Indigenous] title.'[108] The Malaysian Court of Appeal cited comparative and international legal principles to find that the 'precise nature of customary title draws upon the practices and usages of each community.'[109] This approach permitted the court to find that customary titles could be permanent even if the use of the land was territorial and communal.[110] The Belize Supreme Court cited the Malaysian decision with approval and decided that rotational land uses can be recognized as property rights under the Belize constitution.[111] This case also built upon the decision of the Inter-American Commission on Human Rights that came to the same conclusion.[112] The Belize case was also the first judgment in the world to reference the UN Declaration on the Rights of Indigenous Peoples.

The Canadian Supreme Court also recently recognized Aboriginal title in Canada by applying standards that recognized Indigenous peoples' ability to hold land on a territorial basis despite rotating seasonal uses. While the Court did not cite the UN Declaration on the Rights of Indigenous Peoples, it held that 'the court must be careful not to lose or distort the Aboriginal perspective by forcing ancestral practices into the square boxes of common law concepts, thus frustrating the goal of faithfully translating pre-sovereignty Aboriginal interests into equivalent modern legal rights.'[113] Applying Aboriginal legal traditions at the time of contact, the Court was able to find that Indigenous peoples' own laws led to an exclusivity of occupation and regular use sufficient to recognize title despite a small, mobile population.[114]

As these cases imply, when making legal judgments the choice and agency of Indigenous peoples in their movements must be recognized and affirmed. These points are also increasingly being made in the field of Indigenous studies. There are some excellent novels written by Indigenous writers that explore this phenomenon.[115] It could be said that we have new kinds of seasonal rounds that take us away from and around our territories, before we return.[116] These rounds often replicate our ancient patterns of life and apply them to changing circumstances. An example from our history as Anishinaabe people illustrates this phenomenon.

The Anishinaabe historically used land by changing residences three or four times during the year. From mid-March to mid-April, they would move from small winter camps to be with their extended families to tap maple trees and make syrup. Then, from mid-April to May, the Anishinaabe would gather with a few more of their relatives to fish in the tributaries of major streams that ran through their territories. Throughout Great Lakes watersheds, these sites were important spring-time gathering places. The Anishinaabe would harvest the waters using gill nets, spears, hooks, and fish weirs. When the fish run ended, they would congregate in larger numbers with other clan groupings to make summer camps on lakes or at the mouths of rivers in their land. At this time, small crops would be planted and large game would be hunted to supply the community's needs. They would also share knowledge and experience with one another and discuss the challenges they encountered over the winter. They would visit with other peoples too, including the Huron, Cree, and Neutral Indians. The people lived like this for four to five months until the weather turned colder once again. At this point, the Anishinaabe would gather up their goods and disperse to the snow-bound woodlands with their close family kin. They would live like this from October until March, in small clan-based winter camps engaged in small-scale hunting and gathering activities. In late March or early April, the cycle would begin all over again, though different sites in the woods, streams, lakes, and rivers would often be chosen to allow for the replenishment of areas used in previous years. Over a period of twenty to fifty years, most of their territory would be intimately used in this way.

In the present, seasonal rounds persist for many Anishinaabe people who continue to live on reservations.[117] Some continue to follow traditional economic activities while others replicate these ancient patterns in new economic circumstances. For example, in the winter and early spring, many Anishinaabe will spend time on the reserve with their families, engaged in small-scale hunting, gathering, and home-based economic activity. Some will do a little fishing, sugaring-harvesting, and trapping to supplement their families' means. Others will work intensely in the community with internally focused projects and developments. Some will work in band or organizational politics. Others work with community centres, child and family services, medical centres, and in the schools. In the late spring, men might fish more intensively to store food away for the summer. Then, when the warm weather arrives, they will leave their close-knit family-based associations and gather to work with an increasingly larger number of people. In fact, in my own family, my uncles, when they were younger, helped erect high steel structures in Chicago, Detroit, and New York during the summer months.[118] Other relatives presently work away from home in various industrial, construction, or resource sectors in the cash economy during this time. Women also engage in these activities. In the late spring, they too begin to expand their circle of activity and travel to nearby centres to reinforce work developed during the winter months. Finally, in the height of summer, many Anishinaabe gather in larger groups to share and develop ideas across broad kinship-based networks. Conferences, pow-wows, family reunions, retreats, and seminars are all familiar to the Anishinaabe during this season. In the fall, when the colder weather approaches, people might once again work less intensely off the reserve. Men might go to their Nation's traditional hunting grounds for deer or other game to supplement the money saved over the summer. Women might do the same, or in other ways wind down the intensity of summertime interactions outside the reserve. When most people come home at this season, the circle once again begins to repeat itself. While there can be significant variations, this general pattern is sufficiently similar to our ancient seasonal rounds to demonstrate important continuities.[119]

In keeping with the above insights, the best way to ensure that we do not become dominated because of our physical mobility is to recognize and affirm Indigenous patterns of mobility in law, literature, and politics. Indigenous communities can bring these examples to other people's attention, while demonstrating why these movements should not be judged by abstract, inaccurate norms. Legislatures, courts, lawyers, academics, and journalists could also be more sensitive to the consequences perpetuated by inappropriate views of Indigenous mobility. Stereotypes must be jettisoned. Every nation would do well to apply the legal principles found in recent international customs, cases, and conventions.[120] These actions might help others to see us as Indigenous even as we circulate throughout our countries and historic territories in ways that do not appear to fit erroneous perceptions of what it means to be Indigenous.[121] Indigenous peoples must be free to dispute and escape false traditions perpetuated by the state which are often replicated within Indigenous communities and beyond.

E. Recognizing and Affirming Indigenous Conceptual Mobility

Our analysis of mobility now moves from the realm of the descriptive to the probabilistic to suggest two ways in which the above insights, drawn as physical philosophy, could enhance freedom and prospects for pursuing a good life. Based on the foregoing observations, I submit that greater effort should be devoted to facilitating *dibenindizowin* and *mino-bimaadiziwin* on bases which reject false ideas concerning Indigenous physical and philosophical immobility. While Indigenous peoples must have significantly greater political, social, and legal space to craft their own lives, we must also not overlook avenues of freedom which could be 'mutually constructed within Indigenous communities and between them and the people they live amongst.'[122] Since dependence, independence, and interdependence are part of all Indigenous relationships, I submit that we must better learn how to pursue our varied traditions through a continuously interactive process of compromise, resistance, rejection, negotiation, deliberation, and dissent.[123] Thus, the following policies and prescriptions concerning Indigenous mobility are concerned with how Indigenous peoples might practically relate to others and integrate them in their political, legal, and social relationships.

First, to enhance freedom through challenging false traditions, I submit that Indigenous peoples should be permitted to regulate and integrate non-Indigenous peoples on a territorial basis within their communities. Second, to allow Indigenous peoples to harmoniously associate with other political units, I submit that we need better ways of regulating formal political relations between First Nations Indigenous and other governments. To facilitate decision-making that develops harmonized relationships, I suggest that Indigenous peoples should enjoy a measured separation from colonial relationships in structuring their laws and governmental institutions.[124] In making these points, I want to stress that they should not be imposed on Indigenous people, nor should they be regarded as inconsistent alternatives. Furthermore, they should not be universalized nor should they be made to fit all situations Indigenous peoples encounter. They are merely designed to provide further options and alternative pathways to freedom, to make it easier for Indigenous peoples to develop their traditions, free of damaging stereotypes and false limits.

i) Indigenous Governments and Personal Relationships

Indigenous peoples could enjoy greater freedom if they were permitted to legally regulate non-Indigenous people and formally integrate them into their communities. This is already happening to a limited extent when Indigenous peoples welcome others through marriage, adoption, and long association.[125] It also occurs in Nunavut and other territories, where Indigenous peoples are a majority in their homelands and thus govern other people by virtue of their numbers.[126] These practices could be extended by officially recognizing that Indigenous peoples have jurisdictional powers over everyone who lives within their territories, reserves, or villages.[127] Within clear limits, Indigenous peoples could possess broad civil and criminal legislative and adjudicative powers when they regulate others within their homelands. This could more appropriately integrate any person who lives, works, or travels in their territories. This power could also contemplate the formal extension of citizenship to non-Indigenous peoples through mutual, full, free, prior, and informed consent.[128] The incorporation of individuals into Indigenous polities should accord with Indigenous law and values and be correlated with international human rights standards. If political boundaries between communities are ambiguous, they should be demarcated based on developing international and comparative law principles.[129] This approach could guarantee significant freedoms for both Indigenous groups and individuals and generate better processes for political recognition and participation.

One of the largest obstacles to Indigenous peoples' regulation of others lies in a false tradition which holds that such abilities are 'inconsistent with their status.'[130] This tradition has congealed into a legal doctrine which ensures that non-Indians cannot generally be subject to tribal regulation or adjudication in the United States. This tradition does not facilitate peace and order on Indian reserves because it creates incentives for non-Indians to ignore or defy Indigenous laws.[131] The rule also prevents many people from considering themselves as a part of the reservation's political life, people who otherwise would make important contributions to the community. Such limits can inhibit the freer formation of bonds that help people work together for the common good. The denial of First Nations jurisdiction in relation to non-Indians also conceals a colonial boundary that cleverly conscripts Indians into patrolling their own subordination, by fashioning false distinctions between themselves and others on a racialized basis. Internalized colonialism based on these traditions must end. Indigenous peoples must remove this colonial roadblock to enjoy philosophical mobility in pursuing freedom and a good life.

Indigenous peoples should be considered as political societies, by themselves and others. The concept of race has been discredited as a suitable marker of community boundaries;[132] it should be rejected as a marker for Indigeneity as well. As part of rejecting this tradition, Indigenous peoples should be able to adopt people from other parts of the world into their families, and make them citizens of their nations, if that is each party's wish. At the same time, this process must be designed to ensure Indigenous peoples' laws and values are strengthened and not undermined in the process of accepting others into their societies.[133] If proper protections are present, based on self-determination and human rights values, the infusion of new people and their ideas should be considered a healthy part of Indigenous peoples' political life.

Traditions which construct Indigenous societies on an abstract, racialized basis can freeze ideas about who is authentically Indigenous. Such ideas condition us to expect 'real' Indigenous peoples to be racially 'pure.' This can lead to the diminishment of the community's jurisdiction if 'blood' or ancestry becomes too remote from an idealized fullness as people travel through the generations. This is an inappropriate constraint – a false horizon. This view limits mobility by construing Indigenous peoples as 'pure' on the moment of European arrival, with a consequent reduction of 'purity' as they travel beyond this point in time. This racist tradition is harmful to constructing healthy contemporary societies. As the Royal Commission on Aboriginal Peoples observed,

Aboriginal peoples are not racial groups; they are organic political and cultural entities. Although contemporary Aboriginal peoples stem historically from the original peoples of North America, they often have mixed genetic heritages and include individuals of varied ancestries. As organic political entities, they have the capacity to evolve over time and change in their internal composition.

… One of the greatest barriers standing in the way of creating new and legitimate institutions of self-government is the notion that Aboriginal people constitute a 'disadvantaged racial minority' … Only when Aboriginal peoples are viewed, not as 'races' within the boundaries of a legitimate state, but as distinct political communities with recognizable claims for collective rights, will there be a first and meaningful step towards responding to Aboriginal peoples' challenge to achieve self-government.[134]

Freezing contact as the fulcrum point for determining the height of Indigeneity works a nefarious colonial purpose. It allows societies who associate with Indigenous people to perpetually diminish Indigenous rights as they move from that point of time onward and adapt to new circumstances. This standard punishes Indigenous people for any genetic journeying beyond contact, thereby correspondingly diminishing their society's power to move through time.

As one can see, *a priori* ideas of racial 'purity' are related to concepts that construct Aboriginal rights from the moment of contact, before Europeans interacted with Indigenous peoples.[135] Under this approach, European contact is constructed as diminishing Indigenous freedom.[136] Chief Justice Marshall of the United States Supreme Court said contact created limitations that excluded Indigenous political '*intercourse* with any other European potentate.'[137] The last sentence deserves careful re-reading; this troubling tradition lies at one of the roots of Indigenous peoples' domination. To exclude intercourse with others is to preclude freedom. Unfortunately, colonial societies continue to meddle with Indigenous intercourse when they prevent the passage of Indigenous citizenship in accordance with Indigenous peoples' biological and political processes. Under this 'racist' belief, Indigenous peoples cannot give non-Native people lands or membership in their communities without the state's permission. In this light, Justice Marshall's words concerning intercourse take on a more sexualized connotation. Indigenous intercourse without government permission does not allow Indigenous peoples to pass along citizenship to their children if they have too many non-Indians in their family tree.[138] This demonstrates the deeply 'seeded' racism that underlies Doctrines of Discovery and Aboriginal Rights. These traditions obstruct Indigenous travel through the generations. They have severely negative consequences for Indigenous mobility.

This is why we should consider recognizing and affirming Indigenous peoples' regulation and integration of other people into their communities, based on practices of free, prior, and informed consent for Indigenous peoples and those who receive rights, participation, or citizenship from them. These practices would allow Indigenous peoples to travel beyond false racialized borders. We could more freely function as democratic societies that draw their legitimacy from Indigenous peoples' self-determining choices about the nature of our communities, and those who associate with us. Under this approach, *dibenindizowin* and *mino-bimaadiziwin* could more fully animate Indigenous relationships if this kind of fluidity was embedded in our laws. The regulation, integration, or consensual accommodation of peoples from other places into our communities would be a refreshing, generous, and hospitable idea. It would also allow our societies to substantially expand, as free peoples are inclined to do.[139]

ii) Indigenous Governments and Institutional Relationships

Indigenous peoples' ability to travel more freely through physical space and time could be enhanced if there were better ways of regulating and harmonizing institutional relations between Indigenous and other governments. This democratic pursuit could be 'mutually constructed within Indigenous communities and between them and the people they live amongst.'[140] Unfortunately, Indigenous mobility in relation to political power is often frozen by nation states because Indigenous peoples are considered competitors for lands, resources, and political power.[141] The strength of Indigenous peoples' prior occupancy and sovereignty is difficult for states to overcome and thus they seek to constrain Indigenous claims by attempting to relegate them to the past. If Indigenous peoples are construed as politically 'stuck in the past,' then there is no need for the state to involve them in present and future political relationships. For example, one often finds courts applying limitations statutes to Indigenous claims, thereby stifling the contemporary resolutions of disputes.[142] The unilateral handicapping of Indigenous governments in relation to other state actors produces an obvious advantage for non-Indigenous governments, who are not considered as being frozen in time. This approach not only gives advantages to non-Native nations and individuals, it simultaneously creates a significant disadvantage for Indigenous peoples in their relationships with others. This is a tradition which leads to domination.

It becomes harder for Indigenous peoples to freely seek a good life when they are disadvantaged in this way. This result does not comport with any parties' highest moral and legal standards. Steps must be taken to overcome ideas and practices that place Indigenous governments in political and legal museums. As such, nation states should recognize contemporary Indigenous peoples' governments as vital to the modern life of each country. This should be recognized both within and beyond the borders of Indigenous reserves. The ways in which Indigenous peoples should relate to the broader state will vary from country to country. This is because Indigenous peoples have goals that differ from one another, and from those of their non-Indigenous neighbours. Indigenous/state relations are constructed on distinctive historical experiences. For these reasons, the Maori of New Zealand will likely want to pursue different arrangements from First Nations in Canada. Native Americans in the United States will differ from the goals the Sami pursue in Scandinavia, and so forth. The democratic aspirations of other populations within the nation should also appropriately influence the contours of Indigenous representation. The enhancement, regulation, and harmonization of Indigenous peoples' political relationships with surrounding nation states must specifically attend to the particular barriers and opportunities found within each country to better facilitate future Indigenous mobility.

Despite these differences, Indigenous peoples and others could look across national borders to learn what might be possible as we seek to construct better relationships with adjoining nation states. Those who are not strict isolationists or ironically colonial in their orientation to nation states will likely seek healthy intercourse with surrounding societies. Some institutional examples that facilitate Indigenous/state harmonization include treaties, truth and reconciliation commissions, First Nation jurisdictional recognition, representation as Indigenous people in Parliament or the legislature, state-wide holidays and celebrations of Indigenous peoples' contributions, permanent treaty offices, Indigenous recognition legislation, apologies for past injustices, independent land claims tribunals, and other forms of constitutional, legislative, and policy instruments.

Furthermore, in other publications I have written that one device for facilitating harmonization is the recognition and application of First Nations laws to other people in society.[143] The application of Indigenous law to non-Indigenous peoples can help to spread our laws over a greater portion of our traditional territories.[144] I do not believe our legal values should be ghettoized, even as I resist their being universalized. Our ideas about law should be mobilized in practical ways to travel beyond the reserves; they should not be theorized as pure conceptions concerning justice and the good life. Indigenous law should prudently contribute to the formation of binding standards that guide the behaviour of all people on our lands. The point of each innovation is to facilitate non-Indigenous recognition of Indigenous peoples and their political, legal, and cultural participation and representation outside of lands set aside for them within the nation state.

If properly implemented, harmonization could help others see Indigenous governments as part of the contemporary world whose structures must be democratically regenerated and accommodated as they move through space and time among nation states. As it currently stands, the relationship between Indigenous peoples and others is too often characterized by conflict and denial. Certainly, nation states are the main culprits in reproducing these injuries. They bear the lion's share of responsibility for such conflict. However, it must also be pointed out that Indigenous peoples can also contribute to the narrowing of their world. This occurs when they fail to recognize their neighbours' humanity and appropriate aspirations because of past or current colonial treatment. Indigenous peoples turn away from appropriately recognizing others when they place abstract or essentialized theorizing above real-world interdependencies. This further alienates individuals and nations from their land, labour, and material realities. It diminishes Indigenous mobility. It results in domination.

Non-Indigenous government officials worry that the recognition of Indigenous governments and laws will undermine their sovereignty and land claims and will inappropriately intrude on their citizens' liberties.[145] Significantly, Indigenous governments worry about the same thing when considering non-Indigenous governments.[146] An unbalanced focus on these concerns prevents us from adequately accounting for the interdependence of peoples, ecosystems, and economies in the modern world. It also ignores contemporary political forces that work to disable Indigenous attempts to live as separate peoples. Working to create appropriate harmonization and separation between governments can more effectively address the fears we face and facilitate greater freedom within Indigenous/nation state relationships. There must be a much larger place for the proper recognition, separation, and coordination of fields of mutual concern, which recognizes and addresses adverse power imbalances among peoples. As Indigenous peoples move through the world, they should be able to work and learn from those around them. The same should be said of nation states and other international bodies in relation to Indigenous peoples. There may be important ideas that Indigenous peoples can bring to other communities if their views are incorporated into their philosophies and practices.

While Indigenous peoples and their institutions should be permitted to draw closer to the nation states which surround them, this must not result in any person or groups' forced assimilation. Harmonization of governmental relationships should not equal Indigenous termination.[147] The synchronicity I am proposing requires the maintenance of Indigenous societies and envisions their future growth and strength. It contemplates structures and practices that strongly resist colonialism. It allows for measured separations and the pursuit of radically different interests. When music is harmonized, individual notes retain their distinctiveness and resonance; similar keys should be struck in recognizing Indigenous/non-Indigenous governmental relationships. Indigenous governments must retain a healthy degree of independence and control within their communities even as they live interdependently. They should not be generally absorbed into the body politic. Independence is not opposed to interdependence.[148] Self-determination does not require self-abnegation.

Thus, while creating healthy relationships with other governments, Indigenous peoples should be freely responsible for their own autonomous democratic governments, vibrant educational systems, rich ceremonial structures, self-regulating economies, and rigorous internal protection for individual freedoms and collective civil society structures. They should also be free to pursue radically libertarian, socialist, and Marxist options, too – as is the case with all societies. Compulsion should be rejected. This is not to say that Indigenous societies should be without constraint, or beyond the reach of law or the influence of other governments or institutions. There are real and substantial limits on self-determination that are necessary to promote freedom and the search for a good life. These limits are not of the false-horizon type. I am not trying to advance a liberal world view; I am attempting to outline an Anishinaabe view which is open to relational paths to freedom and a good life. I am deeply suspicious of liberalism, conservatism, socialism, Marxism, or any other exclusive organizing first principles for Indigenous or any other peoples.[149] This entire book is devoted to deconstructing grand theories and rejecting essentialized political, social, or legal classifications. Nevertheless, governmental and other institutional and personal limits that recognize legal restraints are prudent because they help reduce domination.[150] Every society should continually recreate boundaries that cannot be crossed, which includes culturally appropriate checks and balances,[151] and applications of international human rights obligations.[152] Indigenous governments must generate beneficial yet extensive legal limitations in exercising autonomous power.[153] These limitations must be free of colonial oversight and yet be subject to self-imposed and democratically developed restrictions that recognize binding obligations to their own and other people and nations.[154] Self-restraint and democratic obligations which bind peoples and individuals are real and important limits in facilitating freedom and the quest for a good life.

Fortunately, many Indigenous legal traditions combine a healthy degree of independence with restraint.[155] For example, historic exercises of Anishinaabe law focus on reciprocity, mutuality, and appropriate self-regulation.[156] These conceptions require Anishinaabe people to attenuate their practices to ensure appropriate balance is maintained in any relationship. Anishinaabe political domination should be as unacceptable as nation state domination. When Indigenous peoples follow their laws they must exercise restraint if anyone's freedom is imperiled. Indigenous peoples must face the consequences any nation encounters when they fail to respect the fundamental dignity of others. Indigenous freedom should not be construed as a licence to live without checks and balances in their relationships. This is the insight implied through *dibenindizowin* and *mino-bimaadiziwin*. When Indigenous peoples make their own decisions – about who they are, where they live, and how they should relate with others – this will facilitate freedom and their quest for a good life. Indigenous governments need a greater degree of control over their own affairs. They also need better relationships with other governments through effective harmonization and separation, to overcome traditions that inappropriately bind them in false, idealized relationships.

F. Conclusion

Indigenous peoples' physical and philosophical mobility must be recognized and affirmed. Traditions that diminish freedom and the quest for a good life must be resisted. This will not take place without taking calculated risks and engaging in much hard work. The proposals for action outlined in this chapter are not self-enforcing and do not flow from *a priori* abstractions. They flow from physically contextual political practices. They require democratic and intersocietal resistance and engagement to make them a reality. *Dibenindizowin* and *mino-bimaadiziwin* are best pursued as living traditions. A pragmatically engaged approach that rejects idealized views of Indigenous life must more thoroughly animate our activities. To return to the words of Hin-hah-too-yah-lat-kekht (Chief Joseph) that graced the introduction to this chapter,

> You might as well expect all the rivers to run backward as that any man who was born free should be contented penned up and denied liberty to go where he pleases. If you tie a horse to a stake, do you expect him to grow fat? If you pen an Indian up on a small spot of earth, and compel him to stay there, he will not be contented, nor will he grow and prosper. I have asked some of the Great White Chiefs where they got their authority to say to the Indian that he shall stay in one place, while he sees the white man going where they please. They cannot tell me ...
>
> Let me be a free man, free to travel, free to stop, free to work, free to trade where I choose, free to choose my own teachers, free to follow the religion of my fathers, free to talk, think, and act for myself – and I will obey every law or submit to the penalty.[157]

Chapter Two

Civil (Dis)Obedience, Freedom, and Democracy

I have always been somewhat suspicious of the notion of liberation because if it is not treated with precautions and within certain limits, one runs the risk of falling back on the idea that there exists a human nature or base that, as a consequence of certain historical, economic, and social processes, has been concealed, alienated, or imprisoned in and by mechanisms of repression. According to this hypothesis, all that is required is to break these repressive deadlocks and man will be reconciled with himself, rediscover his nature or regain contact with his origin, and reestablish a full and positive relationship with himself. I think this idea should not be accepted without scrutiny. I am not trying to say that liberation as such, or this or that form of liberation, does not exist: when a colonized people attempts to liberate itself from its colonizers, this is indeed a practice of liberation in the strict sense. But we know very well, and moreover, in this specific case, that this practice of liberation is not in itself sufficient to define the practices of freedom that will still be needed if this people, this society, and these individuals are to be able to define admissible and acceptable forms of existence or political society. This is why I emphasize practices of freedom over processes of liberation; again the latter have their place, but they do not seem to me to be capable by themselves of defining all the practical forms of freedom.

Michel Foucault[1]

Freedom is not always facilitated through reasoned deliberation in community gatherings, boardrooms, courts, classrooms, or legislatures. When it is not, and enough pressure has built, Indigenous peoples can move into the streets to challenge the domination they encounter. The shift from the assembly hall to the highway highlights another boundary-crossing issue: the relationship between cooperation and rebellion in reproducing domination and freedom. This movement represents another dimension of physical philosophy: the practice of civil disobedience and direct action in response to inappropriate limits on Indigenous–government relationships. This chapter explores this issue in greater detail and asks whether freedom and the quest for a good life can be enhanced when Indigenous peoples disrupt and/or prevent access to land and other resources.

Thus, as a question of practice, this chapter examines nine acts of Indigenous civil disobedience in Canada and evaluates their relationship to self-determination in a free and democratic society. Indigenous peoples often engage in pragmatic non-violent action if a country's rules of law, management, and ethics do not create sufficient space to resist domination. Direct action attempts to pry open new spaces of engagement and turn oppression on its head. In some small measure, civil disobedience allows a subjugated group (like Indigenous peoples) to reflect back to the domineering party the experience of being oppressed.[2] For example, it is important to see how Indigenous peoples' blockade of strategic sites challenges the mobility of other Canadians.[3] 'Blockades are intentionally spatial practices,' as Nicholas Blomley observes.[4] The constraints on movement, enforced through blockades, focuses attention on mobility restrictions faced by Indigenous peoples themselves. Blocking the flow of people and commerce reverses and challenges colonial constraints on mobility.

The effects of Indigenous direct action on other Canadians are not to be overlooked. While they are often minuscule in comparison to governmental restrictions on Indigenous mobility, they are nonetheless significant. Indigenous civil disobedience can be sharply felt by those against whom it is directed, since it reverses the flow of power to some small extent. As Gene Sharp has observed, 'When people refuse their cooperation, withhold their help, and persist in their disobedience and defiance, they are denying their opponent the basic human assistance and cooperation which any government or hierarchical system requires. If they do this in sufficient numbers for long enough, then to a certain degree "that government or hierarchical system will no longer have power."'[5]

The interdependent nature of civil disobedience, if exercised peacefully to establish a less oppressive reengagement, suggests this power's potentially democratic character. However, as the following case studies will demonstrate, democracy and freedom are not always facilitated by this practice. Civil disobedience can also become a false tradition when detached from specific political contexts and idealized as a universal solution. When this occurs civil disobedience can result in further oppression and undermine people's attempts to lead a good life. Thus, despite its positive potential, civil disobedience has its limits. Like other practices of Indigenous freedom, direct political action must take account of context.[6] It must be practised with calibrated care, with strict attention devoted to the particular circumstances in which it is deployed.

A. Moving Beyond Abstractions: Remembering Grounded Histories

This chapter's exploration of the limited and limit-challenging practices of civil disobedience also introduces a key point for understanding this book's thesis. Civil disobedience is placed in perspicuous contrast to the last chapter's discussion of Indigenous mobility for a specific reason:[7] to prevent the focus on mobility from creating another false horizon. This pivotal point must not be overlooked. There is no over-arching theory or practice which can be deployed to enhance relational self-determination. While mobility is a significant Indigenous issue, other priorities come into view when we shift our gaze to other Indigenous practices. We must not get carried away in thinking Indigenous cultures are focused *only* on movement. They are not. Indigenous motivations and actions towards freedom must not be essentialized. This chapter demonstrates how Indigenous practices can be just as strongly focused on 'digging in,' thereby deflecting attention away from the fluidity of Indigenous cultures.

It will be difficult to understand these complexities unless we remind ourselves there is no such thing as an ideal mobilized 'Indian,' Indigenous person or group. Mobility is a practice, not an ideal. It would be a mistake to replace one stereotype about Indigenous peoples with another as a result of the last chapter's reflections. Indigenous peoples cannot be fully captured by any theoretical category, including mobility. In fact, such categorizations would be inaccurate and agonizingly ironic given my caution against non-contextual theorizing. Thus, like mobility, Indigenous politics should not be completely explained by reference to protest, unyieldingness and civil disobedience. Life is more nuanced than ideal forms allow. Utopian conceptions of Indigeneity must be resisted if we want to facilitate freedom (which, of course, includes questioning the meaning of freedom itself). Abstract political theories drawn from rarified first principles do not explain the real world of Indigenous political action. This is why this book focuses on Indigenous practices and uses the term *physical philosophy* to consider these activities.[8]

Actual Indigenous experiences reveal alternative pathways moving towards freedom and a good life. Alternative genealogies of Indigenous practice, relating to both mobility and civil disobedience help guard against creating false traditions.[9] As Richard Rorty has suggested, a study of activity should be prior to theory.[10] In this spirit, the following chapter will briefly discuss select examples of Indigenous practices relating to Indigenous civil (dis)obedience. To highlight the subjective characterization of such conflicts I will use the term *civil (dis)obedience* from this point forward to refer to such conflicts. I have bracketed the first syllable in *dis-obedience* to signal that an act of disobedience in one context may, in another context, be considered obedience to either Indigenous peoples' law or the state's own unenforced or unrealized standards. Thus in some settings disobedience to Canadian law (as interpreted by governments) could well be obedience to Indigenous law. Furthermore, in some situations so-called civil disobedience could also be characterized as obedience to Canadian law 'as it should be,' if such laws applied Indigenous legal principles or the state's own highest standards.[11]

The examples of civil (dis)obedience in this chapter fall into three groups, relating to three results that seem to flow from its exercise. The first explores situations where an Indigenous community achieved greater democratic voice and reduced domination over themselves and others because of their activities. Examples that will illustrate this result can be found at Haida Gwaii, James Bay, Cape Croker, and Clayoquot Sound. The second type of example is drawn from those instances where civil (dis)obedience produced at least some limited benefits for Indigenous peoples and Canadians more generally, but failed to resolve the specific issue giving rise to direct action. Examples showing this result are drawn from Oka and Burnt Church. Finally, the third kind of experience examined in this chapter focuses on instances where civil (dis)obedience did not open up any meaningful democratic space, thereby further eroding Indigenous freedom. These less liberatory results demonstrate the volatility of civil (dis)obedience in enhancing relational freedom and democratic self-determination.

While civil (dis)obedience can be an important democratic practice, these short case studies suggest that it is best used carefully and sparingly in the current Canadian context. It is not an easy tool to deploy, because it often generates grave misunderstandings and toxic backlash.[12] Direct action is never unilateral. It is always inserted into a wider context which cannot be controlled by the group initiating it. It is always relational, just as is freedom (*dibeninidizowin*) itself. While its practitioners hope to promote understanding between people, civil (dis)obedience can broadly shut down deliberation and provide further excuses to justify repression. As is the case with other practices, care must be taken not to romanticize direct action as an 'ideal' pathway to freedom. Nor should we completely reject it. It can be liberating when deployed in carefully calibrated ways. Furthermore, contexts may change and civil (dis)obedience might shift from helpful to harmful, or vice versa. As some of the following examples show, civil (dis)obedience can lead to better relationships in some circumstances and further oppression in others.

Unfortunately, some activists seem to treat civil (dis)obedience in the way some Indigenous lawyers might view rights – as 'the' ideal category to facilitate freedom. It becomes 'the' answer to all problems and its widespread use can be heralded in absolutist terms. 'Idle No More,' a broad-based celebration of Indigenous resistance and survival that spread across Canada and beyond in 2013–14, revealed some of these voices. While most participants viewed these activities in nuanced ways, others used the movement to theorize that it represented a fundamental, foundational or universally necessary response to subjugation and colonialism.[13] A cult of self-sufficiency through direct action surrounds some people's and community's relationship to civil (dis)obedience, transforming it from a context-specific tool into an idealized form, thereby closing off other avenues to freedom because they are deemed less worthy. While we should strongly reject the view that civil (dis)obedience is never justifiable, the cases in our third grouping reveal its limitations as well as strengths.

Places in this chapter's third cluster, where civil (dis)obedience was less successful in changing circumstances, on the ground or more generally, were Anicinabe Park in Kenora, Ontario; Barriere Lake in Quebec; and Temagami in Ontario.[14] The varieties of examples of Indigenous civil (dis)obedience are provided in the following pages to prevent an oversimplification of the consequences of direct actions.

Before we turn to particular examples of civil (dis)obedience, a word of caution is necessary related to the following collection of disputes. The practice and effects of direct action described in the chapter are broad and complex and resist simple categorization. In fact, while the conflicts presented below are grouped into three, this placement must not be regarded as final and conclusive. Comparisons using different criteria from those found in this book could assemble and contrast these disputes in other ways. Moreover, many of these conflicts are ongoing, and could in coming years be shifted in comparative terms with other disputes for many reasons. Thus, the following threefold grouping is merely a point of entry; it is not definitive. These comparisons are provided to give contextual illustrations of this book's thesis – which resists deterministic structuralism and universalism in Indigenous affairs. Recognizing that freedom does not follow predefined pathways is the price we pay for beginning 'where we are' in pursuing a good life.[15] While fictitious certainty is sacrificed by philosophies that take placed-based physicality (rather than abstract metaphysics) as their starting point, materially focused philosophies are more responsive to contextual political realities, which develop through time.

B. Group One: Best Practices (so far) in Indigenous Civil (Dis)obedience

i) Moresby Island, Haida Gwaii, British Columbia

In *R. v. Oakes*, the Supreme Court of Canada described the values of a free and democratic society. The court said these included 'respect for the inherent dignity of the human person, commitment to social justice and equality, accommodation of a wide variety of beliefs, respect for cultural and group identity, and faith in social and political institutions which enhance the participation of individuals and groups in society.'[16] One would expect that civil (dis)obedience informed by these practices would encourage more productive democratic engagement. In fact, this seems to be the case with the Haida people of British Columbia, our first example. In their experience with civil (dis)obedience, many of democratic practices identified in the *Oakes* case are on display.

The Haida people's willingness to engage in civil (dis)obedience is partially rooted in their long presence in the area. For thousands of years, the Haida used and occupied Haida Gwaii, off the west coast of British Columbia. This land was called the Queen Charlotte Islands for over a century before its name was officially redesignated as Haida Gwaii in 2010.[17] Creation stories speak of the Haida's genesis in the area.[18] The Haida believe they were present in the area during the last ice age.[19] They have oral histories about villages that once stood on lands now covered by Hecate Strait during that time.[20] They were on Haida Gwaii when the Spanish arrived.[21] They later greeted and ushered English, Russian, and American explorers into their territories.[22] Throughout this period they traded, socialized and sometimes fought with other Indigenous Nations on the mainland of North America.[23] The Haida existed as a highly organized society in 1846 when the Oregon Treaty was drawn to divide Canada from the United States in the Pacific Northwest.[24]

Unfortunately, British Columbia has never constitutionally recognized Haida ownership and resource use. There has never been any treaty between the Haida and the Crown. In fact, for over 125 years British Columbia claimed the island archipelago as its own. The Crown issued grants, tenures, licences, and permits, and collected royalties for lands and resources on Haida Gwaii without Haida approval.[25] The Haida regard these governmental acts as unjustified examples of occupation of lands they legally own.[26] The government's physical occupation of Haida Gwaii blocks Haida access to their lands and resources. This is a practice of domination. It is a flashpoint for conflict generated by harmful legal traditions that subordinate Haida governance and stewardship in relation to their environment. These factors created the background conditions for the eventual use of civil (dis)obedience by the Haida people.

The specific events preceding their physical confrontation with governments unfolded as follows.[27] In 1973, the Haida initiated negotiations with the federal government for a declaration acknowledging their ownership of Haida Gwaii.[28] As part of these negotiations, Gwaii Haanas, the southern part of the archipelago, was identified as a site of great ecological significance. A series of proposals recommended that this land be protected from development to conserve its natural beauty. In the mid-1970s, seemingly in response to the possibility for protection, the BC Government initiated a land-use planning forum under the Ministry of Forests, ostensibly to determine the future of Gwaii Haanas. While progress was made, this process ultimately proved disappointing to the Haida, because their objectives were not recognized through the forum. 'In fact, government allowed logging to proceed at full pace while a seemingly endless series of land use planning meetings continued for several years.'[29]

Finally, in the mid-1980s, as a result of Haida frustration with the government's process, a blockade was erected to prevent further logging on Gwaii Haanas.[30] This act of civil (dis)obedience attracted national and international attention, and a strong public campaign developed in the mid-1980s to preserve Gwaii Haanas as a national park.[31] Thus, Haida civil (dis)obedience opened up a new democratic space to explore Haida self-determination and freedom. They attempted to work and communicate directly with other Canadians. A cross-country caravan was formed and travelled across Canada to secure support for Haida rights.[32] In short, direct action facilitated wider deliberation and negotiation aimed at reducing government domination in the area and beyond. As a result of these newly minted processes, the Haida removed their blockades to work for broader solutions.

While initial efforts to negotiate new arrangements were encouraging, delays and procedural wrangling eventually built a sense of frustration among the Haida and their supporters. A lack of democratic engagement after a period of initial promise threatened to erase the freedoms they had gained. Since negotiation floundered when the Haida removed their pressure, they decided to redeploy direct action. They erected another set of blockades. At the time of the second blockade, Miles Richardson, president of the Haida Nation, proclaimed the reason for the occupation: 'There will be no logging on the area that the Haida people have designated that are not to be touched. This is Haida land ... It's time, that in the exploitation of resources, and in the management of these islands, that the people who are here sharing these lands with us *respect*, equally with everyone else, the aspirations and values of the Haida Nation. These are our homelands, we have been here for thousands of years and we intend to be here for thousands more.'[33] Haida Elder Ethel Jones echoed similar sentiments when she said, 'At this moment we want our island back. There's no written statement anywhere that we signed this land over to the government.'[34] Diane Brown, a young Haida leader at the time also declared, 'We are a nation of people at risk today ... I want to stress that it's the land that helps us maintain our culture. It is an important part of our culture. Without the land, I fear very much for the future of the Haida Nation.'[35] These views were prominent throughout the reoccupation and they were continually reinforced by other Haida leaders and Elders throughout the ordeal.[36] In these voices and actions, including the arrest of 72 protestors, one can see permanence, not mobility, undergirding Haida engagement.

The impasse between the parties culminated in a court action, which tested Haida rights on the island – but the case proved inconclusive.[37]

It did not address the underlying issues in the conflict. The Haida were looking for an acknowledgment of their special relationship with the territory and an ongoing role in its future use, but they did not find this in the courts.[38] The judicial system was resistant to their claims. Elders dressed in button blankets and ceremonial robes spoke directly to the judge (robed in Canada's ceremonial regalia) about the binding force of Haida law.[39] This was part of a sophisticated strategy to appear in court without the aid of lawyers.[40] Despite the Elders' eloquent legal arguments, the judge concluded that he had 'no alternative' but to apply British Columbia injunction law as the exclusive standard for judgment in the case.[41] He did not regard Haida law as part of British Columbia law, nor did he see alternatives to development within his own legal tradition. This decision demonstrates that courts are usually quite distant from democratic processes when it comes to Indigenous issues. While a case might open up space for further discussion, courts are usually too removed from on-the-ground practices to provide effective remedies. One problem is that courts frame issues in terms that are too abstract and generalized to be of much immediate assistance. As happened in this instance, courts too often rely on ideal forms;[42] they are not sufficiently attuned to the realities of government domination on the ground when dealing with Indigenous issues. Another problem is that court decisions give the impression of finality when conflict is still ongoing. As a result, while legal principles can sometimes play an important role in structuring engagement with courts they are very poor substitute for pragmatic action. In the Haida dispute more than high principle was required to appropriately channel the conflict.

Fortunately, after the legal decision was issued, a more responsive, targeted and contextually sophisticated political process was initiated. Negotiation and democratic interplay between the parties accomplished what the court's abstract theorizing could not. The Haida continued to apply direct pressure through leaders like Guujaaw, Miles Richardson, and Diane Brown, along with the direct actions of the Haida Watchmen Society who managed Gwaii Haanas.[43] In response, in 1986 a group of non-Native leaders, led by Vancouver lawyer and future BC Supreme Court Chief Justice Bryan Williams and in concert with the Haida, proposed the area's preservation. The Social Credit government of Bill Bennett responded by establishing the Wilderness Advisory Committee (WAC) to evaluate the validity of protecting Gwaii Haanas.[44] The creation of another institution to facilitate deliberation about Haida Gwaii's future was an important development.

Subsequent to the Wilderness Advisory Committee's creation, in 1987, the federal minister for national parks, Tom McMillan, worked with Elizabeth May of the Ottawa-based Sierra Club to put considerable pressure on British Columbia to preserve the area.[45] Haida pressure and involvement also remained very strong. Other important contributions were made by the Islands Protection Society, Vicki Husband of the Sierra Club, Paul George and Ken Lay of the Western Canada Wilderness Committee, and Colleen McCrory of the Valhalla Society. This intense campaigning led to an agreement between Prime Minister Brian Mulroney and BC premier Bill Van der Zalm that the area would be protected. Part of the protection package was a substantial buy-out by government of timber rights valued at $37 million.[46] While each party had different goals, their alignment had the effect of furthering Haida freedom.

One of the reasons the Haida Nation was successful in its use of civil (dis)obedience was that the actions of its people initiated a multiparty democratic engagement to help reduce the domination they were experiencing. Haida direct action facilitated partnerships that built on each party's intersecting yet distinct interests. Haida people fought for land, resources, heritage, and governance rights, while non-Native participants generally sought environmental protection. There was no absolute fusion of horizons between the parties, but there was sufficient convergence to reach an agreement. The Haida built wider alliances, and their success in doing so largely explains why direct action helped them partially achieve their goals. Civil (dis)obedience required a broader focus than Aboriginal rights in order to succeed. Ultimately, direct action was a democratic activity – it involved other Canadians and their interests. It aligned with and advanced the values found to be part of a free and democratic society, outlined in the *Oakes* case, including 'respect for the inherent dignity of the human person, commitment to social justice and equality, accommodation of a wide variety of beliefs, respect for cultural and group identity, and faith in social and political institutions which enhance the participation of individuals and groups in society.'[47]

In 1988, as a result of these practices, the Governments of British Columbia and Canada signed the South Moresby Agreement, which designated the area as a national park. While the Haida regarded the park's creation as only a starting point for recognizing their title and sovereignty, this development nevertheless relieved considerable pressure with the cessation of logging.[48] But the Haida did not give up. Between

1988 and 1993, the Haida Watchmen's strong direct action in managing the park pressured the government into further negotiations.[49] This eventually led to the Gwaii Haanas Agreement of 1993, which set out the terms for cooperative management of the area, between the Haida Nation and the Government of Canada.[50] In 2000, the *Gwaii Haanas National Park Reserve* was redesignated by regulation under Schedule 2 to the *Canada National Parks Act*,[51] which further protected the area from development. In 2010, protection was extended to the seabed adjacent to the park under the *Canada National Marine Conservation Areas Act*.[52] Through these agreements, the Haida have achieved many of their goals, including an acknowledgment of their special relationship with the territory and an ongoing role in its future use.[53]

This success was later consolidated in a successful action brought before the Supreme Court of Canada to ensure that governments consulted with and accommodated Haida assertions of rights and title throughout Haida Gwaii. In a decision entitled *Haida Nation v. British Columbia (Minister of Forests)*, the Supreme Court of Canada recognized that the Crown could not replace Tree Farm Licences without nourishing freedom-enhancing, self-determining, democratic relations with the Haida people.[54] The Court held that both sides must deal with one another in good faith and that the Crown must substantially address Haida concerns and thereby avoid any appearance of sharp dealing.[55] A Haida lawyer told the Supreme Court that 'cedar was sister' to her people and that the Haida people's relationship with the Crown and the forest had to recognize this fact. In turn the Supreme Court acknowledged that the Crown's 'duty to consult and accommodate is part of a process of fair dealing and reconciliation that begins with the assertion of sovereignty and continues beyond formal claims resolution.'[56] While Haida people continue to contest troubling implications with the Crown's assertion of sovereignty over them, they have significantly enhanced their freedom through the *Haida* case and their negotiated relationships – generated through direct action and civil (dis)obedience.

Thus, the Gwaii Haanas reoccupation and subsequent actions are noteworthy because they show that civil (dis)obedience can be consistent with the values and principles of a free and democratic society. While central Haida concerns have not been resolved – because their ownership of the island has not been constitutionally or otherwise affirmed – the parties have reduced the level of domination as a result of Haida taking direct action. Civil (dis)obedience worked in this instance because the parties honourably moved beyond hurling 'mere incantations' across the blockade and found practical solutions to their problem through 'concrete practices.'[57] They worked together. This example demonstrates the importance of context and intersocietal interactions in creating spaces to expand Indigenous freedom. It reinforces the point made at the end of the last chapter. The Haida were able to secure a greater degree of control over their own affairs and create better relationships with other governments through effective harmonization and separation of their interests and powers. This helped the parties to partially overcome traditions, doctrines and stereotypes that replicated hierarchical relationships and frustrated democratic engagement. Haida freedom has been enhanced, and Canadians have benefited more generally, through the protection of the internationally environmentally significant Gwai Haanas archipelago.

ii) James Bay

The next example of civil (dis)obedience comes from Northern Quebec. It also illustrates that direct action can benefit local and national constituencies. As in the Haida example, the James Bay action is also rooted in Indigenous practices that do not take mobility as their starting point or subsequent focus. It once again demonstrates that freedom and the quest for a good life can take many shapes.[58] Furthermore, also like the Haida case, the following example shows that democratic engagement and multi-party alliances are important in facilitating freedom. The grounded, place-based nature of the parties' relationships also complicates what can be achieved. Democratically infused direct action can produce positive outcomes but, as with any real-world practice, it simultaneously reproduces less-than-perfect results.[59] The Cree still live with severe constraints, even as they have improved aspects of their lives through their direct action.

The James Bay Cree have occupied lands and used the waters flowing into the eastern coast of James Bay and lower Hudson's Bay for thousands of years.[60] Their livelihood, social organization, spiritual practices, and beliefs are closely related to this ecosystem. When Canada was first settled by non-Europeans, James Bay was considered to be a part of Rupert's Land and part of Hudson's Bay Company territories through a Royal Charter.[61] It was as if Great Britain treated Canada as an empty abstraction, an *a priori* form, into which the Crown could pour its own distant traditions, unrelated to the actual fact of Cree occupation.[62] The James Bay Cree experienced the world differently. They had extensive experience on and with the land. They wondered how the land could belong to another when they continued to use it and had never surrendered it; they felt that such assertions were a troubling *form* of domination.[63]

Nevertheless, when Canada became a Dominion in 1867, there were provisions within the *British North America Act, 1867* requiring that Indian issues in the area be addressed prior to development.[64] In 1868 the Imperial Parliament passed the *Rupert's Land Act,* and the Hudson's Bay Company subsequently surrendered its so-called rights to the land to the Canadian government.[65] When the Cree heard about this transaction, they wondered how the Company had any land to surrender to the Crown. They did not think that it or the Imperial Crown possessed any rights, title, or legally enforceable interests on their lands. The Cree practised their ways throughout the territory, while the Crown only had an abstract, paper land title, which had no basis in physical, on-the-ground realities. Furthermore, an 1870 Imperial Order in Council required that the Canadian government secure surrenders of Indian title in Rupert's Land before it could be used by others. Despite these principles, no land surrender occurred in James Bay in the years following this Order. In 1898 and 1912, when Quebec's boundaries were extended over Cree homelands Aboriginal title remained unextinguished. Nevertheless, Quebec considered Cree and Inuit territory to be provincial land. This history exemplifies that abstract forms resting on false traditions of 'discovery' and 'terra nullius' collided with real-world practices to notionally displace Indigenous peoples. The non-recognition of Aboriginal rights and creeping provincial claims over Indigenous lands cultivated conditions for future conflict.

The moment of physical conflict arrived on 30 April 1971. On that date, Quebec premier Robert Bourassa proposed building a large hydroelectric-power development in Northern Quebec.[66] This decision angered many Cree and Inuit people because it would interfere with their long-established practices. They engaged in civil (dis)obedience and direct action. Nevertheless, Quebec wanted to transform imperial *forms* of ownership into actual activity on-the-ground in the area.[67] The government did this through a coercive process. Hydro-Québec was granted authority by the provincial government to divert major rivers in the area, thereby harnessing power through a series of dams, dikes, reservoirs, and power stations.

The James Bay Cree and Inuit of Northern Quebec vigorously opposed the project, arguing that it would damage the environment and destroy traditional livelihoods. They also maintained that the proposed project lands belonged to them. To the Cree and Inuit, the government's decision was contrary to Indigenous and Canadian law. The government was proposing a permanent blockade of traditional lands and waters without taking account of common law or Indigenous law's obligations. Thus, on 15 November 1973, the Cree and Inuit went to court to supplement their protests and they obtained an injunction to stop the James Bay Project's construction, though it was overturned a week later in the Quebec Court of Appeal.[68] However, the pressure from the short-lived injunction created an atmosphere that allowed for the negotiation of a land claim settlement signed on 11 November 1975.[69] The James Bay Agreement was significant because it initiated a modern era of treaty-making between Indigenous peoples and the Crown in Canada.[70] In this regard, Cree and Inuit action impacted other Indigenous peoples for good and ill.[71] Thus, the action by the James Bay Cree and Inuit of Northern Quebec was important for local and national reasons.[72] It reduced domination in some respects but generated conflict and subjugation in others. For example, while the Cree secured monetary, governance, educational and other social benefits under the agreement, many of their lands were flooded and many people's traditional livelihoods were destroyed. Governments also insisted on the extinguishment of Aboriginal rights and title under the treaty.[73] Requirements to forever cede, release, surrender, relinquish, exchange, or suspend Indigenous rights and interests within traditional territories plague treaty processes down to the present day.[74] Certainty largely flows one way under this framework and unfairly benefits Canadian and provincial governments, because pre-existing rights flowing from Indigenous sources are presumed to threaten government interests – more than Crown rights are assumed to threaten Indigenous interests under these same agreements. Another challenge arising from this process was that the federal and Quebec governments were slow to implement the agreement and disputed aspects of the treaty. In fact, implementation has proven to be a problem in the case of all modern treaties,[75] replicating the challenges faced by Indigenous peoples holding historic treaty rights.[76] These factors, along with widespread destruction of Cree lands and environments through the extensive flooding, were disastrous for many Cree people and many Canadians more generally. These negative effects also created further flashpoints for conflict.

Therefore, when the provincial government announced phase 2 of the James Bay Project (called the Great Whale Project), the Cree again took direct action. They strongly protested Quebec's decision before the national and international media. They engaged in focused and targeted civil (dis)obedience. Their efforts generated empathy and understanding in many places and brought environmental and Indigenous activists together to develop strategies that advanced their different yet intersecting interests. Cree resistance and its wider implications also transformed Quebec's conception of itself in the process.[77] As with the Haida, direct action gained traction when strategic alliances democratically open spaces for challenging government and corporate action.

In 1992, as a result of this pressure, a major potential recipient of the project's power (New York State) cancelled its hydroelectric contract with Quebec. This hurt the Quebec government, because it represented a major loss of future revenue and dimmed its reputation in political circles. As well, at the behest of the federal government, the provincial government had to rework environmental standards related to the proposed dam. The difficulties caused by this protest led Premier Jacques Parizeau to postpone construction of the Great Whale Project.

Litigation and protest dragged on for the better part of a decade.[78] Finally, a new set of negotiations broke the impasse. A deal between the Quebec government and the James Bay Cree was signed on 7 February 2002, permitting further hydro development in Northern Quebec.[79] In exchange, the Cree received $3.5 billion over 50 years and were able to negotiate greater control within their territory. The Paix des Braves Agreement, as it has been called, was designed as 'a global approach in favour of greater autonomy and greater responsibility on the part of the Crees for their development,' so as 'to make possible an active and ongoing participation by the Crees in economic development activities on the James Bay Territory.'[80] Furthermore, the agreement is 'based on a development model which relies on the principles of sustainable development, partnership and respect for the traditional way of life of the Crees, as well as on a long-term economic development strategy.'[81] In addition, the agreement is designed to promote 'the emergence of a Cree expertise in the field of economic development, job creation, and economic spin-offs for the Crees and the population of Quebec in general,'[82] in the context of a 'nation-to-nation' relation with Quebec.[83] Some hail the agreement as a major breakthrough and an international benchmark in the settlement of Indigenous rights.[84] Others have decried its existence, arguing that it completes the process of assimilation and the destruction of land, water, and the traditional Cree way of life.[85]

Thus, the agreement did not signal the conflict's end.[86] Civil (dis)obedience was partially successful in connecting the parties in democratic conversations, but it did not lead to a perfect, idealized solution. The Cree were able to secure important local objectives and benefit other Indigenous peoples by the general policy changes they helped initiate. At the same time other issues remain for future dispute, resistance, 'compromise, negotiation and deliberation.'[87] The practice of physical philosophy demonstrates that 'inevitably there will [always] be dissenting voices.'[88] At least civil (dis)obedience more fully engaged the parties' agency in this instance than would have occurred if the Cree had stood by idly.

When abstract theoretical concepts such as the doctrine of discovery and Aboriginal title dominated the scene, the Cree were less free because governments and courts used these false traditions to exclude Indigenous participation. The situation changed when Cree resistance problematized these abstractions and the Cree insisted that their own priorities be worked into future relationships. Effective harmonization enabled them to secure greater control over their own affairs and develop better relationships with other governments. The physicality of Cree actions produced measurable results for themselves and others. While these results are not unambiguously positive, and could even be considered catastrophic for many Cree, they did enhance the prospects for *dibenindizowin* and *mino-bimaadiziwin* for other Cree and non-Cree people in the territory and beyond.

iii) Chippewas of the Nawash

Civil (dis)obedience can facilitate Indigenous freedom if clear and measurable objectives for fostering change are communicated and understood. At the same time, civil (dis)obedience can clearly be used against Indigenous peoples and lead to oppressive results. This fact is illustrated in our next example, involving the Chippewas of the Nawash First Nation. As discussed in the introduction, this is the First Nation in which I have my membership. It is located four hours northwest of Toronto on the Saugeen/Bruce Peninsula, on the western shores of Georgian Bay.

Examining the experiences of the Chippewas of the Nawash reveals another dimension of Indigenous-Crown conflict related to land. In the last example involving the James Bay Cree, we saw that Indigenous peoples had on-the-ground territorial ownership while the government tried to 'perfect' its theoretical claims through court procedures and a treaty. In the following example, my people found that non-Indigenous peoples used direct action and civil (dis)obedience to 'squat' on Indigenous land in their attempts to challenge Indigenous ownership. In response, the Anishinaabe of Neyaashiinigmiing used direct action to contest settlers' claims and thus highlight breaches of Crown law designed to protect Indigenous peoples.

This example demonstrates that we should resist falsely conceptualizing direct action as an Indigenous-only tactic to secure land, governance, and resources. It has long been a powerful tool in the hands of non-Native people. Direct action and civil (dis)obedience are not unambiguously positive tools from an Indigenous perspective. Settlers from other countries have often erected blockades and have taken actions that excluded Indigenous peoples from Indigenous lands. This form of civil (dis)obedience shows the double-edged nature of this tactic. Civil (dis)obedience can be turned against Indigenous peoples and significantly diminish their freedoms when this occurs. Civil (dis)obedience is not an ideal form.

From the outset, the British acknowledged the problem of settlers taking direct action and displacing Indigenous peoples from their lands. As a result, the Royal Proclamation of 1763 and subsequent associated treaties were designed to prevent Europeans from blocking Indigenous peoples from their territories.[89] The Crown took these actions because the unauthorized occupation of Indigenous peoples' lands was a very significant concern in North America.[90] Direct action by non-Indians threatened trade, travel, and diplomacy and could even lead to war when settlers were unrestrained.[91]

Thus, the Royal Proclamation and Treaty of Niagara contained important legal principles protecting Indigenous peoples against European settlers' actions. For example, the Royal Proclamation and Treaty of Niagara 'reserved' lands west of the Appalachian height of land as Indian Hunting Grounds.[92] These lands were not included in any colony. Non-Indians were expressly forbidden from settling Indian lands – because of 'great Frauds and Abuses' that were committed by them. The Crown reserved to itself exclusive rights to negotiate Indian title to facilitate peace, friendship, and respect. The Treaty of Niagara 'gave treaty recognition to the nation-to-nation relationship between the First Nations and the British Crown.'[93]

In practice, the proclamation often failed to stifle the expansionist ambitions of non-Indian settlers and speculators. They flooded over the

Appalachians and physically occupied and blocked Indigenous peoples' access to Indigenous land, contrary to British and Indigenous law.[94] This is why it may be said that civil (dis)obedience has as long a history among settlers in relation to Indigenous lands as it does among Indigenous peoples. In fact, the desire for westward expansion was a primary reason the thirteen American colonies rebelled against Britain in 1776.[95] Colonists wanted to get their hands on Indian lands, and they used direct action and civil (dis)obedience to advance this goal in the American Revolution. This demonstrates how difficult it was to restrain settlers from directly occupying Indigenous lands despite the Royal Proclamation.

This same problem was present in what became Canada. Turning to our present example, involving the Saugeen Peninsula: prior to the 1850s, settlers physically occupied Anishinaabe lands in the area, contrary to British and Indigenous law.[96] Unfortunately, the Crown's representatives often condoned this form of non-Indigenous civil (dis)obedience. When my ancestors were negotiating with the government during this period, a Crown negotiator insisted that we agree to a treaty's proposed terms. He said the government could not stop non-Indigenous peoples from occupying our lands contrary to their laws. Superintendent W.G. Anderson spoke the following words, regarding the settlers' civil (dis)obedience:

> After talking nearly all day yesterday and nearly all last night on the subject of your reserve, you have concluded not to cede your land to the Government for your benefit ...
>
> You complain that the whites not only cut and take timber from your lands but that they are commencing to settle upon it and you can't prevent them, and I certainly do not think the Government will take the trouble to help you while you remain thus opposed to your own interest – the Government as your guardian have the powers to act as it pleases with your reserve, and I will recommend that the whole excepting the part marked on the map in red be surveyed and sold for the good of yourselves and your children.
>
> The money once secured in your Great Mothers strong box will be safe to you for future generations. Whereas, if it is not sold, the trees and land will be taken from you by your white neighbours and your children will then be left without resource.[97]

This example demonstrates that Crown officers were often unable or unwilling to restrain settlers from occupying Indigenous land. There are numerous examples of this kind of civil (dis)obedience across Canada being practised by newly arriving settler populations.[98] Throughout Southern Ontario, rights to hunt and fish, reserved to the Indians through treaties, were diminished as farmers and merchants physically blocked Indigenous peoples from their traditional harvesting sites.[99] Under the circumstances, it is passing ironic that Indigenous practices of civil (dis)obedience have received the lion's share of attention in the past few years. Non-Aboriginal occupation of Indigenous lands has long overshadowed fleeting Indigenous uses of direct action throughout Canadian history. Non-Indigenous civil (dis)obedience has been astonishingly successful in transferring Indigenous land to non-Indigenous people. This continues to present problems for Indigenous peoples today.

In light of these traditions, we now turn our attention to more recent uses of civil (dis)obedience among my people in their attempts to turn this historic tide. Since treaties recognized rights to hunt and fish throughout our territories, the Chippewas of the Nawash always fished for livelihood purposes.[100] However, over time, governments and local farmers blocked access to land and resources and constrained our freedom to pursue these activities.[101] The situation began to change in the 1980s, as more severe restrictions were placed on Anishinaabe treaty practices. Indigenous rights to fish in the Great Lakes were increasingly being blocked by rigorous government enforcement.[102] The government was encouraged in this position by fishing lobbies, such as the Ontario Federation of Anglers and Hunters.[103] However, Anishinaabe peoples believed that fishery regulations were contrary to time-honoured Aboriginal practices and their existing treaty rights. Thus, they took direct action and fished in the face of potential prosecution. When local fishermen from Neyaashiingmiing were charged with commercial fishing, contrary to government regulations, this presented an opportunity for the Chippewas of the Nawash to test the issue before the courts.

In 1993, the case of *R. v. Jones and Nadjiwon* was issued.[104] It found that licences issued by the Ministry of Natural Resources unjustifiably infringed Anishinaabe rights to fish for commercial purposes. Justice David Fairgrieve held that our treaties reserved rights throughout the territory to engage in a subsistence commercial fishery.[105] The decision generated a greater determination to advance treaties rights among band members and their allies.[106] With an increased resolve to reinforce our treaties, the community turned its attention to preserving an Anishinaabe burial ground in Owen Sound. Houses had been built upon lands specifically reserved as burial grounds under our treaty. The fact that non-Indigenous people were now living on these lands did not prevent the community from taking action. As a result, on 3 December 1993 people from the Cape Croker Indian Reserve physically occupied a residential lot on 6th Avenue West in the city of Owen Sound. They did so in protest of the houses, which were desecrating this protected sacred site. They also protested the fact that artefacts and corpses from the graves had been sent to museums for study and display. They likewise objected to the fact that soil from the site had been used to fabricate bricks for buildings in Owen Sound and surrounding communities.[107] Throughout the occupation, the band sought an apology, demanded the removal of the houses, and insisted that the gravesite be restored and marked with a proper monument.

Unfortunately, a few municipal officials denied that the area was a burial ground, which further fuelled the conflict. The *Jones/Nadjiwon* decision did not immediately prompt the municipality to take the treaty more seriously, though it empowered the people of Neyaashiingmiing to take action. The community's act of civil (dis)obedience was aimed at engaging the public in Owen Sound and beyond through democratic dialogue. It sought to provide knowledge about the continuing importance of treaty rights for land use throughout the territory.

Fortunately, direct action was successful in this instance, because the community clearly communicated its objectives. The burial ground was protected, and the houses that had been built on them were removed. The land now stands free of municipal or other structures. It is once again treaty-protected land and a descriptive plaque marks the resting place of our ancestors. This measurable claim, backed by civil (dis)obedience and coupled with a recent legal victory, enabled the parties to engage in a constructive manner.[108] Professor Darlene Johnston and Chief Ralph Akiwenzie were particularly key figures in helping others become more generally aware of the issues on the reserve and beyond. Furthermore, Elders within the community played an important role in keeping peace and discipline behind the lines of protest.

Though there were some negative feelings expressed towards the protestors, communications were mostly clear and respectful and created the conditions which led to an agreement. This expanded the scope of Anishinaabe freedom with the Saugeen territory by protecting the burial grounds and enabling them to honour their ancestors in a good way. This facilitated both *dibenindizowin* and *mino-bimaadiziwin* for our people. Thus, in this instance, direct action increased Indigenous freedom, because the protests were peaceful, informational, aimed at wider engagement, and built on recognized legal interests. These conditions led to a favourable result. This example demonstrates that civil (dis)obedience can be practised in ways that are consistent with a free and democratic society.

iv) Clayoquot Sound

Our next example comes from Clayoquot Sound on Canada's west coast. The background to the case is rooted in a group's long presence in a territory.[109] Permanence, not mobility, was stressed to enhance freedom. The Nuu-chah-nulth people of Clayoquot Sound in British Columbia are located on the western shores of Vancouver Island and are organized as the Tla-o-qui-aht, Toquat, Ahousaht, Hesquiaht, and Uclelet bands. They live in the midst of one of the 'largest intact rainforests in the world.'[110] The Nuu-chah-nulth comprise 43 per cent of the total population of the area, but from a Canadian legal standpoint they hold only 0.4 per cent of the total land area, because the provincial government regards itself as being the legal owner of territory. The Nuu-chah-nulth of this region never surrendered their lands or resources to the federal or provincial government through treaties or other agreements. Like the Haida and James Bay Cree, they question the Crown's claim of ownership of land that has been theirs for millennia.

Despite long-standing practices of Indigenous ownership,[111] the provincial government leased land in Nuu-chah-nulth territory to resource extraction companies.[112] For decades the Nuu-chah-nulth resisted the alienation of their land, though the province blocked them from accessing their territories through development. The most recent wave of government activity began in 1984, when the Tla-o-qui-aht and Ahousaht bands declared a tribal park on Meares Island.[113] The Nuu-chah-nulth felt they had endured one too many encroachments. The bands took direct action. They blocked access to the island, along with a group called Friends of Clayoquot Sound.[114]

The declaration and the blockade were in response to MacMillan Bloedel's intention to log the area.[115] In response, MacMillan Bloedel served an injunction on non-Native protesters and the Tla-o-qui-aht and Ahousaht bands applied for a counter-injunction. In 1985, the Tla-o-qui-aht and Ahousaht injunction was granted by the British Columbia Supreme Court, though logging continued elsewhere in the Sound.[116] Subsequently, an unknown logging road was discovered in

Sulphur Pass in the Sound, and blockades were erected in the summer of 1985. Fletcher Challenge asked for and was granted an injunction, and 35 people were arrested, including Earl George, Ahousaht hereditary chief. Charges against Earl George were eventually dropped. In 1989, ten protestors were jailed for the Sulphur Pass blockades. After such high-profile confrontations and arrests, Premier Van der Zalm declared logging in Clayoquot Sound a disgrace and formed the Sustainable Development Task Force for Clayoquot Sound. Furthermore, an international campaign for the boycott of MacMillan Bloedel was undertaken by supporters of the protestors in the Sound. The alliances between Indigenous peoples and others show that, in this instance, civil (dis)obedience was very effective in facilitating a broader democratic engagement.

Despite broad public engagement, the first steps to address Indigenous issues within the Sound were not successful. The government failed to sufficiently engage the parties. For example, in April of 1993, the Government of British Columbia released the Clayoquot Sound Land Use Decision, which would have permitted logging the Sound without Nuu-chah-nulth input.[117] The plan contained very scant references to Nuu-chah-nulth concerns, and First Nations were immediately opposed to it. Chief Francis Frank announced, 'I am here to set the record straight, we have never expressed support for this decision.'[118] The Land Use Decision basically allowed logging to go ahead as before, without any recognition of Indigenous peoples' interests. This was a flashpoint for further conflict. The Nuu-chah-nulth once again set up blockades to prevent access to the forest and disrupt plans for it being logged. A support group called Friends of Clayoquot Sound set up the Clayoquot Peace Camp in solidarity with First Nations in the area. The protest attracted 12,000 people in an attempt to halt clear-cut logging of Clayoquot Sound's rainforests.

The dispute soon turned ugly. An injunction was sought and obtained in the British Columbia courts, and people were soon charged for violating the terms of the order as they continued to protest.[119] By the end of the summer of 1993, 856 people had been arrested and charged for violating the terms of the injunction.[120] This is an exceptionally large number of people, making it one of the largest displays of civil (dis)obedience in Canadian history.[121] In making a finding of contempt, the BC court said 'an organized and determined group of people had acted in concert for the purpose of obstructing the plaintiff's lawful operations and that, in so doing, they willfully and flagrantly defied the several orders of this court.'[122] Given that the Aboriginal title issue is unresolved and that other people were using Indigenous land without permission, it is revealing to highlight which traditions the court relied upon to adjudicate the case. It protected corporate interests rather than Aboriginal rights, though the court's reference to 'a willful and flagrant defiance of law' could have easily been applied to those who failed to respect Nuu-chah-nulth legal traditions.

To ease tension and attempt to solve the problem, Premier Harcourt appointed the Clayoquot Sound Scientific Panel to draft 'world-class' logging practices for the Sound, incorporating First Nations traditional knowledge.[123] In 1994, an Interim Measures Agreement was signed with Nuu-chah-nulth, creating a Central Regional Board with approval power over resource development in Clayoquot.[124] The release and adoption of the Scientific Panel recommendations by the government helped defuse the conflict at Clayoquot. The protestors enjoyed a degree of success as a result of the blockade: MacMillan Bloedel had major contracts cancelled as a result of the negative media attention, and Interfor was convicted under the Forest Practices Code for violations of the law. The number of logs cut also fell dramatically in the Sound, and the area was eventually declared to be a UN Biosphere Reserve.[125]

First Nations seem to have positively influenced the way forests were used in the area as a result of their civil (dis)obedience.[126] The protest of the Clayoquot Sound Land Use Decision had at least two important consequences for the Nuu-chah-nulth. First, the provincial ombudsman agreed that the province had failed in its duty to consult the Nuu-chah-nulth in a meaningful and timely manner. Accordingly, on 12 November 1993, he recommended that the government meet with the Nuu-chah-nulth representatives and sign an Interim Measures Agreement to deal with their rights. Forty-three days later, the parties had an agreement that created a cooperative forest management area, economic development opportunities, and joint management processes for land-use decisions. This gave the Nuu-chah-nulth advisory capacity in forest decision-making. While imperfect, this measure enhanced democracy and temporarily reduced government domination. While it was a step in the right direction, Nuu-chah-nulth power continued to be limited; cabinet still had the final decision.

As noted, a second and more substantial result of the Nuu-chah-nulth objection to the Clayoquot Sound Land Use Decision was the creation of the Clayoquot Sound Scientific Panel for Sustainable Forest Practices.[127] This was an innovative development, because it incorporated

Indigenous participation in land-use decisions in a small way. The panel's goal, as defined by then premier Harcourt, was 'to make forest practices in Clayoquot not only the best in the province, but the best in the world.'[128] The panel's creation and its subsequent report demonstrate that civil (dis)obedience can sometimes pry open important democratic spaces.[129] The inclusion of the Nuu-chah-nulth perspective assisted the panel in justifying the development of an inclusive and holistic ecosystem approach to forest management.[130] The Nuu-chah-nulth concept for traditional ecosystem management is called *Ha Huulhi*.[131] The articulation of Nuu-chah-nulth laws was important in reframing relationships in the area.[132] Their views allowed the panel to more fully support ecological planning, which some actors otherwise regarded with suspicion.[133] In applying these ideas, the panel concluded, 'long-term ecological and economic sustainability are essential to long-term harmony.'[134] As a result, the panel adopted some excellent recommendations concerning subregional, watershed and site-level planning.[135]

Blockades came down because First Nations were given the opportunity to inject their values into land-use plans and practices. They created an effective alliance and partnership with environmentalists both nationally and internationally.[136] Once again, engaging broader Canadian and international populations was crucial in successfully deploying direct action. It facilitated a more effective harmonization of governmental powers. Furthermore, the process led to First Nations involvement in resource use. MacMillan Bloedel formed a logging company called Iisaak Forest Resources with First Nations in the area.[137] First Nations own the controlling portion of shares in Iisaak. MacMillan Bloedel later sold their share of Iisaak to logging giant Weyerhaeuser, but First Nations control remained. Environmentalists negotiated a Memorandum of Understanding with Iisaak, and it became the first Forest Stewardship Council eco-certified major licence holder in Canada. In 2000, Clayoquot Sound was designated a UN Biosphere Reserve.

Despite positive language and plans for the better use of Clayoquot Sound forests, more work needs to be done.[138] Domination remains, and Indigenous peoples have not fared well in their lands.[139] This is in line with an earlier observation that conclusions in a democratic society are often partial and incomplete, because we are dealing with actual practices and not ideal, perfect forms.[140] A major shortcoming of the Scientific Panel's report relates to its failure to make provision for Indigenous peoples' continuing participation in decisions about the forests.[141] It laconically concluded that 'several models for participation are useful to consider.'[142] This has been a source of continuing friction in the area. Despite these problems, the report has helped facilitate temporary peace in the Sound, though other factors obviously contributed to this result.[143] The Clayoquot deployment of civil (dis)obedience helped advance democracy and increased freedom with the local area. It also positively heightened awareness of Indigenous issues in British Columbia and beyond and therefore contributed in a small way to Indigenous peoples' movement away from domination in other areas.

C. Group Two: Helping Others, Failing at Home

i) Oka/Kanesatake, Quebec

The next cluster of conflicts deals with disputes that generated wider democratic exchange but failed to significantly reduce domination in the local area. While the previous examples illustrate that even communities who most successfully deploy civil (dis)obedience still face significant challenges, the examples in this section demonstrate the difficulties encountered in increasing freedom in your own backyard, even if you help people in similar circumstances.

The first example in this section comes from Oka, Quebec, where direct action prompted Canadian military intervention.[144] This event intensified democratic debate about the place of Indigenous peoples in Canada, but it did not lead to the return of land claimed by the Haudenosaunee.

There is a question about whether the lands of the upper St. Lawrence Valley around Montreal are the traditional territories of the Haudenosaunee Confederacy.[145] The Mohawks of the Confederacy regard the land as their own. The Province of Quebec takes a contrary view and claims that the land is not subject to Mohawk title.[146] Thus, Indigenous peoples and others in the area have competing notions about the rightful use and occupation of land.[147] This uncertainty generates confusion and causes periodic conflict. The most high-profile disturbance in recent years occurred at Oka/Kanesatake, where an armed confrontation between the police and Mohawk people took place concerning the use and ownership of land called 'The Pines.'

Oka is a Quebec municipality that is intermixed with Mohawk lands in the community of Kanesatake. Oka/Kanesatake is located on the north shore of the Lake of Two Mountains, where it meets the Ottawa River, 53 kilometres west of Montreal. The lands set aside for the

Mohawks are not 'Indian reserve' lands under the *Indian Act*. The surface area of Kanesatake is 1,142 hectares. There are nearly 1,960 people in Kanesatake, with approximately 1,347 residents on the actual territory of the Mohawk.[148]

In the early days of New France, the Sulpicians were granted land in the area by the King of France in order to bring the Mohawks of Kanesatake to the Catholic religion.[149] The seigniory was created by successive grants from the King of France in 1717, 1718, 1733, and 1735. These grants purported to convey land to the ecclesiastics of the Seminary of St. Sulpice, forming part of the seigniory, with a full proprietary title, but on the condition that they should take care of a certain mission they had founded among the Indians. This land was known as the Seigneurie of Lake of Two Mountains. The Mohawks always regarded the land as theirs, while the Sulpicians held that the land had been granted to them.[150] Through the centuries, the Sulpicians sold much of the land to non-Indigenous people. In a 1912 decision – the *Corinthe* decision – the Judicial Committee of the Privy Council found in favour of the Sulpicians against the Mohawks.[151] The Mohawks did not regard the decision as determinative.

In 1977, the Mohawks of Kanesatake filed a claim with the Canadian Office of Native Claims regarding land.[152] The government financed research for the claim's further development, but the case was denied upon final submission because it was held that the claim did not meet the 'criteria' of the Specific Claims Branch. This did not resolve the issue for the Mohawks, and they continued to strive for recognition of their asserted rights.[153]

In March 1990, there was an attempt by Oka's municipal employees to clear some land to build condominiums and expand a golf course. This could have been perceived by the Mohawk as a municipal blockade, because it would have prevented Mohawk access to the land. 'The Pines,' as the proposed development area was called, is connected to a Mohawk burial ground. The municipal workers encountered Mohawk resistance in their attempt to clear the area. While there were significant divisions within Mohawk communities related to issues such as gaming, cigarette sales, traditional versus elected governance, nationalism, sovereignty, militarization, non-violence, and so forth, once the conflict at the Pines began, these issues were largely subsumed with and secondary to the land claims issue in most Mohawk people's eyes.[154] Thus, community differences became much less significant once blockades went up; Mohawk desires to prevent further development and protest the municipality's occupation of the Pines became an overarching focus, eclipsing other concerns.[155] The Mohawk people felt as if other Canadians had already claimed occupation of most of their land, making the preservation of the Pines much more pressing.[156] Not surprisingly, the mayor of Oka took a different view of the matter and submitted the question to the courts to uphold non-Aboriginal title. Oka won; an injunction was granted by the superior court to allow municipal employees to continue their work, thus setting the stage for further conflict. In response, Mohawk protesters reinforced barriers to prevent bulldozers from breaking ground for the golf course.[157]

On 10 July 1990, the mayor of Oka wrote to request help from the provincial police, the Sûreté du Québec, to enforce the Quebec superior court's injunction. The mayor also asked for intervention, because he believed there was criminal activity by some Mohawks at the blockade. The mayor's action and police presence further escalated tensions. On 11 July 1990, the protestors reinforced their positions around the blockade. In order to dismantle the blockade and in an attempt to create confusion among the Mohawks, a police SWAT team fired tear gas and concussion grenades at the barricade. The police actions created confusion, and in the ensuing firefight bullets were exchanged. Tragically, when the smoke cleared Marcel Lemay from the Sûreté du Québec was dead, allegedly slain by a Mohawk bullet.[158] This development further intensified the conflict and led to other Indigenous peoples from across the continent joining the Mohawks in their protest.[159] It also strengthened the resolve of the government against the Mohawks. In an attempt to contain the situation, the Sûreté du Québec established their own blockades to restrict access to Oka and Kanesatake. As in other conflicts noted here, governmental blockades once more became visibly physical, demonstrating the material power of Canadian society to block Indigenous peoples from lands they regarded as their own. In retaliation and in solidarity with the Kanesatake Mohawks, other Mohawks at Kahnawake blockaded the Mercier Bridge between the Island of Montreal and the South Shore suburbs at the point where it passed through their territory.[160] At the peak of the crisis, the Mercier Bridge and Highways 132, 138, and 207 were all blocked, causing enormous traffic jams and frayed tempers in the city.

On 14 August, Premier Robert Bourassa called upon the army for support.[161] This was an exceptionally rare event in Canadian history, and underscored the extremely high level of conflict at Oka.[162] The municipal, federal, and provincial governments justified their actions by saying they were trying to keep law and order in the province, in particular the enforcement of the injunction against the blockade. Mohawk protestors also justified their actions by reference to law and order, asking for an acknowledgment of their rights to occupy land in the area.[163]

On 29 August, the Kahnawake Mohawks dismantled the barricades at the Mercier Bridge, defusing tension among commuters and leaving the Kanesatake Mohawks isolated. After 78 days, on 26 September, the blockades were removed and many of the leaders of the blockade were arrested, but none were ever convicted.

In March 1991, Kanesatake Mohawks and the federal government agreed on an agenda for negotiations.[164] Unfortunately, progress on recognizing the Pines as Mohawk land has been slow. Nothing of great significance has transpired to acknowledge their ownership or control. In 1994, a memorandum of understanding over land purchases was signed between the Mohawks and the federal government. In 1997, the Mohawks established their own police station, and the federal government made land purchases in adjoining areas in the name of Kanesatake. On 21 December 2000, a new land governance agreement was signed between Kanesatake and the federal government. Unfortunately, many aspects of the dispute remain unresolved, including – most distressingly – the status of the burial ground/golf course. Ultimately, though it strengthened Mohawk resolve as a people,[165] civil (dis)obedience did not free the Mohawk from the domination they face in their territory.[166] Thus, we would propagate a false tradition if we were to conclude that direct action always produces favourable results and accomplishes activists' immediate objectives.

Fortunately, the events at Oka provoked a more wide-ranging national debate, thus facilitating democratic deliberation about Indigenous issues in the country.[167] The Oka confrontation prompted the establishment of a Royal Commission on Aboriginal Peoples.[168] The commission's final report was handed down in 1996 and contained over 441 recommendations. Indigenous people were generally disappointed with the federal government response to the report.[169] There was no widespread recognition or affirmation of Aboriginal or treaty rights following its release. However, the government released an ineffectual policy document, *Gathering Strength*, and a subsequent *Inherent Rights of Self-Government Policy* that contained some elements of the Royal Commission's final recommendations.[170] While this policy ultimately proved to be ineffective in any real terms, it did provide avenues for further negotiation. The events at Oka were also a factor in bringing Indigenous peoples to the constitutional negotiating table in an earlier period, when the Charlottetown Accord was being developed in 1992.[171] The leaders of four national Indigenous organizations worked with first ministers to debate and draft a series of amendments to the constitution, including provisions dealing with Aboriginal rights. While the Charlottetown negotiations failed to gain acceptance from the wider Canadian population in a nation-wide referendum, in the short term Indigenous peoples seemed to gain a greater rate of participation in Canadian affairs in the immediate aftermath of Oka.[172] Unfortunately, since most of the activity has been limited to discussion and debate, not much action has taken place on the ground to demarcate Indigenous lands and overcome the domination of Indigenous peoples that persists in many places in the nation.

ii) Burnt Church

The second and final example in our second cluster of disputes relates to civil (dis)obedience in the Maritimes.[173] Conflict erupted in 1999 following the *Marshall* decision, which upheld Mi'kmaq treaty rights to fish and earn a moderate livelihood from this resource.[174] This case provoked Native and non-Native violence, direct action, resistance, and negotiation at Burnt Church/Esgenoôpetitj, on Miramichi Bay in New Brunswick. After four years of conflict, the people of Esgenoôpetitj secured political recognition of their rights to fish for food and ceremonial purposes. They also obtained twenty-one commercial fishing licences and money for training, equipment, infrastructure development, and research related to Mi'kmaq fisheries.

The peace that followed this dispute's resolution benefited Mi'kmaq peoples and Canadians more broadly. The Mi'kmaq now have a slightly stronger place in the Atlantic fisheries, and they participate a little more fully in the region's political economy.[175] At the same time, the conflict's resolution did not significantly advance the interests of many of the most prominent Esgenoôpetitj activists working at the heart of the dispute.[176] Its most prominent leaders regarded the deal as a sell-out. They lament that it did not recognize Mi'kmaq sovereignty and traditional values as the most important point at issue.[177] Unfortunately, their message was not warmly received by the Canadian government and broader non-Native population.[178] In fact, these leaders' views were ultimately secondary to those of other Mi'kmaq community members, who were exhausted by the conflict. Thus, in the shorter term the community seems to have eventually prioritized specific economic development agreements with Canada over broader explicit anti-colonial objectives. The wider group's decision to settle for immediate physical benefits as opposed to 'holding out' for more structural change demonstrates the difficulties encountered in securing more abstract metaphysical victories through direct action and civil (dis)obedience.

Mi'kmaq people of the Atlantic coast have long dealt with resource challenges and encroachments. They have withstood waves of people from across the ocean over the last 1,000 years. The first visitors were from Scandinavia and they were later followed by people from Spain, France, and Great Britain.[179] Early Europeans came to utilize the aquatic resources of this rich maritime environment but did not settle the land. In the early 1600s, the Mi'kmaq, Maliseet, and Passamaquoddy Indians sailed the oceans of the region in distinctive seagoing canoes.[180] A century later, they were also sailing European shallops and exercised wide dominion over trade in the area.[181] They also had productive social relations with the French until 1755, when the English from the American colonies defeated and later removed the Acadians of the region.[182] A tumultuous period set in, as the English sought to challenge Indigenous land and resource use in the area.[183] Wars intermingled with peace treaties, and treaties were signed between 1693 and 1779 to establish peace and friendship between the groups.[184] The Mi'kmaq lived in accordance with these treaty promises for over 200 years, though these promises largely faded from the public memory of the rest of the population.[185]

As noted, in 1999 Maritime treaties suddenly came to wider public attention once again with two judgments issued by the Supreme Court of Canada on one case.[186] The government and other fishers were not prepared for the Court's conclusion that Mi'kmaq treaties protected a right to fish for a moderate livelihood.[187] Thus, in October 1999, 150 non-Native fishermen took to the water and destroyed approximately 3,000 Native lobster traps, which the Esgenoôpetitj Mi'kmaq had set in Miramichi Bay.[188] Most non-Native people from the community adjacent to Esgenoôpetitj made their living through lobster fishing. They felt that their livelihoods were threatened by Mi'kmaq treaty rights. Furthermore, many non-Native fishers did not regard the *Marshall* decision as applying to lobsters, and most were concerned that Mi'kmaq actions would upset the delicate ecological balance in the region's lobster fishery. Thus, in destroying Esgenoôpetitj traps the non-Native residents of the region used civil (dis)obedience and direct action to attempt to blockade Mi'kmaq access to the resource. This included dressing up in Indian warpaint, donning fake Indian regalia, dancing, whooping, and tomahawk-chopping into the air while issuing racist taunts.[189]

Once again, we see that direct action can be a double-edged sword for Indigenous peoples. As this event illustrates, it is just as likely to be used by non-Native people as by Native peoples. Direct action continues to be a powerful tool when non-Native people want to resist outcomes contrary to their perceived interests. Those who romanticize or universalize civil (dis)obedience should more fully take account of this fact. Its use must be judged in context-specific ways; it can never be regarded as an unalloyed good when Indigenous issues are at play.

The people from Esgenoôpetitj resented the actions of their non-Native neighbours because it constrained Mi'kmaq freedoms. Thus, they retaliated by occupying the wharf at Burnt Church and fighting back in other ways. As violence escalated, people from both sides of the dispute were hurt, including one Native youth who was beaten with a baseball bat.[190] Trucks and boats were also burned, and both Native and non-Native people sustained property damage as a result of these altercations.[191] In countering the local fishers' direct action, the Mi'kmaq were generally motivated by a belief that they had a right to enter the lobster fishery, subject to their own laws and regulations dealing with allocation and conservation.[192] Thus, Mi'kmaq fishers did not apply to the government for licences to catch lobsters. They felt that they were acting consistent with the Supreme Court's judgment and that their re-entry into this fishery was constitutionally justified. Once again, this is a case where civil (dis)obedience to one law could be characterized as obedience to another.

The beliefs underlying Mi'kmaq assumptions were further complicated with the release of the *Marshall II* case two months after the Court's initial decision.[193] In *Marshall II* case, the Supreme Court dramatically resiled from the implications of its previous judgment.[194] While *Marshall II* denied the West Nova Fishermen's Association's motion for a rehearing and a stay of the Court's original opinion, it nevertheless unexpectedly issued a 'clarification' of the first decision's meaning. The Court wrote that it had not decided that Mi'kmaq resource rights extended beyond eels.[195] It further wrote that it 'did not hold that the Mi'kmaq treaty right cannot be regulated or that the Mi'kmaq are guaranteed an open season in the fisheries.'[196] *Marshall II* cast doubt on the constitutionality of Esgenoôpetitj people's right to fish for lobster, which was arguably a stronger implication under the Court's first decision.

The Supreme Court's re-entry into this dispute was a shock to many people. The very act of restating its conclusions reframed and reinterpreted the original decision's meaning, because it emphasized some points at the expense of others. Furthermore, the Court's 'clarification' added more information and detail to its former reasons. This had the effect of limiting the conclusions Indigenous peoples might draw from the *Marshall I* case, thereby expanding the powers that governments and non-Native fishers could claim flowed from it to their advantage. The Supreme Court's recontextualization of Mi'kmaq rights largely favoured non-Mi'kmaq interests and changed the balance of power following the decision.

The Court's release of its 'clarification' coincided with the onset of winter, when most Mi'kmaq communities had agreed to a moratorium on fishing for a short period. During the winter of 2000, Mi'kmaq leaders from Esgenoôpetitj negotiated with the federal government to implement fishing rights they believed were recognized in the *Marshall* cases. They maintained that they did not need federal permission to fish, while the Canadian fisheries minister took the view that such recognition was required.[197] As a result of this impasse, the Mi'kmaq eventually walked away from negotiations and called upon their own people to draft laws to manage the fishery. This resulted in the *Draft for the Esgenoôpetitj First Nations (EFN) Fishery Act* and a *Draft for EFN Management Plan*, which advanced more traditional and sovereign views of the Mi'kmaq fishery.[198] Under this plan,

> Burnt Church would fish a total of 15,000 traps per season – 10,000 traps during the spring commercial fishery and 5,000 during a traditional fall fishery. The total would amount to less than 2% of what DFO allocates to fishers in the Miramichi area ... The plan also incorporated extensive environmental monitoring and conservation measures and a habitat restoration program to be administered by band-funded biologists.[199]

Once the community plan was completed, Mi'kmaq people went fishing. Beginning in early May 2000, officers from the Department of Fisheries and Oceans (DFO) became aware that members of the Burnt Church First Nation community were setting lobster traps under Mi'kmaq authority; the traps thus did not carry DFO tags. Following orders from their superiors, DFO officers seized a large number of traps not identified with DFO tags and removed them from the water.[200] This action infuriated Burnt Church fishermen. Violence again flowed in the wake of Crown action. In the process, Mi'kmaq conflict was largely transferred from skirmishes with the local non-Native population to clashes with government officials. Non-Native people no longer had to resort to direct action – the Canadian government largely took up their cause and stood in their place. The violence was raw and disturbing. On 22 August 2000, a fishery officer was injured by a rock thrown during a confrontation with Mi'kmaq fishermen.[201] On 29 August, fisheries officials swamped and sunk two Native boats during a raid on Mi'kmaq lobster traps. On 12 September 2000, government representatives seized four boats and arrested sixteen Mi'kmaq people, including the Burnt Church band chief. As the season closed out, fisheries minister Herb Dhaliwal closed the lobster fishery on Miramichi and gave the Mi'kmaq and Maliseet a twenty-four-hour deadline from 21 September 2000 to remove their traps. Not everyone complied. Thus, on 23 September 2000, three non-Native people were arrested and firearms were seized after shots were fired on the water. Fisheries officials later removed about 800 traps that had remained in the bay. While the violence of the 2000 season was punctuated with brief moments of negotiation and an attempt to resolve the dispute through a government-appointed mediator,[202] the blunt physicality of events dominated the parties' experiences.[203]

The following year, 2001, saw further conflict as the parties consolidated their positions, though the physicality of the violence slowly diminished.[204] The federal government devised strategies which placed further pressure on Esgenoôpetitj to retreat from more sovereigntist views. First, they appointed third-party managers to monitor the band's finances.[205] Second, they further strengthened their negotiation processes through region-wide attempts to consider treaty promises throughout the Maritimes. Third, the federal government issued lobster fisheries licences to Mi'kmaq fishers without their consent so that federal rules coincided with Mi'kmaq self-determined licensing, issued by their own communities.[206] This allowed the DFO to refrain from aggressive enforcement action by making it appear that Mi'kmaq fishers were acting under federal authority. Thus, in August 2001, the Department of Federal Fisheries announced a limited fall food fishery for Natives in waters off Burnt Church reserve. The Mi'kmaq resented Canada's duplicitous manipulation of the situation to the government's advantage. Thus, the violence did not disappear and continued to haunt the parties' interactions. For example, in September at least thirty gunshots were reportedly fired during a weekend duel between

Native and non-Native fishermen. Fortunately, no one was physically hurt though 'the contest' was one-sided, with fifty boats purportedly being used by non-Native fishers, and only ten by Indigenous peoples.

Finally, on 1 August 2002, an agreement-in-principle was reached between Ottawa and Burnt Church regarding the Native lobster fishery. It was worth about $20 million over two years, and the band agreed they would fish under the authority of Fisheries and Oceans Canada. One explanation for the Mi'kmaq policy change is that band elections had brought a new, more conciliatory chief and council into power at Burnt Church. Furthermore, events following terrorist attacks on the United States on 11 September 2001 made it more difficult for many Mi'kmaq fishers to maintain an aggressive stance towards the government. Finally, the agreement pressed the government's advantage in advancing its implicit alliance with non-Native fishers, ensuring that Mi'kmaq fishers did not achieve substantial change in the wider fishery's allocation and regulation. While this agreement produced peace and led to benefits within the Mi'kmaq community and beyond, this outcome did not satisfy those who saw sovereignty and tradition as lying at the heart of this dispute.[207]

The resolution does not effectively allow Mi'kmaq law, governance, and tradition to guide fisheries decisions. Furthermore, the agreement does not address government-backed violations of the rule of law concerning Mi'kmaq treaty rights.[208] When analysing this conflict, one of the book's central points is on display: freedom is at its strongest when it is relational and facilitates democratic self-determination. The Mi'kmaq of Esgenoôpetitj were unable to force or persuade their immediate neighbours (or the country at large) that sovereignty and tradition were a viable base on which to co-manage or regulate fisheries. The parties could not find ways to explicitly transform perceived abstract concepts into practices that would guide future relationships. There was no real harmonization of the parties' governmental relationships nor did the Mi'kmaq secure greater control over their own affairs.

This example shows that freedom must be worked out in context. *Dibenindizowin* is realized through real-world experiences, which themselves are embedded in the diverse cultural relationships in which we live and interact. Good ideas such as sovereignty may be important goals for living a good life, but in this case, they seemed to be insufficient to facilitate further freedom, even when advanced through blockades. When freedom is viewed as being dependent, even predicated, on metaphysical concepts of independence through Indigenous force and civil (dis)obedience, this seems to be an insufficient basis upon which to build change. Freedom must be realized in physically place-based terms in order to expand how we act in material world.

D. Group Three: Diminishing Democracy and Eroding Freedom, Generally and Specifically

i) Anicinabe Park

Our third cluster of cases dealing with civil (dis)obedience demonstrates that direct action often fails to enhance freedom in any meaningful way and can in fact lead to further repression. As I have repeatedly suggested, Indigenous direct action is never pursued in isolation. It is always inserted into ongoing (dysfunctional) relationships, and it draws upon and is carried along by broader societal forces.[209] For example, civil (dis)obedience in Canada is related to the civil rights movement in the United States and the FLQ crisis in Quebec. The many sit-ins, marches, and protests that occurred in the 1960s demonstrated direct action's importance in shaping and changing public attitudes and policy.[210] Actions at Wounded Knee and Alcatraz Island especially engaged Indigenous peoples' attention and participation on both sides of the border.[211] The United States–Canadian border is an abstraction for many First Nations people.[212] It does not reflect the social realities of Indigenous languages, cultures, marriages, trade, and political relationships, which are maintained and continually re-formed across this line. The physical reality of Indigenous mobility has facilitated the intersocietal spread of Indigenous civil (dis)obedience in both countries. For many First Nations people, the so-called international border represents a false horizon because its limits are constantly transgressed in numerous ways. Despite colonial patrol, it is regularly crossed and successfully challenged by grounded Indigenous practices, even in the face of Supreme Court of Canada decisions.[213]

Our first example in this section demonstrates this point. The Ojibwa Warrior Society drew on significant cross-border participation in its occupation of Anicinabe Park in the Northwestern Ontario town of Kenora in 1974. Members of the American Indian Movement (AIM) from Minnesota, Wisconsin, and other states joined their Anishinaabe cousins in Ontario to occupy the site.[214] Following a four-day conference of Native peoples from both countries, a blockade was erected in the five-hectare park to counter the discrimination faced in the region.[215]

The Anishinaabe claimed ownership of the park and used the protest to highlight broader failures to recognize their lands and resources. They argued that they had been unjustly pushed out of their territories by governmental occupations of their land and that Canadian law would never rectify this dispossession.[216] In particular, they claimed that the Park had been purchased by the Department of Indian Affairs in 1929 with the intent of turning it into an urban reserve but that it was sold to the town of Kenora 'without compensation with the natives' for development as a tourist area.[217] While the Minister of Indian Affairs later denied that the department ever intended to create a reserve on the site,[218] the failure to recognize Indigenous peoples' special relationship and attachment to the area was a primary reason for Indigenous resistance.[219] The Anishinaabe 'dug in' in a specific place and refused to sever their relationships to the land. On a second level, the park's occupation was also designed to highlight the troubling discrimination that Indian people faced with regards to health care, education, and housing. The Anishinaabe wanted greater involvement in and influence over decisions that directly affected them in these and other fields. These democratic aspirations were voiced because they desired greater freedom.[220]

Unfortunately, Indigenous peoples' reoccupation of the park did not do much to facilitate democracy or reduce domination in this instance. In fact, the park's reoccupation led to intense conflict with the Ontario Provincial Police (OPP).[221] Unlike examples in the first section of this chapter, the Anicinabe Park conflict did not open democratic space to alter or harmonize the parties' relationships.

Feelings ran high in the area at the time because the protestors threatened to burn the nearby pulp mill and bomb the hydroelectric station if the park was not returned and their social dislocation not addressed.[222] The leaders of the occupation spoke openly about using guns and armed confrontation to win their cause. Furthermore, they espoused universalized, essentialist views about violence as related to their freedom and relationship to land. Louis Cameron, a spokesperson for the occupation, stated, 'If life is to continue for Indian people, life must depend on free land. And our people must take guns and free that land.'[223] These sentiments were publicly evident in many ways, including an inscription on a park wall sign which read,

This piece of land
we stand on, is our
Flesh n' blood

Bone n' marrow
of our bodies. This
is why we choose to die here at
Anicinabe Park.[224]

As the occupation progressed, non-Native people within the town
of Kenora also spoke of using violence in the conflict.[225] Both sides
spoke in increasingly absolutist terms. Local racist speech and chau-
vinistic intransigence among a portion of Kenora's population
was also an obstacle to developing practices of *dibenindizowin* and
mino-bimaadiziwin.[226] When civil (dis)obedience moved beyond non-
cooperation – and into the realm of gross racialization and the permanent destruction of property, with the associated potential of threats
to life – freedom was diminished. One form of domination replaced
another without creating new spaces for deliberation. Freedom was
thereby undermined in the process, and this made it more difficult for
potential allies to respond in constructive ways.

The mayor, news media, Quakers, and Jean Chrétien (as federal minister of Indian Affairs) all had a potentially constructive role to play in
addressing the conflict but were not able to significantly reduce domination, particularly in light of profound expressions of racism and the
wider threats of violence. While the blockade was eventually dismantled through the efforts of AIM leader Dennis Banks, no lasting changes
were made to improve the parties' relationships. Though the government made promises to settle the issue through negotiation, it did not
follow through on these assurances. Thus, life did not change for the
Anishinaabe people in the area. The status quo resumed; the park is still
in Kenora's hands, and Indigenous peoples still encounter significant
discrimination in health care, education, and housing in this area and
beyond.[227] Like confrontation, negotiation did not alter the situation to
the satisfaction of those who had taken matters into their own hands.

Therefore, following the blockade a group of protesters decided to
walk to Ottawa to make their claims more widely known.[228] On 30 September 1974, approximately 1,000 people arrived on Parliament Hill in
Ottawa to complete a march begun in Vancouver on 14 September. People involved in the demonstration demanded treaty rights recognition,
fair and independent land claims processes and settlements, and the
dismantling of the *Indian Act* and of the Department of Indian Affairs.
These goals were consistent with the types of claims made in Kenora
and were supported by many who had occupied Anicinabe Park.

Unfortunately, when the Native People's Caravan arrived on Parliament Hill, the protesters met with fierce resistance. They encountered barricades, armoured Royal Canadian Mounted Police (RCMP), and armed National Guardsmen. In this instance, it is depressingly interesting to note that for Indigenous peoples, the shoe was once again on the other foot, so to speak. It was Indigenous peoples who encountered a blockade when they went to Ottawa – one erected by the police. The police are not above using civil (dis)obedience in securing Crown privileges, even though many Canadians often regard the police as neutral arbiters of what constitutes obedience or disobedience to law. They are not. For the protestors, direct police action made it appear that no one was interested in talking with them or acknowledging their grievances. A subsequent violent clash with riot police resulted in the crowd being tear-gassed, nine officers and protesters being hospitalized, and the caravan retreating from the Hill.

Once again, this case shows that a line protective of freedom and democracy was crossed when conflict turned to physical violence without the realistic possibility of democratic debate. Furthermore, deep emotional wounds were created by this conflict.[229] Thus, in this instance the practice of civil (dis)obedience did not re-engage the parties in democratic dialogue. In fact, the conflict deepened governmental domination of Indigenous peoples. It also brought to light another danger present in situations of civil (dis)obedience. It contributed to the dichotomous construction of Indigenous-government relations. Many Indigenous people, who noted the violent response to the caravan, stored these memories as kindling for later confrontations with the Canadian government and corporations. They viewed Canada and the police as the enemies who were mortally and inherently opposed to their interests. Simultaneously, the police constructed Indigenous protest as threatening to democracy. Thus, civil (dis)obedience did not lead to any democratic re-engagement of any significance in this instance. In fact, it pulled the parties further apart. While the promises of negotiation temporarily dismantled physical blockades, crushing domination remained. In fact, in the *Grassy Narrows* decision of 2014, the Supreme Court even had the temerity to write that 'Ontario has exercised the power to take up lands for a period of over 100 years, without any objection by the Ojibway.'[230] This conclusion not only overlooks the violent conflict over Ontario's land use in the region, it also ignores the decades-long direct actions related to mercury poisoning and forest practices in the wider Treaty 3 area.[231] This example shows that civil (dis)obedience can be deployed and responded to in ways that are counterproductive to the development of a free and democratic society. Direct action is not a panacea; it is not a universal good, because it does not work in all contexts. To conclude otherwise would be to pass along a false tradition.

ii) Algonquins of Barriere Lake

In deciding a case of Indigenous civil (dis)obedience during a particularly intractable dispute, a motions judge of the Ontario court wrote, 'There can only be one law, and that is the law of Canada, expressed through this court.'[232] This narrow view of Canadian law does not reflect the richness of Canada's legal inheritance.[233] Therefore, it also reflects a false tradition. There are three constitutionally significant strands of law in Canada: the common law, the civil law, and Indigenous law.[234] These laws are not always expressed through the courts.[235] Most law relies on customary contexts to gain its force; courts, legislatures, and executive actors are often secondary influences in deciding which laws should operate in society.[236] As noted, when Indigenous peoples participate in so-called civil (dis)obedience, this action is often undertaken in obedience to Indigenous law.[237] Despite this reality, Indigenous legal traditions are rarely recognized as having any formal status by governments, courts, and other parties.[238] These 'on-the-ground' physical authorities have not generally been deployed by state officials to bolster Indigenous communities or Canadians more generally.[239] Thus, unfortunately, they have not been more widely used to create better relationships. Nevertheless, there are occasions when the rule of law is regarded as more than a singular idea and is therefore construed as a complex series of practices.[240] There are times when the rule of law is used to strengthen diversity.[241] For example, in critical response to a narrow construction of the rule of law by another motions judge, the Ontario Court of Appeal noted:

> Other dimensions of the rule of law, however, have a significant role ... These other dimensions include respect for minority rights, reconciliation of Aboriginal and non-Aboriginal interests through negotiations, fair procedural safeguards for those subject to criminal proceedings, respect for Crown and police discretion, respect for the separation of the executive, legislative and judicial branches of government and respect for Crown property rights.[242]

This statement is a better description of the rule of law in the Canadian context than the view expressed by the first motions judge. It focuses on the action-oriented practices that are necessary for law in a free and democratic society: respect, reconciliation, and negotiation.

In the previous examples, we saw that civil (dis)obedience failed to generate meaningful respect, reconciliation, and negotiation concerning Indigenous demands. As a result, no lasting relationships of peace, friendship, or respect were formed through civil (dis)obedience. Unfortunately, this next example, involving the Algonquins of Barriere Lake, contains similar lessons. Despite sustained direct action over a long period of time, the parties have not created meaningful relationships. They have not found sustainable ways of respecting both Canadian law and Algonquin legal traditions. Thus, both parties have failed in their attempts to carve out a good life for those who live in these territories. There has been neither harmonization of the parties' governmental relationships nor any increase in Algonquin control of their own affairs. In fact, in this situation, Canadian governments have largely ignored Algonquin law and at times have actively sought its elimination. The failure to recognize and affirm the practical dimensions of Algonquin law as a tool for building healthier relationships within and beyond the community diminishes freedom for everyone who is interested in seeing Algonquin people prosper in their homelands.

The Algonquins of Barriere Lake are one of ten Algonquin communities in Canada, forming part of the wider Algonquin territories located in the Ottawa River watershed and in adjoining areas on the edge of the Canadian Shield in Northern Ontario and Northwestern Quebec.[243] The Mitchikanibikok Inik,[244] or Barriere Lake people, have a rich history in this region.[245] Their territorial knowledge exhibits a key aspect of this book's thesis; it is physically derived from 'a contextual and experientially driven process rather than a static and timeless content.'[246] In this light, they have long struggled to have their lands and resources acknowledged and protected by Canada and the Province of Quebec.[247]

Barriere Lake is on the shores of Rapid Lake, Quebec, on the bank of the Cabonga Reservoir, 134 kilometres north of Maniwaki.[248] The community has over 500 members on a twenty-eight-hectare reserve.[249] After a century of halting displacement from various parts of their territory, a small twenty-five-hectare reserve was formed in 1961 on land where they were already settled.[250] The Algonquins assert that the land outside the reserve belongs to them. The Mitchikanibikok Inik claim that their traditional territory has never been surrendered[251] and reaches into the headwaters of the Upper Ottawa River in Northwestern Quebec beyond the reserve.[252] Despite strong arguments that this area remains Algonquin land under both Algonquin and Canadian law, Quebec has alienated much of the territory for resource development.[253]

In 1988, the Algonquins deployed direct action by camping on Parliament Hill to protest a provincial proposal to further clear resources from their territory.[254] Since Ottawa is within Algonquin traditional territory, they felt justified in reoccupying this small portion of their land. While camped in Ottawa, the Algonquins urged the federal government to assist them in implementing conservation strategies to protect their traditional territories.[255] The Algonquin action was designed to send the message that it was contrary to Algonquin law for the provincial government to physically occupy Algonquin land and prevent Algonquin people's access to their traditional territories. Through reoccupation of a traditional site, the Algonquins tried to open a self-determining democratic space to engage governments in deliberation, negotiation, and reconciliation of their rights and interests. Unfortunately, they failed in this goal and did not develop any meaningful institutional relationships. In fact, the Algonquins were charged with trespassing on Parliament Hill, and their tents were seized on 28 September 1988. The confiscation of their possessions and the failure to constructively listen to their pleas compounded their conflict with the federal and provincial governments. A vicious cycle continued; further direct action resulted.

In 1989, the Algonquins' actions on Parliament Hill were followed by a blockade of a road through the La Vérendrye Wildlife Reserve in Quebec, which was under pressure from clear-cut logging.[256] Furthermore, toxic pesticides had blanketed important traditional food sites, threatening central livelihood activities. In protest, the Algonquins slowed traffic and asked motorists to sign a petition supporting conservation efforts in the area. In six hours, they received 1,400 signatures. They were also protesting provincial regulations for hunting in the area that did not make any provision for Aboriginal hunting.[257] In response, Canadian Pacific Forest Products, owners of Canadian International Paper Company, applied for and received an injunction from the courts ordering the Algonquins to dismantle their blockades.[258] The Algonquins resisted.[259] Unfortunately, the protests and blockades brought the Algonquins of Barriere Lake into direct conflict with the Sûreté du Québec (provincial police force). This further fanned their frustration and further constrained their freedoms. In their words, 'Relations with the police deteriorated and in October 1989, the SQ, equipped with riot gear and batons, forcefully stormed a logging blockade set up by the Algonquins near Le Domaine in the middle of the La Vérendrye Wildlife Reserve.'[260]

Despite these problems, the Algonquins of Barriere Lake were able to secure some space to negotiate. In 1991, they entered into a Trilateral Agreement with the Canadian federal government and the Quebec provincial government.[261] The purpose of the agreement was to develop an integrated resource management plan (IRMP) for the one-million-hectare traditional Barriere Lake territory.[262] Negotiated in the shadow of the Oka dispute, the agreement was designed to give the Algonquins a decisive role in resource management throughout their lands and a modest share of resource revenues from their territories. Its purpose was to initiate sustainable development in the region within the 'respective jurisdictions' of Canada, Quebec, and the Algonquins of Barriere Lake.[263] The agreement also promised funding for the Barriere Lake people to collect, correlate, analyse, and map the community's traditional knowledge of their land and resources. This process was to lead to an IRMP to guide the territory's future use and development. Given its innovations, the agreement was hailed in many quarters. It was labelled as a 'trailblazer' by representatives of the United Nations Convention on Biological Diversity, and the Royal Commission on Aboriginal Peoples called it a model for coexistence.[264]

Unfortunately, implementation of the agreement broke down because Quebec disregarded, and eventually denied, that Algonquins could use their own laws as a basis for co-managing the territory.[265] The province also came to realize that it would lose significant revenue if it shared a portion of the estimated $100 million from the territory.[266] These facts partially conditioned Quebec's practical withdrawal from the agreement.[267] Furthermore, looming constitutional negotiations (eventually embodied in the Charlottetown Accord) also put Quebec on edge regarding its future political autonomy. This also played into the province's hesitancy to work with Canada and First Nations. Detailed cooperation to harmonize jurisdictions at this level complicated the province's negotiations on the national stage. Thus, as the Oka conflict dissipated and Barriere Lake barricades were dismantled, Quebec was not prepared to share jurisdiction or revenue – despite what it promised in the agreement; the province was not prepared to develop a meaningful real-world relationship. While the agreement did have a brief resurgence a few years later, it was never implemented in a manner consistent with its 1991 written formulation.[268] While the community again blockaded roads through their territory in subsequent years, including 2008 and 2010, they have not been successful in securing further action in relation to the Trilateral Agreement.[269]

Unfortunately, the province was not the only party to frustrate the agreement; Canada also failed in its obligations to fund Barriere Lake's participation in this process. As a result, the people of Mitchikanibikok Inik had to pay professional and other fees to keep the agreement alive. They hired consultants and other experts to collect and communicate information contemplated in the agreement. These expenditures eventually placed great strain on Algonquin financial resources which 'would be used against them in a series of attacks that accused the band and their advisors of mismanagement of funds, embezzlement and corruption. This deficit would also be used to justify placing the community under financial receivership, but at the time, it was all the community could do to keep the Agreement alive.'[270] In addition, the Canadian government also interfered with the internal political structures of community by imposing *Indian Act* rules on the band and disregarding overarching Algonquin laws and customs.[271] Canada also aggressively sought to manipulate the community in other ways that generated insecurity at Barriere Lake.[272] As a result, Barriere Lake has been involved in a decades-long dispute concerning the legitimacy of its customary leadership.[273] This had made it more difficult for the community's allies and supporters to work with them, and has made it easier for governments to focus on this seemingly more pressing concern, thus compromising steps to implement the Trilateral Agreement.

As Canada and Quebec have thwarted Algonquin freedom and thereby impeded their attempts to create meaningful relationships with others, the people of Barriere Lake have been caught in a maelstrom of internal dissension and disorder.[274] This has hampered their ability to effectively use their laws to address their problems by developing healthier relationships in their own backyard and homeland.[275] As noted, much of this dysfunction can be traced to both Canada's failure to honour Algonquin laws concerning leadership *and* Quebec's appropriation of Algonquin land. Political manipulation and economic suffocation have damaged important socio-legal relationships within Barriere Lake.[276] In addition, the Quebec police are also alleged to have played a negative role in fuelling this crisis.[277] They are said to have advanced interests that have prevented people from reaching out to mend frayed relationships. Furthermore, there have been unsubstantiated allegations of sexual abuse, voter fraud, and legal conflicts of interest, which have plagued the community's attempts to implement better relationships through the Trilateral Agreement.[278]

At the same time, the Mitchikanibikok Inik are not passive victims in the face of these forces; they have agency even within constrained circumstances. Unfortunately, the Mitchikanibikok Inik have not always deployed their powers in the most productive ways. Allegations of bitter infighting and lateral violence have challenged the community's ability to break through colonialism's constraints. Leadership is seen to be divided and families pitted against one another in ways that inhibit the practical implementation of their own legal traditions.[279] While there is a small yet relatively robust group of external allies and supporters of direct action at Barriere Lake, and while many people continue to work hard within the community to strengthen their laws and traditions, there has been a failure to channel this power towards productive ends. Excessive energy appears to have been dissipated through internal hostilities, which have thus far have failed to secure good relationships within the band and beyond. While the provincial and federal governments are largely responsible for the inordinate pressure they have created within the community, in the absence of governmental change, the Algonquins are in the best position to attend to their troubled internal relationships.

Unfortunately, thus far, the Barriere Lake people have not been able to sufficiently marshal their resources to expand freedom. Civil (dis)obedience and direct action, pursued over a twenty-year period, has not facilitated *dibenindizowin* and *mino-bimaadiziwin*. It is not a universally ideal form of social and political action. In fact, it could even be argued that for the Barriere Lake people, civil (dis)obedience has eroded liberty within themselves and within their relationships. Power struggles and the sometimes tenuous nature of internal order appear to have made the Algonquins less free in owning and controlling their interactions with others. Through direct action the Algonquins seem to have diminished 'power control' within their broader network of relationships (which would not be the case if the Algonquins were enjoying *mino-bimaadiziwin*).[280]

For many Mitchikanibikok Inik, a key to the future is said to lie with the revival of the Trilateral Agreement. They want governments to use this agreement to work with them in improving territorial, community, and provincial sustainability. They believe the agreement acknowledges a legitimate place for the Algonquins of Barriere Lake relative to their lands and resources. So far, governments do not seem to agree with this assessment.[281] Nevertheless, the agreement holds significant potential for reducing government domination of the Algonquin people in the area. It recognizes the importance of Algonquin peoples' participation in the territory's development. As such, it proposes a process which could build healthier relationships. It could enable the parties to address the technical and psychological aspects of the conflict if it was sincerely acted upon. If this occurred, it may one day herald the recognition of Algonquin law as a legitimate force in the territory if the parties. Until then, Barriere Lake remains in a state of colonially supervised dysfunction,[282] where community members cannot act in ways that threaten Quebec's resource revenues or Canada's jurisdictional concerns.

On-the-ground, civil (dis)obedience has failed to secure a broader recognition of Algonquin law. Governments do not seem to want to have relations on these terms. Yet, as this book argues, freedom must often (though not always) be worked out in relational contexts. There are great needs to both strengthen internal governance and enhance inter-governmental relationships. *Dibenindizowin* is not embedded in the diverse cultural relationships in which the Algonquins, Canadians, and Quebecers live and interact. Good ideas such as sovereignty and tradition are important goals for living a good life, but in this case they seem to be insufficient to facilitate further freedom. I would argue that the parties must move beyond abstract ideas and coercive physical force to advance their goals. The process contemplated by the Trilateral Agreement appears to be a good way to facilitate such movement, but so far Quebec and Canada have been unmoved by the Algonquins' actions. The provincial and federal governments have clung to false traditions related to their own 'integral,' 'distinctive' cultural views of their own laws and jurisdiction in Canada.

iii) Temagami Anishinaabe

As noted in this book's introduction, Anishinaabe people learn important legal lessons from their environments. Key legal concepts, which are inspired by the world around us, are embedded in the Anishinaabe language. The Earth (and the words used to describe her) suggests standards about how to regulate activity and resolve disputes. The Anishinaabe have long taken direction about how we should live through interactions and observations with the environment. People regulate their behaviour and resolve their disputes by drawing guidance from what they see in the behaviour of the sun, moon, stars, winds, waves, trees, birds, animals, and other natural phenomenon. As discussed, the Anishinaabe word for this concept is *gikinawaabiwin*.[283] Another Anishinaabe word for teaching and learning about the Earth is *akinoomaage*. The term is composed from two roots: *aki* and *noomaage*. *Aki* means 'earth.' *Noomaage* means 'to point towards and take direction from.' Thus 'teaching and learning' literally means 'the lessons we learn from pointing to and taking direction from the Earth.' Through terms like *gikinawaabiwin* and *akinoomaagewin*, Anishinaabe people are encouraged to draw analogies from our surroundings and carefully apply or distinguish them in our daily lives. The Earth is a profound resource for legal reasoning. *Akinoomaage* suggests a physical philosophy that requires attentiveness to place-based context in making decisions: parallel situations are correlated, dissimilar situations are distinguished.[284]

Chief Gary Potts of the Temagami Anishinaabe illustrated Anishinaabe legal reasoning through an experience he shared from his territory. He wrote:

> I remember once coming across an old white pine that had fallen in the forest. In its decayed roots a young birch and a young black spruce were growing, healthy and strong. The pine tree was returning to the earth, and two totally different species were growing out of the common earth that was forming. And none was offended in the least by the presence of the others because their own identities were intact.
>
> When you walk in a forest you see many forms of life, all living together. They each have their own integrity and the capability to be different and proud. I believe there is a future for native and non-native people to work together because of the fundamental fact that we share the same future with the land we live on.
>
> We will never be able ... to build another planet like earth or build a covered bridge to another planet and start all over again. We need to acknowledge that the *land is the boss*.[285]

Chief Potts' attempt to describe what he saw in the bush and draw meaning from his experience is an example of *gikinawaabiwin* and *akinoomaagewin*. This is an example of physical philosophy which is aimed at drawing meaning from real-world experiences.

Practices of *akinoomaagewin* led Chief Potts and the Temagami Anishinaabe into a dispute with the Ontario provincial government over the appropriateness of logging through their traditional territory. From an Anishinaabe perspective, the conflict flowed from observing the Earth's legal culture in their lands and taking direction from the Earth's authority as a practical, physical matter. Due to their experiences on the land, the Temagami felt that clear-cutting old-growth forest would clear away long-established Anishinaabe legal authorities. It would be harder to draw messages from the Earth if the land was nearly devoid of life. Thus, as in the previous examples in this section, the Anishinaabe blockaded roads into their territories in obedience to their laws, and in contravention of provincial law. They wanted to protect their legal archive (i.e., land) and not see it destroyed. Unfortunately, as with this section's prior illustrations, the Anishinaabe were unable to diminish their own, the land's, or others' domination – despite sustained direct actions.

The Temagami Anishinaabe people reside in a territory located approximately 160 kilometres northeast of North Bay, Ontario, to the northeast of Georgian Bay.[286] They call their land N'Daki Menan. N'Daki Menan spans a 10,000-square-kilometre height of land, which they claim has sustained them for over 6,000 years.[287] It is populated by ancient white and red pines, studded with deep clear lakes, crossed by rich-flowing rivers, and filled with plants and animals on which the Temagami rely. Jesuit priests entered this territory in 1640,[288] while fur trading posts came and went on the margins of the territory between 1670 and 1848.[289] In 1884 the federal government surveyed a 260-square-kilometre reserve for the Temagami, but the province refused to set any land aside for the group because of the valuable timber resources in the area.[290] As the Friends of Temagami describe it, 'In 1901, in an attempt to protect one of North America's largest pine forests for logging, the Temagami Forest Reserve was established. At over 15,000 km² (5,900 square miles) this Reserve was larger than today's Algonquin Park.'[291] A Temagami Indian reserve was not officially set aside until 1970.

Since the creation of the Canadian state, the Temagami have been subject to government restrictions related to their land use and management.[292] This has diminished their freedom to live a good life. While the government has claimed that the Temagami were parties to the Robinson-Huron Treaty of 1850,[293] the Temagami claim that their lands and resources have never been appropriately recognized by the federal and provincial governments.[294] This has generated significant physical conflict. In 1973, to combat these issues, Chief Gary Potts filed land cautions in 110 townships within their traditional territories, asserting Temagami ownership.[295] He claimed that the land was unsurrendered

Indian land as a result of having been left out of the Robinson-Huron Treaty of 1850 and subsequent adhesions.[296] The cautions were filed in the provincial land registry to prevent further government occupation of their land. The cautions stopped mining but not logging.

In 1978, Ontario sued the Temagami in the Supreme Court of Ontario. The government asked for a declaration that Ontario had clear title to the land in question and that the Anishinaabe had no interest therein.[297] The case dragged on for years. At trial, Mr. Justice Steele eventually found that the Temagami 'had no aboriginal right to the land, and that even if such a right had existed, it had been extinguished by the Robinson-Huron Treaty of 1850, to which the Temagami band was originally a party or to which it had subsequently adhered.'[298] He wrote that the Temagami had

> failed to prove that their ancestors were an organized band level of society in 1763; that, as an organized society, they had exclusive occupation of the Land Claim Area in 1763; or that, as an organized society, they continued to exclusively occupy and make aboriginal use of the Land Claim Area from 1763 or the time of coming of settlement to the date the action was commenced.[299]

The court's decision did not resolve the issue, as is often the case when broad conceptual ideas displace morally justifiable anger in particular contexts or face-to-face deliberation and negotiation. The court's abstract statements did not match the reality on the ground and thus reinforced the government's domination of the Temagami people.

As a result, Temagami civil (dis)obedience soon resumed.[300] In 1986, Ontario planned construction of the Red Squirrel logging road into the Temagami Wilderness area but it was temporarily stopped by further court action and lobbying. The Temagami blockaded the Red Squirrel Road from 1 June 1988 until December 1988, when they were removed pursuant to a court injunction. In 1989, the Ontario Court of Appeal upheld the decision of Justice Steele 'on the assumption that [if] an aboriginal right existed ... [it] had been extinguished either by the Robinson-Huron Treaty or by the subsequent adherence to that treaty by the Indians, or because the treaty constituted a unilateral extinguishment by the sovereign.'[301] The Supreme Court of Canada finally rejected the Temagami's arguments in 1991, holding that the 'right was in any event surrendered by arrangements subsequent to that treaty by which the Indians adhered to the treaty in exchange for treaty annuities and a reserve ... [therefore] the aboriginal right has been extinguished.'[302] Thus, the Court held the Temagami were bound by an agreement simply by accepting its benefits. This decision affirmed an exceedingly casual and informal way for Indigenous peoples to sunder broader relationships with lands and resources. It did not accord with Temagami experiences living on the ground. It does not flow from any process which would apply *akinoomaagewin* reasoning. Thus, the Court's conclusion did not resonate with the Temagami, but it nevertheless cleared the way for removing the cautions filed in the provincial registry.[303]

As has already been noted, there is very little democratic engagement when parties take their conflicts to court. In this case, the Supreme Court decision delayed or prevented the resolution of the conflict. The decision did not apply the 'Aboriginal perspective of the meaning of the right at stake.'[304] Furthermore, it did not take a 'large, liberal, and generous' approach to the characterization of the right at issue. Nor did the decision 'choose from among the various possible interpretations of the common intention [at the time the treaty was made] the one which best reconciles the Anishinaabe interests and those of the British Crown.'[305] The failure to find significant acknowledgment of the Temagami's subjective experiences of being denied access to their land and resources does not enhance *dibenindizowin* or *mino-bimaadiziwin*. This has been a problem more generally when using the Canadian judicial system. In most cases reviewed in this chapter, courts have done a poor job of conveying persuasive reasons for their decisions to Indigenous peoples.[306] Judges could be more effective in writing judgments that address Aboriginal views, yet their decisions rarely address the physicality of Indigenous law. A more informed approach, applying all laws operative on a territory, could facilitate further deliberation, negotiation, and compromise. Citing Indigenous law could enhance democracy, reduce domination, and create greater respect for the common law, constitutional, and Indigenous legal traditions. It may be that judges need more physical experiences with Aboriginal people or issues to effectively write in ways that diminish conflict.[307] Decisions remain unpersuasive when they do not realistically engage with those most negatively affected by them.

While the Temagami lost in court, there was a brief negotiation period with the Crown, because the Supreme Court of Canada ruled that the Crown had 'failed to comply with some of its obligations under this agreement, and thereby breached its fiduciary obligations to the Indians.'[308] Negotiations held the potential to address the larger issues in the conflict and take the parties beyond the specific technicalities of the dispute.[309] These negotiations lasted until 1995, when Premier Mike Harris had them unilaterally terminated. In 1995, the government lifted the cautions against the land, and mine staking began.[310] This hurt those who had tried so hard to make their history, views, and feelings known. The actions of Premier Harris' government were a tremendous setback. Land claims negotiations to recognize land for the Temagami have been ongoing ever since, though at a slow place, but with no present success. Furthermore, co-management regimes proposed at the time were pursued in earnest, but they never recognized any real control or authority resting in the land or with the Temagami First Nation.[311] The Red Squirrel logging road was re-opened in June 2005.

As noted, the practice of the Temagami people in taking direct action to engage other Canadians in their struggle against domination was largely thwarted by decisions to submit these matters to courts. It shows how ill-suited the courts generally are in resolving Indigenous peoples' disputes with the Crown. If I were advising First Nations, I would generally counsel them to avoid the courts whenever possible. I must be clear that I am not making an absolute, essentialized or *a priori* judgment. I believe the courts on rare occasions play an important role in facilitating *dibenindizowin*, as will be explained in later chapters. However, the Temagami dispute shows what we have generally seen with each example in this chapter: there is usually no recognition by either the courts or provincial authorities that the land is the boss, or that *gikinawaabiwin* or *akinoomaagewin* should be taken into account when making use of the land and resources. This has narrowed freedoms for Temagami and Canadians more generally.[312] In this regard, Professor David McNab has observed, 'In spite of this recent litigation, the TAA's aboriginal title and land rights to N'Daki Menan has never been resolved and the situation is much worse now than in 1973 when the cautions were placed on the land. Litigation in the white man's courts [does] not always work.'[313]

While consultation protocols are being developed in relation to territorial mining,[314] the potential for further physical action throughout the territory remains. However, given the dismal results of using civil (dis)obedience to this point, such action will likely be taken only if the Anishinaabe feel they can succeed in temporarily reversing the flow of domination in their territory to turn their lives around. Given their experience so far, they may think twice before engaging in civil (dis)obedience again, because each action they have taken has further suppressed their democratic participation in the Canadian state, leading to a corresponding loss of freedom.

E. Conclusion

The foregoing case studies have been examined to further demonstrate the interdisciplinary methods that can be employed in developing physical philosophies. Each case study in this chapter discussed specific limits and opportunities for freedom in the context of particular disputes.[315] They illustrate the strengths and limitations of direct action. Fortunately, the socio-legal specificity of each case study does not exclude reaching towards tentative generalizations. Of course, we should critique and abandon these generalizations when they do not align with contextually contingent circumstances in particular places. Nevertheless, they may provide a resource for reasoning for people looking to take ownership of their relationships in pursuit of their views of a good life. Patterns can be discerned within and among the events under study to draw particular (though not universal) lessons in relation to Indigenous peoples' relationships with the Canadian state.[316]

In the first cluster of cases, the examples of direct action from Haida Gwaii, James Bay, Cape Croker, and Clayoquot Sound show that it is possible for Indigenous peoples to strengthen democratic self-determination and reduce domination for themselves and others. Each community used civil (dis)obedience to meets its own objectives while simultaneously expanding the space for a broader democratic engagement between governments and other Indigenous peoples. It is interesting to note that, unlike the cases in the second group, the exercise of civil (dis)obedience did not involve the discharge of weapons or other threats to any person's physical bodily integrity.

The examples in the second grouping likewise show that freedom and democracy can be strengthened through civil (dis)obedience, though they also reveal some significant limitations on its practice. The cases from Oka and Burnt Church suggest that physical violence might weaken a group's ability to secure its own objectives, even though these two cases secured limited benefits for other Indigenous peoples and Canadians more generally. Nevertheless, in these particular disputes, violence seemed to limit the local communities' accomplishment in relation to their own goals. They alienated local communities in ways not seen in the first four examples.

However, as noted, care must be taken not to universalize this generalization concerning violence. My conclusions flow from on-the-ground contingent realities of the cases studied; they are not constructed through theorizing about idealized, metaphysically perfect forms. The contingent nature of theorizing through physical philosophy means that we must always be open to other cases potentially showing different results. Violence might not always diminish freedom and democracy,[317] though I reject it in my own practices.[318] However, not everyone is a lawyer and bound by an oath to pursue non-violent actions in relating to the state and other people more generally. However, even if I had not taken this oath, my experience leads me to conclude that there is a greater volatility and disrespect for all forms of life when violence is unleashed. It often requires absolutist conceptualizations and commitments. This causes me to strongly counsel against its use.[319] Nevertheless, at least one example suggests that violence may not be irreconcilable with advancing freedom and democracy, as for example when weapons were discharged and an Anishinaabe man was killed during the Ipperwash dispute in Ontario during the mid-1990s. While much remains to be done, freedom and democracy were partially strengthened as a result of this clash. The Ipperwash people had their land returned and better policy frameworks were created for dealing with conflict between Indigenous peoples and the Crown.[320]

The third cluster of case studies in this chapter focused on instances where civil (dis)obedience did not open up any meaningful democratic space and thus more substantially eroded Indigenous freedom.[321] The case studies from Anicinabe Park, Barriere Lake, and Temagami reveal real limits to the practice of civil (dis)obedience. These examples show that direct action can be anti-democratic and lead to repressive practices if it is disrespectful of Indigenous peoples' laws concerning peace, friendship, and respect.

Thus, while civil (dis)obedience can be an important practice of freedom, we should recognize both its limits and its strengths. As democratic institutions, Indigenous, federal, and provincial governments must learn how to take account of the complexities of Indigenous dissent without trapping themselves or others within dichotomously false limits.[322] 'A democratic system of government [should be] committed to considering those dissenting voices, and seeking to acknowledge and address those voices in the laws by which all the community must live.'[323] Disagreement and dissent can be expressed in many ways, including civil (dis)obedience. Dissent through civil disobedience has an important place in democracy, even within Indigenous communities.[324] There are times when freedom is enhanced and democratic self-determination is reinvigorated through deploying this practice.[325]

The continued eruption of civil (dis)obedience demonstrates that Indigenous peoples will not retreat from taking a direct role in trying to construct their place in the world. The Idle No More movement confirmed this fact in very strong and inspiring ways. As a result, civil (dis)obedience will be a part of the political landscape for quite some time. While we must always be mindful of the differing ways dissent can be turned into opportunities for democratic self-determination, we must also remember that *dibenindizowin* and *mino-bimaadiziwin* can be sought by various means. Conflict between Indigenous peoples and others will likely never be fully at an end, though we can work for and expect greater harmony between the parties if we create better processes for working through disagreements. So far, we have done a very poor job of dealing with Indigenous dissent in Canada, often forcing it to the margins, where it is made illegal and ineffectual. The next chapter will explore what happens when Indigenous rights explicitly enter Canadian affairs through constitutional debates and instruments.

Chapter Three

Indigenous Freedom and Canadian Constitutionalism

Canada's constitutional structure is another place where Indigenous peoples attempt to challenge false horizons. When practices of mobility or civil (dis)obedience fail to effectively address domination, Indigenous peoples pursue other alternatives, along varied pathways. It is often the case that these different roads are travelled simultaneously. Since binary conceptions of Indigeneity are false, diversity of action is not problematically dichotomous or incongruous. In striving for freedom, it is not necessarily inconsistent to pursue varied relationships and simultaneously reject and embrace state, corporate, and other forms of power. There is no 'essential' Indigenous identity that requires Indigenous peoples to think and act in unison. Indigenous peoples live in the midst of complex circumstances. They participate in cross-cutting, parallel, contradictory, and intersectional activities, which appear to be troubling only if judged by theoretically pure conceptions of Indigeneity or 'Indianness.'

This book is a call to more explicitly recognize the fact of Indigenous diversity in all our legal, social, and political circles. When we recall that freedom and the pursuit of a good life is a politically messy process, and not just an idealized end goal, we become less concerned with the abstract purity of any one person's or group's position. Of course, in the process we must always be attentive to state and corporate power and how it may be deployed to take advantage of our diversity. Our contingencies can be used against us. We can be bought off, divided, and pitted against one another when we acknowledge there is no one true path to freedom and a good life. Ambiguity and uncertainty can lead us to lose our will to fight for 'the cause' – because it is so complicated. This is a problem that fundamentalist and unified approaches attempt to solve.

They strive for certainty. As a result, essentialized viewpoints often seem more compelling because they are easy to grasp in the abstract. For instance, we are told we shall overcome our subjugation when we become more traditional, authentic, culturally connected, educated, spiritual, economically self-sufficient, or in touch with ourselves and the Earth. Of course, cultivating these attributes may improve our lives. They may deepen our relationships and enhance freedom. At the same time, our diversity means that they may not; there is no one true foundation on which to base action when dealing with Indigenous issues. This is my thesis. As we remove conceptual stereotypes, we begin to see Indigenous peoples as real human beings, with various options available to them, rather than as some *a priori* category that must act and be acted upon in a particular, universalized way.

Taking this insight to heart, we will now add another dimension to the complexity of Indigenous practices described in this book, alongside mobility and 'digging in.' We will consider Indigenous peoples' troubled and productive relationship to Canada's constitution through the introduction of Aboriginal and treaty rights within section 35(1) of this instrument.

Indigenous peoples interact with Canada's constitution on many different levels, ranging from cautious engagement to outright opposition. As illustrated in the previous chapter many chose to vigorously challenge Canada's constitutional structures because of the domination they experience from the state. In fact, a prominent facet of Indigenous peoples' relationship to the constitution is characterized by persistent dissent.[1] At the same time Canada is conceptualized as a 'free and democratic' society in Section 1 of the Canadian Charter of Rights and Freedoms.[2] Freedom and democracy are paired as complementary values in Canada's highest law. Freedom is not just the absence of coercion or constraint,[3] nor does it necessarily privilege Crown sovereignty and majority rule.[4] Freedom and democracy relate to our abilities to act and constrain ourselves in cooperation with and opposition to others in accordance with rules that we participate in choosing, creating, and changing.[5] At the same time, we must recognize that both freedom and subjugation are relational. This chapter traces this insight and illustrates another path to freedom and a good life for Indigenous peoples in Canada – simultaneous resistance and engagement with Canada's constitutional values, structures, and traditions. Indigenous people seek freedom through rejecting the legitimacy of Canadian constitutionalism *and* working with its more complementary elements. Such approaches can be important channels to facilitate freedom, as long as such views are not universally priorized, essentialized, or considered a fundamental aspect of Indigenous political life in North America.

A. Constitutional Complexities

Canada has many constitutional histories.[6] Some say that Canada was initially formed through the marriage of three British colonies in 1867: Canada, Nova Scotia, and New Brunswick. In their eyes, this union was initially a common-law affair,[7] though it was eventually solemnized by the mother country.[8] Nevertheless, these partners chose not to itemize all constitutional powers in one document, as their neighbours, the United States of America, had done. Canada's constitution is a more complicated arrangement; puritans might even consider it immoral, because it really isn't rooted in any first principles. There is no statement of 'truths we hold to be self-evident,' as in the United States Declaration of Independence. Canada's constitution is rooted in ongoing practice. It is open ended – a perpetual work in progress, a living tree. It is comprised of various written texts, an assortment of established conventions, and a diverse array of oral traditions. It is an open-ended marriage, polyandrous in many ways, allowing for multiple partners. It even has rules that allow the parties to contemplate divorce.[9] In many respects, Canada's constitution is a fluid arrangement, and many people seem to like it that way. Jeremy Webber has called this 'agnostic constitutionalism: a constitutionalism in which contending positions are seen to be essential to the society, animating it, and where these positions are not neatly contained within a comprehensive overarching theory.'[10] As Professor Jim Tully observed, 'The contestable character of constitutional democracy should not be seen as a flaw that has to be overcome.'[11]

The open nature of Canada's constitution is mandated by the preamble to the *British North American Act 1867* (now the *Constitution Act, 1867*), which established it as 'a Constitution similar in Principle to that of the United Kingdom.' The United Kingdom's constitution is largely unwritten and draws upon customs, conventions, and deeply embedded principles to structure government. Since Canada's constitution is similar in principle to that of the United Kingdom, it is obvious that Canada's constitution also contains many unwritten terms. The Supreme Court of Canada has recognized numerous fundamental, unwritten constitutional principles and powers in the *Constitution Act, 1867*.[12] In *Reference re Remuneration of Judges of the Provincial Court of Prince Edward Island (the Provincial Court Judges Reference)*, the Court found that 'the preamble is not only a key to construing the express provisions of the *Constitution Act, 1867* but also invites the use of those organizing principles to fill out gaps in the express terms of the constitutional scheme.'[13]

Indigenous peoples' relationship to the land, its resources, and other peoples could be considered one of organizing features of Canada's unwritten constitution. A British Columbia judgment found that the unique relationship between Indigenous peoples and the Crown is an 'underlying constitutional value' that can be given the force of law.[14] The same court found that Indigenous self-government is another underlying constitutional value, though the Supreme Court of Canada has not been explicit in this regard.[15] While Canada's highest court has been slow to recognize Indigenous governance, this fact has not stopped Indigenous peoples from acting together to influence and manage their relationships relative to Canada's constitution. They certainly exercise a *de facto* measure of governance to advance their causes relative to the Canadian state. As discussed in the last chapter, this often leads Indigenous peoples to disrupt visions of Canada that leave them out of its ongoing formation. As noted, these expressions of dissent can also lead Indigenous peoples to broadly reject Canada's constitutional legitimacy.

Despite Canada's unwritten constitutional practices and traditions, the conventional court-centric view of early constitution-making in Canada has concentrated on formal British Imperial instruments. It has privileged principle over practice. As a result, there is less evidence of Indigenous agency, either for or against constitutionalism, in these written texts. However, even within these documents Indigenous peoples are perceptible, and the texts can be read as providing recognition and room for these groups to act. As noted earlier, the Royal Proclamation of 1763 and subsequent Treaty of Niagara made it illegal to occupy Indigenous lands without consent.[16] The proclamation also mandated that treaties with Indigenous peoples had to be made with Imperial authorities before their land could be settled or used for other purposes. Furthermore, under its terms, local colonies were forbidden from entering into land transactions with Indian Nations.

In 1867, when Confederation occurred, section 91(24) of the *British North America Act* gave the federal government exclusive legislative authority relative to 'Indians and lands reserved to Indians.'[17] Manitoba's entry into Confederation in 1870 contained provisions related to Metis land rights.[18] In 1871, British Columbia's constitutional entry contained federal obligations to liberally manage Indian lands. It also contained provincial obligations to transfer lands to the Dominion for the Indians' benefit.[19] When Alberta, Saskatchewan, and Manitoba were given responsibility over natural resources in their territories in 1930, they were constitutionally mandated to assume legal responsibilities for Indian hunting and fishing rights.[20] Thus, Indigenous legal structures can be found in written Canadian constitutional documents, though their presence only weakly reflects Indigenous aspirations.

A more active story concerning Indigenous constitutional relationships can be told when Canada's unwritten constitutional traditional practices are brought alongside idealized narratives. These other sources clearly reveal Indigenous peoples' struggles in relation to the Crown. In many parts of the country, such as British Columbia, Quebec, and the North, the Crown did not recognize or act upon principles such as those found in the Royal Proclamation and Treaty of Niagara. Thus, Indigenous lands and resources were 'taken' without treaties or other agreements. This led to consistent opposition by Indigenous peoples in these regions.[21] Even in the parts of the country where treaties were signed, Indigenous peoples experienced broad denials of their freedom and autonomy to land, governance, and other vital resources. This also led many Indigenous leaders and communities to set themselves against Canada and its constitutional designs. This opposition could often be disruptive and intense, though Canada's colonial structures tended to mute the power of this resistance.[22] In fact, Indigenous peoples have long withstood government assertions of authority over them by avoiding, attacking, and refusing to recognize Crown land claims and the Crown's assertion of sovereignty.[23] There were and are good reasons to embrace these points of view, given Canada's harsh treatment of First Nations and other Indigenous peoples. These views are based on sound physical evidence regarding the destructiveness of the Canadian state for Indigenous peoples. They demonstrate that Canada has not only done a poor job in reflecting Indigenous peoples within its constitutional order, it has greatly harmed their social, economic, and spiritual relations and practices throughout most of its history. As Chief Justice McLachlin observed, Canada committed cultural genocide in relation to Aboriginal peoples.[24] Colonialism is not only a historic fact of Canadian life – it is a present distressing reality.

At the same time, Canada's unwritten constitutional tradition has other dimensions, and like its textual twin, contains strands of recognition and protection for Indigenous peoples. For example, Canada's constitutional order recognizes the continuity of Indigenous laws after the assertion of Crown sovereignty. In the first year of Canada's Confederation, the case of *Connelly v. Woolrich* affirmed the existence of Cree law on the Prairies and recognized it as part of Canadian law.[25] The legal doctrine applied by Justice Monk is known as the doctrine of continuity and demonstrates that Canada's constitutional law stems from a 'great variety of sources,' including Indigenous law – obligations sustained by practice.[26] The British Court of Appeal recognized this in *R. v. Secretary of State for Foreign and Commonwealth Affairs* when it held: 'These customary laws are not written down. They are handed down by tradition from one generation to another. Yet beyond doubt they are well established and have the force of law within the community.'[27]

> Under this view Indigenous legal traditions also functioned as Canadian constitutional traditions and were given the force of law throughout the country. The continuing weight of Indigenous law has provided jurisdictional space to work out aspects of their constitutional relationships with the Crown, despite the often negative treatment of Indigenous legal orders experienced in the process.[28]

Treaties and agreements between Indigenous peoples and the Crown also have constitutional significance. These also flow from Indigenous practices. Many treaties helped create the country and define key legal relationships.[29] Other treaties attempted to hold Indigenous Nations at arms length from Canada, as First Nations tried to preserve space outside Canada's constitutional order. There have been hundreds of negotiated arrangements throughout Canadian history, and they have drawn from both Indigenous and Crown-directed political legal practices to frame their terms.[30] For some, treaties are perhaps the most significant feature of Indigenous peoples' relationship with the Crown, because they produced promises that the pre-existing population would live together in peace and order with those who followed.[31] They demonstrate the active attempt by Indigenous peoples to create a relationship with the Crown partially based on their own goals.[32]

For example, when Manitoba entered Confederation, negotiation with Indigenous peoples played a prominent role in constitutional development. A dispute between the Metis and the Crown arose when the Dominion Parliament attempted to unilaterally survey the old North-West Territories around the Red River in 1869.[33] The Metis blocked surveyors from their work because they did not want to be forced into the Dominion without their participation and consent. They practised civil (dis)obedience and achieved a democratic result. These actions delayed Canada's expansion into this region and compelled the first government of Sir John A. Macdonald to secure the consent of the region's prior inhabitants.[34] In particular, the Red River Metis vested a provisional government with authority to negotiate terms of union with Ottawa and bring the area into Confederation. Representatives of this government travelled to Ottawa as delegates of the Metis people to negotiate conditions for this portion of western Canada's entry. They brought with them a locally developed bill of rights that expressed their demands. The negotiations were challenging, but an agreement was reached and its terms were embodied in the *Manitoba Act* of 1870.[35] The democratic legitimacy of this process was sealed through the Metis provisional government's acceptance of the agreement before the Dominion and Imperial Parliament's statutory endorsement which made it part of Canada's constitution.[36] The people of the Metis Nation regard the *Manitoba Act* as embodying a treaty that recognizes and affirms their nation-to-nation relationship with Canada,[37] even though its provisions concerning land and resources have not been appropriately fulfilled.[38] Metis agency in Manitoba was thus important to the development of the country.[39]

Indigenous law and treaties, along with other constitutional practices, conventions, and customs can be found in many places throughout Canada, demonstrating the active nature of Indigenous peoples' participation in Canada's constitutional order, behind, against, and beyond the written documents.[40] While they have powerful forces arrayed against them, Indigenous peoples in Canada have worked to resist, shape, and reform Canadian constitutional practice because of the constitution's flexible contours. This illustrates that one should be careful in thinking Canada is constructed only on abstract metaphysical principles; to participate in its ongoing construction requires more than the proper recitation of cases and ancient constitutional theories. Canada is continuously assembled through a physical philosophy that is attentive to the ongoing intersocietal practices and traditions of its peoples.

B. Constitutional Suspicions

As a result of Canada's open-ended system, constitutional reform throughout the country occurs in many different ways: through civil (dis)obedience, formal textual amendment, changing political practices, and shifting legal interpretation. As this book attempts to make clear, there is no singular constitutional history that holistically synthesizes and fully captures the shifting sands of Indigenous experience with this system. The composite nature of Canada's constitution has simultaneously made it both easier and more difficult to create greater space for Indigenous governance. Unfortunately, since the entrenchment of Aboriginal and treaty rights in Canada's constitution, it has been harder for Indigenous peoples to throw off false constitutional limits. As will be further explained in the next chapter, section 35(1)'s jurisprudence frames Aboriginal and treaty rights in essentialized, *a priori* terms. Nevertheless, even in the face of this problem, current Indigenous constitutional practice both directly challenges *and* pieces together transformative interpretations from different documents, conventions, customs, and cases. This is a practice of freedom: *dibenindizowin*. While it requires great skill to traverse these varied domains, Indigenous people have long experience with this structure's subtleties, and thus they continue to work within, between, and around its many fractures to promote their own interests.[41] This is evident in the lead-up to section 35(1)'s inclusion in the constitution.

Constitutional reform was a topic of great interest in Canada from the late 1960s until the early 1990s. In that period, there were numerous debates and formal proposals regarding the country's structure. Indigenous peoples were very active in advancing their aspirations in relation to the Canadian state. Some groups, like the Haudenosaunee, consistently resisted forcible inclusion within Canada. Audra Simpson has referred to this stance as the politics of refusal.[42] The Confederacy generally regards itself as an autonomous entity that has an alliance with the Crown, rather than a relationship of subjugation. While Canadian courts have not accepted this view,[43] it is not uncommon for Haudenosaunee to declare and act as if they were outside Canada's constitutional framework.[44] They regard this as a practice of freedom. Other First Nations have been more willing to consider themselves a part of Canada, particularly those groups such as the Nisga'a, who have recently signed treaties with the state.[45] They regard themselves as having negotiated their way into Canada.[46] Other groups have adopted positions somewhere between those of the Haudenosaunee and Nisga'a. They strategically seek to secure a stronger place within the Canadian state, even as they resist its grasp by pressing for greater autonomy through democratic self-determination. They represent an important challenge to what Jim Tully has labelled 'Imperial constitutionalism, [which involves] the implantation and replication of European forms of organization in Americas.'[47]

The different positions taken by Indigenous peoples in relation to the Canadian state have made it very difficult for them to form a unified front on constitutional reform during the closing decades of the twentieth century.[48] As affirmed throughout these pages, the practice of physical philosophy is a messy affair. There is a great diversity among Indigenous Nations in Canada, with a variety of languages, geographies, cultures, spiritual traditions, and economic practices. Indigenous diversity, coupled with a deep distrust of the Canadian state, has made it very challenging for Indigenous leaders to present constitutional reform to their people in a consistently positive light.

Many Indigenous peoples were suspicious of reform because of the Canadian government's repeated attempts to forcibly eliminate their languages, laws, land, government, and culture. They wondered why they should desire greater integration within a state that had almost shattered their lifeways and community structures. Indigenous peoples wanted to sing their own songs,[49] as it were, yet the government continually worked to teach them so-called better ('correct') ways. Thus, many had concerns that the constitutionalization of Aboriginal rights could lead to a further erosion of Indigenous languages, cultures, and governments. In fact, some saw constitutional entrenchment as an attack on their freedom to make their own decisions in the world. They felt their unique legal personalities would be undermined by being forced to fit others' conceptions of a proper political relationship.

Furthermore, many Indigenous peoples had signed treaties with the British Crown, a nation separate from Canada (at least in practice) from most First Nations' perspectives. Thus, they regarded potential incorporation within Canada's constitution as a breach of broader international relationships. Those holding this position did not want to narrow their political arrangements to North American political authorities. Because many had signed treaties with the British Crown, they felt that their treaties created international obligations, and they were adamant that they did not want to lose access to this wider field of political practice. At the same time, Indigenous people who had not signed treaties broadly regarded themselves as being outside of the Canadian legal framework. They resented being forcibly included within its structures. Thus, Indigenous peoples did not regard constitutional reform as a universal good, even when the goal was formalized entrenchment · of Aboriginal rights in Canada's highest written laws. Many distrusted the uncertain promise of rights. They were reluctant to set their future course in accordance with another group's conception of a 'good' political life.

C. Constitutional Discussions

Of course, the process of constitutional reform was difficult for not only Indigenous peoples. Canadians more generally struggled with its implications.[50] As noted, Canada's constitution has evolved over time, through the mixing of written provisions with unwritten customs, conventions, and judicial interpretation. Many wanted to allow the constitution to continue to evolve along those lines. They did not want a disembedded constitutional form; they did not think it would be a good thing to create further language, with abstract tenets subject to judicial interpretation.[51] The desire for a practice-based constitution stood on solid ground; some of Canada's strongest constitutional protections are unwritten.[52] For example, one of the most significant aspects of Canada's unwritten constitution prior to Confederation was the development of responsible government, which made the executive subject to legislative branch of government. This unwritten constitutional doctrine was carried over into Confederation, though not in written form. Responsible government has served many Canadians well, and there were concerns that executive and legislative accountability would be eroded if new provisions were created.[53] Some felt that formal constitutional entrenchment might unnecessarily restrict the flexibility and strength found in Canada's unwritten constitutional traditions. For these people, responsible government and other associated democratic rights and freedoms were secure without explicit entrenchment.

Of course, Indigenous peoples did not have the same perspective on responsible government. Many will argue that they still do not experience responsible government, which is the subjection of executive power to their own popular sovereignty and agreement. Indeed, executive authority and parliamentary sovereignty have not served Indigenous people very well, due to assimilative legislative forces. For example, most Indigenous people did not get the right to vote in various political jurisdictions in Canada until between 1946 and 1969. Others never wanted to select Members of Parliament or provincial legislators because these people were viewed as members of foreign governments. Most legislation enacted by Parliament does not reflect Indigenous aspirations and priorities. They still cannot implement and control basic governance functions such as education, safety, health and general welfare. Thus, there are many reasons Indigenous peoples have not generally participated in mainstream political institutions or organizations. This is why Indigenous advocacy often occurs outside formal systems, using civil (dis)obedience and unwritten constitutional practices to assert an autonomous, semi-autonomous or unique relationship to the Canadian state. However, during the heightened period of constitutional debate, a small group of Indigenous people regarded written guarantees as a better way to gain greater protection against Canadian intrusions. They viewed formal amendments related to Aboriginal rights as a way to exert pressure from inside the system. Thus, despite distrust among many Indigenous peoples concerning constitutional reform, some saw constitutional entrenchment as an opportunity to formally constrain the government's ability to act contrary to their rights and interests.[54]

The process to formally amend Canada's constitution was not easy. Canadian written constitutional law was dependent on the United Kingdom's legislative process. Canada's written constitution could not be amended without legislative action by the British Parliament (where Canada's constitutional statutes resided). These statutes included the *Constitution Act, 1867*, numerous amendments, various statutes admitting different colonies into Confederation, and the *Statute of Westminster*, which gave Canada equality and a broader degree of legislative independence from Great Britain. While the 1931 *Statute of Westminster* gave Canada some independence, it still did not allow for the amendment of Canada's written constitution without British Parliamentary agreement. Thus, written constitutional reform focused on Britain, and Indigenous peoples were a part of this advocacy. However, Indigenous peoples and Canadians often went to England for different reasons. Most Canadians generally wanted to sever formal links with the United Kingdom; Indigenous peoples were much more resistant to breaking these ties. Many viewed themselves as being in a solemn treaty relationship with the British Crown. As a result, they did not want to lose the protection and political check-and-balance of a more distant government protecting them from local and national political constituencies.

Thus, many Indigenous peoples fought the domestication of their relationships with great vigour.

For most Canadians, the lack of a domestic amending formula led them to seek constitutional reform in 1927, 1931, 1935–6, 1950, 1960–1, and 1964. Indigenous peoples were not part of these efforts, because they were not invited, and may not have even been interested had such an invitation been extended. As noted, many Indigenous people regarded the Queen as their ally and the Canadian state as their oppressor and thus saw domestication as a great political and legal evil. The substitution of the Canadian state for the British Crown would not have been regarded as a positive development. This fact has led many Indigenous peoples through the years to declare that they possessed or desired a stronger constitutional relationship with Britain, as opposed to a diminished one. When the British (rather than the Canadian) Crown was regarded as their partner, a nation-to-nation relationship with the British Crown made greater political sense. Most other Canadians, however, saw the British Crown's continuing control over the country's affairs in a more negative light. However, throughout most of the twentieth century Canada's early efforts at constitutional reform led to failure, though they had the advantage of being tightly focused on procedural questions related to achieving a domestically controlled constitutional amendment formula.

The tide slowly began to turn with the election of Prime Minister Pierre Elliott Trudeau. Under his direction, in 1968 the Liberal government of the day sought to introduce broader substantive issues into the constitutional debate, such as changes to governmental institutions, distribution of powers, and the entrenchment of a bill of rights. At this early stage there was no discussion of Aboriginal rights being explicitly constitutionalized. In fact, the Liberal government planned the exact opposite for Indigenous peoples. The infamous White Paper of 1969 explicitly proposed their assimilation and the elimination of treaty rights and any other special or separate status.[55] This initiative was regarded by most Indigenous peoples in the worst possible light.[56] It was deemed a great offence and has been described as 'the single most powerful catalyst of the Indian nationalist movement.'[57] It was resisted in the strongest possible terms. As a result, exclusion facilitated the development of resistance to the White Paper within many Indigenous political organizations and generated coordination amongst them to strengthen their advocacy.[58] The National Indian Brotherhood (later Assembly of First Nations) came to life and prominence in this period.

The Union of B.C. Indian Chiefs was formed through a fusion of the Indian Homemakers Association of B.C., the North American Indian Brotherhood, and the Southern Vancouver Island Tribal Federation.[59] The Indian Association of Alberta provided leadership through this crisis,[60] and the Manitoba Indian Brotherhood and the Association of Iroquois and Allied Indians also made their views widely known.[61]

Despite Indigenous opposition to the White Paper, wider constitutional debate continued. In 1971, the provinces and federal government managed to obtain a tentative agreement on broader constitutional principles in a document called the Victoria Charter. Once again, there was no mention of Aboriginal issues. Ultimately however, consensus over the Victoria Charter broke down because of changes in political leadership and concerns about Quebec's reaction to specific income security provisions. Other attempts to patriate the constitution in the mid-1970s also ended in failure. Indigenous peoples were largely shut out of these constitutional discussions and were not at all supportive of the entire enterprise to that point.

D. Constitutional Amendment: Strategies and Debates

In 1978, constitutional reform once again came to the forefront of Canadian political life. At the time, it seemed unlikely that Indigenous peoples would find a place in the discussions. The most contentious issue for the country as a whole was who possessed the authority to request an amendment to the constitution. This seemed more of a federal/provincial issue to most people. The written constitution did not provide for amendment procedures, and there was uncertainty in Canada's unwritten constitutional powers about this question. Some assumed that Quebec would need to assent to any constitutional amendment because of its distinct legal and linguistic status.[62] Others believed only a substantial number of the provinces representing a majority of the population needed to consent to constitutional change. At the same time, the federal government of Prime Minister Pierre Elliott Trudeau believed that the federal government alone could request that Britain patriate the constitution, as the domestication of its amending formula was often called. Thus, since the debate was focused along federal/provincial lines, most did not expect Indigenous peoples to have much of a role in this debate.

Despite this perception, Indigenous peoples played an increasingly important role in constitutional debates between 1978 and 1982.

Different Indigenous groups played constitutional politics on both sides of the dissent/engagement line as they attempted to secure their interests. The reasons for this are complex. The federal government wanted to obtain more than a domestic amending formula in patriating the constitution. As had been the case a decade earlier, constitutional reform provided an opportunity to address a variety of other outstanding issues, aside from the amending formula. One of these unresolved issues was the relationship of Indigenous peoples to Canada, a factor that obviously drew some Indigenous groups into the debate. Once again, the parties had wide-ranging discussions about a charter of rights, institutional reform, and separation of powers. Indigenous issues became more prominent as time passed, because some Indian, Metis, and Inuit leaders regarded constitutional incorporation in a positive light. They saw it as a way to resist policies like the White Paper and thereby provide firmer protection against legislative extinguishment of their treaties and unique status.[63]

As a result, in 1978 the National Indian Brotherhood (NIB) formally identified constitutional reform as a priority for Indian bands across Canada.[64] Their two main concerns were the entrenchment of Aboriginal and treaty rights in the constitution *and* participation in the constitutional reform process.[65] The federal government responded to this initiative by inviting the NIB, along with the Native Council of Canada (NCC) and the Inuit Committee on National Issues (ICNI) to attend constitutional negotiations with observer status. Indigenous peoples wanted to be more than observers. Regrettably, the government's invitation did not amount to participation as Indigenous organizations envisioned it, thereby placing First Nations in a more antagonistic role in the process.

This dramatic turn of events brought to the fore those within the NIB and other Indigenous organizations who saw constitutionalization in a less favourable light. As a result, a broad strategy of direct action was developed to block the domestication of Canada's constitution. One of these strategies for expressing opposition to reform was to petition the British Queen and Parliament. While the Queen possessed no real political authority to respond to Indigenous advocacy (because it was expected the British Parliament would 'rubber stamp' Canada's recommendations regarding the constitution) Indigenous opposition threatened to unravel the fragile consensus within Canada. The threat to constitutional partriation posed by Indigenous peoples was considerable. This opposition was on display when over 200 First Nations people visited England in 1979 and successfully raised their concerns before parliamentarians and the British public more generally.[66]

Following these protests, the federal government recognized that further antagonizing Indigenous people could gravely threaten its constitutional objectives. Therefore it promised formal Indigenous involvement in the constitutional process but then proceeded to act without Indigenous organizations in developing priorities for constitutional inclusion.[67] Thus, when a meeting was held between provincial premiers and the prime minister in the fall of 1980, Indigenous organizations once again boycotted official events. They chose to pursue their goals through other means. They held parallel meetings where they decided to further their advocacy in the United Kingdom. The National Indian Brotherhood chose to further press the British Queen, Parliament, and other Commonwealth partners to reject Canada's overtures.

The Union of British Columbia Indians also chose direct action to open up more democratic space to debate their future relationship with Canada. They resolved to organize a 'Constitutional Express,' which would travel from Vancouver to Ottawa raising awareness of their position. This event eventually attracted 500 participants. When the Express arrived in Ottawa, it generated a great deal of press coverage. The arrival also corresponded with a meeting of 2,000 other Indians hosted by the Assembly of First Nations, which generated further media attention. The group drafted a Declaration of the First Nations and presented it to the Governor General as a statement of their inherent rights. It was also decided that some members of the Express would continue on to New York, London, and Rotterdam to create international pressure against constitutionalization without their consent. Finally, the Assembly of First Nations also resolved it would not participate in a Special Joint Committee meeting on the constitution that same week because government did not recognize its position. However, as noted, Indigenous peoples continued to find themselves on different sides of the constitutionalization line. Unanimity was not a feature of Indigenous politics in this period. Thus, when the Special Joint Committee was convened, Indigenous representatives from the Native Council of Canada, the Inuit Committee on National Issues, the Council of Yukon Indians, and the Nisga'a Nation attended. This provided a measure of input into formal constitutional decision-making, despite widespread opposition elsewhere in the process.

After these meetings, the National Indian Brotherhood also tried to find a way to influence internal constitutional reform, even as they fought it from afar in Britain and in other corridors of power. Thus, they joined with the Native Council of Canada and the Inuit Committee on National Issues to develop 'a common position on constitutional

provisions which would entrench treaty and aboriginal rights, recognize aboriginal self-government and require consent to constitutional amendments affecting their rights.'[68] Unfortunately, cooperation
between these groups was tenuous, because particular treaty groups
within the NIB opposed working with the Metis, who were a part of the
Native Council of Canada. Furthermore, the Union of British Columbia
Indians completely rejected constitutional entrenchment as inconsistent with their view of themselves as Nations possessing international
status. One Union participant subsequently put the issue in this way,
'We were fighting for nationhood, not section 35.'[69]

As Indigenous peoples' positions splintered, the provinces and the
federal government also experienced similar fractures. Each party
seemed willing to go its own way to pursue constitutional goals in its
own interests. This frustrated Prime Minister Trudeau, and he increasingly sought to impose a stronger federal role within the process. Thus,
on 6 October 1981 the federal government insisted it had unilateral
authority to request a constitutional amendment from the British Parliament to domesticate the country's amending formula. The provinces
rejected this position and asserted that they had to consent to such a
request. Quebec further assumed it had a veto over the entire process
because of its distinct language, culture, and political history. These
divisions placed the federal government under additional pressure to
seek other strategic alliances. It brought the provinces back to the bargaining table.

As a result of these processes, during the period of 28–30 January 1981,
the federal government struck a deal with the three national Indigenous
organizations to recognize Aboriginal and treaty rights in the constitution. There was further agreement to insert a section in the proposed
Charter of Rights and Freedoms to insulate Aboriginal collective rights
from abrogation or derogation that might result from individual rights
interpretations. Finally, the parties agreed to constitutionalize future
conferences to deal with Indigenous issues. While these provisions
looked promising for both the federal government and Indigenous
organizations, the short-lived trust between the groups quickly eroded.
The federal government subsequently appeared to present these clauses
as capable of amendment without Indigenous consent. Many Indigenous people felt betrayed. This led to a further fracturing within the
NIB. Some regional organizations quit the organization or threatened
to do so, forcing the NIB to reverse its support for the federal proposal.

At this point, during the spring and summer of 1981, Indigenous
peoples intensified their activities in England and Europe. They did not

participate in litigation before the Supreme Court of Canada concerning the constitutionality of the federal government's attempted unilateral patriation.[70] Instead, litigation was launched before the English courts, with various regional Indigenous organizations participating at different points in the suit's development, including the Union of British Columbia Indians, the Indian Association of Alberta, the Federation of Saskatchewan Indian Nations, the Union of Nova Scotia Indians, the Union of New Brunswick Indians, the Four Nations Confederacy of Manitoba, and the Grand Council of Treaty Nine from Ontario. The main case eventually carried the name of the Indian Association of Alberta.[71] Their core arguments were that treaties were domestic, not international agreements, and that the British Crown had never explicitly transferred responsibility for Indians to Canada, making treaty implementation Britain's continuing responsibility. In the end, First Nations organizations from Saskatchewan and British Columbia did not participate in this case because of differences in opinion on legal strategy. The FSIN did not agree their treaties were domestic agreements, and the Union of BC Indians argued they were a part of Canada's constitutional order, but their consent was needed to patriate the constitution.[72]

Despite a strong campaign in England, Lord Denning of the English Court of Appeal eventually rejected the Alberta Indians' arguments on 28 January 1982. He found that:

> ... the Crown was no longer single and indivisible. It was separate and divisible for each self-governing dominion or province or territory.
>
> ... Thus, the obligations to which the Crown bound itself in the Royal Proclamation of 1763 are now to be confined to the territories to which they related and binding on the Crown only in respect of those territories. None of them is any longer binding on the Crown in respect of the United Kingdom.[73]

This was a devastating blow for many First Nations. The failure to win support from British Parliament or the courts mirrored the failure of the provinces before the Supreme Court of Canada to persuade that institution their consent was needed for patriation. On 28 September 1981, the Supreme Court of Canada had written that a 'unilateral' patriation of the constitution was legal. However, it also noted that a 'substantial degree' of provincial consent was required by constitutional convention before the federal-provincial relationship could be fundamentally altered by a request to Britain for constitutional amendment. The Court's politically cunning judgment, coupled with the pressure created by Indigenous peoples in Britain, sent the federal government back to the bargaining table with the provinces, with an additional promise to include Aboriginal and treaty rights in the final document.

This promise did not last long. Aboriginal rights were quickly dropped from the accord when the provinces and federal government sat down to negotiate on 5 November 1981. Indigenous groups who favoured a formal entrenchment of their rights were shocked by this development. Provincial pressure and federal timidity were the cause of this perceived setback. This turn of events further placed the NIB in a tenuous position with its membership. Since the NIB was uncertain about whether it could support the reinstatement of Aboriginal rights provisions without full First Nations backing, the political initiative was taken by other Indigenous groups. As a result, the push for the entrenchment of Aboriginal rights in the constitution was led by other organizations such as the Native Council of Canada, the Inuit Committee on National Issues, the Native Women's Association of Canada, the Dene Nation and the Council of Yukon Indians under the banner of the Aboriginal Rights Coalition (ARC).[74] The federal government responded positively to ARC's submissions but insisted it could not act without provincial consent. Direct action ensued for Indigenous peoples across Canada. The federal government's reticence in the face of provincial opposition to Aboriginal rights resulted in a series of large Indian demonstrations in nine cities across Canada to protest the provincial position. Indigenous direct action never died during the push for constitutional patriation. The provinces reacted to the pressure and reconsidered their position on Aboriginal rights, eventually agreeing to their reintroduction in the accord. All the while, the NIB sat in the background, with many of its members opposed to the entire process.

E. Constitutional Entrenchment

On 17 April 1982, Aboriginal and treaty rights officially became a part of Canada's written constitution. Section 35 in Part II the *Constitution Act, 1982* came into force and read as follows:

(1) The existing Aboriginal and Treaty Rights of the Aboriginal Peoples of Canada are hereby recognized and affirmed.
(2) In this Act, 'aboriginal peoples of Canada' includes the Indian, Inuit and Metis peoples of Canada.

Furthermore, section 25 in Part I of the *Constitution Act, 1982* was enacted to read:

> The guarantee in this Charter of certain rights and freedoms shall not be construed so as to abrogate or derogate from any aboriginal, treaty or other rights or freedoms that pertain to the aboriginal peoples of Canada including
> • any rights or freedoms that have been recognized by the Royal Proclamation of October 7, 1763.

Finally, section 37 of the constitution read:

> (1) A constitutional conference composed of the Prime Minister of Canada and the first ministers of the provinces shall be convened by the Prime Minister of Canada within one year after this Part comes into force.
> (2) The conference convened under subsection (1) shall have included in its agenda an item respecting constitutional matters that directly affect the aboriginal peoples of Canada, including the identification and definition of the rights of those peoples to be included in the Constitution of Canada, and the Prime Minister of Canada shall invite representatives of those peoples to participate in the discussions on that item.
> (3) The Prime Minister of Canada shall invite elected representatives of the governments of the Yukon Territory and the Northwest Territories to participate in the discussions on any item on the agenda of the conference convened under subsection (1) that, in the opinion of the Prime Minister, directly affects the Yukon Territory and the Northwest Territories.

Constitutional conferences would take Indigenous peoples back into the messy realm of on-the-ground politics. The first constitutional conference in 1983 mandated under section 37, produced amendments to sections 35 and 25 of the *Constitution Act, 1982*. As a result of negotiations and agreement during this conference, subsections 35(3) and (4), 25(b) and 37.1(1) were added to the *Constitution Act, 1982* by the *Constitution Amendment Proclamation, 1983*. Thereafter section 35 contained additional amendments which read:

> (3) For greater certainty, in subsection (1) 'treaty rights' includes rights that now exist by way of land claims agreements or may be so acquired.
> (4) Notwithstanding any other provision of this Act, the aboriginal and treaty rights referred to in subsection (1) are guaranteed equally to male and female persons.

Furthermore, section 25 was amended by inserting an additional quali-
fication that Charter rights were not to be construed as abrogating or
derogating from 'any rights or freedoms that now exist by way of land
claims agreements or may be so acquired.'

Finally, section 37 was amended to provide for an additional two First
Ministers conferences with Aboriginal organizations. These provisions,
sections 25, 35, and 37 of the *Constitution Act, 1982* became the primary
sections identifying Aboriginal and treaty rights in Canada's written
constitution, along with section 91(24) of the *Constitution Act, 1867*.

F. Constitutional Conferences and Accords

As an open-ended set of relationships, Canada's constitution is interpreted by many people in civil society, including the courts, Parliament,
legislatures, academics, the media, and interested individuals. Indigenous peoples also participate in this process in conflicting, cooperative, and cross-cutting ways. Nevertheless, despite this diversity – or
perhaps because of it – each group plays an important role in giving
the constitution meaning. Freedom is enhanced when people are free
to believe and act in different ways in relation to our constitution. This
includes the freedom to dissent from being included within this order,
as well as the freedom to join or play coy. It is certain that a 'strange
multiplicity'[75] will continue to characterize Canada's constitutional
order because so many issues were left unresolved that require interpretation after the proclamation of the *Constitution Act, 1982*. The most
prominent national issue was that Quebec did not give its assent to the
new constitutional package, rejecting it through its National Assembly
on 1 December 1981 because it did not recognize Quebec's distinct position in Canadian society. This issue is still with us. At the same time,
the newly minted, so-called Aboriginal peoples in section 35(1) of the
constitution also had problems with the *Act*. Many mourned the loss of
their direct ties with the British Crown and refused to accept the legitimacy of domestication. Thus, they continue to this day to resist forcible
inclusion within Canada and deny the constitution's legitimacy. Other
First Nations were wary about section 35 being seen as forcing their *de
facto* inclusion into Canadian society without their consent. Some felt
the section 37 constitutional conference would fail to produce agreement about the meaning of Aboriginal and treaty rights in section 35.
They were right, as subsequent negotiations would prove. At the same
time, those who were more optimistic about the constitutional package

were concerned about the potential for future limitations of their rights by Canadian courts. They were also justified in being concerned; as we will see in the following chapters, section 35(1) has not produced many gains for Indigenous peoples in line with the broader aspirations they expressed during this period. In particular, most Indigenous peoples thought that section 35's major flaw was its failure to recognize and affirm the pre-existing and ongoing inherent rights to practise self-government. This issue still has not been addressed in any satisfactory way for Indigenous peoples.

Nevertheless, in the decade immediately following the constitution's patriation there were many opportunities to address these concerns. First Ministers conferences were held in Ottawa in 1983, 1984, 1985, and 1987 as directed under section 37(1), to identify, define, and discuss Aboriginal and treaty rights.[76] The amendments generated by this process were discussed above. Four major Indigenous organizations participated in these conferences: the Assembly of First Nations, purportedly representing over 600 Indian Bands in Canada; the Native Council of Canada, representing non-status and Metis people; the Metis National Council, representing Metis people generally; and the Inuit Committee on National Issues, representing Northern territorial Inuit communities. These organizations found it difficult to achieve solidarity on many issues, though an even greater gulf separated them from the provinces and federal government. In particular, Saskatchewan, British Columbia, and Newfoundland were unwilling to accept the concept of 'inherent' Aboriginal rights, and most governments had difficulty recognizing undefined Aboriginal rights to self-government. It seems that while they were willing to recognize abstract, *a priori* rights in other parts of the constitution, they were unwilling to see this happen in relation to Aboriginal and treaty rights. There was a concern that self-government would threaten the territorial integrity of the Canadian community, even though the four major organizations at the constitutional table argued they had an inherent right to self-government within the boundaries of the Canadian political community.[77] While the First Ministers conferences produced only limited success in a substantive sense, they did perform an important educative function as the events received extensive media coverage.[78] In this respect, they opened up important democratic space.

When the dust had settled from the last First Ministers conference in 1987, the federal government immediately initiated a process to secure Quebec's agreement to the constitution. Quebec had signalled its willingness to sign the constitution if its demands were accepted, including recognition of its distinct society status. Thus, negotiations between the provinces and federal government to satisfy Quebec's demands produced the Meech Lake Accord, which was signed on 3 June 1987. The accord set a higher standard for constitutional amendment than set forth in the 1982 constitution. Ordinarily, a measure would become constitutional if it had the agreement of seven provinces representing 50 per cent of the population. However, the Meech Lake Accord required the unanimous agreement of all provinces within three years to become constitutional. The heightened standard for amendment gave greater manoeuvring room for those opposed to its endorsement. In particular, Indigenous peoples lobbied both nationally and provincially for the accord's rejection. This time, there was much greater unanimity among Indigenous politicians, because their positions had been so strongly rebuffed.

Indigenous peoples were opposed to the Meech Lake Accord's ratification because they were not consulted in its development and it did not reference their distinct status and rights to self-government.[79] Many Indigenous peoples saw the accord as a troubling return to situation that existed before 1982, where formalized amendments would affect their future without their participation or consent.[80] As a result of this opposition and through their alliance with other like-minded groups, the Meech Lake Accord was defeated. Indigenous opposition was particularly prominent and important to the accord's defeat because Elijah Harper, a Cree man from Red Sucker Lake who sat in the Manitoba Legislature, became the public symbol of its demise. Elijah Harper consulted widely with Indigenous groups in making his decision to resist the accord. When the time for voting came he signalled his opposition by holding an eagle feather high in his hand. His refusal to endorse the accord in the Manitoba Assembly prevented it from securing the unanimous consent required for its passage throughout the country.

After the defeat of the Meech Lake Accord, constitutional discussions receded for a time from the national stage. However, in 1991 Canada was once again caught up in wide-ranging constitutional debate. This time, unlike with the Meech Lake Accord, there was much greater participation by Indigenous peoples in the deliberations. Once again we see that Indigenous freedom and pursuit of a good life is practised in context and does not necessarily take its cues from abstractly pure principles. Indigenous leaders worked with provincial premiers and the prime minister in laying out the scope of the debate. Indigenous peoples also had a more prominent role in working on its details. Issues dealt with during these discussions were related to Canadian identity, Quebec's distinctiveness, the reform of national institutions, economic union, and clarifying of distribution of powers, including the spending power and the streamlining of government. Most importantly for Indigenous peoples, there were also significant package of powers related to Aboriginal and treaty rights. In particular, the Charlottetown Accord would have recognized an Indian, Inuit, and Metis inherent right of self-government within Canada. However, the accord was not ratified when it was taken to the Canadian public for a nationwide referendum on 28 October 1992.

With the political process having come to a standstill, the courts have been the most active players in recent years in discussing Indigenous peoples' relationship to Canada's constitution. A detailed jurisprudence interpreting Aboriginal and treaty rights was initiated, and the significance of these developments will be addressed in the next chapter. Aside from these court decisions, perhaps the most lasting aspect of the failed 1992 accord was the rise to greater prominence of the Native Women's Association of Canada (NWAC). In the months leading up to the Charlottetown Accord, a parallel process of consultation took place within Indigenous communities concerning constitutional options. NWAC objected to the Canadian government providing funding to only the other four national Indigenous organizations: the Assembly of First Nations, the Native Council of Canada, Metis National Council, and the Inuit Tapirisat of Canada (replacing the Inuit Committee on Native Issues). NWAC claimed it should have been separately represented in constitutional consultations, thereby bringing the distinct views of Indigenous women to the process. NWAC also claimed the other Indigenous organizations were male dominated and thus incapable of presenting their views.[81] While the government, courts, and other Indigenous organizations ultimately rejected this view,[82] over time NWAC has established that its views are a critical part of Indigenous constitutional development in the country. NWAC's voice forcefully sounds along with others seeking to manipulate, reform, or eliminate Canada's constitutional structure relative to Indigenous rights and interests. The implications of these developments will be examined in chapter 5. Yet, despite the gains experienced by Indigenous women's and other organizations through their constitutional advocacy, Canada's constitutional provisions relative to Aboriginal rights are very much still a work in progress, saturated with enormous ambiguity.[83]

G. Conclusion

The drive towards assimilation, where agency is ignored in the process, is a troubling feature of human association. Many people want those around them to be like them.[84] In political terms this means that people are uncomfortable with asymmetry in political organization.[85] This leads to a desire for universally oriented constitutional structures that favour conclusive, once-and-for-all answers, or essentialized, uniform categories for processing disputes. In practice, Indigenous peoples have largely resisted this pull and dissented from this vision, as I have attempted to demonstrate throughout this chapter and book. Fortunately, democracy encourages productive yet interminable practices of deliberation and negotiation because, as the Supreme Court has observed, 'inevitably there will [always] be dissenting voices.'[86] Freedom seems to grow stronger when constitutional structures are contested. Unfortunately, Indigenous peoples suffer tremendously, because Canadian constitutional practice has not more firmly embraced Indigenous visions which arise through such contestation.

Democratic self-determination demands dissent *and* agreement. It requires a continuous process of discussion, compromise, negotiation, and participation.[87] Finality in political affairs is fictional. It is a false form of organization. Countries never achieve certainty and consensual convergence and concurrence among all groups and members of society. As this chapter demonstrates, Canada's constitution is continually open to question. Indigenous peoples are always pressing against its potentially perpetual Eurocentric form. Indigenous peoples' creative relationship to Canada's unwritten constitution shows that the written constitution is not a real limit on how they organize themselves. Indigenous peoples have tried to create their own vision of how they should live, despite Canada's assimilative insistence that they internalize, submit to, and replicate perceived 'correct' constitutional forms.

Unfortunately, the practice of Indigenous dissent has not significantly diminished Canada's colonial domination thus far. As will be discussed in the next two chapters, courts and legislatures continue to confine Indigenous political structures to forms that are not of Indigenous peoples' own choosing. Furthermore, a five-year Royal Commission on Aboriginal Peoples failed to change the deeply undemocratic nature of the Crown's relationship with Indigenous peoples.[88] The 2006 Kelowna Accord, negotiated with First Ministers to improve Indigenous socio-economic conditions also broke down. Formally, there has been political failure at the national level when it comes to Indigenous constitutionalism. As a result, Indigenous advocacy has thus become more prominent before the courts and through negotiated local agreements or regional treaties. More directly, Indigenous peoples have simultaneously continued their focus on also developing unwritten, less formalized means of asserting and protecting themselves and their lands. They continue to be intellectually and physically mobile in their own unique ways.[89]

Chapter Four

(Ab)Originalism and Canada's Constitution

The foregoing chapters have focused on how practice-based philosophical action and reflection can help build productive relationships or resist repressive ones, and thus facilitate freedom. In developing these themes, I have not discounted the immense power of ideas in motivating people to action – they are vitally important, and I will continue to advance this point. Generalizations are critical and should be given appropriate weight when they are built on evidence and sound experience. We must pay attention to observable social phenomena to generate better understandings of tradition. Traditions are composed of practices and generalizations. They create frames of reference that help us evaluate how to act in the real world. When properly used, they can be important tools for enhancing freedom. In so observing, I am outlining a methodology for analysing tradition that favours empirical engagement and critical reflection. I have labelled this approach 'physical philosophy.'

As noted earlier, I have generally been deeply unsympathetic to liberal, conservative, or other categorical accounts of law in my work.[1] Many versions of liberalism largely fail to reflect on unarticulated foundational assumptions that underlie a supposedly neutral and objective treatment of law and tradition. Conservatism can favour tradition in ways that replicate the status quo and troubling hierarchies. I hope my focus on freedom is not read as a liberal trope or as a defence of conservatism.[2] I am attempting to ground my analysis in relationality, through examples of trickster-inspired readings of *dibenindizowin* and *mino-bimaadiziwin*. I am attempting to develop an Anishinaabe account of freedom from a particular school of thought within Anishinaabe tradition. I am not saying freedom exists as an ideal construct; it does not exist outside of our lived experience. Freedom, on my account, is contingent; it is generated through social practices that strive to own and take responsibility for all our relations. Freedom is not an independent state of being in the world. It is not a concept that stands outside of time or beyond human construction. This is why I have been critical of approaches that assume that so-called pure, idealized, abstract, *a priori* ideas inexorably lead to liberty.[3]

Categorical thinking can be oppressive if it prevents people from questioning orthodoxies that seem to flow from such sources. While some ideas are better than others, we cannot always place one concept at the top of the hierarchy and invariably expect that 'proper' thinking about it will solve all our political, social, or legal problems. This is even the case with ideas like Indigeneity, freedom, and the good life. I am not trying to substitute them for alternatives I find less satisfactory, such as Aboriginal, rights, treaty, and self-determination. There is no pure Platonic form or ideology that will lead to a political life that is devoid of conflict, including reflections used in this book. We need to be intellectually mobile and we also need to know when to appropriately 'dig in.' Unfortunately, in my view, there is no set place from which we can make these judgments. We need to be constantly open to alternative approaches that challenge false horizons, even as we embrace life-giving traditions. These alternatives are what I have labelled 'physical philosophy': a practice of reflection and action that flows from the materially grounded conditions in which we find ourselves, but also points us towards more liberating (though ever contingent) generalizations.

Thus, this book has developed a now familiar refrain: freedoms are enhanced by resisting methodologies that confine Indigenous peoples within essentialized, authentic categories and frameworks. This chapter will focus on another restrictive classification as it relates to constitutionalism: originalism. Originalism is a 'first-order' generalization and (as should be clear by this point) I am deeply critical of this kind of preferentially ordinal structuring of thought and action. Thus, this chapter begins by critiquing originalism within Canadian constitutional law and finishes by turning a critical eye on originalism within Indigenous legal traditions. Thus, while the last chapter concentrated on challenges connected with constitutional *formation* (and re-formation), this chapter will critique fundamentalism as it occurs in constitutional *interpretation*.

A. (Ab)Originalism and Living Trees: Analysing Modes of Interpretation

Originalism is judicial philosophy that roots constitutional rights and principles in historic argumentation.[4] The justifications for an originalist approach in constitutional law are varied.[5] Nevertheless, they generally coalesce around an idea that the law has a specific historical meaning to which judges and politicians must defer. Originalism privileges a 'settled' view of a particular moment in the past, concluding that precise constitutional understandings are inherent within some prior declaration or experience. As such, originalism has been called 'a paradigmatic form of legal positivism.'[6] It gives prominence to the so-called subjective intentions and so-called objective public meanings of a constitution's drafters, ratifiers, or receivers.[7] Originalism is often used in an exclusivist, either/or manner, prohibiting and discouraging modes of constitutional interpretation based on other grounds.[8] While attempts have been made to reconcile originalism with other forms of constitutional interpretation,[9] these efforts have met with great scepticism.[10] Originalism generally places dispositive weight on formative historical understandings and meanings, whereas other forms of interpretation draw guidance from history but give it lesser weight.[11] Originalism is perhaps best known for its role in U.S. constitutional law, where many prominent members of the Supreme Court and legal academy strongly support this approach.[12] It has also been the subject of substantial critique in this and other settings.[13]

Originalism does not garner meaningful support in Canadian constitutional circles.[14] It is not a generally accepted mode of interpretation. In fact, the Supreme Court has explicitly rejected this practice.[15] In the *Ontario Hydro v. Ontario (Labor Relations Board)* case, it wrote: 'This Court has never adopted the practice more prevalent in the United States of basing constitutional interpretation on the original intentions of the framers of the Constitution.'[16] Academic commentary has also maintained that 'originalism has never enjoyed any significant support in Canada.'[17]

Despite these observations, the Supreme Court and other constitutional participants might be surprised to discover that originalism is flourishing under our noses, because the practice does not quite go by this name in Canada; in this country, it goes by the name 'Aboriginalism.' The Supreme Court of Canada's abnormal originalism, or (ab)originalism, judges Indigenous peoples by reference to a mythically questionable past. Their cases measure the constitutionality of Indigenous peoples' rights by attributing public meaning to events that are regarded as being foundational to constitutional relations between Aboriginal peoples and the Crown at some dubious historical point.[18] This is mode of reasoning constructs false traditions. It subjects

Indigenous peoples to abstract norms, thereby creating essentialized principles within section 35(1) of the constitution. It is therefore contrary to the approach advocated in this book.

For example, Aboriginal rights can only be claimed if they flow from Aboriginal practices that were 'integral to their distinctive culture' prior to European contact.[19] Similarly, Aboriginal title can only be recognized and affirmed if a group occupied land prior to the assertion of settler sovereignty.[20] Likewise, treaty rights must be proved by reference to the common intention between the parties at the time the agreement was made.[21] In each instance, constitutional rights are contingent upon the Court creating an original public meaning for a past event, when such rights were first recognized,[22] 'crystallized,'[23] or contemplated by the parties (in the case of treaties).[24]

These modes of interpretation fabricate 'fundamentalist' first principles, rather than being open to the organic fluidity that characterizes Canada's constitutional experience, as discussed throughout this work. Thus, holding that rights are solely dependent on past recognition, crystallization or contemplation is a significant break with our country's dominant constitutional traditions. It is also discriminatory, as Indigenous peoples rights are constructed on more restrictive grounds than is the case with other constitutional provisions. This is a problem for Canadian constitutional law more generally, and for Aboriginal peoples in particular. It is contrary to the physical philosophies espoused in this book. Originalism does not foster the freedom to question historically conditioned stereotypical categorizations of Indigeneity based on false (cultural, social, legal, and political) forms. While it is perfectly appropriate to draw upon history in considering Aboriginal and treaty rights, history must not be the source from which all constitutional principles are drawn.

Originalism must therefore be excised from section 35(1) because it creates a troubling double-standard within Canadian constitutional law. Originalism, as applied to Aboriginal peoples, excludes the growth of rights not connected to founding intentions and events, while other rights and freedoms are free to draw their meanings from more contemporary considerations. Originalism's application to Indigenous peoples constructs an unbalanced interpretative landscape. It subjects Aboriginal and treaty rights to greater constitutional constraints than would occur under the Supreme Court of Canada's dominant interpretive approach.

To remedy this problem, the interpretation of Aboriginal and treaty rights in section 35(1) and beyond must draw from the same sources as other constitutional provisions. The metaphor of a living tree is one of these significantly influential sources.[25] The 'living-tree' approach to constitutional interpretation was first adopted by the Judicial Committee of the Privy Council in the so-called Persons Case.[26] The question in the Persons Case was whether a woman could be appointed to the senate under section 24 of the *British North America Act, 1867*, which states that 'the Governor General shall from time to time ... summon qualified Persons to the Senate.'[27] Since women could not hold political office when this section was enacted it was argued that this section's meaning could not be changed to accommodate shifting conceptions of a woman's role in political life. The Supreme Court of Canada accepted this argument and decided that the framer's understanding of the constitution's words could not change with the times.[28] It therefore held that women could not be 'qualified persons,' because they were excluded from political office at the time the constitution was enacted.

On appeal, the Privy Council disagreed with the Supreme Court's conclusion and overturned its decision. It held that women were persons who could be qualified to be summoned to the senate. The Court arrived at this conclusion by adopting a living-tree interpretative approach. Justice Sankey, writing on behalf of the Privy Council, declared:

> The *British North America Act* planted in Canada a living tree capable of growth and expansion within its natural limits. The object of the constitution was to grant a constitution to Canada. 'Like all constitutions it has been subject to development through usage and convention ...' Their Lordships do not conceive it to be the duty of this Board – it is certainly not their desire – to cut down the provisions of the Act by a narrow and technical construction, but rather to give it a large and liberal interpretation so that the Dominion to a great extent, but within certain fixed limits, may be mistress in her own house, as the Provinces to a great extent, but within certain fixed limits, are mistresses in theirs.[29]

In the result, women were held to be persons who could be summoned to the senate because the Privy Council held that the Supreme Court's reliance on the public meaning of 'person' in 1867 was too narrow and technical a construction. A large and liberal interpretation required that any ambiguity about the meaning of the word 'person' should be resolved by including women.[30]

In the intervening years, the Supreme Court further developed the Privy Council's living-tree metaphor and designated it as the dominant approach to constitutional interpretation.[31] Consequently, it has become the dominant mode of analysis in determining the constitution's meaning.[32] As now articulated, this approach allows the Court to look beyond historical understandings of a provision and give it meaning in the light of contemporary circumstances. The Supreme Court has acknowledged this fact in many cases. For example, in *Securities Reference*, the Court wrote, 'This metaphor has endured as the preferred approach in constitutional interpretation, ensuring "that Confederation can be adapted to new social realities."'[33] In *Same-Sex Marriage Reference*, the Supreme Court wrote that '"frozen concepts" reasoning runs contrary to one of the most fundamental principles of Canadian constitutional interpretation: that our Constitution is a living tree which, by way of progressive interpretation, accommodates and addresses the realities of modern life.'[34] This led the Court to conclude that same-sex marriage was not prohibited by the constitution even though 'several centuries ago it would have been understood that marriage should be available only to opposite-sex couples.'[35] In *Attorney General of British Columbia v. Canada Trust Co. et al.*, the Court reaffirmed the living nature of Canada's constitution, declaring that 'there is nothing static or frozen, narrow or technical, about the Constitution of Canada.'[36] This led the Court to deny the idea that the constitution created historically fixed categories. It wrote, 'If the Canadian Constitution is to be regarded as a "living tree" and legislative competence as "essentially dynamic" ... *then the determination of categories existing in 1867 becomes of little, other than historic, concern.*'[37] The Supreme Court reiterated this theme in *Reference Re Provincial Electoral Boundaries (Sask.)* when it wrote: 'The doctrine of the constitution as a living tree mandates that narrow technical approaches are to be eschewed,' which means that 'the past plays a critical but non-exclusive role in determining the content of the rights and freedoms granted by the *Charter*.' As such, the Court wrote, 'the tree is rooted in past and present institutions, but must be capable of growth to meet the future.'[38] These observations led the *Provincial Electoral Boundaries* Court to conclude that the right to vote could not be 'viewed as frozen by particular historical anomalies.' It said: 'What must be sought is the broader philosophy underlying the historical development of the right to vote – a philosophy which is capable of explaining the past and animating the future.'[39] The Supreme Court made a similar point in *Hunter v. Southam*, in relation to Charter interpretation, when it wrote that a 'constitution ... is drafted with an eye to the future' and therefore we must not 'read the provisions of the Constitution like a last will and testament lest it become one.'[40] These and numerous other decisions plainly demonstrate that a future-oriented living-tree approach to constitutional interpretation is dominant in Canada.

There are good reasons for applying the living-tree approach in Canadian law, including in an Aboriginal and treaty rights context. It invites democratic participation because, as we learned in the last chapter, Canadian constitutional law is an open-ended, ongoing activity.[41] Its growth is cultivated on the historical, social, political, cultural, legal, and economic grounds in which the constitution-as-practice is situated.[42] People may be more inclined to get involved in the constitution's development if they realize that it responds to assorted demands on various terrains.[43] It is not just the preserve of legal elites. A living constitution allows people with different interests to prune and graft it in accordance with its broader context. The constitution is not just a dead piece of historical writing; it is a living tradition. It 'facilitates – indeed, makes possible – a democratic political system by creating an orderly framework within which people may make political decisions,' as the Supreme Court wrote in the *Quebec Secession Reference*.[44]

Living-tree analysis is also consistent with Canada's broader constitutional tradition because, as will be remembered, the country does not have a singular founding moment. As noted, Canada's constitution gradually evolved;[45] it adapted to reflect changing social and political values throughout its history.[46] While the passage of the *British North America (BNA) Act* in 1867 marked an important stage in this evolution, section 52(2) of the *Constitution Act, 1982* makes it clear that Canada's constitution includes many other laws.[47] Furthermore, the *Constitution Act, 1867* (as the *BNA Act* is now called) also mandates a dominion with a 'Constitution similar in principle to that of the United Kingdom.'[48] This means Canada's constitution draws on centuries of accreted experience with no one occasion dominating as a founding moment.[49] Even in relation to particularly significant moments, the organic nature of our tradition makes it appropriate to change the constitution's meaning over time.[50] Indeed, we will recall that Canada stands in contrast to the United States experience which ratified a singular constitutional text at a particular historic period.[51] Viewing the constitution as a living tree makes more sense in a country like Canada, which has always been engaged in an 'ongoing process of constitutional development.'[52]

Despite deep problems underlying Aboriginal rights jurisprudence, as noted, the Supreme Court has not employed a living-tree approach when considering the rights of Aboriginal peoples. It has chosen to categorically freeze them in time. It has not continuously woven Indigenous constitutional practices into the ongoing narrative of the nation. In fact, the only time the Supreme Court considered the living-tree approach as applied to Aboriginal peoples, it was rejected on the facts of the case. The case was *R. v. Blais*, where the Court was asked to find that Metis peoples were Indians under sections of the 1930 *Natural Resources Transfer Agreement* (NRTA).[53] The Supreme Court rebuffed this assertion on the grounds that the language, historical context, and views of the NRTA's drafters did not support the Metis' claim.[54] When the Court was asked to apply a living-tree interpretative approach, it did something it rarely does when interpreting the constitution – it refused. In justifying its narrow reading, the Court wrote:

> We decline the appellant's invitation to expand the historical purpose of para. 13 on the basis of the 'living tree' doctrine enunciated by Lord Sankey L.C. with reference to the 1867 *British North America Act*: *Edwards v. Attorney-General for Canada*, [1930] A.C. 124 (P.C.), at p. 136.
>
> This Court has consistently endorsed the living tree principle as a fundamental tenet of constitutional interpretation. Constitutional provisions are intended to provide 'a continuing framework for the legitimate exercise of governmental power': *Hunter v. Southam Inc.*, [1984] 2 S.C.R. 145, *per* Dickson J. (as he then was), at p. 155. But at the same time, this Court is not free to invent new obligations foreign to the original purpose of the provision at issue. The analysis must be anchored in the historical context of the provision … Similarly, Binnie J. emphasized the need for attentiveness to context when he noted in *R. v. Marshall*, [1999] 3 S.C.R. 456, at para. 14, that '"[g]enerous" rules of interpretation should not be confused with a vague sense of after-the-fact largesse.' Again the statement, made with respect to the interpretation of a treaty, applies here.[55]

In the *Blais* case, the Supreme Court held that the application of a living-tree approach would produce a result that was inconsistent with the NRTA's 'original purpose.' An interpretative approach that conveyed 'after-the-fact' generosity was thus rejected. However, 'after-the-fact largesse' is precisely the kind of generosity resulting from the Persons Case, particularly as developed by the Supreme Court over the past seventy-five years. Women were qualified 'persons' to be appointed as senators within the constitution despite a historic context that denied women the right to vote or claim political office.

B. (Ab)Originalism and the Canons of Construction

In refusing to apply a living-tree approach in the *Blais* case, it should be noted that the Court supported its opinion by applying the 'generous rules of interpretation,' which apparently exist to benefit Aboriginal peoples. Ironically, while expansive in one respect, these canons of construction ultimately constrain Aboriginal and treaty rights because they bolster appeals to *a priori* historical truths. Thus, the canons themselves have become a problem for Indigenous peoples because they keep our gaze focused on an essentialized past. This is because the Court says these 'special rules' are only 'dictated by the special difficulties of ascertaining what in fact was agreed to' when law was made.[56] Notice the originalism communicated in the Court's formulation of the canons of construction. Since the distinctive rules for interpreting Aboriginal rights only exist to help the Court weigh evidence of *historic* purposes, these limits pose substantial problems for Aboriginal peoples.[57] They cannot be used to go beyond a law's original meaning, as can occur in living-tree jurisprudence.[58] It is ironic that allegedly generous rules would have the effect of ultimately restricting interpretations of Aboriginal rights, especially when these rules appear very generous on the surface. The canons of construction have themselves become a [problematic] tool to assist the courts in discerning an ephemeral Platonic form.

Generously construing intentions when Aboriginal peoples were viewed as inferior is not the same thing as unequivocally repudiating laws rooted in such discriminatory beliefs. Generosity should lead the Court to acknowledge that many of the government's formative policies were 'wrong, have caused great harm, and have no place in our country,' as the Government of Canada acknowledged in its 2008 Statement of Apology to Aboriginal peoples.[59] Regrettably, the Court has not yet taken this step in relation to the way it developed and applies its canons of construction. Thus, these special rules sustain original intentions and public meanings, though they try to put them in their best light, troubling as these experiences may be. Thus, these special rules apply despite the fact that many of the country's formative laws and policies were designed to undermine Aboriginal peoples' lands,

governance, and lifestyles. This should raise awareness that any interpretive 'generosity' associated with originalism has its limits. It is a
'generosity' that tacitly emphasizes the identification of problematic
past intentions. This is opposed to the forward-looking view of living-
tree jurisprudence, which incorporates Indigenous legal traditions,[60]
adopts a 'progressive interpretation,' 'accommodates and addresses
the realities of modern life,'[61] and rejects historical discrimination.[62]
'Generous' originalism will not produce as many benefits as living-tree
constitutionalism because the framework in which it applies is much
narrower.

i) Treaties, Originalism, and the Canons of Construction

In this section, I have been arguing that distinctive canons of construction applicable to Aboriginal and treaty rights unfortunately do not
function in a manner analogous to the living-tree doctrine because they
have been developed and applied within the context of originalism.
This restricted view is part of a broader history in which the courts
have long deployed distinctive canons of construction when considering Aboriginal issues.[63] To unequivocally show their originalism,
these canons will be examined to demonstrate this point. In the treaty
realm, Chief Justice Marshall of the United States Supreme Court first
articulated special interpretive principles for dealing with Indigenous
peoples in the case of *Worcester v. Georgia*.[64] Justice Marshall developed
this approach to better understand and give effect to the Cherokee
Nation's intentions at the time their treaties were negotiated.[65] Justice
Marshall broadly construed specific provisions within these treaties to
understand the Indian's original intent in entering such agreements.
These rules developed through the years and they were consolidated
in *Jones v. Meehan* in 1899,[66] and have played an important role in the
United States throughout the intervening years.[67] In 1990, the Canadian
Supreme Court approvingly cited these rules in the case of *R. v. Sioui*.[68]
The *Sioui* case also endorsed previous Canadian citations of these canons from the cases of *R. v. White and Bob*[69] and *R. v. Taylor and Williams*[70]
and *R. v. Simon*.[71] The Court has continued to apply these canons to
understand a treaty's original intent in the cases of *R. v. Horseman*,[72] *R.
v. Badger*,[73] *R. v. Sundown*,[74] *R. v. Marshall (I)*,[75] *R. v. Marshall (II)*,[76] *R. v.
Marshall; R. v. Bernard*,[77] and *R. v. Morris*.[78]

A brief review of each of these cases reveals their obvious originalism. The *White and Bob* case focused on original intent to 'bring out

the importance of the historical context, including the interpersonal relations of those involved at the time, in trying to determine whether a document falls into the category of a treaty under section 88 of the *Indian Act*.'[79] The *Taylor and Williams* case canvased original intentions because 'cases on Indian or aboriginal rights can never be determined in a vacuum.' Thus, the Court wrote, 'It is of importance to consider the history and oral traditions of the tribes concerned, and the surrounding circumstances at the time of the treaty, relied on by both parties, in determining the treaty's effect.'[80] The *Simon* case applied the view that 'Indian treaties should be given a fair, large and liberal construction in favour of the Indians' to give effect to the 'intention of creating mutually binding obligations' in a treaty between the Mi'kmaq and the Crown.[81] The *Horseman* case held that the Court 'must be prepared to look at that historical context in order to ensure that they reach a proper understanding of the meaning that particular treaties held for their signatories at the time.'[82] It also wrote that, 'to put it simply, Indian treaties must be given the effect the signatories obviously intended them to have at the time they were entered into even if they do not comply with to-day's formal requirements.'[83] Generous 'back-word' looking rules were also used to assist with originalist interpretations in the *Badger* case, which similarly sought to understand 'the intention of the framers.'[84] *Sundown* likewise held that these rules were in place to 'take into account the First Nation signatory and the circumstances that surrounded the signing of the treaty.'[85] *Marshall I* adopted the point of view of a seventeenth-century 'officious bystander' to ensure that modern treaty interpretations accord with their original public meaning.[86] The same *Marshall* Court also used originalism to 'choose from among the various possible interpretations of the common intention [at the time the treaty was made].'[87] In *Marshall II*, the Court reiterated that the rules of treaty interpretation were aimed at understanding what 'was in the contemplation of either or both parties to the 1760 treaty.'[88] The Court was also firm in indicating that treaties 'cannot be wholly transformed' by engaging in an 'extended interpretation' of their original meaning.[89] This view was reinforced in *R. v. Marshall; R. v. Bernard*, when the Court observed that an Aboriginal group's historic 'activity must be essentially the same' as what was occurring the in past in order to receive recognition.[90] Finally, the *Morris* case highlighted the Court's originalist framework that 'promises in the treaty must be placed in their historical, political, and cultural contexts to clarify the common intentions of the parties and the interests they intended to reconcile at the time.'[91]

From the foregoing review, it is clear that originalism plays a significant role in the Supreme Court's treaty jurisprudence. 'Generous' interpretative rules are consistently referenced but they are deployed to assist the Court's retrospective search for meaning. These rules do not take us out of the past in determining the intentions of the framers or in understanding an agreement's public meaning. They freeze meanings in fundamentalist forms. While treaty interpretation should exhibit a greater deference to history because it respects the parties' agency when assigning them meaning, it should not be used to limit the availability of future rights not discussed during the negotiations.[92] Living-tree jurisprudence does not operate within such limits. It permits 'progressive constitutional development' that, while attentive to a law's roots, also keeps its eye more firmly on the present and future by 'structuring the exercise of power by the organs of the state in times vastly different from those in which it was crafted.'[93]

ii) Aboriginal Rights, Originalism, and the Canons of Construction

Yet originalism is not only practised in section 35(1)'s treaty jurisprudence. It is also present in the Court's treatment of Aboriginal rights and title.[94] For example, in the Supreme Court's first case dealing with Aboriginal rights, it wrote, 'Section 35(1) must be given a generous, large and liberal interpretation and uncertainties, ambiguities or doubts should be resolved in favour of the natives.'[95] A brief review of some of the leading cases in this area similarly shows that the application of these canons are strongly correlated with the Court's originalism, such as in the cases of such as *R. v. Van der Peet*,[96] *Delgamuukw v. British Columbia*,[97] *R. v. Sappier; R. v. Gray*,[98] and *R. v. Marshall; R. v. Bernard*.[99] In fact, most section 35(1) cases do not ground their interpretation of Aboriginal rights in a living-tree approach. As occurs with treaties, the Supreme Court picks an 'original' moment to guide their interpretations and they repeatedly use the canons of construction to elucidate this moment (which the court has itself fabricated). In the *Van der Peet* case, the defining moment for recognizing and affirming Aboriginal rights is the one immediately prior to contact with Europeans[100] because 'the rights recognized and affirmed by s. 35(1) must be temporally rooted in the historical presence – the ancestry – of aboriginal peoples in North America.'[101] Under this formulation, Justice Lamer tautologically concluded that Aboriginal rights possess 'original' rights because Aboriginal peoples are 'Aboriginal.'[102] Thus, on this formulation, Aboriginal rights can be claimed only if they are based on 'practices, customs and traditions that are rooted in the pre-contact societies.'[103] This test forces the parties into an originalist framework with public meaning (recognition and affirmation of Aboriginal rights) being assigned to first contact.

Likewise, in the *Delgamuukw* case, the Supreme Court also placed the proof of Aboriginal title in an 'original' moment. However, *Delgamuukw* moved that moment from contact to sovereignty. In this regard, the *Delgamuukw* court wrote that 'in order to establish a claim to aboriginal title, the aboriginal group asserting the claim must establish that it occupied the lands in question at the time at which the Crown asserted sovereignty over the land subject to the title.'[104] The Court said that 'sovereignty is the appropriate time period' for proving Aboriginal title because 'aboriginal title crystallized at the time sovereignty was asserted.'[105] Thus, as with Aboriginal rights, the proof of Aboriginal title depends on the Court assigning public meaning to a past event; in this case, the original public meaning is said to be the recognition of underlying Aboriginal title when the Crown asserted sovereignty over Aboriginal groups. This demonstrates how the doctrine of discovery lies at the heart of the Court's originalism. Pinning constitutional meaning to the moment that Aboriginal rights were diminished[106] actually makes the Crown the main recipient of the Court's generous interpretive stance. Crown sovereignty and the 'magic moment of European contact,' as Justice McLachlin once critically described it, become the default position for defining the meaning and limits of future Aboriginal rights within an originalist framework.[107]

The Supreme Court reinforced this framework in the cases of *R. v. Sappier; R. v. Gray,* and *R. v. Marshall; R. v. Bernard.* The *Sappier* case held that reference to pre-contact practice is necessary to prove Aboriginal rights in order 'to determine how the claimed right relates to the pre-contact culture or way of life of an aboriginal society.'[108] In fact, the Court stated that the absence of such originalist evidence makes it next to impossible to claim rights under section 35(1). While the Court was careful to declare that 'aboriginal rights are not frozen in their pre-contact form,'[109] any reasonable analysis of the Court's originalism cannot evade the fact that contemporary Aboriginal practices are frozen out of constitutional inclusion if they do not have pre-contact correlations. They become frozen rights despite the Court's reasons to the contrary.[110]

The *Marshall/Bernard* case reaffirmed these principles and observed that the proof of Aboriginal and treaty rights both rested on (ab)originalist premises. Thus, the Court wrote, 'The question is whether the aboriginal practice at the time of assertion of European sovereignty (not, unlike treaties, when a document was signed) translates into a modern legal right.'[111] This sentence reveals the Court's interpretive fusion of Aboriginal *and* treaty rights within an originalist framework. The application of this test led the Court to conclude that Mik'maq people could not claim Aboriginal title because their historic land use did not correspond to common law conceptions of physical occupation when the Crown asserted sovereignty.[112] These tests are problematic because they imagine Aboriginal and treaty rights as containing an authentic preexisting historical essence. These conceptions must be resisted because they do not enhance the living relationships contemplated in Canada's dominant constitutional tradition.

Finally, the *Tsilhqot'in* case dealing with Aboriginal title further confirmed the Court's originalist approach. It did so by working towards the 'goal of faithfully translating pre-sovereignty Aboriginal interests into equivalent modern legal rights.'[113] To accomplish this objective, the Supreme Court followed the '*Delgamuukw* test for Aboriginal title to land [which it wrote] is based on "occupation" prior to assertion of European sovereignty.'[114] One obviously sees the originalism present in this formulation. The Court's gaze is firmly set on interpreting once-upon-a-time Aboriginal interests at the moment of Crown assertion.

Unfortunately, while the outcome was favourable for the Tsilhqot'in people because they secured a declaration of Aboriginal title, the decision replicates one of the worst aspects of originalist fiction. The Supreme Court accepted the proposition that 'at the time of assertion of European sovereignty, the Crown acquired radical or underlying title to all the land in the province.'[115] While the Court qualified this statement by holding that Crown title 'was burdened by the pre-existing legal rights of Aboriginal people who occupied and used the land prior to European arrival,'[116] the Court nevertheless found that the Crown somehow acquired underlying title. In my view, it seems clear that the Court 'granted' the Crown title by an originalist fiction. It is almost certainly the case that, before the Crown asserted sovereignty, the Tsilhqot'in people would have possessed underlying title.

The Court's decision in *Tsilhqot'in* is originalism at its worst. The implications of underlying Crown title are immense: Aboriginal peoples bear the expensive burden of proving title, and Crown sovereignty applies to restrict and discipline Aboriginal self-determination.[117] Indigenous peoples across the world have long critiqued the idea that their lands were legally vacant when Europeans 'discovered' them.[118]

Yet this is how Imperial and Canadian governments treated lands in British Columbia. They applied British law and destabilized Indigenous land holdings and decision-making powers because Indigenous peoples were regarded as inferior political groupings.[119] This is what the Supreme Court of Canada has done in the present day. Colonialism is not only a historic practice, it continues to be acted upon and reinvented in old and new forms to the detriment of Indigenous peoples.

Thus, while the Supreme Court of Canada purported to deny a key aspect of this originalist creed, the fiction persists. Therefore, while the *Tsilhqot'in* case wrote that 'the doctrine of terra nullius (that no one owned the land prior to European assertion of sovereignty) never applied in Canada,'[120] the Crown still magically acquired underlying title by asserting sovereignty.[121] If land was owned by Indigenous peoples prior to the assertion of European sovereignty, it seems impossible to assert that the Crown acquired title in that same land without a version of *terra nullius* being deployed. Yet this is what has been done. Some kind of legal vacuum must be imagined to create the Crown's radical title. Aboriginal title, like other Aboriginal rights and treaty rights explored in this section, continues to be subject to a troubling originalism.

C. (Ab)Originalism as Adverse Discrimination

Attempts have been made to justify the differential treatment of Aboriginal peoples within Canada's constitution based on the Supreme Court's observation that 'Aboriginal rights cannot, however, be defined on the basis of the philosophical precepts of the liberal enlightenment.'[122] This acknowledgment opens important space for recognizing constitutional influences arising from non-European sources.[123] However, as the Court indicates,[124] recognition of Aboriginal difference should not sever Aboriginal rights from broader constitutional traditions that seek to limit the state's reach.[125] Placing limits on government action is clearly an important part of our constitutional regime.[126] This is also the case with Aboriginal rights jurisprudence. As the Supreme Court of Canada observed in the *Sparrow* case, section 35(1) 'gives a measure of control over government conduct and a strong check on legislative power.'[127] Thus, Aboriginal rights should not be placed completely outside of the stream of constitutional history when it comes to considering section 35(1)'s power to constrain governments.[128] While Aboriginal rights do not flow from the 'liberal enlightenment view

[that] rights are held by all people in society because each person is entitled to dignity and respect,'[129] as with other constitutional laws, they configure and constrain government action, and thus are general and universal in an important respect. In this light, in *R. v. Sparrow*, the Supreme Court of Canada explained the place of Aboriginal rights in Canada's constitution as follows: 'Section 35(1) of the *Constitution Act, 1982*, represents the culmination of a long and difficult struggle in both the political forum and the courts for the constitutional recognition of aboriginal rights.'[130] As such, the Court acknowledged that Aboriginal rights placed constraints on the Crown in ways consistent with those which governments encounter in other contexts. As the Court wrote:

> Section 35 calls for a just settlement for aboriginal peoples. It renounces the old rules of the game under which the Crown established courts of law and denied those courts the authority to question sovereign claims made by the Crown.[131]

Thus, though they have a different source, Aboriginal rights parallel constraints on the Crown which flow from the liberal enlightenment, and thus are part of its living tree. Consider how limitations on government action in the broader context are vital to the constitution's development. For instance, in 1215 the issuance of the Magna Carta restricted Crown rights relative to certain classes of individuals (wealthy landowners) which slowly expanded through time.[132] Despite its limitations,[133] Magna Carta's constraint on Crown power is considered to be a pillar of democratic constitutionalism.[134] Similarly, the so-called Glorious Revolution of 1688 circumscribed the Crown's authority and made the monarchy subject to Parliament in many important ways.[135] The English Bill of Rights, which sprang from the revolution, obligated the Crown to raise and spend money with the consent of elected parliamentary officials and not of its own accord.[136] Though these gains were somewhat ambiguous at the time,[137] the 'glorious revolution' has become an important constitutional source and many regard it as a cornerstone of liberty throughout the British Commonwealth.[138] British North Americans enjoyed similar restraints on the exercise of the Crown prerogative when responsible government came to non-Aboriginal Canadians in the 1850s in the Canadian and the Maritime colonies.[139] Furthermore, the American and French Revolutions of the late 1700s, which also purported to restrain Crown sovereignty relative to individual rights, are also regarded as being an essential step in democracy's development. Canada's own Charter of Rights and Freedoms is in this tradition.[140]

While Aboriginal and treaty rights are exercisable only by Aboriginal peoples, and thus do not flow from the liberal enlightenment in this respect, this should not cause us to overlook the truth that they likewise exist to restrain government action. They are living constitutional traditions. While Aboriginal and treaty rights flow from sources beyond the liberal enlightenment, they nevertheless are synchronous with these broader constitutional traditions: they also constrain governments. Thus, we must take care to ensure that while we appropriately define Aboriginal rights as having different contours, we do not place them entirely outside of the constitution's broader framework. Unfortunately, the Court's use of originalism in defining Aboriginal rights is outside the constitution's wider framework.

Not only is originalism out of step with Canada's wider constitutional traditions, it also risks perpetuating the discrimination Aboriginal peoples have encountered throughout the years.[141] This is because originalism links and then limits interpretation to periods when the constitution was formed. Since Canada's legal history is saturated with discrimination towards Aboriginal peoples,[142] constitutional standards should not pass along the troubling attitudes, behaviours, and intentions of past generations of constitutional actors.[143] Again, there is nothing wrong with using history as a constitutional standard if it respects the parties' political agency, and such history is tested, contextualized, and harmonized with our entire constitutional traditions. For example, treaty interpretation generally requires a greater degree of deference to history than do Aboriginal rights cases.[144] Conversely, the weight of history should be diminished in Aboriginal rights cases. This is because Aboriginal agency is severely restricted when the Court interprets rights through the prism of unilateral Crown actions. Quite simply, under current approaches, Aboriginal rights cases do not consider the historic or contemporary perspectives of Aboriginal peoples regarding Crown unilateralism.[145] These cases take no account of Aboriginal views on the negative impacts of perpetually limiting their rights by the moment of Crown contact and sovereign assertion. The fact that the Crown's historic actions are grounded in discriminatory assumptions regarding Aboriginal inferiority should further diminish history's influence. Treaty interpretation, on the other hand, generally purports to respect the parties' agency when assigning them meaning. While treaty history can itself be problematic, due to power imbalances and differences of opinion, its interpretation at least attempts to consider Aboriginal peoples' views at the time they were signed. History should always be calibrated to non-discriminatory standards for judgment when used as a source of constitutional authority; it should rarely be determinative. Contemporary constitutional standards should not replicate views held by past generations of Canadian leaders who regarded Aboriginal peoples as inferior and denied their governance and land rights.[146] Constitutional doctrines that transmit these and other historically discriminatory beliefs should have no place in Canada's highest law.[147]

The Privy Council avoided adopting ancient discriminatory customs as constitutional standards in the Persons Case. It did so after considering the diminished legal and political status of women from before the time of the Roman Empire through the early twentieth century. It noted that 'the exclusion of women from all public offices is a relic of days more barbarous than ours.'[148] It therefore rejected the law's discriminatory history as an aid to constitutional interpretation. The Court wrote that an 'appeal to Roman Law and to early English decisions is not of itself a secure foundation on which to build the interpretation of the *British North America Act* of 1867.' In the face of such bias, the Court held that 'the appeal to history is not conclusive.'[149] In so ruling, the Privy Council discarded arguments rooted in historical discrimination against women. The Supreme Court should take the same approach in relation to Indigenous peoples and similarly reject arguments rooted in historical discrimination.[150] Limiting Indigenous rights to what was integral to their distinctive cultures prior to European contact or Crown sovereignty should 'become a relic of days more barbarous than ours.'

Thus, even though discriminatory customs historically developed among European nations to take land and governance away from Indigenous peoples, such customs should not form part of our law today.[151] As noted, these laws were based on assessments of Indigenous inferiority.[152] They are based on false traditions. For example, past discriminatory assessments of Indigenous peoples' legal and political status are found in North America's leading case on Indigenous peoples' rights, *Johnson v. McIntosh*,[153] where Chief Justice John Marshall wrote the following:

> On the discovery of this immense continent, the great nations of Europe were eager to appropriate to themselves as much of it as they could respectively acquire. Its vast extent offered an ample field to the ambition and enterprise of all; and the character and religion of its inhabitants offered an apology for considering them as a people over whom the superior genius of Europe might claim an ascendancy.[154]

Unilaterally declaring that Indigenous peoples had lesser rights when constitutional principles were formed (due to alleged inferiorities in their character, religion, and genius) does not bode well for originalism. At a minimum, the doctrine of discovery, using the language of the Persons Case, should be considered 'a relic of days more barbarous than ours,' rather than the foundation of the law. It does not respect Aboriginal peoples' agency. Unfortunately, this doctrine explicitly undergirds Aboriginal and treaty rights jurisprudence in Canada to the present day. In 1984, the doctrine of discovery was accepted by the Supreme Court of Canada as one of the country's constitutional foundations. As the Court observed in *Guerin v. R*,

> The principle of discovery ... gave ultimate title in the land in a particular area to the nation which had discovered and claimed it. In that respect at least the Indians' rights in the land were obviously diminished.[155]

The doctrine of discovery has been reaffirmed in subsequent cases.[156] Following the example of the Persons Case, as noted, the Supreme Court should not apply discriminatory customs of this kind in building Canada's highest law. The appeal to history in matters where discrimination has guided past traditions should not be conclusive when deciding the foundation of our current laws.[157] The doctrine of discovery should be challenged as being contrary to Canada's broader constitutional approaches.

For example, when the Crown arrived in North America, Indigenous peoples' territories were not barren and deserted.[158] In fact, despite affirming discovery at most points in the jurisprudence, in at least one instance, the Supreme Court of Canada has written, 'At the time of the assertion of British sovereignty, North America was not treated by the Crown as *res nullius*.'[159] As we have seen in the *Tsilhqot'in* case, the Court misleadingly wrote that the 'doctrine of terra nullius (that no one owned the land prior to European assertion of sovereignty) never applied in Canada.'[160] Canada's Royal Commission on Aboriginal Peoples also recommended the rejection of the doctrine of discovery because it is 'legally, morally and factually wrong.'[161] In light of these observations, and in line with the Privy Council's approach in the Persons Case, we would do well to apply the following caution to the doctrine of discovery: 'Customs are apt to develop into traditions which are stronger than law and remain unchallenged long after the reason for them has disappeared.'[162] It is time to reject archaic and misguided customs and traditions which lie at the heart of Canadian constitutional law, particularly when they rest on Indigenous peoples' legal inferiority. The reasons for considering Aboriginal peoples to be constitutionally inferior have been discredited and should have long since disappeared. It would be incongruous if such approaches continued under the guise of originalism.

Originalism does not tolerate change in relation to 'new social realities' in the same way as a living-tree approach.[163] As I have been arguing, history should not exclusively determine the source and scope of Aboriginal rights. It should not be regarded as both the floor and the ceiling for understanding these rights. While historic legal interpretations should be regarded as helpful by way of analogy when dealing with *sui generis* Aboriginal and treaty rights,[164] they should not be used to deny rights that may spring from other sources.[165] Unfortunately, originalism in an Aboriginal context does not sufficiently draw upon other modes of constitutional interpretation that are also attentive to the constitution's present and future tense.

Aboriginal and treaty rights should be regarded as an important part of Canada's living tree because Indigenous societies have the deepest roots on this continent. While not necessarily a foundational fact of constitutional law, their prior and ongoing connection with the land is a rich soil from which many subsequent relations grow.[166] As with other constitutional provisions, Aboriginal rights should be able to continually expand and mature. They should not be automatically restricted by meanings attached to them at the time of contact, assertion of sovereignty, or negotiation. Such limitations sever Aboriginal relationships from the constitution's broader terrain and threaten the sustainability of Canada's constitutional ecology.

D. Three Alternatives to (Ab)Originalism

The Court does not have to adopt an originalist approach when interpreting Aboriginal and treaty rights. It could adopt approaches more consistent with Canada's physical philosophies. Section 35(1)'s jurisprudence could be brought within the constitutional mainstream by highlighting the contemporary nature of Aboriginal and treaty rights. Lines of authority more consistent with a living-tree approach could be emphasized. This would help to ensure that the 'past plays a critical but non-exclusive role in determining the content of [Aboriginal] rights and freedoms.'[167] In taking this path, the Supreme Court could highlight one of three prominent alternatives to originalism within section 35(1). These three alternatives are arguments relating to (1) the restraint of government authority, (2) the continuity of Aboriginal rights, and (3) the ongoing obligation of the Crown to act honourably in all its dealings with Aboriginal peoples. While history is relevant in each of these approaches, the Court more appropriately focuses on the contemporary aspects of the Crown's relationship to Aboriginal peoples in the following examples.

The first illustration of a living-tree-like approach to Aboriginal rights is found in the leading case in the field, *R. v. Sparrow.* While there are contrary tides in the *Sparrow* case, the Court did not generally link Aboriginal rights to a founding moment. Instead, it held that the meaning of section 35(1) was to be 'derived from general principles of constitutional interpretation.'[168] As a result, the Court explicitly developed these principles within a 'framework for an interpretation ... that ... gives appropriate weight to the constitutional nature of these words.'[169] To accomplish this task, the Court cited the *Manitoba Language Reference* to highlight the fact that section 35(1) was to be interpreted 'in accordance with certain principles held as fundamental and certain prescriptions restrictive of the powers of the legislature and government.'[170] These statements are similar to what was said in the *Edwards* case, which declared, 'The Act should be on all occasions interpreted in a large, liberal and comprehensive spirit, considering the magnitude of the subjects with which it purports to deal in very few words.'[171] Putting canons of construction in this broader, more contemporary approach in the *Sparrow* case, the Court held that Aboriginal rights exist to restrict government action. This demonstrates section 35(1)'s living constitutional status, which operates to both channel and constrain government power. In this light, the Court found that section 35 demanded that the government justify 'any regulation that infringes upon or denies aboriginal rights.'[172] It said that 'such scrutiny is in keeping with the liberal interpretive principle enunciated in *Nowegijick* ... and the concept of holding the Crown to a high standard of honourable dealing with respect to the aboriginal peoples of Canada ...'[173]

These are not the words of originalism; instead, they measure Aboriginal rights by a contemporary purpose which is the 'affirmation of aboriginal rights.'[174] This is more consistent with a living-tree approach. Construing provisions liberally in the *Sparrow* case is aimed at affirming rights, even when they grow significantly beyond their historic roots. Thus, when the *Sparrow* Court appropriately considers the past it does so by simultaneously emphasizing present political realities. As a result, the court used generous rules of interpretation to highlight that 'the relationship between the Government and aboriginals is trust-like, rather than adversarial, and contemporary recognition and affirmation of aboriginal rights must be defined in light of this historic relationship.'[175] To assist in the development of this relationship, the Court wrote that sensitivity to the Aboriginal perspective on the meaning of the right at stake is crucial to its definition.[176] The Court's focus on Aboriginal perspectives and the constitutional nature of the parties' current relationship, as opposed to the search for its origins, is more consistent with the Court's broader living-tree approach to constitutional interpretation.

A second alternative to the Supreme Court's originalism is found in an aspect of the *Mitchell v. M.N.R.* case,[177] which emphasized the continuity of Aboriginal rights.[178] An interpretive approach that emphasizes the contemporary, continuing nature of Aboriginal rights is much closer to a living-tree model. This is because a focus on continuity takes our gaze away from first contact and emphasizes relations between Aboriginal communities and the Crown since their initial encounters.[179] This is also a more generous interpretive approach. It gives the Court some freedom to look beyond the initial roots of an Aboriginal right to see how its branches have 'grown and expanded with their natural limits' (to use the language of the Persons Case). Nevertheless, one has to be careful in considering continuity as an alternative to originalism. Originalism could overtake the continuity thesis if too much weight is given to the common law's initial recognition of Aboriginal peoples' pre-existing law and interests.[180] For example, the *Mitchell* Court is quite clear that Aboriginal rights would only receive protection if they had continuity with 'practices, traditions or customs *that existed prior to contact*.'[181] Nevertheless, if we recognize Aboriginal peoples as complex contemporary communities, the continuity thesis has greater potential to develop along the lines of a living-tree approach because it emphasizes the branches of Aboriginal development, and not their initial recognition. Thus, the *Mitchell* case holds great potential when it observes that

> European settlement did not terminate the interests of aboriginal peoples arising from their historical occupation and use of the land. To the contrary, aboriginal interests and customary laws were presumed to survive the assertion of sovereignty, and were absorbed into the common

law as rights, unless (1) they were incompatible with the Crown's assertion of sovereignty, (2) they were surrendered voluntarily via the treaty process, or (3) the government extinguished them ... Barring one of these exceptions, the practices, customs and traditions that defined the various aboriginal societies as distinctive cultures continued as part of the law of Canada ...[182]

The presumption of the survival and continuous exercise of Aboriginal rights can be a key point in rejecting originalism. While Indigenous peoples would strongly resist the three limitations Chief Justice McLachlin placed on the continuity of their rights,[183] there are sound arguments that Indigenous rights, obligations, and conflict resolution procedures are compatible with the Crown's assertion of sovereignty.[184] Indigenous peoples affirm that many of their most important rights were not surrendered by treaties and were not extinguished by clear and plain government legislation.[185] These facts would be clearer if a living-tree-like reconciliation was the lens through which the courts interpreted the parties' relationships.[186] They hold that their laws coexist with common law and civil law traditions, and that they could be considered a strong part of Canada's constitutional law in the present day.

The continuity thesis is therefore a much stronger ground on which to build the interpretation of Aboriginal rights. It highlights the existing nature of Aboriginal rights, which allows for the growth and development of Indigenous law and tradition as part of the law of Canada.[187] This interpretation is more consistent with the Courts living-tree constitutionalism, which states that 'there is nothing static or frozen, narrow or technical, about the Constitution of Canada.'[188] For this reason, the continuity theory of Aboriginal rights as discussed in the *Mitchell* case is an important alternative to originalism, which is found in most Aboriginal rights cases.

The third alternative to the Supreme Court's originalism comes from the case of *Haida Nation v. British Columbia*.[189] While history is once again relevant in the *Haida* case, the Court's reasons do not inflexibly fasten constitutional rights and obligations to one historic moment. Contemporary obligations are always present under the approach taken in this case. This is apparent when the Court writes that 'in all its dealings with Aboriginal peoples, from the assertion of sovereignty to the resolution of claims and the implementation of treaties, the Crown must act honourably.'[190] The implication of this conclusion is that 'reconciliation is not a final legal remedy in the usual sense ... it is a process.'[191] Under this formulation, rights are not time-bound; the fulfilment of a constitutional obligation does not begin and end by reference to the past. Constitutional obligations must be 'determined, recognized and respected' in the present, especially in circumstances where rights have not yet been reconciled with Crown sovereignty.[192] With the contemporary nature of Aboriginal rights fully on display in the *Haida* case, the Supreme Court developed a test for the contemporary consultation and accommodation of Aboriginal rights. It wrote that constitutional duties arise 'when the Crown has knowledge, real or constructive, of the potential existence of the Aboriginal right or title and contemplates conduct that might adversely affect it.'[193] This test reveals that constitutional rights are related to the Crown's ongoing assessment of the impact of its activities on Aboriginal peoples. The characterization of the Crown's constitutional obligation does not primarily depend on assigning meaning to past events. Since the constitutional relationship does not solely depend on initial assessments of the strength of the Aboriginal group's historically based claims, the Court says this can 'foster a relationship between the parties that makes possible negotiations,' which it regards as 'the preferred process for achieving ultimate reconciliation.'[194] Clearly, the *Haida* case is an alternative to the Court's originalism in the field of Aboriginal rights.

If the Supreme Court further explored the contemporary implications of the three approaches identified in this section, Canada's constitution would be more unified and less discriminatory. Aboriginal peoples' rights would be considered in a broader light, and Canada would be strengthened. This would be more consistent with the Privy Council's living-tree approach, which is that the constitution 'should be on all occasions interpreted in a large, liberal and comprehensive spirit, considering the magnitude of the subjects with which it purports to deal in very few words.'[195]

E. Indigenous Legal Traditions, Living Trees, and Originalism

The Supreme Court and other actors should also consider the nature of Indigenous approaches to constitutional law in adopting living-tree alternatives.[196] This is particularly relevant given the court's declaration that Aboriginal and treaty rights must incorporate the perspective of Aboriginal peoples on the meaning of the right at stake. Living-tree constitutionalism resembles one significant source of Indigenous law grounded in analogies to the natural world.[197] This environmentally based approach to legal interpretation develops rules for regulation and conflict resolution from a study of the world's behaviour.[198] Indigenous peoples who practise this form of law draw analogies from the behaviours of ecosystems, watersheds, rivers, mountains, valleys, meadows, lakes, and shorelines to guide legal actions.[199] It furthers discussions of *akinoomaagewin* and *gikinawaabiwin* discussed elsewhere in this work.

Given this jurisprudential focus, it is no surprise that Indigenous peoples would be attracted to constitutional metaphors based on living things. In fact, one of the strongest metaphors Indigenous peoples use in describing their relations with the Crown is 'as long as the sun shines, the grass grows, and the river flows.'[200] This metaphor, while possessing much deeper meaning,[201] is usually associated with treaties and emphasizes the perpetual nature of agreements to live together in peace, friendship, and respect.[202] An organic, animate, growth-oriented approach to law is also found in the Haudenosaunee constitution, also called *Kaianerekowa* or Great Law of Peace.[203] This constitution binds the Six Iroquois Confederacy together under principles of peace, power, and righteousness.[204] The grand symbol of the *Kaianerekowa* is a great white pine tree with four white roots of peace extending in four cardinal directions.[205] The tree has long needles that grow as the confederacy prospers.[206] The nations and its people are allegorically seated in concentric circles around the tree, also illustrating growth. A great eagle sits atop the tree to watch for the peace and safety of the confederacy. The Great Law is a living tree.[207] Aboriginal peoples of the Pacific north-west also have constitutions related to trees. The Haida, Nisga'a, Gitskan, Wetsuwet'en, Tsimshian, Tahltan, Tlingit, Salish, Heiltsuk, Nuu-Chah-Nulth, and Kwakwaka'wakw all carve poles that communicate their relationships to territory, ancestors, and the natural world around them.[208] Unlike living trees, which metaphorically grow forever, totem poles are designed to eventually fall down and decay as they return to the earth. This reinforces the idea that constitutional laws, though carved from deep histories, are to be reinscribed every few generations to ensure they remain relevant through time.[209] Thus, this metaphor produces effects which are similar with the living-tree doctrine. Other Indigenous peoples in Canada also root their highest laws in analogies related to living beings.[210]

None of the above references suggest that the living-tree doctrine as proclaimed by the Privy Council has its origins in Indigenous peoples' law.[211] Each legal tradition independently embraced living constitutionalism on its own terms. The same could be said about originalism. Unfortunately, Indigenous peoples can be originalists too, in relation to their own laws, and in relation to Canada's broader constitutional traditions. In fact, originalist interpretative practices are present in most traditions. For example, originalism has similarities to biblical and Koranic literalism,[212] and living constitutionalism has parallels with biblical hermeneutics and religious syncretism.[213] These examples often have relevance for constitutional interpretation.[214] Aboriginal peoples' legal perspectives and practices are as varied as other legal traditions in the world, even within particular communities. The identification, celebration, and application of this fact is an important aspect of freedom. Thus, when considering Indigenous peoples' own constitutional traditions it is important to recognize the diversity of approaches within these societies, including originalism.

For example, Indigenous laws privileging originalism in a Cree community are on display in the *Sawridge* decision.[215] This case considered a First Nation's constitutional obligations to accept women as members when they had been disenfranchised and re-enfranchised by the *Indian Act*.[216] Only First Nations women's legal status was at issue because Indian men did not lose Indian status under the act.[217] The Sawridge Band argued they had no obligation to accept First Nations women as citizens if they married non-Indian men. Testimony was given to make the point that it was Cree custom, 'since aboriginal times' until the present day, for women to take their husband's membership status, or lack thereof.[218] Thus, if women 'married out' and lost their Indian status the Band argued this was consistent with original Cree principles. This law, regarded as fundamental to the way the community constituted itself, was that 'woman follows man.' Agnes Smallboy, an Elder in the trial, testified as follows:

Q. MR. HEALEY: How did you come to be a member of the Ermineskin Band?
A. When I was young, I married into the reserve to a man who was named Pete Morin.
Q. What Indian band did you belong to before you married Pete Morin?
A. I was a member of the Sampson Band. In our language, we call it 'the land of the willows.'
Q. MR. HEALEY: Why did you leave your band and join the Ermineskin Band when you married Pete Morin?
A. I did not know the man before I married him. In our system, a woman ... or the parents made arrangements for the marriage of their daughters.

> And when my parents told me that I was to go and live with this man,
> I obeyed my parents …
> Q. Does the woman always go with the man as you did in the Ermineskin
> Band?
> A. Yes, that was the way it was or has been.
> Q. Is that the Indian way today?
> A. It is still the way it is today …[219]

The argument to sustain the practice of 'woman follows man,' as described in this case, can be labelled as originalist. It seeks to maintain the imputed first intentions of Cree ancestors and the Creator,[220] and it vests this practice with public values considered foundational to Cree political organization, at least by those making these arguments.[221] While we should not forget that there are diverse viewpoints within Indigenous law,[222] some of which may vigorously oppose discrimination,[223] other Indigenous communities have also made arguments that originalism requires discriminatory results.[224] As argued throughout this book, (ab)originalism or other forms questionable *'a priori'* reasoning should not be used to sustain discrimination. Discriminatory originalism is problematic, regardless of its nature and source. Whether used by distinguished members of the Supreme Court of Canada, or by respected Elders within Indigenous communities, adverse discrimination should be rejected as contrary to other constitutional approaches within each tradition.[225]

There are also reasons to reject originalism even in cases where discrimination is not at issue. As suggested earlier, it is an unbalanced approach because it does not sufficiently contextualize the present and future tenses of constitutional law. Furthermore, originalism does not offer any greater determinacy than alternative interpretive approaches. Though not a Canadian example, the following illustration raises these issues. It involves the Ottawa First Nation, a people also Indigenous to Canada. The Ottawa are Anishinaabe people who are divided by the border between Canada and the United States. As such, they are found on Manitoulin Island in Ontario and in communities around northern Lake Huron and Michigan. The Little River Band of Ottawa Indians, a subgroup of the larger Nation, resides on the eastern shores of Lake Michigan around Manistee, Michigan. They are organized under a constitution, which consists of a nine-member elected council, an elected Ogimaa (Chief), and a Tribal Court.[226] The Ottawa Tribal Court constantly grapples with different modes of constitutional interpretation in making its decisions, as occurs in the other 330 tribal courts in the United States.[227] This struggle is found in the case of *Champagne v. Little River Band of Indians,* decided before the Little River Band of Indians Court of Appeal.[228]

The issue in the *Champagne* case was whether the Tribal Council's statutory incorporation of certain provisions of Michigan State criminal law was contrary to the Little River Ottawa Band Constitution. A former Tribal Court judge, who had been convicted of the crime of attempted fraud under an Ottawa Band statute, argued that the adoption of Michigan law, which criminalized the crime of attempted fraud, was an unconstitutional 'abrogation of tribal sovereignty and a violation of tribal customs and traditions.'[229] He contended that the Michigan-inspired statute was inconsistent with Anishinaabe traditions and tribal law and was therefore unconstitutional. The Little Ottawa Band Court of Appeal rejected these arguments. While noting it was laudable to seek the development of a 'sophisticated legal system based on Anglo-American legal models [which] preserves the cultural distinctiveness of Ottawa culture through the development of tribal law and the preservation of tribal customs and traditions,' the Court of Appeal nevertheless found that the judge 'attempted to procure money that was not owed to him.'[230] It held that 'Justice Champagne does not and cannot identify an Ottawa custom or tradition that would excuse him for his actions.'[231] The accused judge believed that the Band's statute was unconstitutional because the crime of 'attempt' was not found in their pre-contact laws, whereas the Court of Appeal held that the crime of 'attempt' was consistent with the First Nation's broader powers under the constitution unless there was evidence to the contrary. If the Court had concluded its opinion at this point, the case would have nicely illustrated to two different views of originalism within Anishinaabe constitutionalism. This would have demonstrated originalism's indeterminacy given the contradictory nature of the parties understanding of, and approach to, history.[232] However, the Little River Band Court of Appeal went one step further and held that appeals to originalism would not completely solve the issue. The Court thus wrote, 'It would be a sad day for this community to acknowledge that an action reflecting an intention of an individual to fraudulently procure money from the Band is excused because the word "attempt" does not exist in Anishinaabemowin, as Justice Champagne alleged at oral argument.'[233] Thus, the court concluded that appeals to history alone would not answer the question in this case. For these and other reasons, the court indicated that concerns aside from originalism would guide their reasons.

F. Conclusion

Originalism within an Indigenous legal context can be as problematic as it is within Canada's broader framework. Ultimately, one must make a distinction between historical originalism and living constitutional traditions as sources of authority in our laws. Nothing in this chapter should be construed as rejecting appropriate historical context when interpreting Aboriginal and treaty rights. Aboriginal peoples' laws and relations are important roots of Canada's living tree, and can help nurture its subsequent healthy development. History is an important resource in understanding and developing constitutional relationships; without it we would cease to be ruled by law and be cut off from guidance available from the past. Thus, non-discriminatory historical understandings should influence the interpretation of Aboriginal and treaty rights in the Canadian constitution.

Thus, while this chapter rejects originalism, it does not reject history. My arguments are a matter of emphasis. My objection to originalism is related to how it excludes other modes of interpretation as applied to Indigenous peoples. It has been deployed in narrow and inflexible ways. It has been used to hold that constitutional rights do not exist without historic analogues. When used in this fashion, originalism trumps other modes of constitutional interpretation. Constitutional claims are limited by what was 'integral to a distinctive culture' prior to European contact or the 'assertion' of Crown sovereignty.[234] If an Indigenous group has signed a treaty with the Crown, constitutional rights cannot be claimed unless they are connected to the common intention between the parties at the time an agreement was made.[235] All this is to say that the Court has not just looked to history as a source of authority in Aboriginal cases; it has used history to exclude rights that could be recognized through other interpretative forms. It has deployed a Platonic form that obstructs more contextual modes of interpretation. This approach restricts Indigenous peoples' intellectual and physical mobility and is thus inconsistent with Canada's broader living-tree tradition.

While this this chapter argues for a clear rejection of originalism and other essentialized modes of reasoning, lest I be misunderstood, I want to conclude by re-emphasizing the importance of history as a very important resource for legal reasoning.[236] I will do so by returning

to the *Champagne v. Little River Band of Indians* case, decided before the
Little River Band of Indians Court of Appeal,[237] discussed above. While
this court rejected originalism, it did not turn its back on history. In fact,
the court draws upon historical sources in framing its opinion. It did so
by citing stories related to Nanaboozhoo, the Anishinaabe trickster.[238]
These stories function as law in Anishinaabe communities. Thus, the
court wrote,

> There are many trickster tales told by the Anishinaabe involving the
> godlike character Nanabozho. One story relevant to the present matter is
> a story that is sometimes referred to as 'The Duck Dinner.' *See, e.g.*, John
> Borrows, *Recovering Canada: The Resurgence of Indigenous Law* 47–49 (2002);
> Charles Kawbawgam, *Nanabozho in a Time of Famine*, in Ojibwa Narratives
> Of Charles and Charlotte Kawbawgam and Jacques LePique, 1893–1895,
> at 33 (Arthur P. Bourgeios, ed. 1994); Beatrice Blackwood, *Tales of the
> Chippewa Indians*, 40 Folklore 315, 337–38 (1929). There are many, many
> versions of this story, but in most versions, Nanabozho is hungry, as usual.
> After a series of failures in convincing (tricking) the woodpecker and
> muskrat spirits into being meals, Nanabozho convinces (tricks) several
> ducks and kills them by decapitating them. He eats his fill, saves the rest
> for later, and takes a nap. He orders his buttocks to wake him if anyone
> comes along threatening to steal the rest of his duck dinner. During the
> night, men approach. Nanabozho's buttocks warn him twice: 'Wake up,
> Nanabozho. Men are coming' … Nanabozho ignores his buttocks and
> continues to sleep. When he awakens to find the remainder of his food
> stolen, he is angry. But he does not blame himself. Instead, he builds up
> his fire and burns his buttocks as punishment for their failure to warn him.
> To some extent, the trick has come back to haunt Nanabozho – and in the
> end, with his short-sightedness, he burns his own body.

The relevance of this timeless story to the present matter is apparent.
The trial court, per Judge Brenda Jones Quick, tried and convicted the
defendant and appellant, Hon. Ryan L. Champagne, a tribal member, an
appellate justice, and a member of this Court, of the crime of attempted
fraud. Justice Champagne's primary job during the relevant period in
this case was with the Little River Band of Ottawa Indians. Part of his job
responsibilities included leaving the tribal place of business in his personal
vehicle to visit clients. While on one of these trips, Justice Champagne took
a personal detour and was involved in an accident. The Band and later
the trial judge concluded that his claim for reimbursement from the Band
was fraudulent. Judge Quick found that Justice Champagne 'attempted to

obtain money by seeking reimbursement from the Tribe for the loss of his vehicle by intentionally making a false assertion that he was on his way to a client's home at the time of the accident.' Justice Champagne was neither heading toward the tribal offices nor toward a client's home.

Like Nanabozho, Justice Champagne perpetrated a trick upon the Little River Ottawa community – a trick that has come back to haunt him. It would seem to be a small thing involving a relatively small sum of money, but because the Little River Ottawa people have designated this particular 'trick' a criminal act, Justice Champagne has burned himself ...[239]

After this introduction, the Little River Band Court of Appeal's reasons for judgment go to great lengths to substantiate this conclusion. They demonstrate a positive, non-discriminatory use of history in showing how the crime of attempt is not contrary to Anishinaabe constitutionalism. They simultaneously use history and move beyond it by deploying traditional law in the present tense. Nanaboozhoo's duck dinner case is a significant source of authority for judging the wrongfulness of the judge's attempted fraud.[240] Ironically, the Supreme Court of Canada has not used history in this fashion, to this point because its originalism and 'generous' canons of construction have not allowed Indigenous law to grow in this way.[241] Originalism has thus stunted the growth of Canada's Indigenous Constitution.[242] Fortunately, the citation of Indigenous law, as a past, present, and future-oriented part of Canada's constitution, could help nourish and sustain a living-tree constitutionalism.

In a living-tree mode, Canada's constitutional law can be likened to a verb. It sustains, negates, inflects, modifies, or transforms relationships or states of being. Like a verb, Canada's constitution located us in time – with a past, present, and future tense. It explains what brought us together, and what should happen now and later on to sustain our togetherness and measured separateness. Thus, like a verb, Canada's constitution regulates relationships through time; it link objects (persons, places, and things) to a reciprocal series of obligations in the real world. The word 'constitution' comes from the Latin verb *constituere*, and is made up of two roots: *con*, which means 'together,' and *statuere*, which means 'to establish.' Thus, Canada's constitution could be regarded as an activity of establishing something together. In this light, Canada's constitution acts on persons, places, and things, just like verbs.

The Anishinaabe people of the Great Lakes also characterize constitutional law as a verb. The Anishinaabe use the word *chi-inaakonige* to describe constitutional law. *Chi* means 'great' or 'large' and *inaakonige* means to act on an object through making a judgment, deciding things a certain way, or agreeing on something.[243] Thus, constitutional law is the great way of acting through judgment, guided decision-making and agreement. Since the Supreme Court of Canada also characterizes Canada's constitution as a verb – as an action and a shifting state of being – these activities can be drawn together. A prime activity associated with Canada's constitution is that it 'embraces the entire global system of rules and principles which govern the exercise of constitutional authority.'[244] Embracing, governing, and exercising authority are necessary constitutional actions. Understanding the constitution's fluid state of being is also necessary in regulating governmental practices. As this chapter has emphasized, in pursuing these activities, the Court has said the constitution is organic[245] and animate[246] – a living tree.[247]

Understanding constitutional law as an ongoing activity that nourishes a living entity improves our judgments relating to its genesis, preservation, and growth. Recognizing that a constitution has a temporal existence helps us balance the past, present, and future when regulating our relationships. This chapter contends that Canada's constitution is weakened if too much emphasis is placed on either our origins, or our current obsessions, or our future predictions regarding what they require. It is unhealthy to place too much stress on any one part of the roots, trunk, or branches of any living tree. Each part needs to bear the weight of growth to be strong and durable. Canada's constitution is at its strongest when interpretation is equally attentive to all forms of authority, including arguments that appeal to its history, text, and structure. These modes of argument must be similarly combined with doctrinal authority from previously decided cases, prudential arguments about the costs and benefits of a course of action, and ethical ideas that appeal to the ways Canadians think about their social commitments.[248]

Constitutional interpretation should be non-discriminatory. Unfortunately, Canada's constitution contains a particularly deep and troubling interpretive inconsistency. This flaw exists in relation to Aboriginal and treaty rights within section 35(1) of the *Constitution Act, 1982*. Most constitutional rights are interpreted in accordance with a living-tree approach. Conversely, Aboriginal peoples' rights are largely viewed through an originalist lens. This chapter explains the differences in these approaches, highlights their adverse effects for Aboriginal peoples, and identifies non-discriminatory alternatives consistent with Canada's broader constitutional framework.

If living-tree principles were applied to Aboriginal peoples, we could one day say about Canada's Aboriginal and treaty rights jurisprudence, 'This metaphor has endured as the preferred approach in constitutional interpretation, ensuring "that Confederation can be adapted to new social realities."'[249] We would have an Aboriginal jurisprudence that holds that '"frozen concepts" reasoning runs contrary to one of the most fundamental principles of Canadian constitutional interpretation: that our Constitution is a living tree which, by way of progressive interpretation, accommodates and addresses the realities of modern life.'[250] We would also apply the view that 'there is nothing static or frozen, narrow or technical, about the Constitution of Canada.'[251] Thus, we would say, about Aboriginal and treaty rights, 'If the Canadian Constitution is to be regarded as a "living tree" and legislative competence as "essentially dynamic" ... *then the determination of categories existing in 1867 becomes of little, other than historic, concern.*'[252] This would allow us to reinforce an approach that holds: 'the past plays a critical but non-exclusive role in determining the content of the rights and freedoms' within the constitution.[253] We could then conclude in relation to Aboriginal and treaty rights: 'The tree is rooted in past and present institutions, but must be capable of growth to meet the future.'[254] If originalism was rejected in favour of living-tree constitutionalism in ways consistent with the spirit of this chapter, Aboriginal and treaty rights would be more strongly rooted in 'a philosophy which is capable of explaining the past and animating the future.'[255] Interpreting Aboriginal and treaty rights as living traditions would mark an important maturation point in the ongoing evolution of Canada's organic constitution.[256] This would stand in significance alongside the achievement of responsible government, the extension of women's political rights in the Persons Case, and the extension of civil rights before the Charter came into force.[257] We 'must not read the provisions of the Constitution like a last will and testament lest it become one.'[258] This goes for Aboriginal and treaty rights, as much as it does for other parts of Canada's constitution.

Chapter Five

Legislation and Indigenous Self-Determination in Canada and the United States

An article of faith in many Indigenous political circles is that you cannot trust governments.[1] As this book has shown, there are many good reasons for holding this position. Parliaments, legislatures, and courts have most often acted in ways that are severely detrimental to the health and vitality of Indigenous peoples. On-the-ground facts demonstrate that distrust is well placed.[2] This view should not be jettisoned any time soon. In fact, if anything, Indigenous peoples should continue to prioritize working in most every way possible, beyond governments and legal structures, to bolster their communities. The path to greater freedom and good living does not often run anywhere close to legislative or judicial chambers. 'Avoid them like the plague' would seem to be a sound strategy for any Indigenous group contemplating engaging the Canadian state.

Official state structures seem to carry viruses that are most harmful to Indigenous peoples. Colonialism, imperialism, and inequalities bred through cronyism and unbounded capitalism are deeply entangled with formal state structures.[3] In fact, they appear to be mutually self-reinforcing. These forces have infected Indigenous communities to such an extent that a cure drawn from these structures seems remote.[4] Nevertheless, in the medical field, antidotes are often derived from virulent hosts, which are re-engineered and introduced in small amounts through inoculation. In the technological field, when dealing with corruptible transfers of electronic information, viruses are screened out using other electronic means. In these systems, remedies are often drawn from the problem at hand. While I would resolutely resist the extraction of universal lessons from these analogies, for many of the reasons found in this book and more, they do suggest a potential line of inquiry. While political systems are vastly dissimilar from medical and technological systems, I have argued elsewhere that humans are deeply interdependent on one other for their health and vitality.[5] Anishinaabe and other legal traditions reinforce this message. 'We are all related' is a widespread teaching within Indigenous communities and this tradition will be further developed in the conclusion. At this point in the book, this observation is made to further problematize the assumption that state institutions are irredeemable and do not have any positive role as instruments of change in Canada.

Unless one believes in a Creator who regularly and directly influences formal political affairs in an active way for Indigenous peoples, there seems to be no singular structure or ideology outside of ourselves to whom Indigenous peoples can turn to rescue them from political harm. Even if the Creator is actively involved in Indigenous politics, His or Her designs are subject to many different interpretations that require some level of human discernment. For example, many have wondered why Indigenous communities are subject to colonial oppression if the Creator was a guiding force in their lives. Some have seen divine approval in their decline while others have seen God's hand in their perseverance and resurgence.[6] Whichever interpretation is given, the fact remains that Indigenous communities are subordinated in Canada. The Creator's designs for their decline or deliverance are not unambiguously clear. Since divine rescue seems in short supply on a national basis, it appears as if Indigenous peoples are left to themselves in exercising agency in dealing with others. Thus, while it looks as though Indigenous peoples would be well advised to do almost anything besides turning to the state in securing a great measure of freedom, the fact also exists that Canadian political structures greatly oppress real lives. If the state is ignored, in the hope that it will just wither away, its power may be diminished in some quarters, but in other instances it will continue to steal and despoil Indigenous lands, resources, families, and relationships – without hesitation.

Similarly, if the only response to state power is 'essentialized' resistance at every turn, this may overturn current configurations of powers (though not necessarily so), but such reordering does not inevitably lead to healthier futures. Most revolutions have failed to produce the hoped-for change idealized in pre-revolutionary resistance.[7] Those whom we oppose do not go away if an axis of power shifts. New relationships will be needed that require institutional and structural components. Politics is always with us, and it is usually messy and requires some degree of compromise. While formal political life should be appropriately contested by individuals and groups, ongoing interdependencies suggest a level of engagement with others on less-than-perfect grounds.[8] Sometimes (though not always), engagement is even required in situations that are oppressive, hostile, and adverse to longer-term interests. This requires intellectual and philosophical mobility even in the face of great harm.

Thus, this chapter questions a 'fundamental' article of faith within many Indigenous political circles, concerning whether governments can be productively engaged in pursuing freedom. In interrogating this seemingly essential doctrine, I aim to raise possibilities for a formal, though admittedly limited, state role. I do so in the spirit of facilitating the teachings I received from Basil Johnston and others concerning *dibenindizowin* and *mino-bamaadiziwin*. In pursuing this inquiry, I must again stress that an extremely wide margin of resistance, opposition, and disregard for the state seems appropriate in relating to Canada, given real-life experience. Opposition to colonialism can be a slippery practice. Pathways that seem liberating to Indigenous peoples can be reinvented by the state to reproduce the very oppression they are designed to overthrow.[9] Nothing in this or other chapters should diminish the force of this insight.[10]

At the same time, this book has taken the position that, in politics, 'it depends.' We must always be attentive to context. Whether Indigenous peoples can gain a measure of support from Canada for living free and good lives 'depends' on a complex constellation of real-world factors. Thus, we should not automatically rule out the possibility that aspects of state engagement could aid Indigenous peoples in particular cases, just as we tried not to rule out such possibilities when discussing mobility, direct action, constitutional formation, and constitutional interpretation. The world is full of contingencies. Appeals to first principles and authenticating *a priori* arguments do not sufficiently engage or explain Indigenous political, social, cultural, legal, and economic agency in dealing with the challenges that have and must be encountered. There are reasons to act, even though our interventions will never produce uncontestable certainties, determinacy, and timeless truth.[11]

Thus, I argue that freedom can be secured (though not necessarily) by our being open to a variety of possible courses of action. Freedom can sometimes be found in bobbing and weaving between formal and informal structures and strategically deploying or withholding action in calibrated ways. This book has examined in some detail where such spaces might be found within and beyond formal Canadian political life. My goal is to strengthen freedom so that Indigenous peoples can own and be responsible for themselves and their relationships in more productive ways. Perhaps by not foreclosing or automatically shutting down avenues of action, opportunities can be identified for pursuing these objectives.[12] By being cautious as we proceed, but also careful to not base such wariness on absolute prohibitions, we might find better paths towards a good life.

In this light, this chapter suggests that there may be circumstances where Parliament could take legislative steps to facilitate responsible ownership by Indigenous peoples of their own actions and relationships.[13] Self-determination is implied in such control. Article 3 of the United Nations Declaration on the Rights of Indigenous Peoples expresses a parallel goal in this way: 'Indigenous peoples have the right to self-determination. By virtue of that right they freely determine their political status and freely pursue their economic, social and cultural development.'[14]

As I have argued, democratic self-determination is an important political aspiration for Indigenous people.[15] Indigenous peoples spent decades fighting for its recognition in international forums. It is also something that could be pursued within the bounds of a nation state. For example, Article 5 of the Declaration makes the point that Indigenous peoples 'have the right to autonomy or self-government in exercising their right to self-determination.'[16] Article 5 of the same document states:

Indigenous peoples have the right to maintain and strengthen their distinct political, legal, economic, social and cultural institutions, while retaining their right to participate fully, if they so choose, in the political, economic, social and cultural life of the State.[17]

While self-determination and self-governance are justifiably critiqued for blocking Indigenous aspirations (and can be misused as abstract forms),[18] perfection can also become the enemy of the good if such critiques obstruct the exercise of Indigenous agency in real-world spheres.

Thus, to explore the admittedly limited but nevertheless important role of self-determination in advancing Indigenous agency, this chapter will examine the potential role of legislation in strengthening this power.[19] The context for this exploration is a comparison of federal legislation concerning Indigenous peoples in Canada and the United

States.[20] While very significant problems exist between Indigenous peoples and governments in the United States, this chapter demonstrates that Canada is much less supportive of Indigenous people in the legislative field.[21] Surprisingly, this is true despite the fact that Aboriginal and treaty rights are constitutionally recognized and affirmed in section 35(1) of Canada's *Constitution Act, 1982*, which proclaims, 'The existing aboriginal and treaty rights of the aboriginal peoples of Canada are hereby recognized and affirmed.'[22] The recognition and affirmation of Native American rights does not exist in the United States' constitution.[23] Nevertheless, the constitutions of Canada and the United States are similar in one important respect: both allocate authority for legislation in relation to Indians to the federal government.[24] This power could be used more effectively in both countries but, in spite of the seeming advantage of Canadian constitutional recognition, Native American people in the United States enjoy greater practical legal recognition in relation to governance, culture, and environmental conservation and development.[25]

What explains the relative (though undeniably limited) success of legislative initiatives in the United States? The answer is, quite simply, that Indigenous peoples in the United States have participated in the creation of receptive policy frameworks with congressional allies which builds law to implement self-determination.[26] Indigenous peoples and parliamentarians in Canada have not been successful in this regard.[27] In fact, Canada's record in this field has been abysmal. The U.S. federal government is more willing to use its power to pre-empt state law's application to Indian reservations, thus carving out a space for Indigenous governance.[28] Canadian governments have been extraordinarily reluctant to displace provincial power in favour of Indigenous governmental authority.[29] Canadian constitutionalism seems to revolve around strengthening provincial autonomy to the detriment of Indigenous and other federal responsibilities.

As a result, Indigenous self-determination does not animate Canadian legislation in any significant way.[30] By way of contrast, in the United States it has been observed that 'tribal sovereignty forms the bedrock of the modern courts decisions and statutes.'[31] With this starting point, tribes in the United States are more willing to creatively work with the federal government because it has generally proceeded 'on the principal that Indian tribes are, in the final analysis, the primary or basic governmental unit of Indian policy.'[32] While it is important to emphasize that there are exceedingly difficult policy challenges for

Indigenous peoples in the United States, too,[33] particularly related to a hostile Supreme Court,[34] the modern statutory acceptance of self-determination has made a notable difference for tribes in the United States.[35] It has meant that 'no Indian legislation has been passed over Indian opposition since ... 1968.'[36]

Legislation furthering Indigenous self-determination in the United States has generally focused on three areas: (1) Indigenous control over federal government services for Indigenous people, (2) the protection of Indigenous cultures and communities, and (3) Indigenous control in relation to natural resources and economic development.[37] Each of these three areas will be briefly examined to identify conspicuous deficits in Canadian legislative action. This short review reveals that the broad scope of U.S. law dealing with Indigenous issues dramatically contrasts with the dearth of statutory activity in Canada.[38]

A. Indigenous Control of Federal Services

Like Canada, the United States has experienced a deeply troubling colonial history in its relation with Indigenous peoples.[39] Change has been slow to develop. Many severe problems have plagued tribes in the United States such as war, removal, congressional treaty abrogation, allotment, and termination. These policies lead to political disabilities that rival and perhaps even surpass any challenge suffered by Indigenous peoples in Canada. Nevertheless, over forty years ago, President Nixon began a new chapter in the relationship between Native American tribes and the federal legislative and executive branches of government.[40] He officially renounced past practices that attempted to 'terminate' tribes and undermine Indigenous self-determination.[41] At the same time, he formally announced a national policy goal of 'strengthening the Indian's sense of autonomy without threatening his sense of community.'[42] This was a significant breakthrough. The congress soon followed President Nixon's lead.[43] In 1975, it passed the *Indian Self-Determination and Educational Assistance Act* to facilitate Indian control of federal services.[44] Among the congressional findings, which are embedded in the act and outline its purpose, is the recognition that 'the Indian people will never surrender their desire to control their relationships both among themselves and with non-Indian governments, organizations and persons.'[45] The act enhances Indian control by allowing tribes to enter into contracts and receive grants to administer federally funded services. This placed Indigenous governments at the centre to governmental decision-making concerning many of the most pressing administrative issues within their communities. In 1994, this act was supplemented by the *Tribal Self-Governance Act*, which allows for the transfer of federal programs to tribes and facilitates congressional support of projects designed to enhance self-determination.[46]

These acts compel the federal government to fund tribal programs that are planned and administered by Indian Nations themselves. Legislation facilitating Indian control of government services also extends to tribally controlled colleges and universities,[47] primary and secondary schools,[48] housing,[49] social assistance,[50] policing,[51] and health care.[52] These acts mark a legislative revolution.[53] They are slowly peeling away layers of federal domination in Indian affairs and tribes are acting in ways which take them beyond the state's day-to-day control.[54] When these initiatives began in the early 1970s, tribes only controlled 1.5 per cent of the delivery and administration of federal services to Indian people, whereas today they control over 50 per cent of this sector.[55] While there is much work ahead, Indian control of Indian services has made a significant difference in the United States because it has strengthened the economic, social, and cultural health of Indian tribes.[56]

Indigenous peoples in Canada do not generally plan and deliver services to anywhere near the same degree as in the United States.[57] In fact, First Nations policy development and delivery in Canada is almost exclusively under federal control. Indigenous governments in Canada are not free to set and execute their priorities when it comes to creating colleges, universities, primary and secondary schools, and developing housing, social assistance, policing, and health care. Self-determination is almost absent in the Canadian Indigenous sphere. The main piece of legislation dealing with First Nations governance in the Canadian context is the *Indian Act*.[58] Unlike most of the contemporary suite of U.S. legislation, the *Indian Act* is explicitly designed to break down First Nations sociopolitical relations and forcibly absorb individual Nation members within broader Canadian society.[59] Its provisions narrowly define and heavily regulate Indigenous peoples' citizenship,[60] land rights,[61] succession rules,[62] political organization,[63] economic opportunities,[64] fiscal management,[65] and educational patterns and attainment.[66] Particularly troubling is the fact that the *Indian Act* makes First Nations largely subject to provincial legislation and regulation without their consent.[67] For example, section 88 of the *Indian Act* drastically constrains jurisdictional spaces that should be filled by Indigenous sovereignty.[68] It does so by delegating vast fields of political activity to provincial governments by referentially incorporating, as federal law, provincial laws of general application.[69] This severely limits First Nations' political power in Canada.[70] It also creates very few incentives for the federal government to work with First Nations and pass legislation recognizing and affirming Aboriginal and treaty rights throughout the country.

The federal government's 'transfer' of legislative responsibility from itself and First Nations to provincial governments is a significant reason that Canada lags behind the United States in developing politically healthier Indigenous communities. This is a national tragedy. Section 88 does not enhance self-determination by making provincial laws applicable to 'Indians.' At a federal level, this allows the federal government to almost completely abandon its section 91(24) constitutional responsibility concerning 'Indians and lands reserved for Indians.' By 'passing the buck' to the provinces, the federal government does not face the consequences of its delegation of authority to the provinces. First Nations must comply with provincial laws that they have no real role in crafting or administering. In fact, if provinces were to 'single out' Indians in the passage of provincial legislation, such action would be *ultra vires*, or unconstitutional, because acting in relation to Indians is beyond provincial authority.[71] *Thus, section 88 of the Indian Act removes incentives from both the provincial and federal governments to work with Indians on the detail of laws which most affect Indian peoples' lives.* The 'idea' of assimilation built into the *Indian Act* and other Canadian legislative action usurps First Nations' authority.[72] The *Indian Act* essentializes Canada's treatment of Indigenous peoples in Canada and subjects them to a false 'form' of organization, subordinate to other governments in the land.

As a result of this approach, unlike in the United States, First Nations in Canada largely remain subject to federal day-to-day control when federal services are delivered to their members. The Auditor General of Canada (AGC) identified three problems with this arrangement as it relates to First Nations.[73] First, the federal government has not been clear about the service levels that First Nations receive relative to the general population. This has resulted in First Nations receiving substantially fewer dollars per capita than others when it comes to basic government service. Such glaring disparities raise concerns related to unfairness and discrimination. First Nations and First Nations organizations have challenged this funding gap in court.[74] These discrepancies do more than create the impression that governments are working towards the assimilation of First Nations. Federal law and policy generates negative incentives that impel Indigenous people to leave the reserves and seek services elsewhere.[75] As the AGC wrote, 'It is not always evident whether the federal government is committed to providing services on reserves of the same range and quality as those provided to other communities across Canada.'[76]

Second, First Nations in Canada do not effectively plan and control the delivery of services because the federal government has not created a legislative base to hold themselves accountable in this field. In this respect, the AGC observed,

> For First Nations members living on reserves, there is no legislation supporting programs in important areas such as education, health, and drinking water. Instead, the federal government has developed programs and services for First Nations on the basis of policy. As a result, the services delivered under these programs are not always well defined and there is confusion about federal responsibility for funding them adequately.

When governments act through policy as opposed to legislation, they retain greater discretion in carrying out their plans. This allows them to exercise broader control over those whom their policies affect. In contrast, when governments act through legislation and regulation they signal a higher level of commitment. This is because legal consequences follow when there is a departure from prescribed legislative standards. Acts done contrary to legislation can be challenged in court and remedies can be secured to compel or constrain government or private actors. There are no such consequences when a government acts contrary to its policies. Since the federal government in Canada, unlike the United States, has not committed itself to measurable standards in the provision of services, it is difficult to maintain legal challenges to unequal service delivery. The federal government has not cultivated its own accountability and transparency in relation to First Nations service delivery. This is ironic given the decade-long federal fetish focusing on First Nations accountability–related service delivery.[77] By way of contrast, the United States federal government has held itself to an appreciably higher level of accountability in its relations with Indigenous peoples.[78]

Third, as a result of problems in federal funding mechanisms, First Nations in Canada do not effectively 'control their relationships both among themselves and with non-Indian governments, organizations and persons,' as is the legislative goal in the U.S. context. The failure to provide such mechanisms in Canada has led to great uncertainty about funding levels within First Nations. This makes it nearly impossible for Canadian Indian communities to engage in stable long-term planning. The AGC has noted that the Canadian government's ambiguous funding mechanism also creates problems related to the day-to-day management of reserves. Money to operate First Nations' governments is often received months after approved programs have already begun, placing great strain on community resources. Moreover, most funding agreements only have a one year life-span, which creates high transaction costs that include duplicative and burdensome negotiation and reporting mechanisms. This places further stress on scarce community administrative resources. Finally, in the area of First Nations control of services, the AGC reported that there is a lack of organizational assistance to support local service delivery. As a result, First Nations have not been able to develop a stable and efficient bureaucracy to ensure certainty, transparency, and accountability in the administration of their resources.[79] These three problems alone reveal the stark differences between Canada and the United States when it comes to Indigenous control of Indigenous services. Canada is severely behind the United States in this respect and this has profoundly negative consequences for First Nations administration and governance.

B. Protection of Indigenous Cultures and Communities

Canada also falls drastically behind the United States when it comes to the second area of legislative focus: the protection of Indigenous cultures and communities. Legislation dealing with these issues in the United States is detailed, supportive of self-determination, and calibrated to recognize important differences existing among tribes. One of the most significant pieces of legislation in this regard is the *Indian Child Welfare Act of 1978* (ICWA).[80] The ICWA was designed to prevent high rates of removal of Indian children from their families and communities,[81] and has been very successful in this regard.[82] Congress has also passed legislation related to religious freedoms,[83] cultural heritage,[84] the protection and enhancement of Indigenous languages,[85] the encouragement, development, and protection of Indigenous arts and crafts,[86] and the development of a national museum.[87]

In comparison to these relatively healthy legislative protections, Canadian legislation is exceedingly thin on the ground when it comes to recognizing, protecting, and enhancing First Nations cultures.[88] For example, while the provinces have acted in the field of Indigenous child welfare,[89] there is no national legislation dealing with this issue despite the inordinate number of children in care.[90] Thus, unlike the United States, where the proportion of Native American children in care is now much lower, in Canada an Aboriginal child is 9.5 times more likely than a non-Aboriginal child to be in government-supervised care. The situation is particularly troublesome in the west. In British Columbia, Aboriginal children comprise over 50 per cent of the children in care, though Aboriginal children only make up 9 per cent of the general population. In Manitoba, over 13 per cent of Aboriginal children are not living with their parents but are in government care. In fact, Aboriginal children comprise about 20 per cent of the child population, but represent over 70 per cent of the children in care in Manitoba. In Saskatchewan, approximately 20 per cent of children in the province are Aboriginal, yet they also represent over 67 per cent of the children in care.[91] Lamentably, these numbers are much higher than was the case when the U.S. government passed the ICWA – decades ago, in 1978. Furthermore, Canadian numbers are shockingly higher than contemporary U.S. rates where Indian children now only represent approximately 3 per cent of children in care. Federal law in the U.S. recognizing self-determination seems to have worked to stem the flood of Indigenous children leaving their communities and families, while generally supportive provincial legislation has not made much of a difference in Canada. The crisis in Canada is compounded by the severe underfunding of federal First Nations child welfare services, particularly when compared to the broader population.[92] Litigation is being pursued by First Nations advocates to address these deficiencies.[93] In light of these facts, it is plain to see that, despite the strong provincial presence in the field of Native child welfare, U.S. federal legislative initiatives recognizing tribal jurisdiction are dramatically more effective in keeping families together.[94] By the same measures, child welfare law is basically a disaster in Canada.

Indigenous peoples in Canada also do not enjoy targeted legislative protection in relation to religious freedom. It is true that human rights acts exist in federal and provincial law and have provisions that provide for 'a right to equal treatment with respect to services, goods and facilities, without discrimination because of ... creed.'[95] Furthermore, as a result of section 67 of the *Canadian Human Rights Act*, similar protections apply on First Nations reserves.[96] These provisions make it possible for First Nations to challenge actions that limit their religious freedoms related to non-government action.[97] However, scanning the judgments of these tribunals makes it clear that human rights codes play next to no role in addressing Indigenous religious freedoms.[98] When Indigenous peoples do not sit in judgment related to human rights violations they face in their own communities or in relation to the abuses experienced at the hands of the federal and provincial governments, they do not have effective power to address human rights issues. Governments have frequently undermined Indigenous spirituality throughout the past through the operation of residential schools,[99] the outlawing of potlatches, giveaways, feasts, and dances,[100] and the planning, approval, and implementation of settlement and development on Indigenous sacred sites.[101] The Government in Canada has not passed any stand-alone legislation limiting its own actions relative to such issues. The Canadian government does not hold itself accountable to Indigenous peoples in this sphere. Unlike in the United States, there are no broad-based legislative constraints addressing governmental responsibilities regarding Indigenous religious freedom in Canada. Furthermore, the government has not passed laws that prevent corporations, farmers, developers, provinces, and municipalities from undermining Indigenous religious freedoms, particularly in relation to land and resources.[102] Indigenous spirituality is often tied to lands, rivers, mountains, forests, and other physical sites and should thus be given legislation protection to limit government impact on such practices.

Indigenous peoples in Canada also lack rigorous national legislative protection related to cultural heritage.[103] By way of contrast, the United States has a relatively stronger regime of heritage protection in the *Native American Graves Protection and Repatriation Act* (NAGPRA).[104] The NAGPRA directs federal agencies and museums to return Native American human remains and sacred objects to appropriate Native groups and organizations. It also prevents the appropriation and disturbance of gravesites, and provides for the return or proper care of such objects through consultation with the tribes. While there are clear limits to the act's effectiveness (as is the case with any legislative action), the NAGPRA has been very important in symbolically and practically enhancing respect for historic Native American material culture.[105] As noted, Canada lacks a comparable legislative framework recognizing and affirming broad-based Indigenous cultural and intellectual property protection.[106] Furthermore, provincial legislation in this area has also proven to be significantly deficient in recognizing and affirming Indigenous culture and heritage.[107]

First Nations in Canada also lag appreciably behind the United States in the area of formalized language protection.[108] Language nourishes culture, identity, and health.[109] It encodes unique world views that enhance our understanding of the world around us.[110] Canada is officially bilingual (French and English) but there is no legislation recognizing and affirming the country's original languages. This is deeply and tragically ironic given Canada's somewhat distinctive role as a proponent of linguistic diversity through French and English. Indigenous languages are dying and the federal government is doing next to nothing in the face of this loss. Indigenous peoples have lost ten of their fifty languages in the last 100 years as a result of modernization and colonization.[111] Furthermore, only a minority of Indigenous people within Canada speaks or understands an Aboriginal language.[112] At current rates of support and transmission, it is estimated that only three Indigenous languages will survive until 2100.[113]

Fortunately, there is evidence that endangered languages can be saved.[114] In fact, the strong desire to learn Aboriginal languages is apparent in Canada. There are more second-language Indigenous speakers in Canada than those who speak them as a mother tongue.[115] Canada could build on these developments and officially act to reverse Indigenous language loss throughout the country. A necessary first step would be the development of legislation encouraging Indigenous language retention and uptake.[116] As noted, this has occurred in the United States through the *Native American Languages Act*.[117] Of course, language legislation must be reinforced by financial and administrative mandates, which has not occurred in the United States.[118] Again, it is important to note that in contrasting Canada to the United States, I am not trying to paper over the very real and substantial colonial burden under which tribes function. I hasten to repeat that circumstances in the United States are often very poor for Indigenous peoples. The most successful tribes have been able to set and realize their priorities in ways that deeply challenge the goals, structures, objectives, and aspirations of the broader nation state. However, far too many communities do not enjoy this level of power and remain thoroughly dominated and subjugated to federal and state power. In fact, for many of these communities, the very mechanisms which enable them to exercise inherent powers of self-government further embed them within a troubling set of colonial relationships. They do not own their relationships and they often cannot pursue their own vision of a good life as is contemplated by the terms *dibenindizowin* and *mino-bimaadiziwin* (though this is not always the case). Despite these substantial problems, the *Native American Languages Act* and other legislation referenced in this chapter creates an important framework and starting point for supporting Indigenous language revitalization and other forms of resurgence. While legislation must always be supported by broader action, Canada has not even taken these baby steps towards enhancing Indigenous self-determination in this respect.[119]

Another area that is vital to Indigenous self-determination relates to dispute resolution.[120] When Indigenous peoples practise their own laws, they identify and apply the principles they want to guide their lives.[121] This reinforces respect for community authorities, including ancient teachings and present-day norms.[122] The Canadian Parliament, unlike the federal congress, has not recognized and affirmed inherent Indigenous authority in this field.[123] Thus, Indigenous peoples in Canada have experienced greater difficulty emphasizing and strengthening their own values and aspirations, particularly when individuals and non-Native governments act contrary to their legal orders.[124] In the United States, while tribal courts were initially designed to assimilate Indigenous peoples,[125] tribes are slowly subverting these plans and are making courts vehicles for self-determination.[126] They are slowly transforming communities' conceptualization of their own powers.[127] Again, the most successful are operating parallel to or outside of federal and state structures and ideologies when it comes to their own jurisprudence.[128] These courts have been known to design structures and author opinions that are decidedly illiberal but nevertheless freedom-enhancing if judged from Western legal values. Thus, while the United States Supreme Court has not always been supportive of these institutions,[129] congress has recognized their importance for maintaining law and order for many years.[130] Furthermore, there are many instances when neither congress nor the courts has any influence over tribal courts; tribes are considered to possess sovereign immunity and cannot be disciplined by other state, federal, or judicial forces without an explicit waiver of that sovereignty immunity.[131] In fact, congress recently passed the *Tribal Law and Order Act* to strengthen tribal courts and thereby more effectively confront public safety challenges facing reservation communities.[132] With such support, alongside their continued internal development and sophistication, tribal courts will continue to play a vital role in facilitating self-determination for some time.[133] While there will be much that is distinctive in Canada, as Indigenous peoples continue to develop their legal traditions, they could greatly benefit from U.S. examples if they sought to secure formal recognition of their dispute resolution structures through statutes and regulations.[134] Tribal courts are developing as significant cultural forces in the United States. Canada would do well to facilitate Indigenous dispute resolution in ways that enhance self-determination throughout the country. It should support the grassroots development of communities of fact-finding, reflection, and judgment that are so important to political life in contemporary Indigenous societies.

C. Indigenous Control in Relation to Economic Development, Environment, and Natural Resources

A peoples' self-determination is strongest when their lands and people are physically healthy and self-sustaining and can act in post-colonial ways.[135] This occurs when they have the capacities and resources to work and grow on their own terms in competition against, or cooperation with, others.[136] Indigenous peoples in Canada do not enjoy the same level of legislative support in these matters, when compared to the United States.[137] In fact, the contrast is stark and dispiriting. Canada has done much less to advance Indigenous self-determination in the fields of economic development and natural resource protection. Among the legislative supports enjoyed by Indigenous peoples in the United States related to economic development are the *Indian Gaming Regulatory Act*,[138] *Indian Financing Act*,[139] *Indian Tribal Regulatory Reform and Business Development Act*,[140] *Indian Tribal Economic Development and Encouragement Act*,[141] *Native American Business Development, Trade Promotion and Tourism Act*.[142] Legislation relating to Native American control over the environment and natural resources is found in the *Clean Air Act*,[143] *Clean Water Act*,[144] *National Indian Forest Resources Management Act*,[145] *American Indian Agricultural Resource Management Act*,[146] and the *Indian Mineral Development Act*.[147] While many challenges remain, these legislative initiatives have boosted living standards for Native peoples in the United States.[148] This has also helped them to make significant gains in protecting their lands and resources.[149]

For example, U.S. legislation in the field of gaming has created enormous revenue for Indigenous peoples, growing from $200 million in 1988 to exceed $25 billion in net revenue during the last few years.[150] Furthermore, substantial revenue has been generated as spin-offs from gaming facilities (hotels, restaurants, entertainment, and shopping) to exceed $3 billion.[151] Moreover, 'Indian gaming facilities, including non-gaming operations, directly support approximately 346,000 jobs and pay about $12 billion in wages to employees.'[152] While these benefits are not evenly spread among tribal entities,[153] they do represent a significant gain for reservation economies. In fact, in some areas, tribal growth has significantly benefited entire regions far beyond reservation boundaries.[154] Non-Native people benefit greatly from tribal development where this has occurred.[155] This has not generally occurred in Canada. Indigenous governments, unlike federal or provincial governments or tribes in the United States, have not been allowed to identify, manage, and exploit a competitive advantage in any industry or enterprise. They cannot create incentives or disincentives to secure business investment as most governments can. In particular comparative terms, Indigenous peoples do not have solid federal support for gaming.[156] The federal *Criminal Code* simultaneously prohibits gambling and creates exceptions to allow provinces to regulate the field.[157] Since First Nations were not successful in establishing gaming as an Aboriginal right within section 35(1) of the constitution,[158] Indigenous peoples generally must work with the provinces to participate in this activity.[159] While there have been some limited successes in this regard,[160] provincial control has meant that Indigenous peoples in Canada do not enjoy the wider benefits gaming has created for tribes in the United States. The failure of the Canadian federal government to legislatively recognize and affirm First Nations in any industry (it does not have to be gaming) in a manner similar to the U.S. *Indian Gaming Regulatory Act* represents a significant loss of economic opportunity for Indigenous peoples in Canada.

First Nations in Canada also lack legislative support related to business development. There is an exceedingly weak policy framework for encouraging economic development among First Nations communities that merely focuses on decision-making, assessment, and communications.[161] In contrast, as noted above, the United States has numerous legislative mechanisms to facilitate Native American economic self-determination.[162] The *Indian Reorganization Act* created tribal business committees that enabled communities to have the legal personality necessary to enter into contracts and other transactions.[163] The *Indian Financing Act* creates access to reimbursable private capital funds for economic activities by tribes or tribal members.[164] It also guarantees and insures commercial loans to individual Indians and organizations. The *Indian Tribal Regulatory Reform and Business Development Act* provides mechanisms for congressional review of law and regulations that affect business on reservations.[165] The *Indian Tribal Economic Development and Encouragement Act* removes uncertainty when entering into contracts with tribes by ensuring that congress and the courts do not 'second-guess' tribal bargains.[166] At the same time, the statute mimics consumer protection and fair dealing statutes to facilitate fairness in tribal transactions.[167]

In addition the *Native American Business Development, Trade Promotion and Tourism Act*, enhances tribal sovereignty by providing for financial, technical, and administrative assistance in growing Indigenous economies.[168] The U.S. federal congress regards economic success as vital to tribes. In fact, section 6 of the act is premised on the congressional finding that 'the United States has an obligation to guard and preserve the sovereignty of Indian tribes in order to foster strong tribal governments, Indian self-determination, and economic self-sufficiency among Indian tribes.'[169] There are no similar statements in law regarding Indigenous economic development in Canadian law. While legislative action in any country usually fails to meet legislators' highest aspirations for their laws, these and other U.S. economic development initiatives demonstrate substantial support for tribal businesses. When one examines the Canadian legislative record, it is clear that Canadian Indigenous peoples do not enjoy this same level of support.[170]

The situation is unfortunately similar when one compares U.S. to Canadian legislation in the field of environmental and resource rights and protections. In Canada, there are a very few statutes singling out and recognizing the ability of First Nations to develop and conserve environments and resources in accordance with their own aspirations. There is one exception to this pattern, where Canadian and American law is somewhat similar in oil and gas legislation. In Canada, the *Indian Oil and Gas Act* enables First Nations to manage and develop these resources on reserve land with federal intervention and assistance.[171] In the United States, the *Indian Mineral Development Act* authorizes tribes to enter into agreements for the extraction, processing, or other development of energy resources, including oil and gas.[172] Both jurisdictions seek to maximize energy resource exploitation, though the structures and institutions they employ are somewhat different.

Unfortunately, when it comes to comparing legislation dealing with environmental and resource protection in the two countries, it is clear that Canadian law also significantly lags behind the United States. For example, there is nothing in Canada remotely similar to the *National Indian Forest Resources Management Act*, *Clean Air Act*, *Clean Water Act*, and the *American Indian Agricultural Resource Management Act*.[173] In the United States, each of these acts recognizes significant inherent authority within tribes to exercise all the powers of states in protecting their environments. This sometimes places tribes in direct competition and conflict with states when states fail to promote and implement environmentally sustainable policies and laws. The *National Indian Forest Resources Management Act* allows tribes to protect, conserve, utilize, manage, and enhance their forest lands. It provides for civil actions against trespass that can be enforced in tribal courts, and it mandates that such judgments are required to be given full faith and credit by tribal and state courts.[174] The *American Indian Agricultural Resource Management Act* creates a similar regime in relation to arable and range lands. The *Clean Air Act* and *Clean Water Act* are pinnacle pieces of legislation and both provide that 'tribes shall be treated as states under these laws and have the option of taking over federal responsibility for setting and enforcing environmental standards on reservations.'[175] It is regrettable that similar initiatives have not been undertaken in Canada, despite the unique constitutional protections Indigenous peoples enjoy in Canada. The Canadian government rarely, if ever, facilitates First Nations competition with the provinces nor does it expedite the disruption of provincial laws and policy, as happens in the United States. First Nations must act weakly within federal and provincial legislative mandates, and are not permitted to create policies that step outside of other's desires for them.

In fact, in the Canadian context, Parliament has even rolled backed the relatively weak environmental and resource protections that once existed relative to Indigenous lands. In 2012, two omnibus legislative initiatives made it easier for the Canadian government to develop lands over which Indigenous peoples may have Aboriginal title, rights, or treaty protections.[176] While Parliament cannot avoid constitutional obligations by passing permissive legislation,[177] removing statutory protection makes it more difficult to use the legal system to uphold constitutional rights and interests.[178] In this case, in passing permissive omnibus legislation, Parliament removed specific protections in the *Navigable Waters Protection Act* that previously triggered federal environmental assessments and Crown duties to consult and accommodate Indigenous peoples. Pipelines were also specifically exempted from review under the omnibus bills (although the National Energy Board must still consider navigations issues through its approval process). Furthermore, the *Canadian Environmental Assessment Act* (CEAA) was replaced with changes that completely eliminate environmental assessments for so-called minor projects. In addition, the *Fisheries Act* was modified to more directly protect fish, but not fish habitat, and a definition of 'Aboriginal fisheries' was imposed that requires 'serious harm' to stop developments harmful to such fisheries. Changes that will have negative effects on Indigenous environments and resources were also made to the following acts: the *Hazardous Materials Information Review Act, Canada Oil and Gas Operations Act, National Energy Board Act, Species at Risk Act, First Nations Fiscal and Statistical Management Act,* and *Indian Act.* These acts are not attentive to Indigenous self-determination in structuring Canada's wider policy framework. In fact, this legislation is likely to harm Indigenous peoples' abilities to 'control their relationships both among themselves and with non-Indian governments, organizations and persons,' which is the goal of U.S. legislation and policy.[179]

D. Conclusion

This chapter suggests that Indigenous peoples in Canada could do more to challenge and engage the Canadian state in the formal legislative sphere. In this matter, by reference to particular fields of statutory action, I have argued that articles of faith in Indigenous politics must be questioned. Tribes and First Nations can absolutely or with qualifications embrace the nation state. Similarly they can reject the nation state and attempt to operate outside its parameters. Neither approach leads inexorably to freedom. The trick is to chart the course which is less oppressive in the short and long term, while still leaving broad possibilities for engaging in alternative ways of acting in the real world when better options present themselves. Whether freedom is enhanced and good lives are made more attainable depends on contextual contingencies which must be judged on ever-shifting, complex multidimensional grounds. When considering what path Indigenous peoples take with the nation state, the counsel: 'it depends' might be as close as we get to *dibenindizowin* and *mino-bimaadiziwin* in operationalizing these teachings.

This chapter is based on the recognition that the constitutional rooting of Aboriginal and treaty rights in Canada's constitution has not led to any significant legislative recognition and affirmation of those rights.[180] In my view, it has been another colonial disaster. In contrast, as the foregoing review demonstrates, the U.S. federal congress has at least begun to recognize and facilitate Indigenous peoples' self-determination in the areas of Indigenous control of federal services, culture, and economic development, resources, and the environment. Nevertheless, colonial subjugation is still distressingly pervasive in the United States, despite many positive efforts. This means that the ideas drawn from the United States' experience, for potential application in Canada, must be applied with the knowledge that they will not necessarily address the deeper challenges that exist between the parties. There will always be significant challenges in the relationship between Indigenous peoples and others in Canada, just as occurs in the United States, despite supportive legislation. However, while legislation is never a universal remedy for solving some of the deepest conflicts Indigenous peoples experience, it can be a necessary, though not sufficient, way (in some instances) to begin the process of decolonizing Canada. It might strengthen communities and improve lives, as this chapter has demonstrated. The modest ideas presented herein, if applied with the goal of self-determination at their heart, might provide some valuable assistance in hastening this process.

Chapter Six

Aboriginal and Treaty Rights and Violence against Women*

As should now be clear, this book claims that freedom is enhanced by pursuing brazenly pragmatic paths. These paths are blazed by both celebrating and critiquing conventional understandings about how to best strengthen Indigenous communities. As will be recalled, *dibenin-dizowin* is the Anishinaabe word for freedom. Its meaning encourages responsibility for self and a respectful ownership of one's relationships. It is similar to the Anishinaabe word for citizenship: *diben-jigaazowin*, which implies that a person has duties and obligations to one's self and one's group. Likewise, *mino-bimaadiziwin* (living well in this world) focuses on living well and giving expression to visions of life as we alone understand them, in responsible relationship with others.[1] Living well and living freely can be frustrated by the imposition of so-called pre-political or inherent characteristics. We must recognize that Indigenous politics are always deployed within the constraints and opportunities of our convoluted circumstances. There is no Hobbes-Locke-like state of nature which is free from the messy complexities of life.

As this book repeatedly emphasizes, freedom is diminished by the insistence that Indigeneity must accord with a pre-existing set of values, doctrines, principles, laws, or traditions that have a fundamental, *a priori*, essence. This was the problem discussed in previous chapters through critiques of all-encompassing conceptions of mobility, direct action, constitutional interpretation, constitutional formation, and legislative engagement. Each instance revealed a set of constraining categorizations flowing from a so-called first principle or basic rule about the proper nature of a practice or group.

This chapter continues to question categorical thinking as it relates to Indigenous peoples. This time, our focus will be on issues related to gender and governance. In too many circles, gender is essentialized in ways that limit both men's and women's freedom. This occurs both within and outside Indigenous communities. Indigenous women and Indigenous governments are marginalized through formal laws and institutional practices as well as through informal norms, stereotypes, and ideologies. These patterns of thought diminish everyone's possibilities to own and have responsibility for themselves and their relationships, and this is true for both Indigenous and non-Aboriginal peoples.

Debates surrounding gender and Indigenous governance are strongly influenced by how Indigenous issues are framed by the courts. In particular, section 35(1) of the *Constitution Act, 1982* excludes a wide range of human rights issues, because it has spawned a political approach that largely emphasizes land and resource conflicts. As a result, too many chiefs, parliamentarians, and leaders have become captivated by issues recognized by the courts. This fixation has inadvertently drawn attention away from pressing structural inequalities related to violence against Indigenous women. On the one hand, it is not unreasonable for leaders to devote their attention to matters that have gained broader legal traction in the judicial realm. This is because Canadian governments do not generally respond to Indigenous issues unless courts compel them to take action. On the other hand, since the courts have been largely insensitive to Indigenous peoples' lived realities, Indigenous leaders must ensure that their political agendas are not determined by the courts' jurisprudence.

To help refocus Indigenous political discourse surrounding section 35(1), this chapter argues that Indigenous peoples' constitutional rights must be reframed and transformed in ways that address other pressing needs including, most importantly, violence against women. Our political and legal leaders have been falsely bewitched by the idea that Aboriginal and treaty rights relate only to land. This is a harmful tradition. Aboriginal and treaty rights also directly implicate the health, safety, and welfare of Indigenous people's bodies. Aboriginal and treaty rights exist to promote and protect physical survival.[2] The health, safety, and welfare of Indigenous women are obviously relevant to a community's past, present, and future well-being. Thus, we must see section 35(1) as including much broader protections – even if the courts are slow to do the same. Aboriginal and treaty rights must be construed in philosophically-physical ways to enhance freedom in real world terms.

Such reframing is particularly important, given that section 35(1)'s significance goes beyond the realm of formal litigation. In fact, section 35(1) is relevant only when it relates to the broader political struggles Indigenous peoples encounter, inside and outside their communities.[3] The connections between Indigenous governance and violence against women must be therefore placed more squarely within this light. This approach would allow Indigenous peoples to more fully and responsibly own themselves and their relationships. As such, Indigenous communities should be regarded as possessing shared constitutional responsibility for addressing violence against women.

Acting to address violence against women should not be an either/or choice. Paths to freedom and a good life traverse complex domains. Walking this road is a politically impure and thorny exercise. Unless section 35(1) becomes a site of this kind of action, particularly as it relates to violence against women, Indigenous women will not be sufficiently empowered to affect national and local policies to generate lasting change.[4]

To unpack stereotypes that prevent positive change, the first part of this chapter discusses why responsibility for addressing violence against women has not been considered as lying within section 35(1)'s sphere. The second part analyses the Supreme Court of Canada's exceedingly narrow interpretation of Aboriginal and treaty rights regarding governance. It considers why jurisdiction related to violence against women would not likely be affirmed under the Supreme Court's current dominant interpretive approach. In so doing, the second part identifies alternative means of recognizing and affirming Indigenous peoples' responsibilities for dealing with violence against women within existing section 35(1)'s jurisprudence, including within Indigenous peoples' own legal traditions.

My point is that Canada's constitution *could* readily embrace approaches that put the health, well-being, and safety of Indigenous women at the heart of community life. However, this will occur only *if* we reject habits of thought that regard Indigenous peoples' assumption of such responsibility as being undesirable or impossible. If Indigenous rights were rooted in contemporary jurisdictional concerns, section 35(1) could make a greater difference in addressing violence against women in daily life.

In making this point I am *not* suggesting that Indigenous governance is *the* answer to the problems Indigenous women face. Nor do I believe we should overemphasize the power of Indigenous governance to solve problems within communities, as vital as this exercise might be. In fact, I would reject such a proposition, because I do not see a single path to freedom in any social field of Indigenous life. There is a pressing need to ensure that most of our activity in this field occurs outside of a constitutionalized discourse. The politics of recognition and state-focused activities will not sufficiently carry the load and therefore must be critiqued and even rejected in many instances.[5] Single-path strategies helped get us into this mess. They must be rigorously scrutinized.

This is the reason this book 'rejects' (while noting the seeming irony) political positions which categorically 'reject' options for dealing with our challenges. I am extremely wary of positions presented in the name of Marxism, liberalism, conservatism, nationalism, traditionalism, or any other system of thought that posits a foundational, exclusive, universal approach for dealing with our challenges. Of course, this position strongly colours my tentative invocation of constitutional law. While I find possible help in this field, I do not believe it generates exclusive diagnoses or remedies related to violence against Indigenous women. As a constitutional law professor, I am keenly aware of constitutional law's trap. It can reproduce the very oppression from which we are seeking liberation.[6] Thus to be clear, in this chapter I am proposing only that section 35(1)'s political and legal weight be added to various other, more directly practice-based activities pursued to realize better lives in real-world terms.

A. The Problem and/or the Answer: Indigenous Self-Determination and Violence against Women

Indigenous women in Canada are beaten, sexually assaulted, and killed in shockingly high numbers.[7] They experience violence at rates three times higher than other women.[8] This violence is also extremely brutal in comparison to that experienced by the general population.[9] They are five times more likely to be killed or to disappear as compared to non-Indigenous women.[10] They also experience much higher rates of intimate partner violence than other women.[11] Incarceration rates of Indigenous women are also greater than those of the general population of women due, in part, to their response to this violence.[12] There is a crisis in Canada's criminal justice system relating to this issue,[13] yet there has been no significant constitutional response despite recommendations in numerous high-profile government reports.[14] While federal legislative action has directed judges to consider the special circumstances of Aboriginal peoples in some instances,[15] these efforts are woefully inadequate in addressing broader issues of violence against women within and beyond Indigenous communities.[16]

At the same time, Indigenous women have demonstrated great leadership in bringing issues of violence more fully into the public spotlight.[17] They have established shelters, arranged counselling, organized vigils, volunteered in clinics, coordinated media campaigns, appeared before parliamentary committees, cultivated the arts, worked in the civil service, and been elected as chiefs and councillors – all with a firm public resolve to end violence against women.[18] The Native Women's Association of Canada has long been at the forefront of these efforts.[19] Its advocacy, research, and on-the-ground efforts have made a huge difference for thousands of people.[20] In fact, Indigenous women across the country have creatively developed detailed policy proposals and grassroots models for dealing with violence against women.[21] Their work includes support for Indigenous self-determination which recognizes and affirms women's rights.[22] The knowledge and experience of these women – and, in particular, their poignant calls for structural change – must be heeded.[23]

As I have argued, law and traditions are not pure; they influence and are intertwined with politics.[24] Section 35(1) does not specifically deal with violence against Indigenous women because, thus far, courts have not construed these powers as falling within Indigenous peoples' jurisdiction. At another level, there is no jurisprudence recognizing Indigenous jurisdiction in this field, because Indigenous communities and Indigenous women are both subject to essentializing stereotypes. Indigenous governments are not recognized as having jurisdiction because they are not fully trusted to deal effectively with violence against women.[25] Indigenous women are not recognized as requiring unique protections, because they are subordinated as legal agents within both Indigenous and wider Canadian political and legal circles.[26]

Issues of jurisdiction, trust, and subordination are intertwined when dealing with violence against Indigenous women, and the relationship between them cannot be easily disentangled. For example, if Indigenous governments attempted to more fully assume legal responsibility related to violence against women, a lack of official recognition would leave them without the resources and broader support necessary to realize tangible change related to actual on-the-ground attitudes, activity, and service delivery. Resulting failures would endanger the lives and health of Indigenous women. This would, in turn, further fuel negative perceptions of Indigenous justice and diminish government and community willingness to support official recognition of jurisdiction in the future. Understanding the vital connection between active, supportive recognition of Indigenous jurisdiction and its proper implementation should reinforce our awareness of the fact that law and politics are not distinct fields. It is for this reason that this chapter contextualizes violence against women in a broader constitutional light.[27]

Thus, if communities are going to deal effectively with violence against women, we must understand why Indigenous peoples currently lack official jurisdictional recognition in this field. The first point to note is that the failure to recognize Indigenous governance is part of a broader dilemma that Indigenous people encounter before the courts in trying to assume responsibility for their own affairs. The Supreme Court of Canada has limited its discussion of Indigenous governance to very few cases and has *not* taken a 'large, liberal and generous approach' to this issue.[28] In the governance sphere there is no spirit of reconciliation in the jurisprudence. For example, in *R v. Pamajewon*, the first decision to discuss Indigenous governance explicitly under section 35(1), the Supreme Court held that Indigenous communities could not claim broad management rights over reserve lands.[29] While the Court's reasons have not escaped critical commentary,[30] this narrow framing all but halted the advancement of successful governance claims under section 35(1).[31] The *Pamajewon* decision was reinforced one year later in *Delgamuukw v. The Queen*, in which the Court declined to address issues related to self-governance because of the 'difficult conceptual issues' raised by this claim.[32] Both of these decisions created a void at the centre of section 35(1) jurisprudence. Section 35(1) allows communities to claim rights in relation to historically specific practices but has been interpreted in a way that simultaneously denies them the means to organize their broader social relationships.[33] This distinction has suppressed Indigenous governmental activity. It has weakened local innovation in responding to the crisis of violence against Indigenous women within Indigenous communities and beyond.

Contrast this situation with the constitutional circumstances of Native American tribes in the United States, who possess authority to exercise criminal and civil jurisdiction on their reserves.[34] Tribal power in the United States flows from a legally recognized autonomous source of sovereignty that existed before the country's creation and survives to the present day.[35] While this authority is subject to the judicially created federal plenary power to regulate Native American affairs[36] and is constrained by legislative restrictions crafted in this light,[37] tribes still possess substantial powers of self-determination related to their internal governance.[38] For example, the U.S. Bill of Rights[39] does not directly apply to tribes,[40] and while the federal government has passed legislation directing tribes to protect their members' rights,[41] these laws cannot generally be enforced in federal courts and, therefore, must be secured before tribal courts.[42] Thus, as a practical matter, tribes in the United States have significant jurisdiction to legislate and adjudicate issues related to violence against women.[43] Unlike in Canada, the exercise of broad powers of Indigenous governance is not subject to limiting stereotypes as expressed in the *Pamajewon* case. As a result, tribes and tribal courts have taken important steps in addressing this issue, even as substantial work remains to be done.[44] The recognition that legal rights vest Indigenous governments with responsibilities for dealing with violence against women greatly aids political action in this field.

Unfortunately, Indigenous women in Canada are denied similar rights and related access to political power that are essential to their safety and to their communities' broader health. It is as if Canadian judges and politicians cannot conceive of Indigenous peoples seriously dealing with the issue of violence against women. This must change. Stereotypes and other essentializing views that prevent such action must be abandoned. Indigenous peoples should be regarded as partners in Confederation who are capable of exercising jurisdiction related to the country's most pressing social and political issues.[45] Indigenous women should be constitutionally recognized as having the power to hold accountable their own governments, and Canadian governments more generally, when they experience violence. Indigenous women and Indigenous communities cannot effectively participate in the creation of healthy societies if they do not have the jurisdictional tools to address the violence and social dysfunction which plagues them. Of course, it must be repeated that the exercise of such power will not eradicate violence against women, because causes and solutions go much deeper than constitutional reform. Nevertheless, severe social distress could nevertheless be modestly yet meaningfully curtailed if Indigenous governments had greater authority and resources available to them to address violence against women.[46] Unless Indigenous governance structures such as councils, courts, clans, etc., address issues central to the safety of Indigenous women, they will continue to be marginalized within Canada and within their communities.[47]

Violence against women not only arises from poor interpersonal relationships, it is also connected to larger social structures of inequality that can be found in any society.[48] One prominent structural disability faced by Indigenous peoples is Canada's ongoing colonization of Indigenous lands and bodies. Violence against women is, therefore, intimately linked with the broader colonial context that Aboriginal rights are designed to address.[49] Without recognizing the links between violence against Indigenous women and male-dominated colonial structures, Indigenous women will remain subject to staggeringly high levels of violence, 'since violence against women is one of the key means through which male control over women's agency and sexuality is maintained.'[50] Thus, the web of oppressive and unequal relationships within which Indigenous women are enmeshed must be addressed as part and parcel of violence against women if the issue is to work its way onto the constitutional agenda.[51] We must not act as if it were 'essential' 'or fundamental' or 'necessary' to Canadian law for Indigenous women to engage political and legal power or protections only through the federal government or outside of the state altogether. Power must be available to them at all levels of society and beyond, because such violence is pervasive. Freedom involves the ability to contest universalized assumptions and exercise choice and agency in numerous ways and in relation to multiple sites of oppression and opportunity.

B. Indigenous Governments: Can They Be Trusted?

While the recognition of Indigenous jurisdiction would be an important step in addressing violence against women, one might appropriately ask whether violence against women would receive the attention and action it deserves if Indigenous peoples were recognized as possessing responsibility in this field.[52] To engage with this question is to acknowledge the broader issues of trust in Indigenous governance lying behind the legal discourse. At present, Indigenous communities can be as oppressive and as dismissive of this issue as other levels of government.[53] As is the case with most political communities,[54] male domination is a troubling fact of life.[55] It always has been.[56] In fact, an early report of the Manitoba Justice Inquiry proclaimed that Indigenous political leaders were a large part of the problem in perpetuating violence within Indigenous communities.[57] The commissioners of the inquiry wrote,

The unwillingness of chiefs and councils to address the plight of women and children suffering abuse at the hands of husbands and fathers is quite alarming. We are concerned enough about it to state that we believe that the failure of Aboriginal government leaders to deal at all with the problem of domestic abuse is unconscionable. We believe that there is a heavy responsibility on Aboriginal leaders to recognize the significance of the problem within their own communities. They must begin to recognize, as well, how much their silence and failure to act actually contribute to the problem.[58]

While these words were written over twenty years ago and constructive change has occurred within some Indigenous political circles over the last few decades,[59] there is no reason to believe that Indigenous communities are enlightened havens of gender sensitivity when it comes to addressing violence against women.[60] Significant problems remain,[61] despite encouraging signs of change related to this issue within Indigenous communities.[62]

From many vantage points, therefore, the troubling levels of violence within Indigenous communities might be considered a reason for denying jurisdiction to Indigenous peoples.[63] People will reasonably wonder whether societies with this degree of trauma are capable of dealing with violence against women. These are essential questions that must be squarely addressed. To be certain, safety must be a paramount concern in addressing violence against women.[64] Reserves can be dangerous places at times, and jurisdictional and other reforms should be deployed in light of this fact.[65] They are sites of marginalization, abuse, violence, and death.

At the same time, we must not lose sight of the strength, creativity, and resilience of Indigenous women and their allies on the reserves and beyond; their knowledge and experience is a key source of power in addressing violence at many levels.[66] It must be recognized that there are many places within Indigenous communities where people enjoy safe and healthy lives.[67] Reserves can be places of love, encouragement, healing, and mutual aid. We should take care to avoid painting all Indigenous peoples with the same brush.[68] Trauma, while widespread, is not the norm is every place throughout Aboriginal Canada.[69] Furthermore, we should also reject the *a priori* assumption that communities experiencing deep levels of violence are incapable of dealing with this issue even if they generate the proper resources and legal tools.[70] People are able to change their lives amidst the most trying conditions.[71]

While addressing violence is certainly more challenging in such contexts, and requires a significant level of support as noted above, much can be accomplished.[72] Thus, while we should always be deeply concerned about any (Indigenous or non-Indigenous) community's ability to effectively address violence against women, these issues should always be considered in a more nuanced light.

Second, it must be acknowledged that Canadian Parliament and provincial legislatures have not responded effectively to the nationwide crisis involving violence against Indigenous women.[73] In fact, even as women's organizations across Canada have been advocating for additional attention to, and services for, addressing violence against women, they have suffered drastic across-the-board cuts to their public funding.[74] Furthermore, repeated calls by national Aboriginal organizations for the Canadian government to address violence against Indigenous women have been met with responses that are slow to address the problem's pervasive nature.[75]

The same situation largely prevails within the provinces, where governments have not taken the initiative to address violence against Indigenous women structurally. In fact, even in those rare cases where provinces have acted, their processes have been framed in excessively narrow terms. For example, commissions of inquiry have been established to examine select issues related to violence against Indigenous women in British Columbia[76] and Manitoba,[77] but the governments' limited focus has generally failed to generate support from the most affected Indigenous communities.[78] Moreover, the existence of Charter rights protecting, *inter alia*, life, liberty, security, and equality has had little influence in addressing this issue.[79] Broader change is needed but has not been forthcoming.[80] The failure of federal and provincial governments to deal meaningfully with violence against Indigenous women shows that the status quo is not working.[81] Any even-handed assessment of whether Indigenous jurisdiction related to violence against women should exist must take account of this fact.

Third, in considering Indigenous jurisdiction in relation to violence against women, it should be acknowledged that Aboriginal governance rights exercised under section 35(1) would not be exclusive. I have been arguing that Indigenous peoples do not live in a legally dichotomous world, and this factor should be accounted for in taking stronger actions. For example, the Canadian government could justify infringements of section 35(1) rights if the Crown's actions were honourable, advanced reconciliation, and were in accordance with valid objectives.[82] Thus, if Indigenous governance powers related to violence against women were recognized and deployed, the Canadian government could always aid or modify this exercise through consultation and accommodation in accordance with its other obligations under section 35(1).[83] Nevertheless, this shared framework would not give the Crown an unfettered licence to impose unjustifiable burdens on Indigenous actions addressing violence against women.

Section 35(1) constrains Crown sovereignty by serving as a check against arbitrary government action. As the Supreme Court observed in *Sparrow*, section 35(1) 'gives a measure of control over government conduct and a strong check on legislative power.'[84] The fact that Indigenous sovereignty limits that of the Crown when section 35(1) is at issue should be more explicitly conceded. This is one of the most significant implications of the constitutional requirement that infringements of Aboriginal and treaty rights be justified by valid governmental objectives, which are exercised honourably and in good faith.[85] In this light, Indigenous governance would be regarded as functioning analogously to the checks and balances of federalism – that is, working in a cooperative, coordinated and competitive way with the other levels of government. This means that Crown sovereignty should appropriately constrain Indigenous sovereignty, and vice versa, in dealing with the practical jurisdictional questions concerning violence against women.[86] Such an approach would enhance Indigenous governance as well as Canadian responses to ensure that violence against women is dealt with in ways that draw upon the strengths of all jurisdictions across the land.[87]

Furthermore, it should be noted that Indigenous peoples' governmental responsibilities regarding Indigenous women under subsection 35(1) would also be subject to subsection 35(4) of the constitution, which states, 'Notwithstanding any other provision of this *Act*, the aboriginal and treaty rights referred to in subsection (1) are guaranteed equally to male and female persons.'[88] This provision is an important bulwark against innovations that could otherwise undermine Indigenous women's rights. It must be remembered that this subsection would likely have its greatest impact on political discourse and practices; it would take only one or two cases under section 35(4) to generate a political discourse more explicitly attentive to section 35(1)'s gender equality implications. This would reinforce the idea that distinctions adversely impacting Indigenous women could not be sustained under section 35(1), as they would run contrary to section 35(4)'s protections.[89] Thus,

every time an Indigenous community exercised its governance jurisdiction under the constitution, including matters related to Indigenous
women, such authority would be subject to an overriding constraint
protecting gender equality found in section 35(4).[90] Of course, these
overriding constraints are problematic because the state is not exactly
a neutral and objective arbitrator when it comes to Indigenous issues.
The state's apparatus is just as likely to replicate violence against
women. Nevertheless the Court's oversight could provide an important check against male domination in some circumstances. While not
completely addressing the complex extra-legal factors involved in
violence against women, section 35(4)'s protection could go some distance towards addressing the problem of male domination within some
Indigenous communities and leadership circles. This provision also has
the potential to be a significant political tool for addressing violence
against women long before courts or legislatures get around to recognizing Indigenous jurisdiction relating to this issue.

In fact, difficulties related to gendered violence within Indigenous
communities are likely to remain at higher levels *until* they are subject
to the full legal and political force of section 35(4). Section 35(4) and
Indigenous women's perspectives more generally would play a greater
role in Canada's constitution if Indigenous people exercised jurisdiction
related to violence against women under section 35(1). Section 35(4)'s
requirement for gender equity in exercising governmental power
would place concerns related to gender discrimination more squarely
at the heart of advocacy within section 35(1). While far from being a
cure-all for gender inequality, the fuller promise of section 35(4) would
become more apparent if Indigenous peoples exercised power to deal
with violence against women under section 35(1). It would operate to
expand the protections of Aboriginal women within their communities
whenever women's rights are in question.

Under this reading of section 35(4), there would be no constitutional justification for Indigenous communities using their authority to
engage in any contemporary, traditional, customary, or other practice or
law that subordinates women and subjects them to any form of adverse
discrimination.[91] Such discrimination would be unconstitutional. Section 35(4) could therefore have an important remedial effect, internally
as well as externally, as Indigenous peoples exercise greater authority
under section 35(1). This could further alleviate concerns flowing from
having Indigenous communities deal with violence against women
while still being deeply mired in discrimination in too many quarters.

Finally, experience in the United States suggests that recognizing Indigenous jurisdiction over violence against women at least partially counteracts aspects of gendered discrimination within Indigenous communities. In pointing this out, I must reiterate that I am not suggesting that the United States should be the model for dealing with violence against women in Canada. In fact, distinctive and significant challenges concerning violence against Indigenous women are present in the United States,[92] as is the case with this issue in most societies throughout the world to greater and lesser degrees.[93] Reservations in the United States are places of danger, violence, and death, as well examples of hope, self-help, and healing. Thus, this comparative experience is invoked only to illustrate the fact that we should not essentialize either the potential (or lack thereof) for Indigenous governments to address violence against women. Important political mobilization can occur when Indigenous governments take responsibility over this area, even as problems remain. When the locus of political authority for dealing with violence against women rests with Indigenous governments, they face much greater internal and external pressure to take action in this field.[94]

On the internal side of the equation, chiefs and councils find that their electoral prospects can be tied to their effectiveness in addressing this issue.[95] If they do not take action on this front, their own constituents on the reservations demand that they do so. When Indigenous communities exercise meaningful self-determination, they cannot as easily shift blame to other levels of government when they are faced with such demands. Therefore, if leaders do not listen to these voices, their chances of political success fade in some circumstances. While violence against women is not the only issue competing for attention on Indigenous legislative agendas, it has a high enough profile to be politically salient and generate extensive community legislation. An Indigenous leader who ignores this issue for an extended period of time loses an important base of electoral support within his or her community. If a candidate faces political uncertainty, the failure to take account of this issue could be a swing factor in his or her electoral prospects. The creation of internal incentives to deal with violence against women, which includes the leadership and advocacy of many Indigenous women chiefs, leaders, and organizations, should not be overlooked when Indigenous jurisdiction in this field is considered.

As a result of these and other incentives, Native governments in the United States have acted in significant ways to legislate in this field.[96]

A brief review of tribal statutes demonstrates this fact. When Indigenous governments deal with general issues related to violence against women outside the context of domestic violence, 'it is not common to have a separate law on sexual assault jurisdiction that differs from general criminal jurisdiction.'[97] Thus, while some tribal governments have specific provisions addressing sexual assault,[98] most have all-purpose criminal codes invoking jurisdiction over violent crimes on a broader level.[99] Furthermore, most tribes also take general jurisdiction over this issue through civil statutes.[100]

However, there is one special area of legislative activity that deals specifically with violence against women on reserves: domestic violence codes.[101] In addition to their considerable detail, these ordinances often contain important contextual statements outlining their purposes. In this way, they set the tone for discussion and action related to violence against women within Native American communities. For example, the *Fort Mohave Law and Order Code* expresses faith in the importance of law in reducing and deterring domestic violence.[102] The *Hopi Family Relations Ordinance* identifies the scope and tragic consequences of domestic violence for individuals, clans, and communities while making specific mention of the fact that domestic violence is not just a 'family' matter.[103] The *Domestic Abuse of the Northern Cheyenne Tribal Code* contains strong statements criticizing the tribe's past approaches to domestic violence,[104] while the *Oglala Sioux Domestic Violence Code* contains a bold declaration of purpose that underlines the cultural inappropriateness of violence against women as well as the importance of safety, protection, prosecution, and education in dealing with this issue.[105] These detailed statutes, along with tribal court cases that interpret them, are evidence of the pressure tribes face within their communities to deal effectively with domestic violence.[106] Though progress in overcoming this scourge is slow, these processes and instruments demonstrate that even communities facing high levels of trauma are capable of developing a response to this crisis. Again, these examples are raised to demonstrate the political implications of Indigenous jurisdiction concerning violence against women.

In addition, tribes in the United States encounter external pressures to address gendered discrimination as a result of their authority related to violence against women. People outside of the tribe organize themselves to persuade tribal councils to act more constructively in this field. Externally generated pressure comes from not only academics and policy institutes but also women's organizations;[107] tribal, state, and local governments;[108] as well as international bodies.[109] Moreover, when tribes exercise jurisdiction, the U.S. federal government is significantly more active than its Canadian counterpart in the field of violence against women on reserves, as it works to recognize Indigenous self-determination in this field.[110] Sustained legislative dialogues are developing between the federal and Indigenous governments as violence against women is recognized as an important field of law-making activity within U.S. First Nations communities.[111] This dialogue is leading to further innovation at the tribal level and spawning action at the federal level to create frameworks to address this issue.

For example, tribes are working with the federal government in the United States to recognize more fully inherent tribal jurisdiction to deal with violence against women and the need to provide resources and assistance in this regard.[112] If such power were recognized in Canada, the federal government could likewise consider legislation similar to that currently passed by the United States Congress. The *Stand Against Violence and Empower Native Women Act (SAVE Native Women Act)*, which was proposed as a stand-alone piece of legislation but has since become Title IX of the *Violence Against Women Act (VAWA)*, was designed to allow tribes to make fuller use of their own laws to address violence against women on reserves. This is a good example of the type of action that governments could take to support Indigenous communities in Canada.[113] Since tribes in the United States clearly have inherent jurisdiction over their own members in this sphere,[114] VAWA acknowledges that tribes possess jurisdiction over non-Indians[115] who commit violent crimes against women on Indian lands.[116] At the same time, the *Act* recognizes that significant problems exist for Indigenous women off-reserve. Thus, Title IX seeks to improve Native programs under the *Violence Against Women Act*[117] by enhancing data-gathering programs throughout the United States and increasing tribal resources and jurisdictional authority so that violence against Native women can be better understood and responded to.[118]

It would be a groundbreaking development if section 35(1) recognized that Indigenous communities in Canada possessed similar jurisdictional tools. This recognition would also be important in light of the fact that much of the violence faced by Indigenous women occurs off reserves.[119] In such circumstances, Indigenous peoples might work with the federal government to gather the type of data required under the *Violence Against Women Act*, which would bring resources and attention to bear on issues arising from the over 600 missing and murdered

Indigenous women in Canada. This would make it easier to respond to the national dimension of Canada's current crisis, because action would be taken on a government-to-government basis. There is also great value in VAWA's recognition of the breadth and scope of the problem involving violence against women.[120] Clear acknowledgment of harm is an essential step towards moving beyond it.[121] When the *SAVE Native Women Act* was introduced, its sponsor, Senator Akaka, said,

> According to a study by the Department of Justice, two in five women in Native communities will suffer domestic violence, and one in three will be sexually assaulted in their lifetime. Furthermore, four out of five perpetrators of these crimes are non-Indian, and cannot be prosecuted by tribal governments. This has contributed to a growing sense of lawlessness on Indian reservations and a perpetuation of victimization of Native women.[122]

Thus, while the legal context of the two countries is somewhat different, the sociocultural conditions between them are not greatly dissimilar when it comes to Indigenous issues. In this light, Title XI of the *Violence Against Women Act* is an important example of how Indigenous groups could work with governments to address domestic violence while enhancing community self-determination.[123]

C. Section 35(1) and Violence against Women

Having discussed reasons why Indigenous communities should not be excluded from exercising jurisdiction related to violence against women, I turn now to the important question of how this issue could be framed within section 35(1) jurisprudence. As noted, attention to the issue of violence against women will be enhanced if Indigenous and Canadian governments treat it as a constitutional issue while continuing to address its other dimensions (social dislocation, poverty, colonialism, male domination on and off reserve, deficient fiscal policy, etc.). In raising this issue's importance in the constitutional realm, Indigenous peoples would have at least two options for asserting jurisdiction over violence against women: they could bring a claim as either an Aboriginal right or a treaty right. Unfortunately, given the narrow way in which the Supreme Court currently frames both of these rights, it is unlikely that a community would succeed under the dominant interpretations of section 35(1). This conclusion may be viewed as a reason for abandoning the constitution's Aboriginal provisions when dealing with violence against women.

There is no question that section 35(1) has largely become a dead end in challenging Canada's continued colonial practices, particularly beyond cases that involve the allocation of resources between the Crown and First Nations. The constitutionalization of Aboriginal and treaty rights has been a huge disappointment when it comes to addressing human rights violations. Despite its current weaknesses, however, I believe that there are at least two crucial reasons for considering jurisdiction related to violence against women under 35(1). First, an application of the prevailing tests in section 35(1) jurisprudence highlights fatal constitutional defects in present interpretive approaches. This is an important critique, because it highlights our constitution's failings and may cause people to search for non-state or extra-constitutional alternatives. Second, a discussion of section 35(1)'s interpretive flaws exposes latent alternative readings that can be used to build a healthier jurisprudence. To be sure, it must be continually emphasized that action in the field of violence against women must always be broader than constitutional argument.[124] However, it is also important that constitutional avenues not be abandoned, because Indigenous women deserve and require protection at the highest levels of constitutional law as well as within the mundane details of everyday community life.

Thus, in considering Aboriginal peoples' claims to section 35(1) rights in relation to violence against women, the Supreme Court's current tests in the field of Aboriginal and treaty rights will be outlined to reveal their critical defects. After a review of the Court's dominant tests in each area, alternative arguments within the existing jurisprudence will be reviewed to demonstrate how current laws could be interpreted to protect against violence and enhance Indigenous self-determination in this important field.

i) Aboriginal Rights: Violence against Women and the 'Integral to the Distinctive Culture' Test

Under the Court's current approach for establishing Aboriginal rights (other than Aboriginal title)[125] within section 35(1), Indian, Metis, or Inuit groups must demonstrate that a practice, custom, or tradition was 'integral to their distinctive culture' prior to European contact.[126] In considering Indigenous jurisdiction in relation to violence against women, a court would apply this test and insist on precision in relation to the claim's exact nature.[127] This means that the potential right must be framed as narrowly as possible in the first instance. Thus, jurisdictional claims may not be framed with an excessive level of generality and 'must be looked at in light of the specific circumstances of each case, and in light of the specific history and culture of the Indigenous group claiming the right.'[128]

As noted above in section one of this chapter, *R. v. Pamajewon* held that Aboriginal people could not claim 'broad management rights over reserve lands.'[129] As a result of this specificity requirement, a community may not be able to claim jurisdiction 'for any and all purposes'[130] related to domestic violence. Thus, under the dominant approach, the courts may insist that a group plead the smallest increments of jurisdiction, such as the prevention of violence or the punishment of people who have been violent towards Indigenous women.[131] Once a court has identified the correct (narrow) characterization of the claim, it would require detailed evidence that violence against women, its prevention, and the punishment of people who engage in it were 'integral to the distinctive culture of the Aboriginal group claiming the right.'[132]

At this point, the test gets exceedingly problematic for any Indigenous group claiming domestic violence jurisdiction. For example, for an Indigenous group to succeed in proving its claim it would have to demonstrate that violence against women and proactive responses to this problem were vital to the means by which it sustained itself prior to European contact.[133] It would have to show that its society would have been 'fundamentally altered' if it did not abuse women and prevent or punish people who were violent towards them.[134] In addition, it would be essential for an Indigenous group to introduce detailed proof of such facts in support of its claim, because a significant number of Aboriginal rights cases have not succeeded due to findings that insufficient evidence was presented at each stage of the test.[135] Notice the requirements for *a priori*, conceptual categorizations of Aboriginal rights mandated by the Court's test.

The spectacle of such a case about violence against women and the evidence it would highlight is difficult to imagine. First, a group would likely have to produce both oral and written history demonstrating the structural nature of violence against women in traditional Aboriginal society prior to European contact and its responses to it. Thus, lawyers would likely have to introduce gruesome and widespread examples of pre-contact violence towards women along with proactive (preventative or punitive) responses in order to it to show its 'centrality' to the community. To further complicate proof of jurisdiction, a community would next have to establish a 'reasonable degree of continuity' of violence and response from contact to the present day, and demonstrate that modern practices of violence towards women, and responses to it, have essential similarities to past violence.[136] An Indigenous group claiming this right would thus find itself spending millions of dollars on experts and legal fees to shame themselves before the courts with such evidence.[137]

It is difficult to contemplate the prospect that any Indigenous group would be willing to sustain such an inquiry due to the stereotypes it could generate or reinforce in the public consciousness. Images of Indigenous men living in the pre-contact forests of North America marginalizing, sexually assaulting, beating, and killing Indigenous women would be difficult for any community to highlight, even if their purpose was to focus on remedial practices. Furthermore, even if a group surprisingly decided to expose themselves to this process and managed to escape the media circus raised by such evidence, they would still be faced with the next-to-impossible task of demonstrating that such activities, and proactive or defensive responses to them, made their society what it was.[138]

Not to put too fine of a point on this process, but it is both racist and sexist in the extreme to require Indigenous peoples to subject themselves to this spectacle in order to prove that they have inherent constitutional power to prevent and sanction members of their communities who are violent towards women today. Violence against women has been deeply rooted in many societies throughout the ages,[139] yet non-Aboriginal governments do not have to subject themselves to this historical analysis in order to exercise jurisdiction.[140] The process Indigenous peoples would have to follow to take effective legislative and judicial action in this sphere reveals a deep defect in Canada's constitutional jurisprudence; it is a flawed tradition. The Court's jurisprudence illustrates how reliance on so-called essentially integral characteristics diminishes freedom. It stands in the way of Indigenous women and their governments pursuing good lives.[141] These arguments reduce Indigenous governments and their constitutional status to the crudest caricatures and stereotypes, characterizing Indigenous peoples as innocent children of the land or as brutal, uncivilized savages of the forest.[142] These stereotypes should be rejected.

Yet, according to the dominant reading of section 35(1) of the constitution, it would be necessary to frame discussions of violence against women in precisely this way. Section 35(1) requires Indigenous people to claim that their societies possessed fundamental characteristics prior to European contact. Under the Court's test, for Indigenous peoples to properly follow the jurisprudence, they must demonstrate *a priori* (in this case prior to European arrival) violence against Indigenous women. One would hate to think this is the point of section 35(1) – to shamefully essentialize and marginalize Indigenous governments. It is hard to imagine that section 35(1)'s purpose would prevent Indigenous peoples from addressing their most pressing legal and social issues – particularly when reconciliation and decolonization are presumed constitutional goals.[143] Thus, the Supreme Court's current approach cannot be right, particularly when one remembers that the gender equality provisions of section 35(4) are part of this constitutional mix. In light of the foregoing analysis, it is clear that the 'integral to a distinctive culture test' is fatally flawed when read in light of the constitution's broader structure and purpose, and in the face of present-day needs.[144] It constructs a false tradition, which stands in the way of people living freer lives.

ii) Violence against Women and Treaties

Now that we have examined how violence against women would be addressed under the dominant Aboriginal rights jurisprudence, we will briefly examine how treaty rights might be deployed to deal with the same issue. We will see that the constitution's treaty provisions are just as problematic as its so-called Aboriginal rights protections. The Court's treaty jurisprudence also emphasizes questionably essentialized historic experience (rather than engaging meaningfully with the real-world, contemporary challenges faced by Indigenous women and Indigenous communities today).

At present, treaty rights must be proved by reference to an *a priori* first principle: the common intention between the relevant parties at the time the agreement was made.[145] If a claimed right was not 'within the contemplation of the parties to the treaties,' it will not be recognized and affirmed under section 35(1).[146] Thus, in order for Indigenous peoples to succeed in claiming that they exercised jurisdiction over people who were violent towards women, they would have to prove that such power was naturally within the contemplation of the parties when the treaty was signed.[147] Once this claim is proven, the Indigenous group would next have to establish that the specific manner in which Aboriginal peoples wanted to exercise the right was a 'logical evolution' of the traditional practice contemplated by the signers of the treaty.[148] The scope of such evolution, however, must occur 'within limits [since their] subject matter cannot be wholly transformed.'[149] While the court will interpret treaties in a large, liberal, and generous manner, resolving ambiguities in favour of Indians,[150] it will not recognize treaty rights unrelated to historic context,[151] as we discussed in greater detail in chapter 4.

As one might imagine, establishing Indigenous jurisdiction in relation to violence against women on the basis of this test would likely be difficult. There is no explicit treaty language guaranteeing a right to deal with violence against women. As a result, a court would have to inquire into whether this power was implied by the broader context of the treaty.[152] Such intention may be difficult to discern, given that First Nations and the Crown were not often bargaining about the other party's internal relations, particularly on the Indigenous side of the agreement;[153] they were largely focused on rights to land, trade, and resources.[154] They simply did not negotiate an entire way of life or how they would live together in the future.[155] Thus, it would be exceedingly unfair to construe an agreement's silences as a surrender of jurisdiction related to the health, safety, and welfare of women in Indigenous communities.[156]

Since Indigenous peoples owned the land and exercised governance powers prior to European arrival, treaties should be seen as a grant of rights from Indians to the Crown, leaving Indians with a residual claim over all jurisdictions not ceded through negotiations.[157] Furthermore, women's rights were not likely within the contemplation of non-Aboriginal negotiators when treaties were signed, given the troubling attitudes towards women in English common law.[158] While courts may attempt to construe the peace and order clauses in the numbered treaties as recognizing jurisdiction in this broad way,[159] the Supreme Court has given guidance on this point, stating that that '"generous" rules of interpretation should not be confused with a vague sense of after-the-fact largesse.'[160] In making this observation, we see that the Court once again fails to apply Canada's living-tree metaphor to treaty rights under Canada's constitution. The Court's (ab)originalism, even within treaty cases, discriminates against Indigenous peoples, because it denies them the more generous standard applied in all other constitutional cases. Given the judiciary's hesitancy to recognize broad jurisdiction in relation to other claims,[161] it is unlikely that treaties will be a source of Indigenous power to deal with violence against women.[162] As in the case of Indigenous rights, this too represents a significant flaw in Canada's current reading of the constitution.

D. Conclusion

As the above review demonstrates, the Court's dominant interpretation of treaty rights flowing from section 35(1) contains many similarities to the test for Aboriginal rights. In order to succeed, claims in both categories must be rooted in historical understandings of the right at the time of European interaction (through either contact or negotiation). There are significant problems with this approach, as discussed above. It relies upon and reproduces many false traditions. Fortunately, genuine alternatives are available for construing Aboriginal and treaty rights within the existing jurisprudence that would allow Indigenous peoples to possess greater responsibility for addressing violence against women. As discussed in previous chapters, there are at least two related strands of contemporary law that could be applied to hold that Indigenous peoples retain rights to exercise jurisdiction in relation to violence against women.

First, as discussed in chapter 4, the courts could reject the idea that Aboriginal and treaty rights must be solely rooted in the past.[163] They could instead apply living-tree jurisprudence in recognizing and affirming Aboriginal and treaty rights under section 35(1). Interpreting section 35(1) as part of Canada's living tree would help eliminate the flawed jurisprudence relating to Aboriginal and treaty rights relating to violence against women.[164] If living-tree principles were applied to Indigenous peoples, the needs of Indigenous women in the present context could be addressed without reference to the Court's (ab) originalism.

Second, even if the Court applied (ab)orginalism it could assume that Indigenous governments possessed jurisdictional responsibility for the health, safety, and well-being of their members,[165] including Indigenous women, without requiring strict proof of such power.[166] These are reasonable assumptions, given how jurisdiction is generally treated in the wider Canadian context.[167] As noted, there is also the legal justification for the exercise of native self-governance on this basis in other jurisdictions.[168] Even with the Canadian Supreme Court's own jurisprudential record, there have been moments when Indigenous peoples were assumed to exercise broader jurisdictional powers.[169] Indigenous peoples were 'organized in societies' prior to the arrival of Europeans, and this could imply that Indigenous governance, which includes the power to deal with violence against women (in an admittedly imperfect way),[170] was an important element of their 'pre-contact' societies.[171] It could be argued that these governance powers were not voluntarily surrendered as a result of the Crown's own assertion of sovereignty.[172] In this light, Indigenous women could claim Aboriginal rights to safety within their societies under the doctrine of continuity. This approach does not require Indigenous peoples to prove the historical exercise of each small increment of jurisdiction under the 'integral to a distinctive culture' test. It also demonstrates that Canada's constitution does not have to be read in ways that are inconsistent with its broader aims. *Pamajewon* does not have to be the last word in defining Aboriginal governance rights under section 35(1),[173] and the prominence of the doctrine of continuity could be an important antidote to the flaws outlined earlier in this section.[174]

While aspects of section 35(1)'s current internal workings could be invoked to address violence against women, considering the power of Indigenous peoples' own responsibilities in this field could also enhance freedom. As noted in the U.S. context, Indigenous laws and philosophies can provide important standards for judgment, which could be effectively applied to address violence against women. The exercise of Indigenous jurisdiction can help to facilitate a process pluralism that is consistent with the book's thesis, which rejects single-source or single-path approaches for dealing with Indigenous issues.[175] It is important to argue and act 'in the alternative.' When Indigenous peoples deploy their own laws alongside other authorities in this field, they develop practically creative alternatives for dealing with violence within their communities. They also generate diverse viewpoints in addressing the problems they encounter, which also provides further resources for decision-making.[176] Again, this is a key to this book's thesis. It demonstrates that Indigenous law has many sources, is subject to healthy disagreements, and can be a living, dynamic, non-essentialized resource for reasoning.[177]

Thus, we should abandon traditions that regard violence against women as lying within the sole purview of federal or provincial governments.[178] Violence against Indigenous women is a very complex and serious socio-legal issue that has significant implications for how jurisdiction, law, and legal traditions are taught, practised, critiqued, and reformulated.[179] This chapter has argued that violence against

Indigenous women must be confronted at all levels of society. In particular, this issue should be addressed from a jurisdictional perspective, since violence is linked to the inequalities Indigenous peoples face within Indigenous communities and Canadian society more generally.

Unfortunately, as noted, at least two stereotypes stand in the way of such action. One is the misperception that Indigenous communities would be incapable of effectively addressing this issue due the high levels of violence they encounter. The second relates to the courts' interpretive misperception that history must be the sole source of Indigenous jurisdictional claims under section 35(1) of the constitution. While there are important truths underlying each viewpoint (violence within communities does raise distinct challenges in dealing with this issue, and attentiveness to history is crucial, though not determinative, in understanding Aboriginal and treaty rights), current tests overstate their case.

In view of this, this chapter has attempted to calibrate a more precise and nuanced approach to dealing with violence against Indigenous women in the light of broader policy and jurisprudential possibilities.[180] In taking this path, I must once again reiterate one of this book's central themes: no single theory is likely to capture the entirety of what must be taken into account when working with Indigenous legal issues. This includes theories and approaches that place jurisdictional issues related to violence against Indigenous women at their centre. As helpful as most theories may be in particular contexts, the world of Indigenous politics is much more complicated than single approaches usually allow. Across-the-board theories reach their limits at some point in their application. I maintain that this would occur even within the realm of Indigenous feminist theory, with its significant potential for important insight and action on many fronts. Any striving to own and control ourselves and our relationships (*dibenindizowin*), and live out our own visions of life (*mino-bimaadiziwin*), suggests that we should regard any single approach as partial, limited, and open to manipulation if it is used to conceal or eclipse other fields of inquiry. I would suggest that this is the case even in relation to the issues discussed in this chapter. It should be triangulated with approaches found elsewhere in this book, and beyond. This must be done to ensure that the insights found in this chapter remain a contextual resource for reasoning, and not an absolute necessity or prohibition in dealing with violence against women, or any other Indigenous issue raised in this book.

Conclusion

This book began by describing Anishinaabe practices of *dibenindizowin* (freedom) and *mino-bimaadiziwin* (good-life). These teachings aim to help people responsibly own and influence how they interact with others. In this light, they are focused on facilitating the pursuit of a good life. Through each chapter, I have argued that there is no one idea or practice which necessarily results in *dibenindizowin* or *mino-bimaadiziwin*. This occurred through examining practices of mobility, direct action, constitutional formation, constitutional interpretation, legislative creation, and gendered constitutionalism. In these discussions, I have attempted to demonstrate how freedom and the pursuit of a good life are multifaceted and contingent activities. They are context-dependent and best pursued in relational ways.

Furthermore, I have argued that freedom and the pursuit of a good life must always be realized within 'traditional' spaces, even as I have subjected these spaces to critique. Some of these spaces are explicit about which traditions are in play in any given situation. Other 'traditional' spaces implicitly configure the background circumstances in which actions are taken, and thus are far more difficult to identify and control. They can impose unnecessary constraints even as they might also enhance our lives. This includes those traditions which are related to Canadian legal and political life. Since there is no constitutional, Indigenous, or other space which is tradition-free, we must regularly interrogate how we receive and act upon them in real-world contexts. Though I do not claim this is universally true, this point may also hold for traditions beyond those discussed in this book, as found in the areas of economic, religious, psychological, and scientific life. We must seek out those traditions that enhance our relationships and increase our abilities to live in accordance with our own dreams, while simultaneously rejecting any tradition which thwarts the realization of these goals. We must attend to the physicality of our circumstances, even as we reach towards more emancipatory generalizations and alternatives. This book has argued that Indigenous legal traditions should be key referents in making these choices.

In this context, I conclude this book by relating an Anishinaabe story to illustrate and summarize these themes. This story is an important resource for understanding the pursuit of freedom and a good life. As with most Anishinaabe teachings, there are many cross-cutting and contradictory lessons within its narrative structure. As time and circumstances change, new insights can emerge from the story as its lessons are transformed through their application in real-world settings. These experiences then create feedback loops that further deepen our understanding about how to challenge and work within our varied traditions.

The story I will relate is most prominently told by Dr. Basil Johnston, an Elder from my reserve. It is about a character known as Pitchii and it is found in his book *Ojibway Heritage*.[1] While the story is old and recounts other people's experiences, and summarizes this book's constitutional themes, it is also, partially, a story about my own life. It has become part of my family's broader experiences, though it originates in another time and place. The story does not just communicate an abstract set of ideas; it has continually re-embedded itself in my family's history throughout the years. As a result, the story has a lived, physical dimension, even as it contains speculative themes. I must also point out that it is not *the* story of my life. Other stories compete for my attention and cause me to reject it as the 'fundamental' life lesson. The story is not necessarily applicable across all space and time. It must be triangulated with other stories and experiences. I have learned to be cautious of single stories as guides for action, including the following story. I apply these caveats even as I believe this story contains very important lessons in the particular circumstances discussed in this book.

Despite these qualifications, I have noted that this story was present in the lives of my great-grandparents, grandparents, and parents.[2] It is physically rooted in the contours of our experiences. I saw it in relation to my own mother and father. I first told my daughters this story when they started elementary school. I know they heard it many times through the intervening years. I distinctly recall telling my youngest daughter about Pitchii when she started secondary school. I also remember recounting it as she was leaving for college half a continent away.[3] The last time I formally told her the story was immediately before she started law school. I was teaching in Val Napoleon's Indigenous Law Clinic at the University of Victoria Law School and my youngest daughter was in that group. Each time I told the story, I wanted her to recognize that she was free to pursue her own paths in life. While I had hopes about how she might help others through her education, I wanted her to pursue her own vision. Thus, I hoped the story would help her sift through what she learned. I wanted her to choose to live by those traditions that would most help her respectfully own herself and her relationships. Conversely, I hoped she would reject paths that lead away from these possibilities, including what she had learned in our family – if these teachings led her away from a good, responsible, relational life.

As my daughter was on the cusp of these educational adventures, I never directly told her that I hoped she would be open to rejecting or transforming what she learned from us, though I am sure she figured this out. I did not want to be an overbearing father. I was trying to live in accordance with the best traditions of Anishinaabe fatherhood, about which I was continually learning. My sister had completed her PhD on Ojibway fathering practices at Kansas State University and I learned a lot from her on this subject.[4] My wife was also my best support in helping me pursue this goal. Furthermore, I have become intrigued by the old Anishinaabe word for father: *noo-se*. My friend Basil defines the word *noo-se* as meaning 'one that creates paths which make it easier for his family to follow.' When I learned this word, I was asked to imagine a man walking through deep snow. As he blazed a trail through snow or ice-encrusted terrains, his children would find it easier to move. They would find sustenance as a result of his efforts. Fathers who were successful in helping to nurture their children in this way would eventually see them move onto their own paths, strengthened by their experiences in walking with him. At this point, children would then make their own trails, thus helping others who followed in their wake too, and renewing the cycle of life once again. This was my greatest desire as a father, though I am sure I have fallen far short of my goals many times. Thus, when I told my daughter the story of Pitchii, I did not interpret what I hoped she would learn from it. Constitutional law is a personal, family, clan, and national affair.

While aspects of the story are not particularly subtle upon first hearing, I wanted my daughter to be as free as possible in receiving the story. I wanted her to find her own meanings. Thus, as I mentioned, I did not initially speculate on how the story might apply to her experience at school. I did not tell her the story was not just about her or our family, but that it was about entire nations and peoples, and how they interact with one another. It is the story told in this book. Of course, it was also about so much more. My interpretive silence was in accordance with my usual approach with these kinds of stories. As noted, Anishinaabe stories convey numerous meanings that can vary through time, thereby assisting us in different seasons of our lives. I reminded myself that these stories' meanings were primarily for my daughters to determine. While I might introduce the characters and conflict in a story, and spin them in a certain way, they had their own responsibility to create proper applications for themselves and others. In any event, I knew I would not be present to help them interpret life in their new settings, nor did I have any desire to run their lives. Furthermore, I recognized that their circumstances would be very different from what I imagined they would encounter. My abstractions and *a priori* assumptions about their educational choices would probably not serve them well, even though I have been around universities for many years. They would have to learn how to act in the context of their new surroundings. While I was also happy to offer my own tentative observations, should they ask for them, most often they would have to choose from this and other stories to determine how to best govern themselves. I could only hope I had provided a sufficient range of possibilities from which they could choose, which placed freedom and goodness within their grasp.

In discussing this pedagogy, I should note that there are times I am very direct in my teaching (and writing). As this book has maintained, freedom is often best enhanced if we are open to alternative ways of acting well in the world, as we perceive each context's demands. There are a variety of pedagogies within Anishinaabe thought. I would not want my daughters or future readers to essentialize Anishinaabe teaching methods as always taking a somewhat indirect form. I and other Anishinaabe people obviously teach in more direct ways, choosing from a spectrum of approaches to facilitate learning that suits each occasion. However, in the context of my daughter's circumstances, at the start of distinct educational journeys, I thought that recounting the story in this manner would best help her on her way.[5] Since the message might not have been immediately clear, I hoped it would encourage further contemplation, broader study, and self-examination, *through time.*

Since lessons found within stories are not 'once-and-for-all' conclusive determinations, their meanings are worked out through deliberation, negotiation, and comprise, as circumstances continually change around us. In this regard, this form of Anishinaabe storytelling is a practice of physical philosophy that engages the democratic impulses related to freedom described throughout this book.

Thus, in line with this approach, I will not provide any further commentary in this book, after I recount Pitchii's story.[6] I hope independent ideas about the story will emerge from each reader that (either positively or negatively) relate to the significance of the themes discussed in this book. As has been my goal throughout this work, my purpose is to facilitate practices of *dibenindizowin* and *mino-bimaadiziwin*, and the uptake or abandonment of Indigenous and other legal traditions relevant to these themes.

Pitchii

Akii and Niibi were from different Nations. They met and fell in love despite their differences, or perhaps even because of them. Niibi was continually on the move, with only the winds and woodlands for company. Akii lived with her people, and was at the centre of their every gathering. She was strong and her life was stable. They never would have met but for their sense of obligation. For a time, Niibi left his peripatetic life to follow a great teacher. Akii left the comfort of her village in response to the same voice. When they met, their love came quickly, and it was not long before their hearts were knit together.

Akii and Niibi soon married and moved to a new place. It was his great-grandfather's traditional territory, but it had changed in the last hundred years. It now was a crowded place. People spoke many languages and their ways were varied and confusing. This wasn't the quiet forest, nor was it the familiar village. They weren't quite sure how to relate to those around them. It was a peculiar place. Nevertheless, Akii and Niibi were happy, lost together in their new world.

In time, a child was born to them. Pitchii came a year after their marriage. He was a quiet child, coming into the world with long, black hair, fair skin, and exceedingly delicate features. Pitchii was an old soul, and his piercing brown eyes captured every detail as life unfolded around him. He was different from the other children. His watchfulness made others uncomfortable. His parents barely noticed. They loved him deeply. They did all they could to make his life full.

When Pitchii was five years old, his father decided to teach him new skills. Niibi longed for his son to follow his ways. He wanted him to develop his own flowing ability of quickly moving through the world – running, jumping, and throwing. This is what made Niibi happy in his youth. It gave him the freedom to master his world. Niibi wanted his son to excel at athletics. He wanted his boy to be the best at every sport.

Akii, ever pragmatic, solidly stable, was concerned about Niibi's plans. They spoke often of Niibi's intentions. 'I think he is gifted in this way. He won't be a real son of mine,' Niibi argued, 'unless he properly masters these skills.' This was the couple's first quarrel. Akii did the best she could to change her husband's mind, but it was to no avail.

Every day, Niibi taught Pitchii what he knew about rushing head-long into the world. They spoke of victory, winning, and fame. Energy surged through them like a flood. They would frenetically practise, and then they would sit down and review the bounds of each sport. 'You must understand each rule in its proper light, Pitchii, if you want to win these games. It is the only way you'll succeed in each contest.' Pitchii enjoyed the attention of his father. The hours they spent together felt like minutes. They were happy together. Pitchii absorbed Niibi's every teaching and worked his hardest to please him.

Then, in the evenings, when the formal lessons were over, Niibi would leave his son alone. During these stolen moments, Pitchii would practise what he had been taught by his father. Pursuing his own rigorous course of exercise, he pushed himself to his limits each time.

As the young boy grew, he became strong. The contests he entered were his to win. He was powerful. He could easily defeat his opponents, but every so often he would let others cross the line before him. He would let them jump and throw further. He wanted others to succeed. While he enjoyed each event, his heart was just not set on winning.

In time, Niibi noticed his son's approach. He saw how he'd hold back and let others take first place. This angered the father and he redoubled his efforts. Niibi's intensity would overflow. It would almost overwhelm his son. For a time, the pressure worked, but Pitchii would eventually hold back in a contest or two, and let others enjoy the thrill of accomplishment and success.

Eventually, Niibi realized his son would never be the best athlete. He talked to Akii and she encouraged him to let the boy find his own course. Niibi agreed, and said he would teach his son to be the most spiritual person in the land, if he would not be the best athlete. Akii protested, and said that is not what she meant, but Niibi barely lis-tened. He set out to raise his son to a higher life.

'I've noticed how you help others in your games, Pitchii. It's an admi-rable quality to want others to succeed. I've decided to train you to be the most spiritual person in the land. Let's get to work.' With these words, Pitchii, now ten years old, joined his father in another rigorous course of study. Niibi taught his son everything he knew about how to be free and how to live well. Over the next two years, he had his son memorize every prayer, song, and ceremony that his people knew. 'You must learn the proper way to understand these teachings, Pitchii. There is only one way to get it right. If you don't understand these principles in their purest form, you will not succeed. You must grasp their essence.'

Pitchii was an excellent student. He committed to memory every idea that was placed before him. Through time, he came to understand every rite associated with his tradition. He also continued to enjoy his father's attention. He did what he could to please him. While the young boy sometimes wished he could learn more about the songs, his father would discourage him when he raised the point. So Pitchii followed his father's will. He became very knowledgeable about his people's spirituality.

The day came when it was time for the young boy to practise the teachings he had learned. Pitchii was now fourteen, the age at which young boys would seek their vision quest. Niibi had his son prepare a shelter in the appointed place. 'Here you will stay for four days while you fast. Our preparation will surely bring you a great vision. I will return in four days to hear of your success.' Niibi then left the young boy to his duties.

Four days later, Niibi returned.

Pitchii was dejected and it was evident to the father that his son had not received a vision. This also discouraged Niibi, and he vowed he would redouble his efforts to assist his son.

The next year, they repeated many of the same teachings from the previous twelve months. While Pitchii still enjoyed his lessons and time with his father, there were times he felt weary of his subject. It felt so isolating to live as he did. He was lonely; he wanted to live among oth-ers and practise what he was learning. He wanted to experience life in other ways. He tried to speak to his father about his feelings but Niibi would not entertain any debate. So the young man kept working, doing all he could to keep building their relationship.

Thus, a year later, when Pitchii again returned to the site of the ceremony, father and son looked forward to a great manifestation. Each was excited about what lie before them, and Niibi left his son for the four-day ritual.

Four days later, when Niibi returned, he immediately knew his son had not seen a vision. It was as before. Niibi felt more work was needed. He suspected his son was still not thinking about their teachings in the proper way. He vowed to stress, ever more deeply, the right way to meditate on their sacred laws. He promised his son they would not deviate from their path. Thus, as before, the training recommenced. Pitchii obediently followed his father, though he was tiring of his lessons. When his father was not around, the young boy turned his attention to his songs and other entertainment. He liked the creativity that flowed through them. Pitchii was caught a few times lingering over the songs he was learning and his father scolded him for it.

The following year, as Pitchii fasted, the result was the same. No vision. Thus, another year of training took place as the young man kept preparing to succeed at his father's quest. At the end of this year – the fourth one – Pitchii was again prepared to fast.

Pitchii was now sixteen. He had been in intensive training with his father for four years. He could perfectly recite every rite but he was slowly growing to be a very unhappy young man. The past year had been a struggle with his father. At times, they even fought with one another. Niibi took his son's budding resistance as evidence that the young man needed further discipline. Now they were at the place of visions for the fourth time.

'I will leave you as before, and return in four days. I am sure you will be successful this time.' As they parted, Pitchii awkwardly tried to hug his father. Niibi half-heartedly reciprocated.

Four days later Niibi returned. It was early in the morning.

Niibi could see no sign of his son.

Niibi sat down to wait for Pitchii to return, thinking that his fast might have taken him into the surrounding woods. He noticed the beauty of the day. A brightly coloured bird was singing above him, the wind was calm, and fragrant cedars surrounded the clearing. It reminded him of his time before marriage. He had spent years alone in similar settings. Now he felt alone again.

Niibi waited through the morning, increasingly worried as time passed. He began searching around the site, trying to find some sign of his son's whereabouts. As afternoon turned into evening, Niibi began to despair. Perhaps some evil has come upon my son, he thought to himself. But I'll wait here longer; maybe he'll come back under the moon. All through the night, Niibi worried, and he tossed and turned through a short, fitful sleep.

The next morning, the sun dawned brightly. Niibi was awakened by the song of a nearby bird, greeting the new day. Thinking his son had returned, Niibi momentarily felt a thrill of excitement in the sound. The father roused himself and once again searched around the camp, yet he found no sign of Pitchii.

Niibi walked home dejectedly. He told his wife of their son's disappearance and Akii was heartbroken. Niibi returned the next day to the site of his son's camp. It was as empty as before. Niibi repeated his vigil each day over the next month, finding nothing each time. Except for the bird-song, a strange silence had fallen over the place of visions. Niibi could hardly bear to be there anymore, his loss was so profound. Nevertheless, Niibi kept his watch over the place, returning each month, searching for a sign of his son's whereabouts.

Months turned into years, and Pitchii did not return. Niibi began wandering further from the site he last saw his son. He searched far and wide for Pitchii through the years, but no one reported ever seeing him. Except for the brief times he returned to Akii, Niibi lived a lonely, isolated life. Sadness filled his soul.

The years turned into decades, as Niibi wandered the earth.

Forty years later, on the anniversary of Pitchii's disappearance, Niibi returned to the vision site as usual. Bowed over with age, the old man fell to ground in front of the lodge.

As he lay on the earth, he looked up and noticed a bird singing in the tree above the lodge. It was here each time he visited. He remembered it had been his only companion over his years returning in this place.

Suddenly, a flash of light blurred Niibi's vision and his son stood before him.

The old man looked at Pitchii in disbelief. 'Ningosis. Son. Aandi gaa-ezhayan? Where have you been all these years?' was all he could manage to say.

Pitchii smiled. 'I have always been here father. Yet you never saw me. Every time you returned I tried to catch your attention, but you wouldn't listen to me. I didn't receive the vision like you wanted, all those years ago. I took a different course. I have been trying to tell you who I am.'

Niibi looked at his son with new eyes, a vague understanding washing over him.

Pitchii continued, 'The day you left me here, so long ago, I tried praying as you taught me. I recited the words exactly – truly – just as you wanted. It was to no avail. There was no power in them for me. They meant nothing, just empty words. But as I began singing our songs in my own way, my soul suddenly found a new voice. I discovered they could be sung differently.

'At that moment, I seemed suddenly transfused with light. An orange glow encircled me. It grew brighter as it radiated out from me. Suffused within this presence, I looked around; the colour was brilliant, eventually fading out to black at the outer edges. I felt renewed. It was like nothing I had ever experienced. I was taken up, lifted over the lodge. I had found my heart-song. I was transformed. My own voice was different from anything we had memorized. It grew as I experimented, and exchanged voices with other birds in the woods.

'When you returned to get me that day, years ago, I was here. You didn't recognize me. I saw your confusion, your anger, your melancholy. I witnessed your sadness. I tried to reach out to you but you wouldn't hear me. You never recognized my presence.

'Each year when you returned, I was here. I grew in joy with my newfound love. Life was good. My songs echoed through the woods and made people happy. I joined with others and I was free. My family has always surrounded you. They have been with you each morning as you rose. We have always been here. We have always been here. We are the keepers of the eastern door. We greet the sun as it rises each day. From the tops of the trees we practise our songs. We sing for everyone who will hear us, and learn our story. We are Pitchiiwak – the robins.'

Notes

Miigwech

1 An earlier version of the first chapter was published as John Borrows, 'Physical Philosophy: Mobility and the Future of Indigenous Rights,' in *Indigenous Peoples and the Law: Comparative and Critical Perspectives*, ed. Shin Imai, Kent McNeil, and Ben Richardson (Oxford: Hart Publishing, 2009). Earlier drafts of parts of chapter 2 were published in John Borrows, 'An Analysis of and Dialogue on Indigenous and Crown Blockades,' in *Philosophy and Aboriginal Rights: Critical Dialogues*, ed. Sandra Tomsons and Lorraine Mayer (Toronto: Oxford University Press, 2013). Chapter 3 is a revised version of John Borrows, 'Aboriginal Political Advocacy and the Canadian Constitution,' in *Indians in Contemporary Society: Handbook of North American Indians*, vol. 2, ed. Garrick Bailey (Washington: Smithsonian Institution, 2008). Pieces of the second chapter were posted on the Web by the Ontario government; see John Borrows, *Crown and Aboriginal Occupations of Land: A History and Comparison*, October 2005, http://www.attorneygeneral.jus.gov.on.ca/inquiries/ipperwash/policy_part/research/pdf/History_of_Occupations_Borrows.pdf; John Borrows, *Seven Generations, Seven Teachings: Ending the Indian Act*, May 2008, at http://fngovernance.org/resources_docs/7_Generations_7_Teachings.pdf.

2 For instance, an earlier version of chapter 4 appeared in *From Recognition to Reconciliation: Essays on the Constitutional Entrenchment of Aboriginal and Treaty Rights*, ed. Patrick Macklem and Douglas Sanderson (Toronto: University of Toronto Press, 2016). Chapters 5 and 6 were revised from articles published in the *Supreme Court Law Review* and the *Osgoode Hall Law Journal*: see John Borrows, '(Ab)Originalism and Canada's Constitution' (2012) 58 *Supreme Court Law Review* 351–98; John Borrows, 'Aboriginal and Treaty Rights and Violence against Women' (2013) 50(3) *Osgoode Hall Law Journal* 699–736.

Introduction

1 Franz Boas observed, 'The causal conditions of cultural happenings lie always in the interaction between individuals and society, and no classificatory study of societies will solve this problem.' Franz Boas, 'The Aims of Anthropological Research,' in *Race, Language and Culture* (Chicago: University of Chicago Press, 1940) at 256.

2 U.S. Census Bureau, The American Indian and Alaska Native Population: 2010 17 tbl. 7 (2010), http://www.census.gov/prod/cen2010/briefs/c2010br-10.pdf.

3 Statistics Canada, *Aboriginal Peoples and Language, National Household Survey*, 2011, http://www12.statcan.gc.ca/nhs-enm/2011/as-sa/99-011-x/99-011-x2011003_1-eng.pdf at 7.

4 See Helen Hornbeck Tanner, *Atlas of Great Lakes Indian History* (Norman: University of Oklahoma Press, 1982) at 58–9.

5 Ibid.

6 See Diamond Jeness, *The Indians of Canada* (Ottawa: Queen's Printer, 1967) at 277.

7 People of the Three Fires are now found in other places in North America. Odawa people live in Kansas and Oklahoma because of the Removal Policies of the U.S. government in earlier periods. Potawatomi people also live in Oklahoma for the same reason, though there are some communities in their traditional territories in Michigan and Wisconsin. Contemporary Ojibway communities can also be found surrounding Lakes Superior and Michigan, and on the north shores of Lakes Erie and Ontario.

8 In this book, I develop the point that tradition can be used to poison or remedy our circumstances. The issue thus becomes how tradition is used; see Jacques Derrida, 'Plato's Pharmacy,' in *Dissemination*, trans. Barbara Johnson (London: The Athlone Press, 1981) at 125–7.

9 Leanne Simpson, *Dancing on Our Turtle's Back: Stories of Nishnaabeg Re-Creation, Resurgence, and a New Emergence* (Winnipeg: Arbeiter Ring, 2011) at chap. 4: 'Within Indigenous thought, there is not a singular vision of resurgence, but there are many.'

10 For a discussion of unique communication patterns within some Ojibway communities, see Roger Spielman, *You're So Fat: Exploring Ojibwe Discourse* (Toronto: University of Toronto Press, 1998).

11 Ibid. at 107–28.

12 These are not Basil Johnston's exact words, but the essence of them to the best of my recollection. I later found a similar sentiment expressed in Basil Johnston, *Honour Mother Earth* (Cape Croker Indian Reserve, ON: Kegedonce Press, 2003) at 147:

To our ancestors it was self-evident that all creatures were born equal and free to come and go and fulfil their purposes as intended by Kitchi-Manitou. All were entitled to a place on this earth where they might raise their off-spring and offer thanksgiving to the Creator.

Kitchi-Manitou has done no less for men and women. The Creator has made us equal, given us freedom to come and go, a place to grow in spirit and nurture our dreams, and leave to talk to the manitous in our way whenever it was meant to do so.

And so the Anishinaubeak came and went as they pleased ...

13 I have explored these interdependencies elsewhere in John Borrows, 'Landed Citizenship: Narratives of Aboriginal Political Participation,' in *Citizenship in Diverse Societies*, ed. Will Kymlicka (Oxford: Oxford University Press, 2000); reprinted in *Citizenship, Diversity and Pluralism*, ed. Alan Cairns (Montreal: McGill-Queen's University Press, 2000).

14 See D'Arcy Rheault, *Anishinaabe Mino-Bimaadiziwin: The Way of a Good Life* (Peterborough, ON: Debwewin Press, 1999). Anishinaabe author Winona LaDuke has written that *mino-bimaadiziwin* is central to Anishinaabe value systems. She observed that

in minobimaatisiiwin, we honor one another, we honor women as the givers of lives, we honor our Chi-Anishinabeg, our old people and ancestors who hold the knowledge. We honor our children as the continuity from generations, and we honor ourselves as a part of creation. Implicit in mino-bimaatisiiwin is a continuous habitation of place, an intimate understanding of the relationship between humans and the ecosystem and of the need to maintain this balance.

Winona LaDuke, 'Minobimaatisiiwin: The Good Life,' (1992) 16(4) *Cultural Survival Quarterly* 69–72.

15 *Mino-bimaadiziwin* has been described as 'the substantive form of the verb that indicates to "move by" or "move along" ... [which] can be rather flatly translated as "life" or "living" but a richer rendering shows it to be a window into the traditional goal of Ojibwe religion: to live well and to live long in this world, and this is in contrast to eschatological traditions stressing the afterlife for the transformation of the natural world.' See Michael D. McNally, *Honoring Elders: Aging, Authority, and Ojibwe Religion* (New York: Columbia University Press, 2009) at 49.

16 See Thomas Peacock, *The Four Hills of Life: Ojibwe Wisdom* (Afton, MN: Afton Historical Press, 2006) at 105–44; Thomas Peacock and Marlene Wisuri, *Ojibwe: Waasa Inaabidaa, We Look in All Directions* (St. Paul: Minnesota Historical Society, 2009) at 90–111.

17 Thomas Peacock, *The Four Hills of Life* at 105. 'People who live a good life, or *bimaadiziwaad*, can be called "those who have power."' McNally, *Honoring Elders*, at 50.
18 McNally, *Honoring Elders*, at 50.
19 Hannah Arendt, *Between Past and Future* (Toronto: Penguin Books, 2006) at 145.
20 Ibid. at 150.
21 Anishinaabemowin is the original language of the northern and western Great Lakes of North America. Citations to *dibenindisowin* can be found at Frederik Baraga, *Dictionary of the Otchipwe Language* (Cincinnati: Printed for Jos. A. Hermann, 1853) at 110, where Baraga says the word means 'liberty, freedom, independence'; see also the *Ojibwe People's Dictionary*, which gives the meaning 's/he is independent, is h/ own master' for the word *dibenindizowin* at http://ojibwe.lib.umn.edu/main-entry/dibenindizo-vai.
22 Lenore Keeshig-Tobias, quoted in *Contemporary Challenges: Conversations with Canadian Native Authors*, ed. Hartmut Lutz (Saskatoon: Fifth House Publishers, 1991) at 85. Lenore Keeshig-Tobias is an Anishinaabe storyteller from my reservation.
23 William Jones, *Ojibwa Texts*, vol. 1 (New York: E.J. Brill, 1917) at 7. I applied the stealing fire story to Canadian law in John Borrows, *Recovering Canada: The Resurgence of Indigenous Law* (Toronto: University of Toronto Press, 2002) at 74.
24 Basil Johnston, *The Manitous: The Spiritual World of the Ojibway* (Toronto: Key Porter Books, 1995) at 58–69.
25 Johann Georg Kohl, *Kitchi-Gami: Life Among the Lake Superior Ojibway* (St. Paul: Minnesota Historical Society Press, 1985) at 431–8.
26 There are many stories related to the gifts Nanaboozhoo gives to other animals. See 'Nanabush and the Skunk,' in Verna Patronella Johnston, *Tales of Nokomis* (Toronto: Stoddart Publishing, 1975) at 5; 'Nanabushu Breaks the Necks of Dancing Geese,' in William Jones, *Ojibwa Texts* (New York: E.J. Brill, 1917) at 101; Basil Johnston, *Ojibway Heritage* (Toronto: McClelland and Stewart, 1976) at 46–58.
27 Donald Smith, *Sacred Feathers: The Reverend Peter Jones (Kahkewaquonaby) and the Mississauga Indians* (Toronto: University of Toronto Press, 1897) at 23.
28 Peter Jones, *History of the Ojibway Indians with Especial Reference to their Conversion to Christianity* (London: A.W. Bennett, 1861) at 62, 75; Elizabeth Simcoe, *Mrs. Simcoe's Diary*, ed. Mary Q. Innis (Toronto: McMillan Canada, 1965) at 158, 308; Pierre-Francois-Xavier de Charlevoix, *Histoire*

et description generale de la Nouvelle France (Paris: Giffart, 1744) at 3:207 as cited in Smith, *Sacred Feathers* at 267.

29 Oral history, Fred Jones, Neyaashiinigmiing, 17 June 2010.

30 For more information about Margaret McLeod, Charles' mother, see John Borrows, 'A Genealogy of Law: Inherent Sovereignty and First Nations Self-Government' (1992) 30 *Osgoode Hall Law Journal* 291 at 312–18.

31 For a discussion of law and language revitalization, and the importance of 'tongues,' see Lindsay Borrows, *Otter's Journeys: Indigenous Law and Language Revitalization* (Vancouver: UBC Press, under consideration).

32 While patterns must definitely be followed for a person to enjoy the freedom to speak a language, I have learned that strict and essentialized codes for learning can get in the way of fluency.

33 Michel Foucault, 'What is Enlightenment?' in *The Politics of Truth*, ed. Sylvere Lotringer and Lysa Hochroth (New York: Semiotext(e), 1997) at 133.

34 For a discussion of freedom as it relates to capabilities, see Amartya Sen, *The Idea of Justice* (Cambridge: Belnap Press, 2009).

35 What constitutes a 'good life,' and what constitutes such a life has long been a concern of philosophers. Discussions about the good life have long been a staple of philosophical debate. See John Cottingham, *Philosophy and the Good Life: Reason and the Passions in Greek, Cartesian and Psychoanalytical Ethics* (Cambridge: Cambridge University Press, 1998), as well as Indigenous practitioners in this field: Raymond J. DeMalli, ed., *The Sixth Grandfather: Black Elk's Teachings Given to John G. Neighart* (Lincoln: University of Nebraska Press, 1984); Arthur C. Parker, *The Code of Handsome Lake, the Seneca Prophet* (Albany: University of the State of New York, 1913); Dennis H. McPherson and J. Douglas Rabb, *Indian from the Inside: Native American Philosophy and Cultural Renewal* (Jefferson, NC: McFarland, 2011).

36 James Tully expresses the idea in this way:

> A 'limit' can mean either the characteristic forms of thought and action that are taken for granted and not questioned or contested by participants in a practice of subjectivity, thereby functioning as the implicit background or horizon of their questions and contests, or it can mean that a form of subjectivity (its form of reason, norms of conduct and so forth) is explicitly claimed to be a limit that cannot be otherwise because it is universal, necessary or obligatory (the standard form of legitimization since the Enlightenment) … Humans can develop the capacities of thought and action to question and contest both types of limit …

> James Tully, *Democracy and Civic Freedom*, vol. 1 of *Public Philosophy in a New Key* (Cambridge: Cambridge University Press, 2008) at 75.

37 As Michel Foucault has written, 'The problem ... [of politics] is to give oneself the rules of law, the techniques of management, and also the ethics, the *ethos*, the practice of the self, which would allow these games of power to be played with a minimum of domination.' Michel Foucault, in *The Final Foucault*, ed. James Bernauer and David Rasmussen (Cambridge, MA: MIT Press, 1988) at 18, cited in Tully, *Democracy and Civic Freedom* at 121.

38 As James Tully has observed:

> Cultures are interdependent, overlapping and internally complex. Cultures exist in a dynamic process of interaction, negotiation, internal challenge and reinterpretation and transformation. As a result, humans are always members to varying degrees of more than one culture. They experience misunderstandings and differences within their first cultures, such as between genders, generations and classes, that are not completely different in kind from misunderstandings and differences across cultures. Cultural understanding and identity is thus enormously more complex, open-textured, interactive and dynamic that the old vision of closed and homogeneous cultures. So, when Aboriginal and non-Aboriginal people meet on the middle ground, they are not trapped in mutually incommensurable world-views ... Interaction has shaped the cultural identities of both in complex ways.

Tully, *Democracy and Civic Freedom* at 240.

39 Ibid. at 205–9.

40 John Rawls, *Political Liberalism* (New York: Columbia University Press, 2005), citing Tully, *Democracy and Civic Freedom* at 175. In my approach, I am also following Felix Cohen's counsel to turn away from metaphysical legal reasoning; see Felix Cohen, 'Transcendental Nonsense and the Functional Approach' (1935) 35 *Columbia Law Review* 809.

41 Tully, *Democracy and Civic Freedom* at 240.

42 The Anishinaabek call these practices the Seven Grandfathers. For more information about these ideas, see Edward Benton-Banai, *The Mishomis Book: The Voice of the Ojibway* (Hayward, CA: Red School House Publications, 1988) at 64.

43 See Edna Manitowabi, 'Grandmother Teachings,' cited in Simpson, *Dancing on Our Turtle's Back* at 35–9.

44 These teachings stress the importance of living in harmony with all your relations; see Benton-Banai, *The Mishomis Book* at 66. The quest for freedom to live a good life should not essentialize any core aspect of these or other Anishinaabe teachings and traditions.

45 The word *akinoomaage* is composed by combining two roots: *aki* and *noomaage*. *Aki* means 'earth'; *noomaage* means 'to point towards and take direction from.' Thus, philosophical inquiry within Anishinaabe tradition can literally refer to the lessons we learn from understanding the earth. Basil Johnston, personal communication.

46 Anishinaabe language professor and linguist Brenda Fairbanks traced the etymology of *gikinoo'amaage* as follows (personal correspondence, 17 January 2014):

- *gikinaw* – 'learn, know, recognize'
- *i* – 'by instrument'
- *amaw* – 'applicative'
- *ge* – detransitive (to general people)

47 Basil Johnston, *Anishinaube Thesaurus* (East Lansing: Michigan State Press, 2007) at 73.

48 Ogimaawigwanebiik (Nancy Jones), *Gakina Dibaajimowinan Gwayakwaawan* (All Teachings Are Correct), in Great Lakes Fish and Wildlife Commission, *Dibaajimowinaan: Anishinaabe Stories of Culture and Respect* (Odahana, WI: Great Lakes Indian Fish and Wildlife Commission, 2013) at 9–12.

49 Remember that reification prompts us to treat abstractions as if they existed as real and tangible objects.

50 This book resists the acceptance of unjust power relations at every stage of its analysis. While I argue that we should reject state engagement in many instances, I do not essentialize any set of relationships as being invariably negative. I believe absolutist approaches lead us away from potential paths to freedom and a good life when we lock ourselves into structures that do not allow us make nuanced judgments as circumstances may require. Those who view these issues from universalistic and idealistic perspectives will likely reject this approach. Nevertheless, this book contains strong critiques of *imperialist* readings of political life, regardless of whether they are generated through colonial *or anti-colonial* rhetoric.

51 In valuing disagreement, counsel can be taken from the Supreme Court of Canada words: 'Inevitably there will be dissenting voices. A democratic system of government is committed to considering those dissenting voices, and seeking to acknowledge and address those voices in the laws by which all the community must live.' In *Reference Re Secession of Québec*, [1998] 2 S.C.R. 217 at 68. For further discussion about the role of dissent in democracy see Tully, *Democracy and Civic Freedom* at 198.

52 Democracy is evolutionary and is best facilitated when it promotes self-government; accommodates cultural and group identities; appeals to moral values; requires a continuous process of discussion, compromise, negotiation and participation; and rests on a legitimate legal foundation. See *Reference Re Secession of Québec*, [1998] at paras. 63–9.

53 *Canada Act 1982*, U.K., 1982, c. 11. In this respect, the Charter builds upon the Universal Declaration of Human Rights, which states, 'All human beings are born free in dignity and rights.' The Declaration was adopted and proclaimed by General Assembly of the United Nations, Resolution 217 A (III) of 10 December 1948 and is available at http://www.un.org/en/documents/udhr/. For a discussion of the Canadian Charter's connection to the international network of states and peoples see Alan Cairns, *Charter Versus Federalism: The Dilemmas of Constitutional Reform* (Montreal: McGill-Queen's University Press, 1992) at 12–20; Walter Tarnopolsky, 'A Comparison between the Charter and the International Covenant' (1983) 8 *Queen's Law Journal* 211.

54 *R. v. Big M. Drug Mart Ltd.*, (1985), 1 S.C.R. 295 at 336.

55 Tully, *Democracy and Civic Freedom* at 196–7, citing John Rawls, *The Law of Peoples with the Idea of Public Reason Revisited* (Cambridge, MA: Harvard University Press, 1999) at 140–3.

56 Indigenous peoples do not generally seek secession. Secession is often a colonist's activity. It is rare for Indigenous communities to seek secession. See the work of Natividad Gutierrez Chong, *Mujeres y nacionalismo: de la Independencia a la nación del nuevo milenio* (Coyoacan, Mexico: Universidad Nacional Autónoma de México-Instituto de Investigaciones Sociales, 2004). For conditions of exit from Canada, see *Reference Re Secession of Québec*, [1998] at para. 138:

> In summary, the international law right to self-determination only generates, at best, a right to external self-determination in situations of former colonies; where a people is oppressed, as for example under foreign military occupation; or where a definable group is denied meaningful access to government to pursue their political, economic, social and cultural development. In all three situations, the people in question are entitled to a right to external self-determination because they have been denied the ability to exert internally their right to self-determination.

> For a discussion of these principles in relation to Aboriginal peoples see John Borrows, 'Questioning Canada's Title to Land: The Rule of Law, Aboriginal Peoples and Colonialism,' in *Speaking Truth to Power: A Treaty Forum*, ed. Law Commission of Canada and British Columbia Treaty Commission

(Ottawa: Law Commission of Canada, 2001). For one example of an Indigenous group's experience with secession, see Grand Council of the Crees, *Never without Consent: James Bay Crees' Stand against Forcible Inclusion into an Independent Québec* (Toronto: ECW Press, 1998).

57 *R. v. Sappier; R. v. Gray*, [2006] S.C.J. No. 54, [2006] 2 S.C.R. 686 at para. 38: 'I can therefore find no jurisprudential authority to support the proposition that a practice undertaken merely for survival purposes cannot be considered integral to the distinctive culture of an aboriginal people. I find that the jurisprudence weighs in favour of protecting the traditional means of survival of an aboriginal community.'

58 For a similar approach see Val Napoleon and Hadley Friedland, 'Indigenous Legal Traditions: Roots to Renaissance,' in *Oxford Handbook of Criminal Law*, ed. Markus Dubber (London: Oxford University Press, 2014).

59 This is also a book about law, yet it focuses on freedom and the good life to critique and rebalance the rights-centric approach to Indigenous issues found in the legal literature. For a critique of the prevalence of rights discourse in Canadian law, see Andrew Petter, *The Politics of the Charter: The Illusive Promise of Constitutional Rights* (Toronto: University of Toronto Press, 2010). For a discussion of the limitations of rights discourse in an Indigenous context, see Christopher Manfredi, 'Fear, Hope and Misunderstanding: Unintended Consequences and the Marshall Decision,' in *Advancing Aboriginal Claims: Visions/Strategies/Direction*, ed. Kerry Wilkins (Saskatoon: Purich Publishing, 2004). For a discussion of how Indigenous peoples can pursue rights but still be attentive to challenging the particular historical and contingent elements of power see Paul Patton, 'Foucault, Critique and Rights' (2005) 6 *Critical Horizons* 267.

Chapter One

1 Hin-hah-too-yah-lat-kekht (Chief Joseph), 'Chief Joseph Recounts His Trip to Washington, D.C. (1879),' in *Voices of a People's History of the United States*, ed. Howard Zinn and Anthony Arnove (New York: Seven Stories Press, 2004) at 147–8.

2 For an excellent discussion of this issue see, generally, Wayne Warry, *Ending Denial: Understanding Aboriginal Issues* (Toronto: University of Toronto Press, 2008).

3 Eric Hobsbawm and Terence Ranger, eds., *The Invention of Tradition* (Cambridge: Cambridge University Press, 1983); Bruce Trigger, *Socio-Cultural Evolution: Calculation and Contingency* (Oxford: Blackwell Press, 1998);

Ronald Niezen, *The Origins of Indigenism, Human Rights, and The Politics of Identity* (Berkeley: University of California Press, 2003) at 6; Andrea Smith, *Native Americans and The Christian Right: The Gendered Politics of Unlikely Alliances* (Durham, NC: Duke University Press, 2008).

4 For a case discussing the concept of 'Indianness' in Canadian law, see *Dick v. The Queen*, [1995] 2 S.C.R. 309.

5 Michel Foucault, 'What is Enlightenment?' in *Ethics: Subjectivity and Truth*, vol. 1 of *The Essential Works of Michel Foucault*, ed. Paul Rabinow (New York: New Press, 1997) at 315, cited in James Tully, *Democracy and Civic Freedom*, vol. 1 of *Public Philosophy in a New Key* (Cambridge: Cambridge University Press, 2008) at 158.

6 This chapter explores my methodological approach for understanding the themes in this book. For further discussions of Indigenous research methodologies, see Shawn Wilson, *Research Is Ceremony: Indigenous Research Methods* (Halifax, NS: Fernwood Publishing, 2008); Margaret Kovach, *Indigenous Methodologies: Characteristics, Conversations, and Contexts* (Toronto: University of Toronto Press, 2009); Wendy Makoons Geniusz, *Our Knowledge Is Not Primitive: Decolonizing Botanical Anishinaabe Teachings* (Syracuse, NY: Syracuse University Press, 2009); Linda Smith-Tuhiwai, *Decolonizing Methodologies: Research and Indigenous Peoples* (New York: Zed Books, 2009); Kathleen Absolon, (Minogiizhigokwe), *Kaandossiwin, How We Come to Know* (Halifax, NS: Fernwood Publishing, 2011).

7 For an excellent study of the issue of Indigenous peoples and mobility, see John Taylor and Martin Bell, *Population Mobility and Indigenous Peoples in Australasia and North America* (New York: Routledge, 2004). See also Martin Cooke and Daniele Belanger, 'Migration Theories and First Nations Mobility: Towards a Systems Perspective' (2006) 43 *Canadian Journal of Sociology* 141.

8 Discussions of Aboriginal culture that promote this view include James Clifton, ed., *The Imaginary Indian: Cultural Fictions and Government Policy* (New Brunswick, NJ: Transactions Publishers, 1996); Thomas Flanagan, *First Nations, Second Thoughts* (Montreal: McGill-Queen's University Press, 2000); Frances Widdowson and Howard Adams, *Disrobing the Aboriginal Industry: The Deception Behind Indigenous Cultural Preservation* (Montreal: McGill-Queen's University Press, 2008).

9 For a critical view of how the law views cultures as unmoving, see Brent Olthius, 'Defrosting Delgamuukw: (or "How to Reject a Frozen Rights Interpretation of Aboriginal Title in Canada")' (2001) 12 *National Journal of Constitutional Law* 385; J. Borrows, 'Frozen Rights in Canada: Constitutional Interpretation and the Trickster' (1997) 22 *American Indian Law*

Review 37; Robert Williams Jr., *Like a Loaded Weapon: The Rehnquist Court, Indian Rights and the Legal History of Racism in America* (Minneapolis: University of Minnesota Press, 2005); Lindsay Robertson, *Conquest by Law: How the Discovery of America Dispossessed Indigenous Peoples of their Lands* (New York: Oxford University Press, 2005).

10 For a discussion of this issue in historic context, see Henry Reynolds, *The Law of the Land*, 2nd ed. (Toronto: Penguin Books, 2001). For a contemporary treatment, see the past tense discussion of Aboriginal civilization in Flanagan, *First Nations, Second Thoughts*. For a static interpretation of Indigenous culture, see Widdowson and Adams, *Disrobing the Aboriginal Industry*.

11 Alan Duff, *Maori: The Crisis and the Challenge* (Auckland, New Zealand: HarperCollins, 1993).

12 First Nations culture might be regarded as too weak to enter into ordinary legal relationships; see *Harry v. Kreutziger*, (1978) 9 B.C.L.R. 166. (B.C.C.A.); Russell Means, 'The Same Old Song,' in *Marxism and Native Americans*, ed. Ward Churchill (Boston: Southend Press, 1983).

13 Lewis Henry Morgan, *Ancient Society, or, Researches in the Lines of Human Progress from Savagery, through Barbarism to Civilization* (Gloucester, MA: P. Smith, 1974).

14 For a judicial expression of these views, see *Sawridge Band v. Canada*, [1996] 1 F.C. 3 (F.C.T.D.). For judicial censure of these views, see *Sawridge v. Canada*, [1997] 3 F.C. 538 (F.C.A.).

15 One must be careful, however, not to romanticize this view of time and conclude that Indigenous peoples have no history. In my view, this was a problem in the work of Claude Levi-Strauss, *The Elementary Structures of Kinship* (London: Eyre and Spottis-woode, 1969).

16 John Borrows, 'Fourword/Foreword: Issues, Individuals, Institutions, Ideologies' (2002) 1 *Indigenous Law Journal* 1. This pattern is also one of the underlying themes in John Borrows, *Drawing Out Law: A Spirit's Guide* (Toronto: University of Toronto Press, 2010).

17 I am intrigued by the Mayan calendar, which is described in Ronald Wright, *Time Among the Maya: Travels in Belize, Guatemala and Mexico* (Toronto: Penguin Books, 1989).

18 Thomas Peacock, *The Four Hills of Life: Ojibwe Wisdom* (Afton, MN: Afton Historical Society Press, 2006).

19 My wife, Kim, says to me, 'Even when you travel, you travel. You don't just pick one place to visit, but when you get to a place you visit all around.'

20 My father was a very important influence in my life because of the love and security he gave me, but he was a quiet man, and did not share much of his history or teachings with me in my early life. It is only over the past fifteen years that I have gotten to know him in greater depth.

21 For a further exploration of these cyclical views of time and the law, see Borrows, 'Fourward /Foreword'; Leroy Little Bear, 'Jagged Worldviews Colliding,' in *Reclaiming Indigenous Voice and Vision*, ed. Marie Battiste (Vancouver: UBC Press, 2000) at 77– 85.

22 My most recent reflections in this regard come from work I did for the National Centre for First Nations Governance, where I researched and reflected on what it means to be Anishinaabek; see John Borrows, 'Seven Generations, Seven Teachings: Getting Rid of the Indian Act' [unpublished], retrieved 1 April 2014 from http://fngovernance.org/resources_docs/7_Generations_7_Teachings.pdf.

23 Ethno-nationalism often feeds this view. Under this view, individuals might stress their blood lines, national exclusivity, native language prowess, origin teachings, ceremonial degree, and authority, etc. See Great Lakes Fish and Wildlife Commission, *Dibaajimowinaan: Anishinaabe Stories of Culture and Respect* (Odahana, WI: Great Lakes Indian Fish and Wildlife Commission, 2013) at 13, 167. For other constructions of ethnonationalism, see Waziyatawin, *What Does Justice Look Like? The Struggle for Liberation in Dakota Homeland* (St. Paul, MN: Living Justice Press, 2008).

24 For an example of work that places Indigenous peoples in a essentialized light, and then (ironically) critiques Indigenous peoples for being fundamentalist, see Widdowson and Howard, *Disrobing the Aboriginal Industry*.

25 Fortunately, for reasons developed in this book, most Anishinaabe people I know do not subscribe to this view.

26 For a more developed discussion of self-conscious traditionalism, see Taiaiake Alfred, *Wasase: Indigenous Pathways to Action* (Peterborough, ON: Broadview Press, 2005). Taiaiake's views are different from my cousin's and students' ideas and I believe they misinterpret the broader objectives of his work.

27 Emily Snyder, Val Napoleon, and John Borrows, 'Gender and Violence: Drawing on Indigenous Legal Resources' (2014) 47 *University of British Columbia Law Review* 593–653.

28 Darlene Johnston, *Litigating Identity: The Challenge of Aboriginality* (Vancouver: UBC Press, 2008).

29 Eddie Benton Benai, *The Mishomis Book* (Hayward, WI: Indian Country Communications, 1988).

30 John Borrows, 'A Genealogy of Law: Inherent Sovereignty and First Nations Self-Government' (1992) 30 *Osgoode Hall Law Review* 291. For example, Widow Sakeon's brother, Tecumseh, constantly travelled throughout eastern North America in his attempts to create a better world.

31 Ibid.

32 Ibid.

33 For a description of this return, see Gunda Lambton, *Sun in Winter: A Toronto Wartime Journal, 1942–1945* (Montreal: McGill-Queen's University Press, 2003) at 155–9.

34 K.R. Howe, *The Quest for Origins: Who First Discovered and Settled New Zealand and the Pacific Islands* (Auckland, New Zealand: Penguin Books, 2003) at 159–82.

35 Ranginui Walker, *Ka Whawhai Tonu Matou: Struggle Without End* (Auckland, New Zealand: Penguin Books, 2004) at 24–77.

36 G. Irwin, *The Prehistoric Exploration and Colonisation of the Pacific* (Cambridge: Cambridge University Press, 1992).

37 R. Berndt and C. Berndt, *The Speaking Land* (Melbourne, Australia: Penguin Books, 1989).

38 Steinar Pederson, 'The State and the Rejection of Saami Customary Law: Superiority and Inferiority in Norwegian – Saami Relations,' in *On Customary Law and Saami Rights Process in Norway*, ed. Tom Svensson (Tromso, Norway: Senter for Saamike Studier, 1999) 127 at 132–4.

39 Paul Zolbrod, *Dine bahane: The Navajo Creation Story* (Albuquerque: University of New Mexico Press, 1984); Ronald Towner, ed., *The Archeology of Navajo Origins* (Salt Lake City: University of Utah, 1996); Jerrold Levy, *In the Beginning: The Navajo Genesis* (Berkeley: University of California Press, 1998).

40 Frank Waters, *Book of the Hopi* (New York: Penguin Books, 1977).

41 Michael Coe, *The Maya*, 7th ed. (New York: Thames and Hudson, 2005); *Popol Vuh, The Definitive Edition of the Mayan Book of the Dawn of Life and the Glories of Gods and Kings*, trans. Dennis Tedlock (Toronto: Simon and Schuster, 1996).

42 Ann Wrightman, *Indigenous Migration and Social Change: The Forestaros of Cuzco, 1570–1720* (Durham, NC: Duke University Press, 2000).

43 Paige Raibmon, 'Meanings of Mobility on the Northwest Coast' in *New Histories for Old: Changing Perspectives on Canada's Native Pasts*, ed. Ted Binnema and Susan Neylan (Vancouver: UBC Press, 2007) 176 at 177.

44 Howard Meredith, *Dancing on Common Ground: Tribal Cultures and Alliances on the Southern Plains* (Lawrence: University of Kansas Press, 1995);

Philip Duke, *Points in Time: Structure and Event in a Late Northern Plains Hunting Society* (Niwot: University of Colorado Press, 1999).

45 Keith Basso, *Wisdom Sits in Places: Landscape and Language Among the Western Apache* (Albuquerque: University of New Mexico Press, 1996).

46 Alan Taylor, *American Colonies: The Settling of North America* (New York: Penguin Books, 2001) at 235.

47 Radisson, Des Grosseilliers, La Salle, Nicollet, MacKenzie, Jacques Marquette, 'Récit des voyages et découvertes du Père Marquette,' in *Relations inédites de la Nouvelle-France (1672–1679) pour faire suite aux anciennes relations*, vol. 2 (Montreal: Éditions Élysée, 1974); Henri Joutel, *Journal historique du dernier voyage que feu M. de la Sale fit dans le golfe de Mexique [...]* (Paris: Estienne Robinot, 1713); Lawrence Burpee, ed., *Journals and Letters of Pierre Gaultier de Varennes de La Vérendrye and His Sons: With Correspondence Between the Governors of Canada and the French Court, Touching the Search for the Western Sea* (Toronto: The Champlain Society, 1927); Sir Alexander Mackenzie, *Voyages from Montreal [...] to the Frozen and Pacific Oceans, in the Years 1789 and 1793* (London: R. Noble, 1801); Arthur Adams, ed., *The Explorations of Pierre Esprit Radisson: From the Original Manuscript in the Bodleian Library and the British Museum*, modernisation of the text by Loren Kallsen (Minneapolis, MN: Ross and Haines, 1961).

48 Bianet Castellanos, *Cancun and the Campo: Indigenous Migration and Tourism Development in the Yucatan Peninsula in Holiday in Mexico: Essays on Tourism and Tourist Experience* (Durham, NC: Duke University Press, under review). Similar experiences are present with Indigenous peoples in Sarawak, Malaysia; see Ose Murang, 'Migration in Sarawak: The Kelabit Experience' (1998) 3(1) *Sarawak Development Journal* 1–11. For further information about traditions of mobility in Borneo (*bejalai*), see Peter Kedit, *Iban Bejalai* (Kuching, Malaysia: Sarawak Literary Society, 1993); Ramy Bulan, *Native Title in Sarawak, Malaysia: Kelabit Land Rights in Transition* (PhD diss., Australian National University, 2005) at 116 [unpublished].

49 Bonita Lawrence, *Real Indians and Others: Mixed Blood Urban Native Peoples and Indigenous Nationhood* (Lincoln: University of Nebraska Press, 2004).

50 Evelyn Peters and Chris Andersen, *Indigenous in the City: Contemporary Identities and Cultural Innovation* (Vancouver: UBC Press, 2013).

51 Evelyn Peters, 'Three Myths About Aboriginals in Cities' (paper presented at Breakfast on the Hill Seminar Series, Canadian Federation for the Humanities and Social Sciences, Ottawa, 25 March 2004).

52 Peter Dinsdale, Jerry White, and Calvin Hanselmann, eds., *Urban Aboriginal Communities in Canada: Complexities, Challenges, Opportunities* (Toronto: Thompson, 2011).

53 For further discussion, see Evelyn J. Peters, *Urban Aboriginal Policy Making in Canadian Municipalities* (Montreal: McGill-Queen's University Press, 2012).

54 Maximilian Christian Forte, *Indigenous Cosmopolitans: Transnational and Transcultural Indigeneity in the Twenty-First Century* (New York: Peter Lang, 2011) at 1–17.

55 See *Snowden v. Saginaw Chippewa Indian Tribe of Michigan*, Appellate Court of the Saginaw Chippewa Indian Tribe of Michigan, No. 04-CA-1017, 32 I.L.R. 6047, 7 January 2005; *In Re Menefee*, Grand Traverse Band of Ottawa and Chippewa Indians Tribal Court, No. 97-12-092-CV, 2004 WL 5714978, 5 May 2004.

56 The process of internalizing the commands of a hegemonic power has been labelled 'imperialism'; see Tully, *Democracy and Civic Freedom* at 264–7.

57 I agree with the observations of Raymond Geuss, *Philosophy and Real Politics* (Princeton, NJ: Princeton University Press, 2008) at 60–70. I would prefer to see rights as socially constructed and politically contextualized; for a discussion of rights as relationships, see Jennifer Nedelsky, 'Reconceiving Rights as Relationships' (1993–1994) 1 *Constitutional Forum* 1. For a discussion of how rights discourse can monopolize public discourse, see Michael Ignatieff, *The Rights Revolution* (Toronto: Anansi, 2000).

58 For example, in Canada Indigenous peoples can only prove they have rights if their rights are 'Aboriginal,' which has been defined as practices that were integral to their culture prior to the arrival of Europeans. See *R. v. Van der Peet*, [1996] 2 S.C.R. 507 at paras. 20 and 46.

59 I employ the word 'damned' in a dual sense: to be punished and to be stopped or blocked in one's social progress.

60 *Delgamuukw v. British Columbia*, [1997] 3 S.C.R. 1010 (S.C.C.) at para. 153.

61 *Tsilhqot'in Nation v. British Columbia*, 2014 S.C.C. 44 at paras. 33 and 44.

62 *Mabo v. Queensland No. 2*, (1992), 107 A.L.R. 1 at para. 66 at (H.C.). For a U.S. example, see *State of Vermont v. Elliott*, 616 AL 2d 210 (1992), *certiorari* denied 113 S Ct 1258 (1993), which held that grants, historical events, and legislative acts, culminating in the admission of Vermont as a U.S. state in 1791, extinguished Western Abenaki Aboriginal title. For commentary, see J.P. Lowndes, 'When History Outweighs Law: Extinguishment of Abenaki Aboriginal Title' (1994) 42 *Buffalo Law Review* 75; J.W. Singer, 'Well Settled?: The Increasing Weight of History in American Indian Land Claims' (1994) 28 *Georgia Law Review* 481.

63 *Members of the Yorta Yorta Aboriginal Community v. Victoria*, (2002) 194 ALR 538 (H.C.) at 561. For commentary, see Kirsten Anker, 'Law in the Present Tense: Tradition and Cultural Continuity in *Members of the Yorta Yorta*

Aboriginal Community v. Victoria' (2004) *Melbourne University Law Review* 1. For a U.S. example, see Jo Carillo, ed., *Recalling the Rhythm of Survival: Readings in American Indian Law* (Philadelphia: Temple University Press, 1998) at 19–50.

64 Frederick Hoxie, *A Final Promise: The Campaign to Assimilate the Indians, 1880–1920* (Lincoln: University of Nebraska Press, 1984); Wilcomb E. Washburn, *The Assault on Indian Tribalism: The General Allotment Law (Dawes Act) of 1887* (Philadelphia: Lippincott, 1975); Donald Fixico, *Termination and Relocation: Federal Indian Policy, 1945–1960* (Albuquerque: University of New Mexico Press, 1986).

65 Nan Seuffert, *Jurisprudence of National Identity: Kaleidoscopes of Imperialism and Globalism from Aotearora New Zealand* (Burlington, VT: Ashgate, 2006) at 11–27; Henry Minde, 'Assimilation of the Sami: Implementation and Consequences' (2005) 3 *Journal of Indigenous Peoples Rights* 3–51; Lisa Valenta, 'Disconnect: The 1988 Brazilian Constitution, Customary International Law and Indigenous Land Rights in Northern Brazil' (2003) 38 *Texas International Law Journal* 643; Richard Hitchcock and Diana Vinding, *Indigenous Peoples' Rights in Southern Africa* (Copenhagen, Denmark: International Work Group for Indigenous Affairs, 2004) at 113–34; Geoffrey Benjamin and Cynthia Chow, eds., *Tribal Communities in the Malay World* (Singapore: Centre for Southeast Asian Studies, 2003); Milca Castro Lucic, 'Challenges in Intercultural Policies, Indigenous Rights and Economic Development' (2005) 28 *PoLAR* 112.

66 For an excellent discussion of this issue, see Jérémie Gilbert, 'Nomadic Territories: A Human Rights Approach to Nomadic Peoples' Land Rights' (2007) 7 *Human Rights Law Review* 681.

67 *Tee Hit Ton Indians v. United States,* (1955) 345 U.S. 272.

68 Williams Jr., *The American Indian in Western Legal Thought* (Oxford: Oxford University Press, 1990).

69 John Locke, *Two Treatises of Government* [1689], ed. Peter Laslett (Cambridge: Cambridge University Press, 1988), second treatise, at chap. 5, paras. 32, 37, and 41. See also James Tully, *An Approach to Political Philosophy: Locke in Contexts* (Cambridge: Cambridge University Press, 1993) at 137.

70 *R. v. Bernard; R. v. Marshall,* [2005] 2 S.C.R. 220.

71 Ibid. at para. 77.

72 *R. v. Van der Peet,* [1996] at paras. 55–9.

73 Ibid.

74 Ibid. at para. 73.

75 *Delgamuukw v. British Columbia,* [1997] 3 S.C.R. 1010; *Tsilhqot'in Nation v. British Columbia,* 2014 at paras. 74–5.

76 *Members of the Yorta Yorta Aboriginal Community v. Victoria*, [2002] (H.C.) 194
    ALR 538 at para. 53: 'When the society whose laws or customs existed at
    sovereignty ceases to exist, the rights and interests in land to which these
    laws and customs gave rise, cease to exist. If the content of the former laws
    and customs is later adopted by some new society, those laws and customs
    will then owe their new life to that other, later, society and they are the
    laws acknowledged by, and customs observed by, *that later society*, they are
    not laws and customs which can now properly be described as being the
    existing laws and customs of the earlier society' (emphasis in original).

77 *Morton v. Mancari*, (1974) 417 U.S. 535 at 554 (U.S.S.C.); *Oliphant* v. *Suqua-
    mish Indian Tribe*, (1978) 435 U.S. 191 at 196 (U.S.S.C); *Montana v. United
    States*, (1981) 450 U.S. 544 at 564 (U.S.S.C.); *Nevada v. Hicks*, (2001) 533 U.S.
    353 at 359–360 (U.S.S.C.).

78 *Brendale v. Confederated Tribes of Colville*, (1989) 492 U.S. 408 at 426–7
    (U.S.S.C).

79 *Atkitson Trading Post v. Shirley*, (2001) 532 U.S. 645 at 649–51 (U.S.S.C.).

80 For an overview of tribal court jurisdiction in the United States, see Justin
    Richland and Sarah Deer, eds., *Introduction to Tribal Legal Studies* (Lanham,
    MD: Altamira Press, 2004); Carrie Garrow and Sarah Deer, eds., *Tribal
    Criminal Law and Procedure* (Lanham, MD: Altamira Press, 2004).

81 Gerald Gall, *The Canadian Legal System* (Toronto: Thomson, 2004) at 35–53;
    George Alexandrowicz et al., eds., *Dimension of Canadian Law: Canadian and
    International Law in the 21st Century* (Toronto: Emond Montgomery, 2004)
    at 48; Peter Hogg, *Constitutional Law of Canada* (Toronto: Thomson, 2005) at
    1–28; Margaret McCallum, 'Problems in Determining the Date of Reception
    in Prince Edward Island' (2006) 55 *University of New Brunswick Law Jour-
    nal*. 3. For an interesting study of the interaction of colonial and Indigenous
    laws, see Peter Karsten, *Between Law and Custom: High and Low Legal Cultures
    in the Lands of the British Diaspora – The United States, Canada, Australia and
    New Zealand – 1600–1900* (Cambridge: Cambridge University Press, 2002).

82 Arthur Ray, 'Native History on Trial: Confessions of an Expert Witness'
    (2003) 84 *Canadian Historical Review* 253 at 263; Robin Riddington, 'Field-
    work in Courtroom 53: A Witness to *Delgamuukw v. BC*' (1992) 95 *BC Stud-
    ies* 12–24.

83 *Attorney-General for Ontario v. Bear Island Foundation et al. Potts et al. v.
    Attorney-General for Ontario*, 1984 CanLII 2136 (ON SC); 15 D.L.R. (4th) 321
    at 340.

84 For commentary, see Hamar Foster, 'Letting Go the Bone: The Idea of
    Indian Title in British Columbia 1849–1927,' in *Essays in the History of
    Canadian Law*, vol. 6, *The Legal History of British Columbia and the Yukon*, ed.
    Hamar Foster and John McLaren (Toronto: University of Toronto Press,

1995) at 28; Paul Tennant, *Aboriginal Peoples and Politics in British Columbia: The Indian Land Question in British Columbia, 1849–1989* (Vancouver: UBC Press, 1990) at 289.

85 The Supreme Court quoted the following passage from the trial court judgment: 'The defendants have failed to prove that their ancestors were an organized band level of society in 1763; that, as an organized society, they had exclusive occupation of the Land Claim Area in 1763; or that, as an organized society, they continued to exclusively occupy and make aboriginal use of the Land Claim Area from 1763 or the time of coming of settlement to the date the action was commenced'; *Bear Island Foundation*, at 373, quoted [1991] 2 S.C.R. 570, 574. Commenting on this at 574–5, the Supreme Court judges said that although they did 'not take issue with the numerous specific findings of fact in the courts below,' it did 'not necessarily follow, however, that we agree with all the legal findings based on those facts. In particular, we find that on the facts found by the trial judge the Indians exercised sufficient occupation of the lands in question throughout the relevant period to establish an aboriginal right.'

86 See *Bear Island Foundation*, above:

> Chief Potts, who is thirty-eight years old, has a white mother and a father who is not of pure Indian ancestry, and whose Indian ancestry descended from persons who arrived on the lands about 1901, long after most of the issues in dispute had occurred. It could not be said that his own ancestors had any direct oral knowledge of the events in question. He was therefore merely giving evidence of oral history he had accumulated from other members of the band. He cannot speak the native language and therefore has difficulty in communicating fully with some of the oldest members, although they speak English.

87 Ibid.

88 Anthony Hall, 'Where Justice Lies: Aboriginal Rights and Wrongs in Temagami,' in *Temagami: A Debate on Wilderness*, ed. Matt Bray and Ashley Thomson (Toronto: Dundurn Press, 1990) at 223 at 237–9.

89 *R. v. Van der Peet*, [1996] at para. 68.

90 *Delgamuukw v. British Columbia*, [1997] 3 S.C.R. 1010 at para. 82.

91 Ibid. at paras. 84, 87.

92 John Borrows, 'Listening for a Change: The Courts and Oral Tradition' (2001) *Osgoode Hall Law Journal* 1.

93 *R. v. Marshall; R. v. Bernard*, [2005] S.C.C. 43 at paras. 62–5; see also Val Napoleon, 'Delgamuukw: A Legal Straightjacket for Oral Histories?' (2005) 20 *Canadian Journal of Law and Society* 123.

94 *Mitchell v. M.N.R.*, [2001] 1 S.C.R. 911 at para. 51. In arriving at this conclusion, the Supreme Court focused on the inadequacy of non-Indigenous experts and inferences drawn from their research.

95 The one citation Chief Mitchell is given at the Supreme Court of Canada is as follows: 'According to our traditions it had always been one of our areas where we did all our planting, we did our fishing and we did our hunting'; ibid. at para. 48.

96 Ibid. at 41. In dissent, Justice Binnie held, at para. 163, 'In my view, therefore, the international trading/mobility right claimed by the respondent as a citizen of the Haudenosaunee (Iroquois) Confederacy is incompatible with the historical attributes of Canadian sovereignty.'

97 Melvin Smith, *Our Home or Native Land? What Governments' Aboriginal Policy is Doing to Canada* (Victoria, BC: Crown Western, 1995) at 264–8.

98 Ibid.

99 Michael Lieder and Jake Page, *Wild Justice: The People of Geronimo v. The United States* (New York: Random House, 1997).

100 Te Puni Kokir, Legislative Reform Treaty of Waitangi 1975, http://www.legislation.govt.nz/act/public/1975/0114/latest/DLM435368.html.

101 See, generally, Michael Belgrave, Merata Kawharu, and David Williams, eds., *Waitangi Revisited: Perspectives on the Treaty of Waitangi* (Oxford: Oxford University Press, 2005).

102 *Amodu Tijani v. Secretary, Southern Nigeria*, [1921] 2 A.C. 399 at 402–4 (JCPC).

103 Ibid.

104 *Western Sahara Advisory Opinion*, (1975) I.C.J. 12.

105 *Case of the Mayagna (Sumo) Awas Tingni Community v. The Republic of Nicaragua*, (2001) Inter-American Court of Human Rights, reproduced in (Spring 2002) 19 *Arizona Journal of International and Comparative Law* 415.

106 *Case of Mary and Carrie Dann v. United States Case No. 11.140 (Judgment on the Merits)*, (December 27, 2002) Inter-American Commission on Human Rights No 75/02, at para. 130.

107 Convention (N° 169) Art. 14(1) states that 'the rights of ownership and possession of the peoples concerned over the lands which they traditionally occupy shall be recognized. In addition, measures shall be taken in appropriate cases to safeguard the right of the peoples concerned to use lands not exclusively occupied by them, but to which they have traditionally had access for their subsistence and traditional activities. Particular attention shall be paid to the situation of nomadic peoples and shifting cultivators in this respect.'

108 *Alexkor Ltd v. Richtersveld Community*, (2003) 12 B.C.L.R. 130 at para. 99.

109 *Kerajaan Negeri Selango v. Sagong Bin Tasi,* [2005] 6 M.L.J. 289 Malaysian Court of Appeal (Putrajaya) (Gopal Sri Ram JCA) at para. 12.

110 Ibid. at paras. 30–3. See also *Adong bin Kuwau & Ors v Kerajaan Negeri Johor & Anor,* [1997] 1 M.L.J. 418, which provided compensation for restricting Indigenous land rights and movement.

111 *Maya Villages of Santa Cruz and Conejo v. Belize,* (Claim 171/172 of 2007) (Supreme Court of Belize).

112 *Maya Indigenous Communities of the Toledo District v. Belize,* Report No. 40/04 of October 12, 2004.

113 *Tsilhqot'in Nation v. British Columbia,* 2014 at para. 32.

114 Ibid. at paras. 55, 58.

115 Witi Ihimaera, *The Rope of Man* (Auckland, New Zealand: Raupo Books, 2005).

116 Brenda Child, 'A New Seasonal Round: Ojibwe Familes and the Great Depression,' in *Enduring Nations: Native Americans in the Midwest,* ed. David Edmunds (Urbana: University of Illinois Press, 2008) at 182–94.

117 I should be clear that the pattern I am describing relates to those who live on the reserve. Those who live off the reserve have the tendency to move in the opposite direction, from being among larger groups in the winter, to returning home to be with their comparatively smaller family groups for holidays in the summer.

118 Indigenous people from Borneo in Malaysia also have similar experiences when it comes to oil wells; see Ryoji Soda, *People on the Move: Rural-Urban Interactions in Sarawak* (Melbourne, Australia: Trans Pacific Press, 2007).

119 These patterns of life have caused some people to stereotype the Anishinaabe as unreliable because we do not always hold year-round jobs. Furthermore, we sometimes hear charges that we are lazy, thinking that we do not work all winter, or all summer as the case may be, in the cash economy. These and other such assumptions misperceive Anishinaabe culture. They fail to appreciate what may be hidden to those unfamiliar with aspirations people have towards the land and the uses to which the Anishinaabe want to put it.

120 Including section 13 of the UN Universal Declaration of Human Rights, which states,'(1) Everyone has the right to freedom of movement and residence within the borders of each state. (2) Everyone has the right to leave any country, including his own, and to return to his country.'

121 It is not the Indigenous peoples who are outdated; it is those who view them in this old-fashioned, stereotypical way.

122 Tully, *Democracy and Civic Freedom* at 240; see also John Borrows, 'A Separate Peace: Strengthening Shared Justice,' in *Intercultural Dispute Resolution in Context,* ed. Cathy Bell (Vancouver: UBC Press, 2004).

123   *Reference Re Secession of Québec,* [1998] 2 S.C.R. 217 at paras. 64 and 68.
124   Borrows, 'A Separate Peace.'
125   For an excellent set of narratives exploring this issue, see Audra Simpson, 'Paths Toward a Mohawk Nation: Narratives of Citizenship and Nation-hood in Kahnawake,' in *Political Theory and the Rights of Indigenous Peoples,* ed. Duncan Ivison, Paul Patton, and Will Sanders (Cambridge: Cambridge University Press) at 113–36.
126   For a critique related to the ineffective nature of Inuit values-based gov-ernance, see Jeanette Gevikoglu, *Sentenced to Sovereignty: Sentencing, Sov-ereignty and the Inuit Court of Justice* (LL.M. thesis, University of Victoria, 2011) [unpublished].
127   John Borrows, *Canada's Indigenous Constitution* (Toronto: University of Toronto Press, 2010) at 155–65.
128   For a discussion of free, prior, and informed consent in international law, see Joji Carino, 'Indigenous Peoples' Right to Free, Prior, Informed Con-sent: Reflections on Concepts and Practice' (2005) 22 *Arizona Journal of International and Comparative Law* 22; UNDRIP (2007) Articles 10, 28, 29, 32, http://undesadspd.org/. IndigenousPeoples Article 19 of UNDRIP reads: 'States shall consult and cooperate in good faith with the indig-enous peoples concerned through their own representative institutions in order to obtain their free, prior and informed consent before adopting and implementing legislative or administrative measures that may affect them.'
129   For cases supporting demarcation, see *Awas Tingni Inter-American Com-mission on Human Rights,* Report 40/04, Case 12.053 (Maya Indigenous Communities of the Toledo District of Belize), Annual Report of the Inter-American Commission on Human Rights 2004, O.A.S. Doc. OEA/Ser.L/V/II.122, Doc. 5 rev. 1 (2005); *Belize Aurelio Cal, et al. v. Attorney General of Belize, Supreme Court of Belize,* (Claim 121/2007) (18 Oct 2007); *Mayanga (Sumo) Awas Tingni Community v. Nicaragua,* Inter-American Court of Human Rights (ser.C) No. 79 (August 31, 2001).
130   *Morton v. Mancari,* (1974); *Oliphant* v. *Suquamish Indian Tribe,* (1978); *Mon-tana v. United States; Nevada v. Hicks,* (2001).
131   Kevin Washburn, 'American Indians, Crime and the Law' (2006) 104 *Michigan Law Review* 709; Joseph William Singer, 'Canons of Conquest: The Supreme Court's Attack on Tribal Sovereignty' (2003) 37 *New England Law Review* 641.
132   Menno Boldt, *Surviving as Indians: The Challenge of Self-Government* (Toronto: University of Toronto Press, 1993) at xv–xvii.
133   Borrows, 'Seven Generations, Seven Teaching'; Borrows, *Canada's Indig-enous Constitution.*

134 Royal Commission on Aboriginal Peoples, *Restructuring the Relationship*, vol. 2 of *The Final Report of the Royal Commission on Aboriginal Peoples* (Ottawa: Supply and Services, 1996), at chap. 3.

135 *R. v. Van der Peet*, [1996]; *Tsilhqot'in Nation v. British Columbia*, 2014 at para. 69.

136 For example, in *Calder v. A.G.B.C.*, [1973] 3 S.C.R. 313, Justice Hall of the Canadian Supreme Court wrote the following: 'The dominant and recurring proposition stated by Chief Justice Marshall in *Johnson v. McIntosh* is that on discovery or on conquest the aborigines of newly-found lands were conceded to be the rightful occupants of the soil with a legal as well as a just claim to retain possession of it and to use it according to their own discretion, but their rights to complete sovereignty as independent nations were necessarily diminished and their power to dispose of the soil on their own will to whomsoever they pleased was denied by the original fundamental principle that discovery or conquest gave exclusive title to those who made it.' For more commentary on the Calder case, see Hamar Foster, Heather Raven, and Jeremy Webber, eds., *Let Right Be Done: Aboriginal Title, The Calder Case and the Future of Indigenous Rights* (Vancouver: UBC Press, 2007).

137 *Worcester v. Georgia*, (1832) 31 U.S. 515 at 519 (emphasis mine).

138 A clear instance of Indian Act status rules. For a similar process in Malaysia, see Ramy Bulan, 'Native Status and the Law,' in *Public Law in Contemporary Malaysia*, ed. Wu Min Aun (Singapore: Longman, 1999) at 248–92.

139 Fortunately, on the ground and away from these metaphysical abstractions, many Indigenous peoples are already practising these values in the present day. For example, throughout North America, 50 per cent of 'Indians' marry non-Indians. It is time that Canadian and Indigenous laws and policies caught up with these practices. Indigenous communities are not diminished if they are composed of people who are integrated into an Indigenous sociopolitical, cultural, and legal context. In the Americas, the term 'Indian' is a government, racialized, conceptual tradition. It is a universalized ideal, a Platonic form, that does not exist in any living Indigenous community. It is a false limit that impedes Indigenous peoples' freer movements, as they cycle over the vast territories of time. As such, it blocks their journeys over difficult conceptual terrain. It is tool that facilitates domination. It should be removed.

140 Tully, *Democracy and Civic Freedom* at 240.

141 John Borrows, 'Aboriginal Title and Private Property' (2015, forthcoming) 68 *Supreme Court Law Review*.

142 *Canada (Attorney General) v. Lameman*, 2008 S.C.C. 14 (S.C.C.); *Wewaykum Indian Band v. Canada*, [2002] 4 S.C.R. 245 (S.C.C.); *City of Sherill (New York) v. Oneida Indian Nation* (2005) 544 U.S. 197 (U.S.S.C.).

143 John Borrows, 'Indigenous Legal Traditions in Canada' (2006) 19 *Washington Journal of Law and Policy* 167; Borrows, *Canada's Indigenous Constitution*.

144 Law Commission of Canada, *Indigenous Legal Traditions* (Vancouver: UBC Press, 2007); John Borrows, 'Creating an Indigenous Legal Community' (2005) 50 *McGill Law Journal* 153.

145 *Oliphant v. Suquamish Indian Tribe*, (1978) at 210.

146 J.D. Crawford, 'Looking Again at Tribal Jurisdiction: Unwarranted Intrusions on Their Personal Liberty' (1993) 76 *Marquette Law Review* 401.

147 For a discussion of the negative consequences of termination in the U.S. context, see Kenneth Philip, *Termination Revisited: American Indians on the Trail to Self-Determination, 1933–1953* (Lincoln: University of Nebraska Press, 1999); Warren Metcalf, *Termination's Legacy: The Discarded Indians of Utah* (Lincoln: University of Nebraska Press, 2002); Roberta Ulrich, *American Indian Nations from Termination to Restoration, 1953–2006* (Lincoln: University of Nebraska Press, 2010).

148 John Borrows, 'Landed Citizenship: Narratives of Aboriginal Political Participation,' in *Citizenship in Diverse Societies*, ed. Will Kymlicka (Oxford: Oxford University Press, 2000), reprinted in *Citizenship, Diversity and Pluralism*, ed. Alan Cairns (Montreal: McGill-Queen's University Press, 2000). Stephen R. Covey also makes this point: 'Independence is vital; however, the problem is that we live in an interdependent reality. Our most important work, the problems we hope to solve or the opportunities we hope to realize require working and collaborating with other people in a high-trust, synergistic way …'; 'Managing Fear and Insecurity,' Thursday, 19 March 2009, *Stephen R Covey* [blog] at http://www.stephencovey.com/blog/?tag=interdependence.

149 I do not consider myself a liberal, conservative, or Marxist theorist. I would like to be considered an Anishinaabe legal practitioner, but I do not believe the application of Anishinaabe methods, practices, or ideas inexorably lead to one view of the world. There are schools of thought and practice within Anishinaabe tradition and life, which I have tried to capture by my emphasis on the trickster, *dibenindizowin* and *mino-bimaadiziwin*.

150 Michel Foucault, *The Final Foucault*, ed. James Bernauer and David Rasmussen (Cambridge, MA: MIT Press, 1988) at 18.

151 Borrows, 'A Separate Peace.'

152 John Borrows, 'Traditional Contemporary Equality: The Impact of the Charter on First Nations Politics,' in *Charting the Consequences: The Impact of Charter Rights on Law and Politics in Canada*, ed. David Schneidermn (Toronto: University of Toronto Press, 1997); Ignatieff, *The Rights Revolution*.

153 Matthew Fletcher, 'Indian Culture and Tribal Law' (2007) 2 *Yellow Medicine Review* 95.

154 Rights are open to manipulation and should never be regarded as pure or absolute; see Alexandre Kiss, 'Permissible Limitations on Rights,' in *The International Bill of Rights: The Covenant on Civil and Political Rights*, ed. L. Henekin (New York: Columbia University Press, 1981) at 290; Jennifer Nedelsky, 'Reconceiving Rights as Relationships' (1993) 1 *Review of Constitutional Studies* 1–26; J. Griffin, 'Discrepancies between the Best Philosophical Account of Human Rights and the International Law of Human Rights' (2000) 101 *Proceedings of the Aristotelian Society* 1–28.

155 For example, see K. Llewellyn and E.A. Hoebel, *The Cheyene Way: Conflict and Case Law in Primitive Jurisprudence* (Norman: University of Oklahoma Press, 1941); E. Adamson Hoebel, *The Law of Primitive Man* (New York: Atheneum, 1974); Max Gluckman, *Politics, Law and Ritual in Primitive Society* (Chicago: Aldine, 1965); Rennard Strickland, *Fire and the Spirits: Cherokee Law from Clan to Court* (Norman: University of Oklahoma Press, 1982); Antonio Mills, *Eagle Down Is Our Law: Witsuwit'en Law, Feasts and Land Claims* (Vancouver: UBC Press, 1994).

156 Michael Coyle, 'Traditional Indian Justice in Ontario: A Role for the Present?' (1986) 24 *Osgoode Hall Law Journal* 605–33.

157 Hin-hah-too-yah-lat-kekht (Chief Joseph), 'Chief Joseph Recounts His Trip to Washington, D.C. (1879).'

Chapter Two

1 Michel Foucault, 'The Ethics of the Concern for Self as a Practice of Freedom: An Interview with Michel Foucault,' in *Ethics: Subjectivity and Truth*, vol. 1 of *The Essential Works of Michel Foucault* (New York: New Press, 1997) 281 at 282. For commentary, see Aurelia Armstrong, 'Beyond Resistance: A Response to Žižek's Critique of Foucault's Subject of Freedom' (2008) 5 *Parrhesia: A Journal of Critical Philosophy* 19–31, http://www.parrhesiajournal.org/parrhesia05/parrhesia05_armstrong.pdf.

2 Gene Sharp in *The Role of Power in Non-Violent Struggle* (Boston: Albert Einstein Institution, 1990) describes the use of power through non-violent action in the following way:

'Power' is used here to mean the totality of all influences and pressures, including sanctions, available to a group or society for use in maintaining itself, implementing its policies, and conducting internal and external conflicts. Power may be measured by relative ability to control a situation, people, and institutions, or to mobilize people and institutions for some activity. Such power may be used to enable a group to achieve a goal; to implement or change policies; to induce others to behave as the wielders of power wish; to oppose or to maintain the established system, policies, and relationships; to alter, destroy, or replace the prior power distribution or institutions; or to accomplish a combination of these. (3–4)

(www.aeinstein.org/wp-content/uploads/2013/09/TheRoleofPowerin NonviolentStruggle-English.pdf)

3 Nicholas Blomley, '"Shut the Province Down": First Nations Blockades in British Columbia, 1984–1995' (1996) 111 *BC Studies* 5–35.

4 Ibid.

5 Sharp writes that withholding cooperation 'is the basic political assumption of nonviolent action.' Gene Sharp, 'Nonviolent Action: An Active Technique of Struggle,' in *Nonviolence in Theory and Practice*, 2nd ed., ed. Robert L. Holmes and Barry L. Gan (Long Grove, IL: Waveland Press, 2005) at 253.

6 Val Napoleon, 'Behind the Blockades' (2010) *Indigenous Law Journal* 9 at 10–11.

7 For a discussion of the role of contrast in political philosophy, see Charles Taylor, 'Understanding and Ethnocentricity,' in *Philosophy and the Human Sciences*, vol. 2 of *Philosophical Papers* (Cambridge: Cambridge University Press, 1985) at 125.

8 Analysis of structures and superstructures are resisted in this account because this kind of analysis tends to produce hierarchies for action, which may constrain people and lead to their own kinds of oppression. I thus reject first-principle adoptions of liberalism, Marxism, or any other system of political, economic, or moral thought. In my own practices of freedom and self-determination, I do not want to be captured by any one Western or Indigenous school of thought or world view. I attempt to concretely participate with Indigenous and other communities to enhance and nourish better relationships in particular contexts. For a discussion of the contextual nature of right relationships, see the work of Aaron Mills, 'Anishinaabe Treaty Constitutionalism: On the Invitation to Right Relations and the Violence of Contract,' in *The Right(s) Relationship? Reimagining the Implementation of Historical Treaties*, ed. Michael Coyle and John Borrows (University of Toronto Press, under consideration).

9 While mobility must be acknowledged and enhanced to facilitate freedom, we must resist detached theoretical abstractions of such practices. For a discussion of language games in philosophy, see Ludwig Wittgenstein, *Philosophical Investigations*, 2nd ed., trans. G.E.M. Anscombe (Oxford: Oxford University Press, 1997) at para. 100; James Tully, *Democracy and Civic Freedom*, vol. 1 of *Public Philosophy in a New Key* (Cambridge:

Cambridge University Press, 2008) at 135–45; Dale Turner, *This Is Not a Peace Pipe: Towards an Understanding of Aboriginal Sovereignty* (Toronto: University of Toronto Press, 2006).

10 Richard Rorty, 'The Priority of Democracy to Philosophy,' in *Objectivity, Relativism and Truth*, vol. 1 of *Philosophical Papers* (Cambridge: Cambridge University Press, 1991).

11 For greater discussion on this issue, see John Borrows, *Canada's Indigenous Constitution* (Toronto: University of Toronto Press, 2010).

12 For an example of work in this regard, see Christie Blatchford, *Helpless: Caledonia's Nightmare of Fear and Anarchy, and How the Law Failed All of Us* (Toronto: Doubleday Canada, 2010). For commentary, see Timothy Winegard, 'Book Review, Christie Blatchford *Helpless: Caledonia's Nightmare of Fear and Anarchy, and How the Law Failed All of Us* (Toronto: Doubleday Canada, 2010)' (2011) 20 *Native Studies Review* 117 at 119: '*Helpless* does provide a one-sided account of a peripheral component of these larger issues facing Six Nations/Caledonia.' For an account of the media's role in direct action, see Rima Wilkes, Catherine Corrigall Brown, and Daniel Myers, 'Packaging Protest: Media Coverage of Indigenous People's Collective Action' (2010) 47 *Canadian Review of Sociology* 327.

13 For a broad and cross-cutting description and analysis of Idle No More and the different motivations for people's participation, see The Kino-nda-niimi Collective, eds., *The Winter We Danced: Voices from the Past, the Future and the Idle No More Movement* (Winnipeg: APR Books, 2014).

14 This work adds to information I compiled as a researcher for the Ipperwash Inquiry into the death of Dudley George in Ontario. For more examples of civil (dis)obedience that falls into this third category, see John Borrows, 'Crown and Aboriginal Occupations of Land: A History and Comparison' (Toronto: Ipperwash Inquiry, 2005), https://www.attorney general.jus.gov.on.ca/inquiries/ipperwash/policy_part/research/pdf/ History_of_Occupations_Borrows.pdf.

15 For further information about Ipperwash conflicts see Edward J. Hedican, *Ipperwash: The Tragic Failure of Canada's Aboriginal Policy* (Toronto: University of Toronto Press, 2013); The Honourable Sidney B. Linden, *Report of the Ipperwash Inquiry* (Toronto: Queen's Printer, 2007), http://www.attorney general.jus.gov.on.ca/inquiries/ipperwash/report/index.html.

16 *R. v. Oakes*, [199\86] 1 S.C.R. 103 at 136.

17 *Haida Gwaii Reconciliation Act*, S.B.C. 2010, c. 17.

18 Robert Bringhurst, trans., *Story As Sharp As a Knife: The Classical Haida Mythtellers and Their World* (Toronto: Douglas and McIntyre, 1999).

19 Guujaaw, Foreword, in *Haida Gwaii: Human History and Environment from the Time of Loon to the Time of the Iron People*, ed. Daryl W. Fedje and Rolf Mathewes (Vancouver: UBC Press, 2005) at xii; Bill Reid, 'The Shining Islands,' in *Islands at the Edge: Preserving the Queen Charlotte Islands Wilderness* (Toronto: Douglas and McIntrye, 1984) at 23–30.

20 Sean Kane, *Wisdom of the Mythkeepers* (Peterborough, ON: Broadview Press, 1986) at 169.

21 Robin Fisher, *Contact and Conflict: Indian-European relations in British Columbia, 1774–1890* (Vancouver: UBC Press, 1992) at 2–3; Arthur Ray, *I Have Lived Here since the World Began: An Illustrated History of Canada's Native Peoples* (Toronto; Lester Publishing, 1996) at 112–13.

22 Ibid.

23 Margaret Blackman, 'Haida Traditional Culture,' in *Handbook of North American Indians: Northwest Coast*, vol. 7 of *Handbook of North American Indians*, ed. William C. Sturtevant (Washington: Smithsonian Institution, Government Printing Office, 1978) at 246.

24 For a discussion of the consequences of the Oregon Treaty of 1846, see Stuart Banner, *Possessing the Pacific: Land, Settlers, and Indigenous People from Australia to Alaska* (Cambridge: Harvard University Press, 2007) at 231; Kent McNeil, 'Negotiated Sovereignty: Indian Treaties and the Acquisition of American and Canadian Territorial Rights in the Pacific Northwest,' in *The Power of Promises: Rethinking Indian Treaties in the Pacific Northwest*, ed. Alexandra Harmon (Seattle: University of Washington Press, 2008) at 35.

25 Jean Barman, *The West Beyond the West: A History of British Columbia* (Toronto: University of Toronto Press, 1996) at 66; Cole Harris, *Making Native Space: Colonialism Resistance, and Reserves in British Columbia* (Vancouver: UBC Press, 2002) at 213.

26 For a complete report of the presentation by the Haida to the McKenna McBride Commission in 1913, concerning government failures to recognize Haida title, see 'Royal Commission on Indian Affairs: Skidegate, BC, September 13th, 1913,' *Haida Laas Journal of the Haida Nation*, September 2010, at 18, http://www.haidanation.ca/Pages/haida_laas/pdfs/journals/jl_sept.01.pdf: 'As far back as we can remember we can claim that the Islands fairly belong to us and as far back as we can remember there was never any treaty with respect to this land, between the Government and the Indians. We have never had a fight for the Islands. No nation ever came and fought us for them and won them from us.'

27 See 'Athlii Gwaii: 25 Years Down the Road,' *Haida Laas Newletters*, Special Issue, November 2010, http://www.haidanation.ca/Pages/haida_laas/pdfs/journals/jl_nov.10.pdf.

28 During this same period, the premier of British Columbia said that a logging license on Haida Gwaii would not be renewed; see Susan Porter-Bopp, *Colonial Natures? Wilderness and Culture in Gwaii Haanas National Park Reserve and Haida Heritage Site*, M.E.S., York University, 17 October 2006 at 44.

29 See the Great Wild Spaces website, http://www.spacesfornature.org/greatspaces/moresby.html.

30 For further context, see Elizabeth May, *Paradise Won: The Struggle for South Moresby* (Toronto: McClelland and Stewart, 1990).

31 David Rossiter, 'The Nature of a Blockade: Environmental Politics and the Haida Action on Lyell Island British Columbia,' in *Blockades or Breakthroughs: Aboriginal Peoples Confront the Canadian State*, ed. Yale Belanger and P. Whitney Lackenbauer (Montreal: McGill-Queen's University Press, 2015).

32 Jeremy Wilson, *Talk and Log: Wilderness Politics in British Columbia, 1965–96* (Vancouver: UBC Press, 1998) at 219.

33 'Loggers Confront Haida Blockade,' *CBC News* Archives, http://www.cbc.ca/archives/entry/loggers-confront-haida-blockade.

34 'Haidas Face Action in Blocking Loggers,' *Globe and Mail*, 15 November 1985.

35 *Vancouver Sun*, 10 November 1985, cited in Porter-Bopp, *Colonial Natures?* at 56 [unpublished].

36 Ian Gill, *All That We Say Is Ours: Guujaaw and the Reawakening of the Haida Nation* (Toronto: Douglas and McIntyre, 2009) at chap. 7: '[Haida Elder] Ethel Jones says: "This is our land and, you know, we definitely aren't afraid of going to jail. Maybe that'll open our government's eyes. Look at this little old lady sitting in jail. For what? For protecting their land? We've slept long enough." [Another Elder] Ada Yovanovich [said]: "We're here to protect our land, and if that's a crime, I'm willing to go [to jail] … I'm over sixty. It doesn't really matter as long as I have some fancywork to do. No, I don't mind at all."'

37 *West Forest Prod. v. Collinson*, [1985] B.C.W.L.D. 4340, subsequent proceeding, [1986] B.C.W.L.D. 609, [1986] B.C.W.L.D. 2365 (B.C.S.C.).

38 Further context is found in Michael Dean, 'What They Are Doing to the Land, They Are Doing to Us: Environmental Politics on Haida Gwaii' (master's thesis, University of British Columbia, 2009), http://www.collectionscanada.gc.ca/obj/thesescanada/vol2/BVAU/TC-BVAU-13912.pdf.

39 The Haida defence in the case is discussed in Norbert Ruebesaat, 'Speaking with Diane Brown' (master's thesis, Simon Fraser University, 1987). Specific discussions about Haida law occur at page 132.

40 Guujaaw, president of the Haida Nation, said of this strategy, 'We didn't use lawyers. We represented ourselves. We certainly weren't trying to beat it on technicalities or deny that we did it. We went into court to explain why we felt we had to do it.' See 'Lyell Island, 25 Years Later,' 17 November 2010, https://wildernesscommittee.org/news/lyell_island_25_years_later.

41 *West Forest Prod. v. Collinson*, [1985] B.C.W.L.D. 4340, subsequent proceeding, [1986] B.C.W.L.D. 609, [1986] B.C.W.L.D. 2365 (B.C.S.C.).

42 Justice McEachern refused to accept Haida legal arguments because he said he 'must do justice according to the law.' John Cruikshank, 'Haida Not Criminals Judge Tells BC,' *Globe and Mail*, 29 November 1985, A2, cited in Pamela Joanne Bush, 'See You in Court: Native Indians and the Law in British Columbia' (master's thesis, University of British Columbia, 1987) at 148.

43 For a discussion of the Haida Watchmen, see Nancy J. Turner, *The Earth's Blanket: Traditional Teachings for Sustainable Living* (Vancouver: Douglas and McIntyre, 2005) at 224–5.

44 Great Wild Spaces website as at note 29 above.

45 May, *Paradise Won* at 147–56.

46 Great Wild Spaces website as at note 29 above.

47 *R. v. Oakes*, [199\86] 1 S.C.R. 103 at 136.

48 Porter-Bopp, *Colonial Natures?* at 66.

49 Ibid. at 73.

50 For an analysis of the forest management aspects of the Gwaii Haanas Agreement, see D.B. Tindall, Ronald Trosper, and Pamela Perreault, eds., *Aboriginal Peoples and Forest Lands in Canada* (Vancouver: UBC Press, 2013) at 242.

51 R.S.C. 2000, c. 32.

52 R.S.C., 2002. c. 18. The Haida also reached a strategic land-use agreement with the British Columbia government in 2007, and in 2010 the parties entered into an agreement entitled Kunst'aa guu – Kunsta'aayah. This agreement deals with the issue of land-use planning and economic development with strong Haida decision-making structures through the creation of a Haida Gwaii management council.

53 Gill, *All That We Say Is Ours* at 158–9.

54 *Haida Nation v. British Columbia (Minister of Forests)*, [2004] 3 S.C.R. 511 at para. 25:

Put simply, Canada's Aboriginal peoples were here when Europeans came, and were never conquered. Many bands reconciled their claims with the sovereignty of the Crown through negotiated treaties. Others, notably in British Columbia, have yet to do so. The potential rights embedded in these claims are protected by s. 35 of the Constitution Act, 1982. The honour of the Crown requires that these rights be determined, recognized and respected. This, in turn, requires the Crown, acting honourably, to participate in processes of negotiation. While this process continues, the honour of the Crown may require it to consult and, where indicated, accommodate Aboriginal interests.

55 *Haida Nation v. British Columbia (Minister of Forests)*, [2004] 3 S.C.R. 511 at para. 42.
56 Ibid. at para. 32.
57 Ibid. at para. 16, referring to the role of the Crown's honour in Aboriginal rights cases.
58 For a discussion of more general experiences in the James Bay region that illustrate this point see, generally, Colin Scott, ed., *Aboriginal Autonomy and Development in Northern Quebec and Labrador* (Vancouver: UBC Press, 2001).
59 For an analysis of the James Bay Indigenous experience between 1975 and 1999, see James F. Horning, *Social and Environmental Impacts of the James Bay Hydroelectric Project* (Montreal: McGill-Queen's University Press, 1999).
60 For a discussion of the James Bay Cree people's relationship with their land, see Hans M. Carlson, *Home Is the Hunter: The James Bay Cree and Their Land* (Vancouver: UBC Press, 2008).
61 For a discussion of early relations between the James Bay Cree and Europeans, see Daniel Francis and Toby Morantz, *Partners in Furs: A History of the Fur Trade in Eastern James Bay, 1600–1870* (Montreal: McGill-Queen's University Press, 1983).
62 For a further discussion of the vacuously abstract nature of the doctrine of discovery, see Robert J. Miller, Jacinta Ruru, Larissa Berendht, and Tracey Lindberg, *Discovering Indigenous Lands: The Doctrine of Discovery in the English Colonies* (Oxford: Oxford University Press, 2010).
63 Boyce Richardson, *Strangers Devour the Land* (New York: Alfred Knopf, 1985).
64 *Constitution Act, 1867*, 30 & 31 Victoria, c. 3, section 146.
65 *Rupert's Land Act*, 1868, 31–32 Victoria, c. 105 (U.K.).
66 For a further discussion of the development of the James Bay hydro projects, see Sean McCutcheon, *Electric Rivers: The Story of the James Bay Project* (New York: Black Rose Books, 1991).
67 One lesson to draw from the triumph of *law* over *the factual reality of Indigenous practical use* is that grounded Indigenous practices can be displaced

by ideal forms (such as the government's paper claim of ownership) if governments act on the so-called reality of legal forms. False horizons can turn into substantial restrictions when they are embedded in law.

68 *Kanatewat v. James Bay Dev. Corp.*, (1974) Que. R.P. 38; reversed (1979) (C.A.) 166; leave to appeal dismiss (1975) 1 S.C.R. 48; see also Richardson, *Strangers Devour the Land* at 242–59.

69 Richard Salisbury, *A Homeland for the Cree: Regional Development in James Bay, 1971–1981* (Montreal: McGill-Queen's University Press, 1986) at 53–63.

70 For a sociological account of the James Bay Cree's efforts to protect their land and governance, see Ronald Neizen, *Defending the Land: Sovereignty and Forest Life in James Bay Cree Society* (Boston: Allyn and Bacon, 1998).

71 Paul Rynard, '"Welcome In, But Check Your Rights at the Door": The James Bay and Nisga'a Agreements in Canada' (2000) 33 *Canadian Journal of Political Science* 211–43; Paul Rynard, 'Ally or Colonizer? The Federal State, the Cree Nation and the James Bay Agreement' (2001) 36 *Journal of Canadian Studies* 8–48.

72 For further commentary, see Martin Thibeault and Steven Michael Hoffman, *Power Struggles: Hydro Development and First Nations in Manitoba and Quebec* (Winnipeg: University of Manitoba Press, 2008).

73 For a strong critique of this requirement from a Cree perspective, see Grand Council of the Crees (of Quebec), *Sovereign Injustice: Forcible Inclusion of the James Bay Crees and Cree Territory into a Sovereign Quebec* (Nemaska, QC: Grand Council of the Crees, 1995).

74 The Union of British Columbia Indian Chiefs (UBCIC) has criticized the 'certainty' provisions available within the BC Treaty Process:

> Canada, the province, and third parties have their rights and interests recognized and protected. These rights are not defined or in any way limited by the Agreement. The Indigenous group, on the other hand, have all of their rights reduced to the written word of the Agreement.
>
> These certainty provisions are far more restrictive than any of the 'extinguishment language' which has been used in other modern land claims agreements to date.

See UBCIC, *Certainty: Canada's Struggle to Extinguish Aboriginal Title*, http://www.ubcic.bc.ca/print/Resources/certainty.htm. For further critique of 'extinguishment clauses,' see Royal Commission on Aboriginal Peoples, *Treaty Making in the Spirit of Coexistence: An Alternative to Extinguishment* (Ottawa: Royal Commission on Aboriginal Peoples, 1995).

75 Christopher Alcantra, 'Old Wine in New Bottles? Instrumental Policy Learning and the Evolution of the Certainty Provision in Comprehensive Land Claims Agreements' (2009) 35 *Canadian Public Policy*, 325–41.

76 For detailed documents discussing implementation problems with modern land claims agreements, from the claimants perspectives, see the Land Claims Agreements Coalition website, http://www.landclaimscoalition. ca/coalition-members/. For an assessment of implantation challenges with historic treaties, see Jill St. Germain, *Indian Treaty-Making Policy in the United States and Canada, 1867–1877* (Toronto: University of Toronto Press, 2001).

77 Caroline Desbiens, *Power from the North: Territory, Identity, and the Culture of Hydroelectricity in Quebec* (Vancouver: UBC Press, 2013).

78 Daniel Salée and Carole Lévesque, 'Representing Aboriginal Self-Government and First Nations/State Relations: Political Agency and the Management of the Boreal Forest in Eeyou Istchee' (2010) 41 *International Journal of Canadian Studies Review* 99 at paras. 29–34.

79 The Paix Des Braves Agreement, as it has come to be known, gives $3.5 billion over fifty years plus a share of the benefits from natural resources taken from Cree land; see *Agreement Concerning a New Relationship between le Gouvernement du Québec and the Crees of Québec*, http://www.autochtones. gouv.qc.ca/relations_autochtones/ententes/cris/entente-020207_en.pdf.

80 Ibid. at preamble.

81 Ibid.

82 Ibid.

83 Ibid. at chap. 2: 'This Agreement marks an important stage in a new nation-to-nation relationship, one that is open, respectful of the other community and that promotes a greater responsibility on the part of the Cree Nation for its own development within the context of greater autonomy.'

84 Salée and Lévesque, 'Representing Aboriginal Self-Government and First Nations/State Relations.'

85 Gabrielle A. Slowey, 'Federalism and First Nations: In Search of Space,' in *Constructing Tomorrow's Federalism: New Perspectives on Canadian Governance*, ed. Ian Peach and Roy Romano (Winnipeg: University of Manitoba Press, 2007) 157 at 166–7.

86 The 1975 James Bay Agreement created a settlement that initially satisfied some of the Cree people in the territory. However, the government's failure to effectively implement the terms of the agreement turned many against it. The treaty became a tool of further government domination when its democratic potential was not embraced by the federal government.

87 *Reference Re Secession of Québec*, [1998] 2 S.C.R. 217 at para. 68.

88 Ibid.

89 For more detail about the historic development of the Royal Proclamation from a First Nations perspective, see John Borrows, 'Wampum at Niagara: The Royal Proclamation, Canadian Legal History, and Self-Government,' in *Aboriginal and Treaty Rights in Canada*, ed. Michael Asch (Vancouver: UBC Press, 1997) at 155.

90 In the United States, the successor policies to the Royal Proclamation were the *Northwest Ordinance* of 1787 and the *Indian Trade and Intercourse Act* of 1790; see Francis Paul Prucha, *The Great Father: The United States Government and the American Indians* (Lincoln: University of Nebraska Press, 1984) at 89–114.

91 Kevin Kenny, *Peaceable Kingdom Lost: The Paxton Boys and the Destruction of William Penn's Holy Experiment* ((New York: Oxford University Press, 2009); Gary Nash, *The Unknown American Revolution: The Unruly Birth of Democracy and the Struggle to Create America* (New York: Viking, 2005) at 345.

92 Anthony Hall, *American Empire and the Fourth World: The Bowl with One Spoon, Part One* (Montreal: McGill-Queen's University Press, 2003) 336–46.

93 *Chippewas of the Sarnia Band v. Canada (A.G.)* 195 D.L.R. (4th) 135; [2001] 1 C.N.L.R. 56 (Ont. C.A.) at para. 56; John Borrows, 'Constitutional Law from a First Nation Perspective: Self-Government and the Royal Proclamation' (1994) 28 *University of British Columbia Law Review* 1–48.

94 See Lindsay Robertson, *Conquest by Law: How the Discovery of America Dispossessed Indigenous Peoples of Their Lands* (New York: Oxford University Press, 2005); Stuart Banner, *How The Indians Lost Their Land: Law and Power on the Frontier* (Cambridge, MA: Harvard University Press, 2005).

95 Colin Calloway, *The Scratch of a Pen: 1763 and the Transformation of North America* (New York: Penguin, 2006) at 60–5; Sidney L. Harring, 'The Six Nations Confederacy, Aboriginal Sovereignty, and Ontario Aboriginal Law, 1790–1860,' in *Earth, Water, Air, Fire: Studies in Canadian Ethnohistory*, ed. David McNab for Nin.Da.Waab.Jig (Waterloo, ON: Wilfrid Laurier University Press, 1992) 181 at 182.

96 Peter Schmalz, *The Ojibway of Southern Ontario* (Toronto: University of Toronto Press, 1991) 140–6.

97 PAC RG 10, v. 213, pp. 126, 356–7. 'T.G. Anderson, Superintendent of Indian Affairs, responding to the Owen Sound and Saugeen Indians,' 2 August 1854.

98 For example, private land in British Columbia was almost entirely taken up through non-Aboriginal occupation of Aboriginal lands, as settlers were permitted and indeed encouraged to take up Indian lands through

'pre-emption.' When the Indians tried to resist this injustice through blockade and occupation, they were not supported by the government. In 1864,
Chief Klatsassin led what has come to be known at the Chilcotin War in
the interior of British Columbia. Aboriginal peoples in the area refused to
allow non-Aboriginal people to survey what they regarded as their land.
The chief and other Indians allegedly attacked and killed thirteen surveyors planning a road to the Cariboo gold fields from the head of Bute Inlet.
The Chilcotin physical occupation of lands that Canada was attempting to
chart ended when Klatsassin and four other chiefs who arrived at Quesnel
to negotiate a treaty with a promise of safe conduct were seized, tried, and
hanged. Furthermore, the colonial legislature of British Columbia passed
statutes that permitted non-Aboriginal people to 'legally' register land in
their own names if they 'occupied' Aboriginal land for a certain period
and made small 'improvements,' such as building a house or clearing the
bush. An ordinance to further define the law regulating the acquisition of
land in British Columbia, 1866 (B.C.), 29 Vict., No. 24, s. 1, provided

> the right conferred ... on British Subjects or aliens ... of pre-empting
> and holding land in fee simple unoccupied and unsurveyed and unre-
> served Crown lands in British Columbia, shall not (without the special
> permission of the Governor first had in writing) extend or be deemed to
> have been conferred on ... any Aborigines of this Colony or the Territo-
> ries neighbouring thereto. A further amendment passed by the Legisla-
> tive Council on 22 April 1870 extended the denial to 'any of the Aborigi-
> nes of this Continent.' Disturbingly, pre-emption was a right denied to
> Aboriginal peoples in the same period. This double standard permit-
> ted non-Aboriginal people to physically occupy Aboriginal land to the
> detriment of its original owners. Occupations and physical blockades
> were the primary mode of non-Aboriginal settlement in the province of
> British Columbia. This form of physical removal of Aboriginal people
> created a province, despite the existence of Aboriginal use and occupa-
> tion prior to the arrival of settlers in these traditional territories. British
> Columbia's experience shows that civil (dis)obedience through block-
> ades can be effective, even if their morality and legality is sometimes
> questionable.

99 Michael Thoms, 'Ojibwa Fishing Grounds: A History of Ontario Fisheries
Law, Science, and the Sportsmen's Challenge to Aboriginal Treaty Rights:
1650–1900' (PhD diss., University of British Columbia, 2004) [unpub-
lished]. For an overview of the history of treaties in Southern Ontario,
see James Miller, *Compact, Contract, Covenant: Aboriginal Treaty-Making in
Canada* (Toronto: University of Toronto Press, 2009) at 93–122.

100 John Borrows, 'A Genealogy of Law: Inherent Sovereignty and First Nations Self-Government' (1992) 30 *Osgoode Hall Law Journal* 391.

101 Peggy J. Blair, 'Solemn Promises and Solum Rights: The Saugeen Ojibway Fishing Grounds and *R. v. Jones* and *Nadjiwon*,' *Ottawa Law Review* 28 (1996–1997) 125–43; Peggy J. Blair, '"Taken for Granted": Aboriginal Title and Public Fishing Rights in Upper Canada,' *Ontario History* 92, no. 1 (2000) at 31–55.

102 Peggy Blair, *Lament for a First Nation: The Williams Treaties of Southern Ontario* (Vancouver: UBC Press, 2008).

103 Edwin Koenig, *Cultures and Ecologies: A Native Fishing Conflict on the Saugeen-Bruce Peninsula* (Toronto: University of Toronto Press, 2006) at 116–17, 125.

104 *R. v. Jones and Nadjiwon*, [1993] 3 C.N.L.R. 182 (Ont. Prov. Div.).

105 Ibid.

106 Rick Wallace, Marilyn Struthers, and Rick Cober Bauman, 'Winning Fishing Rights: The Success and Challenges of Building Grassroots Relationships between the Chippewas of the Nawash and their Allies,' in *Alliances: Re/envisioning Indigenous and Non-Indigenous Relationships*, ed. Lynne Davis (Toronto: University of Toronto Press, 2010).

107 The press release from the Chippewas of the Nawash (available at https://www.attorneygeneral.jus.gov.on.ca/inquiries/ipperwash/policy_part/projects/pdf/under_siege.pdf) gave the reason for the occupation as follows:

> 'These reserve lands contain the remains of our dead,' says Chief Akiwenzie of the Chippewas of Nawash. 'They were reserved as Indian lands in the treaty of 1857, but were never protected by the Department of Indian Affairs. As a result, they were illegally sold and are now the sites of modern houses. For all the desecration these grounds have suffered, they are still sacred to us. They are still Indian Land. We have waited for over 100 years for them to be restored to us. We will not wait any longer.'
>
> Over the years the burial ground at 6th Avenue West in Owen Sound has been disturbed in a most sacrilegious way. Graves were looted, artifacts (including a corpse) were sent to museums, and the soil from the 6th Avenue West site was used to make bricks for construction in Owen Sound.
>
> The Department of Indian Affairs has known of the Band's concerns for over a year and of Nawash's six point plan for correcting the situation (only the survey was done, confirming the land is Nawash's).
>
> Darlene Johnston, land claims researcher and Nawash Band member, said, 'Sure the Department of Indian Affairs has said they will prosecute

the current occupants if they cannot come to a settlement. But it's time we, as a First Nation, stood up and defended our lands ourselves. It should be us who take the heat for court action – not the federal government. But it should be the federal government who funds the court action. Trouble is, they won't. Taking our white neighbours to court won't make us very popular in the area. But then we've never been very popular here anyway.'

Chief Akiwenzie said, 'It is time for non-Native governments to truly recognize our right to self-government and back off enough to let First Nations assert their own jurisdiction and authority. That's mostly what this occupation is all about. We are symbolically taking back our land and honouring those who have become part of it.'

The Saugeen Ojibway do not believe the Department of Indian Affairs is acting in their best interests and therefore demand the following:

1. Immediate control of the process of returning the lands to reserve status, including no further monetary offers without Nawash approval.

2. A commitment to remove the structures currently desecrating the burial grounds.

3. A commitment to restore, protect and maintain the burial grounds.

4. A commitment to fund a monument recognizing these burial grounds as unceded territory.

Until Nawash is satisfied the other governments recognize the First Nation's jurisdiction and authority over these lands, the sacred fire of the vigil will not go out.

108 The biggest challenge in taking direct action to reoccupy our burial site was found in the reaction of a few municipal officials. Acknowledgment of ancestral human remains on the site was slow in coming. There were also questions about the plot of land's ownership, despite the burial ground's having been set aside as a reserve in treaty. Fortunately, in this case civil (dis)obedience opened doors for further discussion with federal and provincial officials. The blockade remained in place for a week, and the issue was resolved when federal officials intervened and negotiated to meet Nawash demands. In this instance, direct action increased Indigenous freedom because the protests were peaceful, informational, aimed at wider engagement, and built on recognized legal interests. These conditions led to a favourable result. This demonstrates that civil (dis)obedience can be practised in ways that are consistent with a free and democratic society.

109 For a discussion of Nuu-Chah-Nulth creation discourses and their inter-action with Canadian law, see Umeek of Ahousaht (Richard Atleo), 'Dis-courses in and About Clayquot: A First Nations Perspective,' in *A Political Space: Reading the Global Through Clayoquot Sound*, ed. Warren Magnusson and Karena Shaw (Minneapolis: University of Minnesota Press, 2003) at 199.

110 Michaela Killoran Mann, '"Clearcut" Conflict: Clayoquot Sound Cam-paign and the Moral Imagination' (master's thesis, Saint Paul University, 2013) at 4.

111 See Daniel Clayton, *Islands of Truth: The Imperial Fashioning of Vancouver Island* (Vancouver: UBC Press, 2000) at 131–49.

112 Peter Pearse, 'Evolution of the Forest Tenure System in British Columbia,' February 1992, Vancouver, BC [unpublished] at 9–12, www.for.gov.bc.ca/hfd/library/documents/bib49592.pdf.

113 For a more general discussion of tribal parks in this region, see Grant Mur-ray and Leslie King, 'First Nations Values in Protected Area Governance: Tla-o-qui-aht Tribal Parks and Pacific Rim National Park Reserve' (2012) 40 *Human Ecology* 385–95.

114 For a first-person environmentalist perspective on Friends of the Clayo-quot, see Tzeporah Berman and Mark Leiren-Young, *This Crazy Time: Liv-ing Our Environmental Challenge* (Toronto: Random House, 2011).

115 For a discussion of forestry practices and conflict, see Patricia Marchak, *Logging the Globe* (Montreal: McGill-Queen's University Press, 1995) 94–5, 105–7.

116 *MacMillan Bloedel v. Mullin; Martin v. The Queen in right of British Columbia*, (1985) 3 W.W.R. 577 (B.C.C.A.); leave to appeal to S.C.C. refused (1985) 5 W.W.R. lxiv. For commentary, see Douglas Harris, 'A Court Between: Aboriginal and Treaty Rights in the British Columbia Court of Appeal' (2009) 162 *BC Studies* 137 at 148–50.

117 *Clayoquot Sound Land Use Decision* (Victoria, BC: Queen's Printer, 1993).

118 *Vancouver Sun*, 1 May 1993.

119 Ronald MacIsaac and Anne Champagne, *Clayoquot Mass Trials: Defending the Rainforest* (Gabriola Island, BC: New Society, 1994).

120 See Friends of Clayoquot Sound, 'About Us,' at http://www.focs.ca/1newsroom/sprnl20031.html (checked 29 June 2005).

121 Bruce Braun, *The Intemperate Rainforest: Nature, Culture, and Power on Can-ada's West Coast* (Minneapolis: University of Minnesota Press, 2002) at 1–2.

122 *MacMillan Bloedel Ltd. v. Simpson*, 1992 CanLII 1593 (BC S.C.). See also *McMillan Bloedel v. Simpson*, [1996] 2 S.C.R. 1048.

123 The operative principles of the Scientific Panel were judged to be 'based on sound ecological science, a holistic philosophy ... and a respectful

acknowledgement of the Nu-Chah-Nulth's rightful role in decision-making regarding forest use.' See Herb Hammond and Alix Flavelle, 'Major Points from an Initial Analysis of the Reports of the Scientific Panel for Sustainable Development in Clayoquot Sound' (1995) 11:2/3 *International Journal of Ecoforestry* 79 at 81. This acknowledgment helped to create a supportive social context for the resolution of the dispute. It was a form of recognition that was welcomed by First Nations in the area. This endorsement does not mean that the work of the panel was perfect. In fact, the report suffers from limited terms of reference. Furthermore, the panel did not go far enough in addressing some issues even within its mandate. However, the affirmation of Nu-Chah-Nulth science was at least a partial fulfilment of this report's potential to change forestry practices by including First Nations in forest planning processes.

124 Tara Goetze, 'Empowered Co-Management: Towards Power-Sharing and Indigenous Rights in Clayoquot Sound, BC' (2005) 47 *Anthropologica* 252 at 254.

125 See Friends of Clayoquot Sound, 'History,' at http://www.focs.ca/history_focs/timeline.html (checked 29 June 2005).

126 The potential destruction of the forests surrounding First Nations threatens more than just Indigenous communities. The network of life that the forest sustains is equally imperilled, including the local non-Native and non-human communities. Inadequate forest protection can also harm relationships of provincial and national trade. The great danger in forest resource extraction is that wood stocks can be drawn down to a level far below efficient investment returns. Subsidies and low stumpage rates may contribute to and encourage this depletion. See William Freudenberg, 'Addictive Economies: Extractive Industries and Vulnerable Localities in a Changing World Economy' (1992) 57(3) *Rural Sociology* 305.

127 Premier Mike Harcourt announced the creation of this panel on 22 October 1993.

128 The Scientific Panel for Sustainable Forest Practices in Clayoquot Sound, *Progress Report 2: Review of Current Forest Practices in Clayoquot Sound*, 10 May 1994 at 4.

129 For further discussion of Clayoquot Sound in the context of conflict transformation, see Killoran Mann, '"Clearcut" Conflict,' accessed 1 April 2014, https://www.ruor.uottawa.ca/en/bitstream/handle/10393/24042/Mann_Michaela%20Killoran_2013_thesis.pdf.

130 As briefly noted, the articulation of ecosystem goals for forest management was assisted by the complimentary uses of the Nu-Chah-Nulth phrase 'everything is one.' This philosophy contributed to a framework

for an ecosystem based resource usage. The approach has been described by Haiyupis in the following terms: 'Respect is the very core of our traditions, culture and existence. It is very basic to all we encounter in life. ... Respect for nature requires a state of stewardship with a healthy attitude. It is wise to respect nature. Respect for the Spiritual ... It is not human to waste food. It is inhuman to over-exploit. "Protect and Conserve" are the key values.' The Scientific Panel for Sustainable Forest Practices in Clayoquot Sound, *Report 3: First Nations' Perspectives Relating to Forest Practice Standards in Clayoquot Sound*, March 1995 at 6.

131 Ibid., *Report 3* at 51.

132 For further information discussing Nuu-Chah-Nulth principles, see Eugene Richard Atleo, *Principles of Tsawalk: An Indigenous Approach to Global Crisis* (Vancouver: UBC Press, 2011).

133 Jeffrey Vincent and Clark Binkley, 'Forest-Based Industrialization: A Dynamic Perspective,' in *Managing the World's Forests*, ed. N. Sharma (Dubuque, IA: Kendall-Hunt Publishing, 1992).

134 The Scientific Panel for Sustainable Forest Practices in Clayoquot Sound, *Report 3* at 6.

135 The Scientific Panel for Sustainable Forest Practices in Clayoquot Sound, *Report 5: Sustainable Ecosystem Management in Clayoquot Sound, Planning and Practices*, April 1995.

136 All of Clayoquot's 'turning points involve the development of new relationships.' See Killoran Mann, '"Clearcut" Conflict' at 67.

137 For information about Iisaak, see Alisa Stern and Tim Hicks, *The Process of Business/Environmental Collaborations: Partnering for Sustainability* (Westport, CT: Greenwood Publishing, 2000) at 16–17.

138 Emily Walter, 'From Civil Disobedience to Obedient Consumerism: Influences of Market-Based Activism and Eco-Certification on Forest Governance' (2003) 41 *Osgoode Hall Law Journal* 531.

139 For commentary in this regard, see Johnny Mack, 'Hoquotist: Reorienting through Storied Practice,' in *Storied Communities: Narratives of Contact and Arrival in Constituting Political Community*, ed. Hester Lessard, Rebecca Johnson, and Jeremy Webber (Vancouver: UBC Press, 2011) at 287.

140 For an industry perspective on the events at Clayoquot, see Gordon Butt and Don McMillan, 'Clayoquot Sound: Lessons in Ecosystem-based Management Implementation from an Industry Perspective' (2009) 10 *BC Journal of Ecosystems and Management* 13 at 19: 'Looking back from an industry perspective, the process was cumbersome, inefficient, and costly. Industry has a focus on the financial bottom line, so it is natural that the industry

perspective largely reflects the effects of changes on timber revenues and costs.'

141 While the report has many references to First Nations input, the panel's recommendations did not make it clear *how* First Nations would participate in decision-making processes. For example, see R4 of The Scientific Panel for Sustainable Forest Practices in Clayoquot Sound, *Report 3* at 50: 'All decision-making process relating to ecosystem use and management in the Clayoquot Sound Decision Area must be undertaken in full consultation with the Nuu-Chah-Nulth.'

142 The Scientific Panel for Sustainable Forest Practices in Clayoquot Sound, *Report 5* at 155. The panel did not recommend any particular form of participation. The parties did not have the advantage of the court's developing principles regarding consultation outlined above. The panel's lack of attention to ongoing participation is a troubling point for First Nations' potential influence over forestry. Given the current allocation of power, wealth, and authority, it is difficult for First Nations to convince others to adopt different priorities.

143 Ongoing treaty negotiations have absorbed the Nuu-Chah-Nulth efforts to hold their place within their territory. There have been few physical occupations or blockade protests in the area because of the presence of negotiated alternatives. The Nuu-Chah-Nulth had some success as a result of their protest and had certain of their interests recognized in the report that allowed them to address larger land-use issues in their wider territory. This focus on other priorities has meant the implementation of the Scientific Panel's report has not received the attention it might have if it were the only item on the table. Nevertheless, First Nations are having a small influence over the way forests are actually utilized in Clayoquot Sound. The Interim Measures Agreement was an important step in this regard, and while the measures identified still have their problems, there is a greater measure of forest protection present because of their existence. For example, the Clayoquot Interim Measures Agreement restricts harvest rates to 300,000 cubic metres a year.

144 Essays discussing its implications are found in *This Is an Honour Song: Twenty Years since the Blockades*, ed. Kiera Ladner and Leanne Simpson (Winnipeg: Arbeiter Ring, 2008).

145 James Pendergast, 'The Confusing Identities Attributed to Stadacona and Hochelaga' (1998) 32 *Journal of Canadian Studies*; Darlene Johnston, 'Litigating Identity: The Challenge of Aboriginality' (master's thesis, University of Toronto, 2003) [unpublished].

146 For the Supreme Court of Canada's statement on Aboriginal rights in New France and Quebec, see *R. v. Adams* [1996] 3 S.C.R. 101 at paras. 31–3; *R. v. Côté*, [1996] 3 S.C.R. 139 at paras. 42–54.

147 See Geoffrey York, *People of the Pines: The Warriors and the Legacy of Oka* (Toronto: Little Brown, 1991) at 43.

148 See Kanasatake Fact Sheet, http://www.aadnc-aandc.gc.ca/eng/110010 0016305/1100100016306 (checked 19 September 2005).

149 Linda Pertusati, *In Defense of Mohawk Land: Ethnopolitical Conflict in North America* (Buffalo: SUNY Press, 1997) at 29.

150 Amelia Kalant, *National Identity and the Conflict at Oka* (New York: Routledge Press, 2004) at 207–10.

151 *Corinthe v. Le Séminaire de Saint-Sulpice* [1911] 21 C.B.R. 316.

152 See James Miller, 'Great White Father Knows Best: Oka and the Land Claims Process' (1991) 7 *Native Studies Review* 24.

153 As with all communities, there have long been different approaches concerning how to best resolve political issues. For more discussion in this context, see Gerald F. Reid, *Kahnawa:ke: Factionalism, Traditionalism, and Nationalism in a Mohawk Community* (Lincoln: University of Nebraska Press, 2004).

154 Patricia Monture, 'The Human Right to Celebrate: Achieving Justice for Aboriginal Peoples,' in *This Is an Honour Song*, ed. Ladner and Simpson, at 291; Ellen Gabriel, 'Epilogue: Fraudulent Theft of Mohawk Land by the Municipality of Oka,' ibid. at 345; Gerald Alfred, *Heeding the Voice of Our Ancestors: Kahnawake Politics and the Rise of Native Nationalism* (Toronto: Oxford University Press, 1995).

155 Alanis Obomsowin, *Kanehsatake: 270 Years of Resistance*, Film (Ottawa: National Film Board of Canada, 1993); Donna Goldleaf, *Entering the Warzone: A Mohawk Perspective on Resisting Invasions* (Penticton, BC: Theytus Books, 1995).

156 Jane Dickson Gilmore, 'Always About the Land: The Oka Crisis of 1990,' in *Canada: Confederation to the Present*, ed. Bob Hesketh and Chris Hackett (Edmonton: Chinook Media, 2001).

157 It is important to note the involvement of a Warrior Society in the blockades at Oka; see Pertusati, *In Defense of Mohawk Land*; Rick Hornung, *One Nation under the Gun* (Toronto: Stoddart Publishing, 1991).

158 A coroner's report into the shooting death of Marcel Lemay concluded that the shot was fired by a Mohawk warrior. But the report failed to identify the killer, and no one was charged with Lemay's murder. P. Whitney Lackenbauer, 'The Mohawks, The Canadian Forces and the Oka Crisis' (2008) 10 *Journal of Military and Strategic Studies* 1 at 17, footnote 36.

159 Tony Hall, 'Blockades and Bannock: Aboriginal Protests and Politics in Northern Ontario 1980–1990' (1991) 7 *Wičazo Ša Review* 58.
160 Dean R. Snow, *The Iroquois* (Cambridge: Wiley-Blackwell, 1996) at 211.
161 Premier Bourassa invoked section 276 of the *National Defence Act* to request military support 'in aid to civil power,' which provinces are permitted to do under the act. While Prime Minister Mulroney seemed reluctant to involve the federal government, he applied the *National Defence Act* to allow the Canadian Army to get involved in the conflict; see Pertusati, *In Defense of Mohawk Land* at 110.
162 Note, however, that the army had had previous involvement at Oka three months before the crisis; see Timothy Winegard, 'The Forgotten Front of the Oka Crisis: Operation Feather/Akwesasne' (2009) 11 *Journal of Military and Strategic Studies* 1. The prior operation involved 248 personnel, 81 vehicles, 3 rafts, various boats, and 2 CH-135 helicopters and was aimed at intelligence-gathering related to economic activities, including gaming and cigarette sales.
163 This point was reinforced by the Indigenous Bar Association, 'Presentation by the Indigenous Bar Association to the Standing Committee on Aboriginal Affairs Regarding the Events at Kanesatake and Kahnawake During the Summer of 1990' (1991) 2 *Canadian Native Law Reporter* 1–10.
164 For a government insider's view on the Oka conflict, see Harry Swain, *Oka: A Political Crisis and Its Legacy* (Vancouver: Douglas and McIntyre, 2010).
165 Taiaiake Alfred, 'Then and Now, For the Land' (2010) 6 *Socialist Studies: The Journal of the Society for Socialist Studies* 93.
166 Douglas George-Kanentiio, *Iroquois on Fire: A Voice from the Mohawk Nation* (Lincoln: University of Nebraska Press, 2006); Robert Campbell and Leslie Pal, 'Feather and Gun: Confrontation at Oka/Kanesatake,' in *The Real Worlds of Canadian Politics: Cases in Process and Policy*, 2nd ed. (Peterborough, ON: Broadview Press, 1991).
167 Alexa Conradi, 'Uprising at Oka: A Place of Non-identification' (2009) 34 *Canadian Journal of Communication* 547.
168 Graham Fraser, 'PM Unveils Indian Agenda,' *Globe and Mail*, 26 September 1990.
169 For an analysis, see John Borrows, 'Domesticating Doctrines: Aboriginal Peoples after the Royal Commission' (2001) 46 *McGill Law Journal* 615.
170 For an evaluation of this report, see Alan Cairns, *Citizens Plus: Aboriginal Peoples and the Canadian State* (Vancouver: UBC Press, 2000) at 121.
171 Pertusati, *In Defense of Mohawk Land* at 136.

172 David Martin and Chris Adams, 'Canadian Public Opinion regarding Aboriginal Self-Government: Diverging Viewpoints as Found in National Survey Results' (2000) 30 *American Review of Canadian Studies* 79.

173 For a fuller description of this dispute, see Sarah King, 'Contested Place: Religion and Values in the Dispute, Burnt Church/Esgenoôpetitj, New Brunswick' (PhD diss., University of Toronto, 2008) [unpublished], http:// www.collectionscanada.gc.ca/obj/thesescanada/vol2/002/NR39916.pdf.

174 *R. v. Marshall* [1999] 3 S.C.R. 456 and *R. v. Marshall* [1999] 3 S.C.R. 533. See *Simon v. The Queen*, which helped break interpretive ground for the Marshall decisions, [1985] 2 S.C.R. 387.

175 Jacquelyn Thayer Scott, *An Atlantic Fishing Tale, 1999–2011* (Ottawa: Macdonald-Laurier Institute, February 2012), http://www.macdonald-laurier.ca/files/pdf/An-Atlantic-Fishing-Tale-February-2012.pdf.

176 For an analysis of how this dispute created greater Mi'kmaq dependence on Canada, see Melanie Wiber and Chris Milley, 'After Marshall: Implementation of Aboriginal Fishing Rights in Atlantic Canada' (2007) 55 *Journal of Legal Pluralism & Unofficial Law* 163.

177 James Sakej Ward, 'The Mi'kmaq and the Right to Self-determination' (2004) 1 *Ćelánen: A Journal of Indigenous Governance*, http://web.uvic.ca/ igov/research/journal/articles_ward_p.htm.

178 David Bedford, 'Emancipation as Oppression: The Marshall Decision and Self-Government' (2010) 44 *Journal of Canadian Studies* 206–20.

179 Annette Kolodny, *In Search of First Contact: The Vikings of Vinland, the Peoples of the Dawnland, and the Anglo-American Anxiety of Discovery* (Durham, NC: Duke University Press, 2012). Jacques Cartier entered Miramichi Bay in 1534; see H.P. Biggar, *The Voyages of Jacques Cartier* (1924), amended and augmented by Ramsay Cook (Toronto: University of Toronto Press, 1993) at 18; Wilson Dallam Wallis, Ruth Otis (Sawtell) Wallis, *The Micmac Indians of Eastern Canada* (Minneapolis: University of Minnesota Press, 1955) at 10.

180 Olive Dickason, *Canada's First Nations: A History of Founding Peoples from the Earliest Times* (Toronto: McClelland and Stewart, 1992) at 107.

181 Ibid.

182 John Mark Faragher, *A Great and Noble Scheme: The Tragic Story of the Expulsion of the French Acadians from Their American Homeland* (New York: W.W. Norton, 2006).

183 For descriptions of Mi'kmaq-Crown relations in this period, see William Wicken, 'Re-examining Mi'kmaq-Acadian Relations 1635–1755,' in *Vingt ans après, Habitants et marchands: Lectures de l'histoire des XVIIe et XVIIIe siècles canadians*, ed. Sylvie Dépatie, Catherine Desbarats, Danielle Gauvreau,

Mario Lalancette, and Thomas Wien (Montreal: McGill-Queen's University Press, 1998); William Wicken, 'Heard It from my Grandfather: Mi'kmaq Treaty Tradition and the Syliboy Case of 1928' (1995) 44 *U.N.B. Law Journal* 146.

184 William Wicken, 'The Mi'kmaq and Wuastukwiuk Treaties' (1994) 44 *U.N.B.L.J.* 241.

185 *R. v. Syliboy*, [1929] 1 D.L.R. 307 (N.S.Co.Ct.); William Wicken, *The Colonization of Mi'kmaw Memory and History, 1794–1928: The King v. Gabriel Sylliboy* (Toronto: University of Toronto Press, 2012).

186 Thomas Issac, *Aboriginal and Treaty Rights in the Maritimes: The Marshall Decision and Beyond* (Saskatoon: Purich Publishing, 2001); Alexander M. Cameron, *Power without Law: The Supreme Court of Canada, the Marshall Decisions, and the Failure of Judicial Activism* (Montreal: McGill-Queen's University Press, 2009).

187 Ken Coates, *The Marshall Decision and Native Rights* (Montreal: McGill-Queen's University Press, 2000).

188 For further context, see http://nvdatabase.swarthmore.edu/content/new-brunswick-burnt-church-first-nation-campaign-defend-their-fishing-rights-1999-2002.

189 For a fuller discussion of racism and fisheries conflicts, see Bonita Lawrence, 'Aboriginal Harvesting Rights and White Resistance' (2000) 24 *Atlantis: Critical Studies in Gender, Culture & Social Justice* 153–6.

190 Sarah J. King, 'Conservation Controversy: Sparrow, Marshall, and the Mi'kmaq of Esgenoôpetitj' (2011) 2(4) *International Indigenous Policy Journal* 1 at 5, http://ir.lib.uwo.ca/iipj/vol2/iss4/5.

191 Ibid.

192 For a discussion of Mi'kmaq environmental law, see Jaime Battiste, 'Understanding the Progression of Mi'kmaw Law' (2008) 31 *Dalhousie Law Journal* 311.

193 *R. v. Marshall*, [1999] S.C.J. No. 66, [1999] 3 S.C.R. 533, 179 D.L.R. (4th) 193 (S.C.C.) ('*Marshall No. 2*').

194 For critique, see Bruce Wildsmith, 'Vindicating Mi'Kmaq Rights: The Struggle before, during and after Marshall' (2001) 19 *Windsor Yearbook of Access to Justice* 203–40.

195 '*Marshall No. 2*' at para. 57.

196 Ibid. at para. 2.

197 For discussion of jurisdictional issues concerning Mi'kmaq fisheries, see Kiera Ladner, 'Up the Creek: Fishing for a New Constitutional Order' (2005) 38 *Canadian Journal of Political Science* 923–53.

198 For an in-depth discussion of Mi'kmaq traditions related to resource use, see K. Prosper, L.J. McMillan, A.A. Davis, and M. Moffitt, 'Returning to Netukulimk: Mi'kmaq Cultural and Spiritual Connections with Resource Stewardship and Self-Governance' (2011) 2(4) *The International Indigenous Policy Journal.*

199 Martha Stiegman, 'United We Fish' (2003) 29(4) *Alternatives Journal: Canadian Environmental Ideas and Action.*

200 For an argument that the government had a duty to regulate Maritime fisheries under the Marshall decision, see Tom Isaac, 'The Marshall Decision and the Government's Duty to Regulate' (2001) *Policy Options* 57, http://archive.irpp.org/po/archive/apr01/isaac.pdf.

201 On 4 May 2001, Rayburn Joseph Dedam, a Native man arrested during the previous year's violence, pled guilty to an assault charge stemming from confrontation between Natives and fishery officers. On 29 May 2000, two Native men from Burnt Church, Clifford Larry and Jason Barnaby, were fined $1,000 each for obstructing fisheries officers in June 2000.

202 Bruce Johansen, *Enduring Legacies: Native American Treaties and Contemporary Controversies* (Westport, CT: Greenwood Publishers, 2004) at 6.

203 For representations of the physical nature of the conflict at Burnt Church, see the film by Alanis Obomsawin, *Is the Crown at War with Us?* (Ottawa: National Film Board of Canada, 2002), http://www.nfb.ca/film/is_the_crown_at_war_with_us/.

204 King, '*Contested Place*' at 36.

205 Ibid. at 38.

206 Ibid.

207 King, 'Conservation Controversy' at 10–11.

208 For a fuller discussion of Canadian failures to abide by the rule of law in Aboriginal and treaty rights disputes, see Andrew Orkin, 'When the Law Breaks Down: Aboriginal Peoples in Canada and Governmental Defiance of the Rule of Law' (2003) 41 *Osgoode Hall Law Journal* 445.

209 Colonization is always a factor in any Indigenous act of civil (dis)obedience; see Mark Cronlund Anderson and Carmen Robertson, 'The "Bended Elbow" News, Kenora 1974: How a Small-Town Newspaper Promoted Colonization' (2007) 31 *American Indian Quarterly* 410–40.

210 Saul Alinsky, *Rules for Radicals: A Practical Guide for Realistic Radicals* (New York: Vintage Books, 1971); and the film by Peter Pearson, *Encounter with Saul Alinsky – Part 2*, (Ottawa: National Film Board of Canada, 1967), http://www.nfb.ca/film/encounter_with_saul_alinsky/.

211 Troy Johnson, Joane Nagel, and Duane Champagne, eds., *American Indian Activism: Alcatraz to the Longest Walk* (Chicago: University of Illinois Press, 1997).

212 First Nations located on both sides of the United States-Canadian border include the Mi'kmaq, Passamaquoddy, Abenaki, Haudenosaunee, Anishinaabek, Dakota, Assinaboine, Blackfoot, Scewepmec, Kunatax, Salish, Nuu-Chah-Nulth, Tlingit, and Haida. The Inuit are also located in Canada and Alaska. For a discussion of the historic context of the border's development, see Anthony Rees, *Arc of the Medicine Line: Mapping the World's Longest Undefended Border across the Western Plains* (Vancouver: Douglas and McIntyre, 2012).

213 *Mitchell v. M.N.R.* [2001] 1 S.C.R. 911.

214 Further information on AIM is found in Dennis Banks and Richard Erdoes, *Ojibwa Warrior: Dennis Banks and the Rise of the American Indian Movement* (Norman: University of Oklahoma Press, 2011). Banks spoke at Kenora during the occupation and eventually helped to mediate the dispute, which resulted in the removal of the blockades.

215 For further details, see Scott Rutherford, 'Canada's Other Red Scare: The Anicinabe Park Occupation and Indigenous Decolonization,' in *The Hidden 1970s: Histories of Radicalism*, ed. Dan Berger (New Brunswick, NJ: Rutgers University Press, 2010) at 77.

216 AIM spokesperson Louis Cameron said, 'We can't go into their courts and say: "We come here to say that you have killed our people, that you've raped people because you're destroying our land: you're destroying our people – people's homes" … Their decision IS predetermined by their set of laws and they cannot understand our position when we speak of sovereignty and independence.' In *Ojibway Warrior's Society in Occupied Anicinabe Park Kenora, Ontario, August 1974* (Toronto: Better Read Graphics, 1974) at 9.

217 Olive Patricia Dickason, *Canada's First Nations: A History of Founding Peoples from Earliest Times* (Toronto: McClelland and Stewart, 1992) at 392.

218 Hedican, *Ipperwash* at 97.

219 Lyle Ironside of the Ojibway Nation travelled to South Dakota in the summer of 1973 to join Crowdog's support camp for Wounded Knee. In the years that followed, Ironside remained at the centre of actions for Native rights. He participated in the office occupations in Kenora and Ottawa and the armed occupation of Anicinabe Park. He remembers Anicinabe Park as 'a sort of Ojibway unity conference, where they wanted the opinions of the old people.' Ironside was acquitted of weapons charges arising from the occupation of Anicinabe Park. When asked about the effect of Anicinabe Park on the people with power, he said, 'They didn't give a

shit. They were elected people but they didn't give a shit about what was happening with the people in Kenora because they never even showed their damn ass in the park except for the pow-wow. Like they didn't give a fuck at all because they figured here was only reservation people all getting together and they don't really have no say with the Department of Indian Affairs and the provincial government of Ontario and the federal government. It's just one of those big get-togethers of something that's not going to prove fuck-all.' Cited in 'The Occupation of Anicinabe Park 1974; Two Interviews reprinted from *Oh-Toh-Kin*, Volume 1 Number 1, Winter/ Spring 1992' at http://sisis.nativeweb.org/sov/oh11occ.html.

220 See 'The Occupation of Anicinabe Park 1974; Two Interviews reprinted from *Oh-Toh-Kin*, Volume 1 Number 1, Winter/Spring 1992' at http:// sisis.nativeweb.org/sov/oh11occ.html. For further information, see Vern Harper, *Following the Red Path: The Native People's Caravan, 1974* (Toronto: NC Press, 1979).

221 An interview with participants of the reoccupation is found at http:// sisis.nativeweb.org/sov/oh11occ.html and reprinted at *h-Toh-Kin* (Winter/Spring 1992) 1(1).

222 *Ojibway Warrior's Society in Occupied Anicinabe Park Kenora, Ontario August 1974* at 15. For further context, see Sean Atkins, 'The River, the City, and the Yellow Line: Reimagining Associative Landscapes in Post-War Northwestern Ontario' (2008) 17 *Native Studies Review* 115.

223 *Ojibway Warrior's Society in Occupied Anicinabe Park Kenora, Ontario August 1974* at 15.

224 Anna J. Willow, *Strong Hearts, Native Lands: The Cultural and Political Landscape of Anishinaabe Anti-Clearcutting Activism* (Albany: University of New York Press, 2012) at 57.

225 Rutherford, 'Canada's Other Red Scare' at 81.

226 For an analysis of the racism expressed during this conflict, see Anderson and Robertson, 'The "Bended-Elbow" News.'

227 See J.B. Waldram, D.A. Herring, and T.K. Young, *Aboriginal Health in Canada: Historical, Cultural, and Epidemiological Perspectives*, 2nd ed. (Toronto: University of Toronto Press, 2006); *2011 June Status Report of the Auditor General of Canada*, chap. 4, at 23–5, http://www.oag-bvg.gc.ca/internet/ docs/parl_oag_201106_04_e.pdf.

228 Once again, the relationship of events which had taken place in the U.S. is evident, as the caravan mirrored the AIM Trail of Broken Treaties of 1972, which was a walk from San Francisco to Washington. For further information, see Robert Burnett and John Koster, *The Road to Wounded Knee* (New York: Bantam, 1974).

229 Petti Fong, 'Vancouver's Kelly White a Native Activist for 40 Years,' *Toronto Star*, 12 January 2013, http://www.thestar.com/news/canada/2013/01/09/vancouvers_kelly_white_a_native_activist_for_40_years.html:

> At 16, White was one of the youngest participants in the Native People's Caravan, a group of activists trekking to Ottawa from Vancouver to demand recognition and respect for aboriginal rights.
>
> When they arrived in Ottawa, the group was met by riot police. Pushed against log barricades, White says, she received blows to her head and suffered a gash to her face.
>
> 'It enraged me. I remember that anger now when I see what we're trying to do in 2013.'

230 *Grassy Narrows First Nation v. Ontario (Natural Resources)*, 2014 S.C.C. 48 at para. 40.

231 For example, on 11 September 2003, community members set up a roadblock at the Abitibi Consolidated access road on Highway 671 (approximately 5 kilometres from the community of Grassy Narrows). They claimed they were never properly consulted about the licence granted to Abitibi Consolidated for clear-cutting activities on Grassy Narrows treaty lands. They also claimed that clear cutting infringed on their inherent treaty rights to hunt, fish, and trap in their traditional territories. Some continue to assert Aboriginal rights to the area, claiming that Treaty Three is illegitimate because the Crown did not negotiate with honour in 1873. They have maintained direct action for at least twenty years, for example, see 'Idle No More Targets Canadian Travel Routes,' *CBC News*, 5 January 2013. Furthermore, members of the Grassy Narrows First Nations have long used direct action to protest their mercury poisoning suffered through Crown logging practices; see Anastasia Shkilnyk, *A Poison Stronger than Love: The Destruction of an Ojibwa Community* (New Haven, CT: Yale University Press, 1985); Leanne Simpson, 'Grassy Narrows First Nation: Survivors, Not Victims,' *CBC News*, 31 July 2015; Masazumi Harada, Masanori Hanada, Masami Tajiri, Yukari Inoue, Nobuyuki Hotta, Tadashi Fujino, Shigeru Takaoka, and Keishi Ueda, 'Mercury Poisoning in First Nations Groups in Ontario, Canada: 35 Years of Minimata Disease in Canada' (2012) 3 *Journal of Minimata Studies* 3–30.

232 *Frontenac Ventures Corp. v. Ardoch Algonquin First Nation*, [2008] 3 CNLR 119 (Ont.C.A.) at para. 40.

233 For a general discussion of this issue, see John Borrows, *Canada's Indigenous Constitution* (Toronto: University of Toronto Press, 2010).

234 Law Commission of Canada, ed., *Indigenous Legal Traditions in Canada* (Vancouver: UBC Press, 2008).
235 Roderick A. Macdonald, 'Custom Made – For a Non-chirographic Critical Legal Pluralism' (2012) 26 *Canadian Journal of Law and Society* 310; Brian Z. Tamanaha, Caroline Sage, and Michael Woolcock, eds., *Legal Pluralism and Development: Scholars and Practitioners in Dialogue* (Cambridge: Cambridge University Press, 2012).
236 Jeremy Webber, 'The Grammar of Customary Law' (2009) 54 *McGill Law Journal* 4.
237 See *Frontenac Ventures Corp. v. Ardoch Algonquin First Nation*, [2008] 3 CNLR 119 (Ont.C.A.) at para. 27.
238 Minnawaanagogook Giizhigook (Dawnis Kennedy), 'Reconciliation without Respect, Section 35 and Indigenous Legal Orders,' in *Indigenous Legal Traditions*, ed. Law Commission of Canada (Vancouver: UBC Press, 2007). For a discussion of this problem in the U.S. context, see Bruce Duthu, *Shadow Nations: Tribal Sovereignty and the Limits of Legal Pluralism* (New York: Oxford University Press, 2013).
239 For a prominent example of the Supreme Court's failure to recognize individual exercises of Indigenous law see *Behn v. Moulton Contracting Ltd.*, 2013 S.C.C. 26. In this case, the Supreme Court of Canada held that the duty to consult was owed to communities, not individuals, and that individuals did not have standing to raise treaty rights as a defence.
240 Roderick Alexander Macdonald, *Lessons of Everyday Law* (Montreal: McGill-Queen's University Press, 2002); Roderick Macdonald, 'Critical Legal Pluralism as a Construction of Normativity and the Emergence of Law,' in *Théories et émergence du droit: pluralisme, surdétermination et effectivité*, ed. Andrée Lajoie, Roderick A. Macdonald, Richard Janda, and Guy Rocher (Montreal: Thémis, 1998) at 9. ('Explicitly made legal rules ... are not the only vehicles of normativity, but compete with a variety of indigenous and customary rules, practices and purely implicit interactional expectancies,' at 15); Webber, 'The Grammar of Customary Law' at 579.
241 *Reference re Secession of Quebec*, [1998] 2 S.C.R. 217 at para. 43; *Bruker v. Marcovitz*, [2007] 3 S.C.R. 607.
242 *Henco Industries Ltd. v. Haudenosaunee Six Nations Confederacy Council* (2006), 82 O.R. (3d) 721 (Ont.C.A.) at paras. 140–2.
243 Maurice Ratelle, 'Location of the Algonquins from 1534 to 1650,' in *The Algonquins*, ed. Daniel Clement (Ottawa: Canadian Museum of Civilization, 996). For a description of Algonquin territory in its perhaps most generous terms, see *ICTMN* Staff, 'Quebec Algonquins Planning Canada's Biggest Land Claim Ever,' *Indian Country Today Media Network*, 16 December

2011, http://indiancountrytodaymedianetwork.com/2011/12/16/quebec-algonquins-planning-canadas-biggest-land-claim-ever-67972.

244 *Mitcikinabikong* means 'the place of the stone fence or weir.'

245 James Morrison, 'Algonquin History in the Ottawa River Watershed,' *Omàmiwininì Pimàdjwowin Cultural Heritage Edition* (Ottawa, ON: Sicani Research and Advisory Services, 28 November 2005), accessed 23 July 2013, www.thealgonquinway.ca/pdf/algonquin-history.pdf.

246 Scott Nickels, 'Importance of Experiential Context for Understanding Indigenous Ecological Knowledge: The Algonquins of Barriere Lake, Quebec' (PhD diss., McGill University, November 1999), http://digitool.library.mcgill.ca/R/?func=dbin-jump-full&object_id=36667&local_base=GEN01-MCG02.

247 Boyce Richardson, in collaboration with Russell Diabo, 'Canadian Hunters Fights for the Forest: The Algonquins Striving for Territory and Good Management, in *Forests for the Future: Local Strategies for Forest Protection, Economic Welfare and Social Justice*, ed. Paul Wolvekamp (London: Zed Books, 1999), 209.

248 Elsie Shenkier and Thomas Meredith, 'The Forests and Barriere Lake,' in *Canadian Issues in Environmental Ethics*, ed. Wesley Cragg, Allan Greenbaum, and Alex Wellington (Peterborough, ON: Broadview Press, 1997) at 67.

249 For a self-description of the community from those working to stop logging in the territory, see 'FAQs and Resources' on the Barriere Lake Solidarity website, http://www.barrierelakesolidarity.org/2008/03/resources.html.

250 For a discussion of the complex federal recognition processes faced by the Algonquins more broadly, see Bonita Lawrence, *Fractured Homeland: Federal Recognition and Algonquin Identity in Ontario* (Vancouver: UBC Press, 2012); Paula Sherman, *Dishonour of the Crown: The Ontario Resource Regime in the Valley of the Kiji Sìbì* (Winnipeg: Arbeiter Ring, 2009).

251 The Crown acknowledged the Algonquins' land rights in 1760–4, and there have been no subsequent treaties surrendering these rights in Quebec; see James Morrison, *Report on Treaties from 1760–1764* (Notre-Dame-du-Nord, QC: Algonquin Nation Secretariat, March 2006).

252 Roland Chamberland, *Terra incognita des Kotakoutouemis: l'Algonquinie orientale au XVIIe siècle* (Montreal: Presses de l'Université Laval, 2004) at 122.

253 Peter Di Gangi, 'Algonquins of Barriere Lake: Man Made Impacts on the Community and Fish and Wildlife, 1870–1979' (Ottawa: Sicani Research and Advisory Services, 24 March 24, 2003), web.resist.ca/~barrierelakesolidarity/resources/man-made-impacts-final-draft.pdf.

254 Chief Jean-Maurice Matchewan, 'Mitchinkanibikonginik Algonquins of Barriere Lake: Our Long Battle to Create a Sustainable Future,' in *Drum Beat: Anger and Renewal in Indian Country*, ed. Boyce Richardson (Ottawa: Summerhill Press, 1989) at 137–66.

255 Ottawa is also claimed to be within the traditional territory of the Algonquin Nation.

256 See the film by Boyce Richardson, *Blockade: Algonquins Defend the Forest* (Ottawa: National Film Board of Canada, 1990).

257 The failure to take account of Algonquin last use in this period is chronicled in Rebecca Aird, 'Quebec's New Forestry Policy: Its Implications for the Algonquins of Barriere Lake and for Nature and Wildlife Conservation in Quebec.' Presentation to the Annual Meeting of the Canadian Parks and Wilderness Society, October 1988 at 4, cited in Shiri Pasternak, 'From Jurisdiction as Property to Jurisdiction as Indigenous Law: The Algonquins of Barriere Lake against the Federal Land Claims Policy' (PhD diss., University of Toronto, 2013).

258 *PF Solved Canada inc. c. Wawatie*, 2012 Q.C.C.S. 4968.

259 See Chief Jean-Maurice Matchewan, 'Mitchinkanibikonginik Algonquins of Barriere Lake' at 137–66.

260 See the website of the Algonquin Nation Tribal Council, accessed 13 September 2005, www.algonquinnation.ca/barrierelake/logging.html.

261 Claudia Notzke, 'The Barriere Lake Trilateral Agreement,' *A Report Prepared for the Royal Commission on Aboriginal Peoples – Land, Resource and Environment Regimes Project* (Barriere Lake Indian Government, October 1995) 21.

262 Claudia Notzke, *Aboriginal Peoples and Natural Resources in Canada* (Toronto: Captus Press, 1994) at 80–1.

263 *ABL Trilateral Agreement*, 26 May 1995, accessed 1 April 2014, http://www.scribd.com/doc/102041306/ABL-Trilateral-Agreement.

264 Shiri Pasternak, 'On Jurisdiction and Settler Colonialism: The Algonquins of Barriere Lake against the Federal Land Claims Policy' (PhD diss., University of Toronto, 2013) at footnote 310.

265 Notzke, 'The Barriere Lake Trilateral Agreement,' at Executive Summary:

> While the provincial government acknowledged that the Agreement was 'a process for change,' it nevertheless insisted that the Agreement be implemented within the rigid confines of existing laws and regulations. This insistence created a crisis from the very beginning, resulted in overt non-compliance on the part of Quebec with the terms of the Agreement, made effective protection of the territory's resources im-

possible, and created a hostile climate between the Algonquins, industry and government.

266 Cogesult, 'Quantification de la valeur économique des industries de la foret, du tourisme, des loisirs et des autres industries et activités dans la region de l'Outaouiais et le secteur couvert par l'entente trilateral, Rapport Final,' March 1996, cited in Pasternak, 'On Jurisdiction and Settler Colonialism' at footnotes 310 and 754.

267 On 15 September 1991, Quebec Superior Court Judge Rejean Paul was appointed by the Quebec government as mediator in the conflict. His report supported many of the Algonquin claims. He wrote, 'The Algonquins of Barriere Lake have, from their own Band budget and to the detriment of their other programs, unilaterally funded certain anthropological studies and have produced maps of an excellent quality, indicating, among other things, their sensitive zones and their sacred territories ... It is David and not Goliath who is attempting to sustain the Agreement.' Research Report at 8.

268 Richardson, in collaboration with Diabo, 'Canadian Hunters Fights for the Forest,' at 209

269 Norman Matchewan, 'Barriere Lake Indians Set Up Blockades as Last Resort: It was the only way to get governments to listen to us, Algonquins say,' *Montreal Gazette* Op-Ed, 8 October 2008; Jorge Barrera, 'Ontario Chiefs Criticize Quebec Police Action in Blockade,' *Canwest News Service*, 11 October 2008.

270 Pasternak, 'On Jurisdiction and Settler Colonialism' at 126.

271 The Minister of Indian Affairs sought to impose section 74(1) of the *Indian Act* at Barriere Lake. This section reads as follows: 'Whenever he deems it advisable for the good governance of a band, the Minister may declare by order that after a day to be named therein the council of the band, consisting of a chief and councillors, shall be selected by elections to be held in accordance with this Act.'

While interference with Barriere Lake leadership has been upheld by the Canadian courts, it has not been denied that such intervention occurred; see *Wawatie v. Canada* (Indian Affairs and Northern Development), 2008 F.C. 975 (CanLII); *Wawatie v. Canada (Indian Affairs and Northern Development)*, 2009 F.C. 8 (CanLII); *Wawatie v. Canada (Indian Affairs and Northern Development)*, 2009 F.C. 374 (CanLII).

272 Andrew Crosby and Jeffrey Monaghan, 'Settler Governmentality in Canada and the Algonquins of Barriere Lake' (2012) 43.5 *Security Dialogue* at 421–38.

273 For an example that recounts this history, see *Wawatie v. Canada (Indian Affairs and Northern Development)*, 2009 F.C. 8 (CanLII).

274 Brett Popplewell, 'The Algonquins of Barriere Lake and Their Battle with Indian Affairs,' *Toronto Star*, 29 October 2010, http://www.thestar.com/news/investigations/2010/10/29/the_algonquins_of_barriere_lake_and_their_battle_with_indian_affairs.html.

275 Judge Rejean Paul's Mediation Report, 15 May 2007, in Pasternak, 'On Jurisdiction and Settler Colonialism' at footnote 589.

276 For a discussion of the implications of these changes, see *Mitchikanibikok Inik v. Thusky*, 1999 CanLII 8724 (F.C.).

277 Pasternak, 'On Jurisdiction and Settler Colonialism' at 134–6.

278 Ibid. at 136–43.

279 These fractures mirror division at the broader Algonquin Nation level; see Theresa Smith, 'Chief Urges Meeting to Foster Unity among Algonquins,' *Ottawa Citizen*, 23 July 2013, http://www.cfne.org/modules/news/article.php?storyid=23313.

280 Michael D. McNally, *Honoring Elders: Aging, Authority, and Ojibwe Religion* (New York: Columbia University Press, 2009) at 50.

281 See 'Report: Special Ministerial Representative to the Algonquins of Barriere Lake,' document submitted to The Honourable Chuck Strahl, Minister of Indian Affairs and Northern Development Canada, 20 December 2007 at 5, cited in Pasternak, 'On Jurisdiction and Settler Colonialism' at note 760.

282 Pasternak, 'On Jurisdiction and Settler Colonialism' at 273.

283 Anishinaabe language professor and linguistic Brenda Fairbanks traced the etymology of *gikinoo'amaage* as follows (personal correspondence, 17 January 2014):

- *gikinaw* – 'learn, know, recognize'
- *i* – 'by instrument'
- *amaw* – 'applicative'
- *ge* – 'detransitive' (to general people)

284 For a more general discussion of analogical reasoning, see Cass R. Sunstein, 'On Analogical Reasoning,' Commentary (1993) 106 *Harvard Law Review* 741.

285 Gary Potts, 'Growing Together From the Earth,' in *Nation to Nation: Aboriginal Sovereignty and the Future of Canada*, ed. Diane Engelstad and John Bird (Toronto: Anansi, 1992) 199.

286 For a historic description of the Temagami people and land, see F.G. Speck, *Family Hunting Territories and Social Life of Various Algonkian Bands of the Ottawa Valley* (Ottawa: Government Printing Bureau, 1915).

287 Contrary to the Temagami view, the Ontario courts expressed doubts about whether the Temagami were the land's ancient inhabitants, raising questions about their recent arrival in the territory, see *Ontario (Attorney General) v. Bear Island Foundation* [1991] 2 S.C.R. 570.

There is a reference in the *Jesuit Relations* of 1640 to an organized band around Lake Temagami called the Outemagami, but its authenticity as the original Temagami Band is doubtful.

288 Charles Bishop, 'North Algonquians, 1550–1760,' in *Aboriginal Ontario: Historical Perspectives on the First Nations*, ed. Edward S. Rogers and Donald B. Smith (Toronto: Dundurn Press, 1994) at 276. The people encountered were called the Otemagami.

289 *Ontario (Attorney General) v. Bear Island Foundation* [1991] 2 S.C.R. 570.

290 Temagami Anishinaabe, 'The Native Dimension: Key Dates,' in *Temagami: A Debate on Wilderness*, ed. Matt Bray and Ashley Thomson (Toronto: Dundurn, 1996) at 185.

291 Friends of Temagami, *Temagami Overview*, 17 April 2008, http://www.oldsite .friendsoftemagami.org/index.php/overview.

292 Jocelyn Thorpe, *Temagami's Tangled Wild: Race, Gender, and the Making of Canadian Nature* (Vancouver: UBC Press, 2012).

293 For more information about the historical context of the Robinson-Huron Treaty, see Janet Chute, *The Legacy of Shingwaukonse: A Century of Native Leadership* (Toronto: University of Toronto Press, 1998) at 130–7.

294 David McNab, *No Place for Fairness: Indigenous Land Rights and Policy in the Bear Island Case and Beyond* (Montreal: McGill-Queen's University Press, 2009) at chap. 3.

295 For Chief Potts' own views on this issue, see Chief Gary Potts, 'Teme-Augama Anishnabai: Last-Ditch Defence of a Priceless Homeland,' in *Drum Beat: Anger and Renewal in Indian Country*, ed. Boyce Richardson (Ottawa: Summerhill Press, 1989) 203–30.

296 These arguments were made with the assistance of Bruce Clark. For a discussion of his work and influence, see Bruce Clark, *Native Liberty, Crown Sovereignty: The Existing Aboriginal Right of Self-government in Canada* (Montreal: McGill-Queen's University Press, 1990); Bruce Clark, *Justice in Paradise* (Montreal: McGill-Queen's University Press, 1999).

297 *Ontario (Attorney General) v. Bear Island Foundation* (1984), 49 O.R. (2d) 353. (Ont.S.C.).

298 *Ontario (Attorney General) v. Bear Island Foundation* [1991] 2 S.C.R. 570.

299 *Ontario (Attorney General) v. Bear Island Foundation* (1984), 49 O.R. (2d) (Ont. S.C.) 353 at 373.

300 For more insight into these confrontations, see Bruce W. Hodgins, David McNab, and Ute Lischke, eds., *Blockades and Resistance: Studies in Actions of Peace and the Temagami Blockades of 1988–89* (Waterloo, ON: Wilfrid Laurier University Press, 2003).

301 *Ontario (Attorney General) v. Bear Island Foundation* [1991] 2 S.C.R. 570.

302 Ibid.

303 Kent McNeil, 'The High Cost of Accepting Benefits from the Crown: A Comment on the Temagami Indian Land Case,' in *Emerging Justice? Essays on Indigenous Rights in Canada and Australia* (Saskatoon: Native Law Centre, 2001) 25 at 56.

304 *R. v. Sparrow*, [1990] 1 S.C.R. 1075 at 1112.

305 *R. v. Sioui*, [1990] 1025 *per* Lamer J. at 1069; *R v. Marshall* [1999] 3 S.C.R. 456 at para. 15.

306 See Kent McNeil, 'The Temagami Indian Land Claim: Loosening the Judicial Straightjacket,' in *Temagami: A Debate on Wilderness*, ed. Matt Bray and Ashley Thomson (Toronto: Dundurn, 1996) at 185.

307 For a thoughtful paper addressing judicial engagement with Indigenous legal traditions, see The Honourable Lance Finch, Chief Justice of British Columbia, 'The Duty to Learn: Taking Account of Indigenous Legal Orders in Practice,' presented at the CLEBC Indigenous Legal Orders and the Common Law Conference, 15 November 2012.

308 Ibid.

309 Mary Laronde, 'Co-Management of Lands and Resources in N'Daki Menan,' in *Rebirth: Political Economic and Social Development in First Nations*, ed. Anne-Marie Mawhiney (Toronto: Dundurn Press, 1993) at 93.

310 See Potts, 'Teme-Augama Anishnabai: Last-Ditch Defence' at 203–28.

311 Patrick W. Matakala, 'Decision-making and Conflict Resolution in Co-management: Two Cases from Temagami, Northeastern Ontario' (PhD diss., University of British Columbia, 995), https://open.library.ubc.ca/cIRcle/collections/ubctheses/831/items/1.0088332.

312 For a discussion of how Court decisions, which were unfavourable to the Temagami, could negatively affect others, see Barbara Jane Davy, 'Ethics and Justice in Daki Menan' (2006) 15 *TOPIA: Canadian Journal of Cultural Studies* 5.

313 David McNab, 'Remembering an Intellectual Wilderness: A Captivity Narrative at Queen's Park 1988–1989,' in *Blockades and Resistance: Studies in Actions of Peace and the Temagami Blockades of 1988–89*, ed. Bruce W. Hodgins, David T. McNab, and Ute Lischke (Waterloo, ON: Wilfrid Laurier University Press, 2003) at 32–3.

314 Tammy Cole, Land and Resources, 'Mining Consultation Protocol and Exploration MOU Documents,' Thursday, 18 April 2013, http://www.temagamifirstnation.ca/index.php?option=com_content&view=article&id=60&Itemid=56.

315 This chapter contains a level of historical, political, and legal context that may not readily be found in approaches based on abstract, conceptual, ideal categories. Instead, this chapter has drawn philosophical ideas from grounded experiences. It has highlighted how ideas can flow from practices that engage with the real world's constraints and opportunities.

316 I did so only after I had considered each case herein in some detail, and many others as well. In fact, I wrote the case studies five years prior to the development of this three-pronged analytical categorization. The material in this chapter was originally produced for the Ipperwash Inquiry and did not attempt to discuss the relationship of civil (dis)obedience to a free and democratic society. My first cut at these case studies is John Borrows, 'Crown and Aboriginal Occupations of Land: A History and Comparison,' 15 October 2005, http://www.attorneygeneral.jus.gov.on.ca/inquiries/ipperwash/policy_part/research/pdf/History_of_Occupations_Borrows.pdf.

317 John Morreall, 'The Justifiability of Violent Civil Disobedience,' in *Civil Disobedience in Focus*, ed. Hugo A. Bedau (London: Routledge, 1991) at 130–42; Joseph Raz, *The Authority of Law: Essays on Law and Morality* (Oxford: Clarendon Press, 1979) at 267.

318 In terms of my professional commitments, I am called to the British Columbia Bar and thus have pledged by oath to 'uphold the rule of law and the rights and freedoms of all persons according to the laws of Canada and the province of British Columbia.' Furthermore, in applying this oath I subscribe to the British Columbia Canon of Legal Ethics, chapter 1, section 1: 'A lawyer owes a duty of care to the state, to maintain its integrity and law. A lawyer should not aid, counsel, or assist any person to act in any way contrary to the law,' accessed 1 April 2014, https://www.lawsociety.bc.ca/page.cfm?cid=2637&t=Chapter-2---Standards-of-the-Legal-Profession. See also John Rawls, *A Theory of Justice* (Cambridge, MA: Harvard University Press, 1971) at 366: 'Any interference with the civil liberties of others tends to obscure the civilly disobedient quality of one's act.'

319 While we know that, on the world stage, certain wars of liberation or independence may facilitate freedom in rare moments, we nevertheless find flaws in every state – even those that regard themselves as liberating. The United States War of Independence has still not generally liberated blacks and Native Americans. Furthermore, the counter-examples painfully

crowd out those few instances when violence succeeded in nourishing a good life – the French, Latin American, and African Revolutions come to mind. People may rationalize that their cause is an exception to these patterns, and they may be right, but given my experience, study, and professional commitments, I would not counsel or support such approaches.

320 The executive summary of the Ipperwash Inquiry frames the dispute as follows:

> Anthony O'Brien George, known as Dudley George, was an Aboriginal man whose parents, relatives, and ancestors were from Stoney Point Reserve. He was 38 years old. He and other First Nations men, women and children occupied Ipperwash Provincial Park on Labour Day, September 4, 1995, primarily to protest the federal government's refusal to return the Stoney Point Reserve. The federal government had appropriated this reserve as a military training site in 1942 pursuant to the *War Measures Act* and had promised to return it to the Aboriginal people after World War II. But over 50 years had passed and the federal government had not returned the Stoney Point Reserve. Despite persistent attempts by the Aboriginal people to persuade the Canadian government to return its land, it had not done so. Frustration steadily increased for over five decades.
>
> The occupation of Ipperwash Provincial Park by former residents of the Stoney Point Reserve, their descendants, and other First Nations people occurred in the early evening of September 4, 1995. Two days later, a confrontation occurred between the Ontario Provincial Police and the Aboriginal people outside the park. Dudley George was shot by the police and died. (http://www.attorneygeneral.jus.gov.on.ca/in-quiries/ipperwash/index.html at 1)

Beneficial policy developments were facilitated because of civil (dis)obedience at Ipperwash. For a discussion of the implementation of some of these findings, including the transfer of Anishinaabek law back to the First Nation, see the Ontario Aboriginal Affairs website, http://ocap.ca/sup porttmt/files/amnesty_report.pdf.

321 While not discussed in the specific cases, a cross-cutting general point can also be drawn from this review, which is that civil (dis)obedience can be undemocratic and restrict freedom if it foments racial and ethnic stereotyping. When the parties move beyond face-to-face deliberation and opt to literally erect physical barriers between them, this may construct binary categories, creating further distance between them. Dichotomies can be dangerous. One of the threats of civil (dis)obedience as a political *practice*

is that it could turn into a political *form*, in the Platonic sense of the word. For a discussion of Plato's forms, see Sir David Ross, *Plato's Theory of Ideas* (Oxford: Oxford University Press, 1951). For criticism of Plato's forms, see Gail Fine, *On Ideas: Aristotle's Criticism of Plato's Theory of Forms* (Oxford: Oxford University Press, 1992).

322 Domination deepens when contestants are characterized in abstract, static, universalizing ways. Labels such as 'the opposite side,' 'foe,' 'freedom fighter,' 'terrorist,' 'enemy,' 'soldier,' and 'warrior' can obscure the interdependent and intersubjective relationships that usually exist between the parties. If limiting labels replace life's genuine complexities, this can create false horizons that restrict people's freedom. Labels can be generalized and made to appear permanently real, as individuals and groups are placed in rigid, closed, or fixed identities (and then start acting on them).

323 *Reference Re Secession of Québec*, [1998] 2 S.C.R. 217 at 68. For further discussion about the role of dissent in democracy, see Tully, *Democracy and Civic Freedom* at 198.

324 Cass Sunstein, *Why Societies Need Dissent* (Cambridge, MA: Harvard University Press, 2003) at 48.

325 Daniel Markovits, 'Democratic Disobedience' (2005) 114 *Yale Law Journal* 1897–1952.

Chapter Three

1 James Tully, *Democracy and Civic Freedom*, vol. 1 of *Public Philosophy in a New Key* (Cambridge: Cambridge University Press, 2008) at 189.

2 *Canada Act, 1982*, U.K., 1982, c. 11. In this respect, the Charter builds upon the Universal Declaration of Human Rights, which states, 'All human beings are born free in dignity and rights.' The Declaration was adopted and proclaimed by the General Assembly of the United Nations, Resolution 217 A (III) of 10 December 1948 and is available at http://www. un.org/en/documents/udhr/. For a discussion of the Canadian Charter's connection to the international network of states and peoples see Alan Cairns, *Charter Versus Federalism: The Dilemmas of Constitutional Reform* (Montreal: McGill-Queen's University Press, 1992) at 12–20; Walter Tarnopolsky, 'A Comparison between the Charter and the International Covenant' (1983) 8 *Queen's Law Journal* 211.

3 *R. v. Big M. Drug Mart Ltd.*, (1985), 1 S.C.R. 295 at 336.

4 'It would be a grave mistake to equate legitimacy with the "sovereign will" or majority rule alone, to the exclusion of other constitutional values.' *Reference Re Secession of Québec*, [1998] 2 S.C.R. 217 at para. 67.

5 Tully, *Democracy and Civic Freedom* at 196–7, citing John Rawls, *The Law of Peoples with the Idea of Public Reason Revisited* (Cambridge, MA: Harvard University Press, 1999) at 140–3.

6 Jeremy Webber, *The Constitution of Canada: A Contextual Analysis* (Oxford: Hart Publishing, 2015) at 1.

7 See J.E. Cote, 'The Reception of English Law' (1977) 15 *Alberta Law Review* 29 at 38. For critical commentary on this view, see John Borrows, *Canada's Indigenous Constitution* (Toronto: University of Toronto Press, 2009).

8 *Constitution Act, 1867*, 30 & 31 Victoria, c. 3 (U.K.), R.S.C. 1985, App. II, No. 11.

9 *Reference Re Secession of Québec*, [1998].

10 Webber, *The Constitution of Canada* at 8.

11 James Tully, *Imperialism and Civic Freedom*, vol. 2 of *Public Philosophy in a New Key* (Cambridge: Cambridge University Press, 2008) at 110.

12 Ibid.

13 *Reference Re Provincial Judges*, [1997] 3 S.C.R. 3 at 75. In *Reference Re Secession of Québec*, [1998] at 239, the Court referred to the *Provincial Court Judges Reference* and reaffirmed that the constitution 'embraces unwritten as well as written' rules.

14 *Campbell v. A.G. (B.C.)*, (2000), 189 D.L.R. (4th) 333 at para. 81.

15 *R. v. Pamejewon*, [1996] 2 S.C.R. 821.

16 Brian Slattery, *The Land Rights of Indigenous Canadian Peoples, As Affected by the Crown's Acquisition of Their Territories* (Saskatoon: University of Saskatchewan, Native Law Centre, 1979) at 191–349.

17 The *British North America Act, 1867* is now called *the Constitution Act, 1867*.

18 *Manitoba Act, 1870* (U.K.), 32 & 33 Vict., c. 3., ss. 30–2.

19 Frank Tough, 'The Forgotten Constitution: The *Natural Resources Transfer Agreements* and Indian Livelihood Rights, ca. 1925–1933' (2003) 41 *Alberta Law Review* 999.

20 *Natural Resources Transfer Agreement, 1930*, S.C. 1930, c. 3.

21 For a discussion of Indigenous resistance in British Columbia, Quebec, and the North, see Paul Tennant, *Aboriginal Peoples and Politics: The Indian Land Question in British Columbia, 1849–1989* (Vancouver: UBC Press, 1990); Georges Sioui, *For an Amerindian Autohistory: An Essay on the Foundations of a Social Ethic* (Montreal: McGill-Queen's University Press, 1992); Peter Kulchyski, *Like the Sound of a Drum: Aboriginal Cultural Politics in Denendeh and Nunavut* (Winnipeg: University of Manitoba Press, 2005).

22 Robin Brownlie, *A Fatherly Eye: Indian Agents, Government Power, and Aboriginal Resistance in Ontario, 1918–1939* (Toronto: University of Toronto Press, 2003); Keith Smith, *Liberalism, Surveillance, and Resistance: Indigenous*

Communities in Western Canada, 1877–1927 (Edmonton: Athabasca University Press, 2009); James Daschuk, *Clearing the Plains: Disease, Politics of Starvation, and the Loss of Aboriginal Life* (Regina, SK: University of Regina Press, 2013).

23 Taiaiake Alfred, *Wasáse: Indigenous Pathways to Action* (Peterborough, ON: Broadview Press, 2005); Taiaiake Alfred, *Peace, Power, Righteousness: An Indigenous Manifesto* (Toronto: Oxford University Press, 1999); Glen Coulthard, 'Subjects of Empire: Indigenous Peoples and the "Politics of Recognition" in Canada' (2007) 6 *Contemporary Political Theory* 437.

24 Sean Fine, 'Chief Justice says Canada Attempted Cultural Genocide on Aboriginals,' *Globe and Mail*, 30 May 2015 at 1.

25 Justice Monk wrote, 'Will it be contended that the territorial rights, political organization such as it was, or the laws and usages of Indian tribes were abrogated – that they ceased to exist when these two European nations began to trade with [A]boriginal occupants? In my opinion it is beyond controversy that they did not – that so far from being abolished, they were left in full force, and were not even modified in the slightest degree.' *Connolly v. Woolrich*, (1867) 17 R.J.R.Q. 75 at 79 (Quebec Superior Court), affirmed as *Johnstone v. Connelly*, (1869) 17 R.J.R.Q. 266 (Quebec Queen's Bench).

26 Royal Commission on Aboriginal Peoples, *Partners in Confederation: Aboriginal Peoples, Self-Government and the Constitution* (Ottawa: Supply and Services, 1993) at 8.

27 *R. v. Secretary of State for Foreign and Commonwealth Affairs, ex parte Indian Association of Alberta and others*, [1982] 2 All E.R. 118 at 123.

28 Borrows, *Canada's Indigenous Constitution* at 210.

29 Sakej Henderson, 'Empowering Treaty Federalism' (1994) 58 *Saskatchewan Law Review* 241.

30 For the text of many of these treaties, see *Canada: Indian Treaties and Surrenders, from 1680 to 1890* (Ottawa: Brown Chamberlin, 1891; reprinted, Toronto: Coles, 1971).

31 John Borrows, 'Creating Countries: Indigenous Treaties in Canada and New Zealand' (2006) *New Zealand Universities Law Review*. For a discussion of Canadian treaty history, see Jim Miller, *Compact, Contract, Covenant: Aboriginal Treaty-Making in Canada* (Toronto: University of Toronto Press, 2009).

32 Freedom is enhanced, and domination decreased, when states, institutions and societies invent their own governance structures, that 'do not draw their [sole] inspiration from Europe or the United States.' See Tully, *Imperialism and Civic Freedom* at 22, paraphrasing Frantz Fanon, *The Wretched of the Earth* (New York: Grove Press, 1961) at 313.

33 The Dominion's unilateral attempt to add the old Northwest Territories to Canada were legislated in the *Rupert's Land Act, 1868*, U.K., 1868, c. 105. For historical context, see Maggie Siggins, *Riel: A Life of Revolution* (Toronto: HarperCollins, 1994).

34 *Manitoba Metis Federation Inc. v. Canada (Attorney General)*, 2013 S.C.C. 14, [2013] 1 S.C.R. 623 at paras. 1 and 150.

35 *Manitoba Act*, U.K., 1870, 32 & 33 Vict. c. 3. The act provided for the creation of the Province of Manitoba, French-language rights, protection for settled and common lands, distribution of 1.4 millions acres of land to Metis children, and amnesty for those who participated in the provisional government.

36 The Imperial Parliament passed the *Constitution Act, 1871*, U.K., 1871, c. 28 to give effect to the provisions embodied in the *Manitoba Act*.

37 *Manitoba Metis Federation Inc. v. Canada* (Attorney General), 2013 at para. 92: 'To understand the nature of s. 31 as a solemn obligation, it may be helpful to consider its treaty-like history and character.'

38 See *R. v. Dumont*, (1988) 52 D.L.R. (4th) 25 (Man.C.A.); rev'd (1990) 67 D.L.R. (4h) 159 (S.C.C.); *Manitoba Metis Federation Inc. v. Canada* (Attorney General), 2013.

39 For a discussion of Metis constitutional history and the Crown's obligation in relation to this history, see *Manitoba Metis Federation Inc. v. Canada* (Attorney General), 2013.

40 *Campbell v. A.G. (B.C.)* (2000) 189 D.L.R. (4th) 333 (BCSC).

41 John Borrows, 'Indian Agency: Forming First Nations Law in Canada' (2001) 24 *PoLAR* at 9.

42 Audra Simpson, *Mohawk Interruptus: Political Life Across the Borders of Settler States* (Durham, NC: Duke University Press, 2014).

43 *Logan v. Styres*, (1959), 20 D.L.R. (2d) 416.

44 Alfred, *Wasáse*.

45 Tom Molloy, *The World Is Our Witness* (Calgary: Fifth House, 2000) at 121.

46 Chief Gosnell's Historic Speech to the British Columbia Legislature Official Report of the Legislative Assembly (B.C. Hansard), Wednesday, 2 December 1998, Vol. 12, No. 17; Douglas Sanders, 'We Intend to Live Here Forever: A Primer on the Nisga'a Treaty,' (1999) 33 *University of British Columbia Law Review* 103–28.

47 Tully, *Imperialism and Civic Freedom* at 211.

48 The National Indian Council (NIC) was formed in 1961 to represent three major groups of Aboriginal people in Canada: Treaty and Status Indians, Indians not recognized by the federal government as possessing status, and the Metis people (the Inuit were excluded). Since the NIC's formation, there has been a national lobby group for Indians to engage in political

advocacy. The NIC's purpose was to promote 'unity among all Indian people'; however, the diversity within the NIC often made it difficult to accomplish this goal.

49 For the role of song in Indigenous legal traditions, which include singing the law, see Leslie Hall Pinder, *The Carriers of No: After the Land Claims Trial* (Vancouver: Lazara Press, 1991).

50 Peter H. Russell, *Constitutional Odyssey: Can Canadians Become a Sovereign People?* (Toronto: University of Toronto Press, 1992).

51 Tully, *Imperialism and Civic Freedom* at 201.

52 For an example of Parliament's traditions protecting executive branch accountability to Parliament, see Peter Milliken, Speaker of House of Commons, Canada, 'Ruling on the Questions of Privilege Raised on March 18, 2010, by the Member for Scarborough–Rouge River (Mr. Lee), the Member for St. John's East (Mr. Harris), and the Member for Saint-Jean (Mr. Bachand) concerning the Order of the House of December 10, 2009, Respecting the Production of Afghan Detainee Documents,' http://www.scribd.com/doc/30588430/Speaker-s-ruling-April-27-2010.

53 People become concerned when states use their sovereignty to separate the executive from both the people and the constitution; see Tully, *Imperialism and Civic Freedom* at 203. For a critique of executive authority in Canada, see Peter Aucoin, Mark Jarvis, and Lori Turnbull, *Democratizing the Constitution: Reforming Constitutional Government* (Toronto: Emond Montgomery, 2011).

54 Perhaps they saw this process as a way 'to give oneself the rules of law, the techniques of management, and also the ethics, the *ethos*, the practice of the self, which would [allow constitutional power to be exercised] with a minimum of domination.' Michel Foucault, in *The Final Foucault*, ed. James Bernauer and David Rasmussen (Cambridge, MA: MIT Press, 1988) at 18, cited in Tully, *Democracy and Civic Freedom* at 121.

55 Peter Cumming and Neil Mickenburg, *Native Rights in Canada*, 2nd ed. (Toronto: Indian-Eskimo Association, 1972) at 331.

56 Harold Cardinal, *The Unjust Society: The Tragedy of Canada's Indians* (Edmonton: Hurtig, 1969).

57 Sally Weaver, *Making Canadian Indian Policy: The Hidden Agenda 1968–1970* (Toronto: University of Toronto Press, 1981) at 171.

58 James Frideres, *Native Peoples in Canada: Contemporary Conflicts*, 4th ed. (Scarborough, ON: Prentice-Hall, 1993) at 286.

59 Ibid.

60 Laurie Drees, *The Indian Association of Alberta: A History of Political Action* (Vancouver: UBC Press, 2002).

61 Weaver, *Making Canadian Indian Policy* at 188.
62 Kenneth McRoberts, *Québec: Social and Political Crisis* (Toronto: McClelland and Stewart, 1988).
63 Frideres, *Native Peoples in Canada* at 317.
64 Doug Sanders, 'The Indian Lobby,' in *And No One Cheered: Federalism, Democracy and the Constitution Act*, ed. Keith Banting and Richard Simeon (Toronto: Metheun, 1983) 301 at 303.
65 Ibid. at 304.
66 Ibid. at 306.
67 Ibid. at 309.
68 Ibid. at 313–14.
69 Mildred Poplar, 'We Were Fighting For Nationhood, Not Section 35,' in *Box of Treasures or Empty Box: Twenty Years of Section 35*, ed. Ardith Walkem and Halie Bruce (Pentiction, BC: Theytus Books, 2003) at 23.
70 Sanders, 'The Indian Lobby' at 322.
71 *R. v. Secretary of State for Foreign and Commonwealth Affairs, ex parte Indian Association of Alberta and others*, [1982].
72 Sanders, 'The Indian Lobby' at 322.
73 *R. v. Secretary of State for Foreign and Commonwealth Affairs, ex parte Indian Association of Alberta and others*, [1982] at 916.
74 Doug Sanders, 'The Indian Lobby' at 320.
75 James Tully, *Strange Multiplicity: Constitutionalism in an Age of Diversity* (Cambridge: Cambridge University Press, 1995).
76 See, generally, Brian Schwartz, *First Principles, Second Thoughts* (Montreal: Institute for Research on Public Policy, 1986).
77 Aboriginal Constitutional Matters, *Transcript of Proceedings* (Ottawa, 26 and 27 March 1987) at 25, 39, 42–3, 329–40.
78 Kathy Brock, 'The Politics of Aboriginal Self-Government: A Canadian Paradox' (1991) 34 *Canadian Public Administration* 272.
79 David Hawkes and Bradford Morse, 'Alternative Methods for Aboriginal Participation in Constitutional Reform' in *Options for a New Canada*, ed. Ronald Watts and Douglas Brown (Toronto: University of Toronto Press, 1991) 161 at 166–8.
80 J.E. Chamberlin, 'Aboriginal Rights and the Meech Law Accord,' in *Competing Constitutional Visions: The Meech Lake Accord*, ed. Katherine Swinton and Carol Rogerson (Toronto: Carswell, 1988) at 11.
81 John Borrows, 'Traditional Contemporary Equality: The Impact of the Charter on First Nations Politics' (1994) 43 *University of New Brunswick Law Journal* 19–48.
82 See *Native Women's Association v. Canada* [1994] 3 S.C.R. 627.

83 John Borrows, 'Uncertain Citizens: The Supreme Court and Aboriginal Peoples' (2001) 80 *Canadian Bar Review* 15; John Borrows, 'Measuring a Work in Progress: 20 Years of Section 35,' in *Box of Treasures or Empty Box: Section 35 and the Canadian Constitution*, ed. Ardith Walkem and Halie Bruce (Penticton, BC: Theytus Press, 2003) at 223.

84 Stephen Coleman, *Popular Delusions: How Social Conformity Molds Society and Politics* (Amherst, NY: Cambria Press, 2007).

85 For a discussion of asymmetrical federalism, see Reg Whitaker, 'The Dog that Never Barked: Who Killed Asymmetrical Federalism?' in *The Charlottetown Accord, the Referendum, and the Future of Canada*, ed. Kenneth McRoberts and Patrick Monahan (Toronto: University of Toronto Press, 1993) at 114; Tom Kent, 'Recasting Federalism' (1991) 12 *Policy Options* 3; Will Kymlicka 'Multinational Federalism in Canada: Rethinking the Partnership,' in *Beyond the Impasse, Toward Reconciliation*, ed. Roger Gibbins and Guy Laforest (Montreal: Institute for Research on Public Policy, 1998) at 15; Philip Resnick, 'Toward a Multinational Federalism: Asymmetrical and Confederal Alternatives,' in *Seeking a New Canadian Partnership: Asymmetrical and Confederal Options*, ed. F. Leslie Seidle (Montreal: Institute for Research on Public Policy, 1994) at 71; Hudson Meadwell, 'Is a "True" Multination Federation a Cure for Our Ills?' in Donald Abelson, *The Myth of the Sacred: The Charter, the Courts, and the Politics of the Constitution in Canada* (Montreal: McGill-Queen's University Press, 2002) at 219–38.

86 *Reference Re Secession of Québec*, [1998] at 68.

87 *Reference Re Secession of Québec*, [1998] at paras. 63–9.

88 John Borrows, 'Domesticating Doctrines: Aboriginal Peoples After the Royal Commission' (2001) 46 *McGill Law Journal* 615.

89 This review demonstrates that Indigenous peoples have a complicated relationship to Canada's constitution. While they extract small jurisdictional spaces for greater community autonomy, the formal constitution's largely oppressive formal structure prevails. The rocky road to reform has caused Indigenous peoples to be very suspicious of others' constitutionalization of their rights. Thus, while Indigenous people have participated in constitutional discussions, they have not done so enthusiastically or with one voice. The search for certainty within Canada's written constitution has become a metaphysical form that limits people's imagination. It thwarts action about alternatives that would be more liberating. This has led to a situation where some Indigenous peoples want to work within Canada's constitutional structure, while others are much more ambivalent. On the opposite end of the spectrum, a significant number of Indigenous groups just want to be left out of the country entirely. Furthermore, Indigenous

issues have sometimes been overshadowed by the constitutional politics of Quebec separatism and federal policies of Indigenous assimilation. Nevertheless, in 1982 Aboriginal and treaty rights were entrenched
in Canada's constitution. For a few years, their inclusion strongly influenced national Indigenous leaders and organizations to negotiate with
the Canadian government about the meaning underlying the recognition
and affirmation of their rights. While these negotiations ultimately failed
to have much of a substantive impact, they did educate a section of the
public about broader Indigenous aspirations regarding further autonomy
and self-government. The higher profile that Indigenous peoples obtained
in this period also prepared the ground for further engagement with the
Canadian state at regional and local levels, as just discussed. However,
while the entrenchment of Aboriginal rights has drawn an increasing
number of Indigenous people into internal Canadian debates, one should
not ignore the great ambivalence with which they have participated.
In fact, the effects of formally constitutionalizing Aboriginal and treaty
rights are still being analysed two decades after their entrenchment. It is
still too early to tell whether, on balance, the entrenchment of Aboriginal
rights was a positive development that will benefit Indigenous peoples.
Politically, entrenchment has produced nothing of national significance
from Canada's Parliament. Jurisprudentially, the results are mixed. On
the positive side, section 35(1) seems to prevent Canada from unilaterally extinguishing Aboriginal and treaty rights. On the negative side, the
Crown's broad power to infringe Aboriginal and treaty rights seems to
undermine much of the autonomy and powers of governance many were
seeking prior to section 35's entrenchment. Furthermore, constitutionalization seems to have led some Canadians to believe that Indigenous peoples' rights are best protected through Canadian formalized constitutional
instruments. Since many Indigenous people do not hold this opinion, the
future will be clouded by continuing disputes over this issue.

Chapter Four

1 I try to resist categorization because I believe categorizations are often
   inaccurate and do not capture the fluidity, ambiguity, and contradictory
   aspects of human nature, or my life more specifically. However, I do not
   consider myself a liberal theorist. If I had to be labelled, I could be considered an 'Anishinaabe legal practitioner,' at least in the last thirty years
   of my life. In my first book, *Recovering Canada: The Resurgence of Indigenous
   Law* (Toronto: University of Toronto Press, 2002), I attempted to judge and

critique Canadian law by Anishinaabe methodologies. I emphasized the trickster and the contingencies of practice and interpretation that arise when this method is used to evaluate Aboriginal and treaty rights in Canada. I argued for a 'Declaration of Interdependence' in *Recovering Canada* (138) to place relationality, rather than abstract, first-principle theorizing, at the heart of my inquiries. In *Canada's Indigenous Constitution* (Toronto: University of Toronto Press, 2010), I argued that Canadian law should not be built on the acceptance of Crown sovereignty and abstract principles related to doctrines of discovery, occupation, adverse possession, or conquest. As with my first book, I subtly tried to undermine and overthrow this view of the world by demonstrating how Anishinaabe and other Indigenous legal traditions could challenge a neutral view of law that presumed it was built on principles, justice, equality, and objectivity. I described law as a 'social activity' (ix) and insisted that 'fundamentalist interpretations of law should be rejected' (219). The overall text attempts to show that law in Canada is not abstract, neutral, or objective, nor does law flow from fundamental, foundational, or essentialized first principles. Canadian law is a very human, social activity that requires the infusion of other Indigenous practices and traditions to generate healthier relationships. Law is a social phenomenon that requires struggle and 'on-the-ground' hard work to produce better results (274–82). Finally, in *Drawing Out Law: A Spirit's Guide* (Toronto: Univeristy of Toronto Press, 2010), I am deeply critical of liberal accounts of law. The work is meant to be read alongside *Canada's Indigenous Constitution* (xiv) to further demonstrate that concepts of agency, autonomy, and freedom are socially constructed and dependent on the practices and stories we tell ourselves about those practices. It focuses on relationality as a key source of law and tradition, and not on abstract ideas of freedom and equality. Its style is purposefully embedded in Anishinaabe stories and traditions to disrupt neutral accounts of law, and to help people see my work in an Anishinaabe theoretical light. Nevertheless, because I sometimes (though certainly not always) draw positive conclusions about possible contingent future courses of action for Canadian law, I believe my work can be misread. Some might regard my work as advancing a 'liberal' agenda because some of my work may support the Canadian state (albeit in a very different relational form than constituted at present). Just because you sometimes find a cause for optimism in the law does not mean you are a liberal. Liberals have not 'cornered the market' on optimism, or scepticism for that matter. Liberalism itself is a complex social constructon that can be turned to many purposes. I hope this book shows that I can be simultaneously hopeful and deeply cynical about Canadian law and its possible future relationships to

Indigenous peoples. I arrive at these conclusions not through liberal theorizing but through the application of Anishinaabe insghts, even if they are not always explicitly visible in the architecture of my reasoning. Of course, I might change my views on the matter tomorrow.

2 Val Napoleon, 'Demanding More of Ourselves: Indigenous Civility and Incivility' (November 2014), on file with author.

3 In this respect, I am critical of theories that work from abstractions, such as those found in John Rawls, *A Theory of Justice* (Cambridge, MA: Harvard University Press, 2005).

4 The Supreme Court has concluded that Aboriginal and treaty rights are limited by the parties' historic intentions and the public meaning attached to original actions. While non-discriminatory understandings of history are an important guide to constitutional interpretation, the Supreme Court of Canada's current approach to Aboriginal rights overemphasizes the past by restricting the constitution's meaning to certain foundational moments. This method, which goes by the name 'originalism,' is alive and well within section 35(1) of the constitution.

5 The people or group whose intentions count in understanding constitutional meaning at a foundational moment can vary. See Thomas B. Colby and Peter J. Smith, 'Living Originalism' (2009) 59 *Duke Law Journal* 239. For a discussion of the distinction between old and new originalists, see Randy E. Barnett, 'An Originalism for Non-originalists' (1999) 45 *Loyola Law Review* 611. Old originalism is perhaps best represented by the writings of Robert Bork, *The Tempting of America* (New York: Free Press, 1990). New originalism is represented by Randy Barnett, *Restoring the Lost Constitution: The Presumption of Liberty* (Princeton, NJ: Princeton University Press, 2004); Keith E. Whittington, 'The New Originalism' (2004) 2 *Georgetown Journal of Law and Public Policy* 599.

6 Peter Smith and Robert Tuttle, 'Biblical Literalism and Constitutional Interpretation' (2011) 86 *Notre Dame Law Review* 693 at 695.

7 '"Meaning" is a capacious concept, and indeed, it has many different meanings, including semantic content, purposes, intentions, practical entailments, and cultural associations. Conceived most broadly, "meaning" includes a vast array of cultural associations, traditions, conventions, and background assumptions.' Jack Balkin, 'Nine Perspectives on Originalism' (2012) *University of Illinois Law Review* 101 at 113.

8 Peter Hogg, *Constitutional Law of Canada* (Toronto: Thomson, 2012) at 15.9(f) and 60.1(e).

9 Books and articles have been written trying to convince originalists that originalism is consistent with other modes of interpretation; see Jack

Balkin, *Living Originalism* (Cambridge, MA: Harvard University Press, 2011). In Canada, there have also been attempts to argue that originalism and living-tree constitutionalism need not be mutually exclusive; see Bradley Miller, 'Origin Myth: The Persons Case, The Living Tree, and the New Originalism,' in *The Challenge of Originalism: Theories of Constitutional Interpretation*, ed. Grant Huscroft and Bradley Miller (Cambridge: Cambridge University Press, 2011) at 120; Bradley Miller, 'Beguiled by Metaphors: The "Living Tree" and Originalist Constitutional Interpretation in Canada' (2009) 22 *Canadian Journal of Law and Jurisprudence* 331.

10 Steven G. Calabresi and Livia Fine, 'Two Cheers for Professor Balkin's Originalism' (2009) 103 *Northwestern University Law Review* 663; John McGinnis and Michael Rappaport, 'Original Interpretive Principles as the Core of Originalism' (2000) 24 *Constitutional Commentary* 371 at 381; Joel Alicea, 'Originalism in Crisis: The Movement Towards Indeterminate Originalism,' 22 May 2010, available at http://papers.ssrn.com/sol3/papers.cfm?abstract_id=1613065.

11 *B.C. Motor Vehicle Act Reference*, [1985] S.C.R. 486 at 507–9.

12 See Steven G. Calabresi, ed., *Originalism: A Quarter-Century of Debate* (Washington, DC: Regnery, 2007); Keith Whittington, *Constitutional Construction: Divided Powers and Constitutional and Meaning* (Cambridge, MA: Harvard University Press, 1999).

13 Paul Brest, 'The Misconceived Quest for the Original Understanding' (1980) 60 *Boston University Law Review* 204; Mitchell N. Berman, 'Originalism Is Bunk' (2009) 84 *New York Law Review* 1; David A. Straus, *The Living Constitution* (New York: Oxford University Press, 2010); Robert W. Bennett and Lawrence B. Solum, *Constitutional Originalism: A Debate* (Cornell, NY: Cornell University Press, 2011); Thomas Colby, 'The Sacrifice of the New Originalism' (2011) 99 *Georgetown Law Journal* 713.

14 Ian Binnie, 'Constitutional Interpretation and Original Intent,' in *Constitutionalism in the Charter Era*, ed. Grant Huscroft and Ian Brodie (Markham, ON: LexisNexis, 2004) 345 at 348. However, for an argument that Canada's dominant constitutional modes of interpretation are consistent with originalism, see Miller, 'Origin Myth' at 120. For an argument that originalism existed within Supreme Court Justice Wilson's judgments, see Adam Dodek, 'The Dutiful Conscript: An Originalist View of Justice Wilson's Conception of Charter Rights and Their Limits' (2008) 41 *Supreme Court Law Review* 321.

15 For commentary, see Justice Ian Binnie, 'Constitutional Interpretation and Original Intent' (2004) 23 *Supreme Court Law Review* (2d) 345. Furthermore, the Supreme Court of Canada did not respond positively to interpreting

the Canadian Charter of Rights and Freedoms in light of the drafter's intent; see *British Columbia Motor Vehicle Act Reference*, [1985] at 509: 'The rights, freedoms and values embodied in the Charter in effect become frozen in time to the moment of adoption with little or no possibility of growth, development and adjustment to changing societal needs ... If the newly planted "living tree" which is the Charter is to have the possibility of growth and adjustment over time, care must be taken to ensure that historical materials ... do not stunt its growth.'

16 *Ontario Hydro v. Ontario (Labour Relations Board)*, [1993] 3 S.C.R. 327.

17 Peter W. Hogg, 'Canada: From Privy Council to Supreme Court,' in *Interpreting Constitutions: A Comparative Study*, ed. Jeffrey Goldsworthy (Oxford: Oxford University Press, 2006) 55 at 83.

18 It may be argued that originalism is textually necessary in Canada's constitution because the word 'Aboriginal' comes from the Latin *ab origine*, meaning from the beginning, or *ancestraux* in the French version; see *R. v. Van der Peet*, [1996] 2 S.C.R. 507 at para. 32. However, the word 'Aboriginal,' like the label 'Indian,' is a European invention, and the Courts have held that non-Native concepts should be applied with great caution when discussing the application of 'Western' law to Native peoples; see *Amodu Tijani v. Secretary (Southern Nigeria)*, [1921] 2 A.C. 399 at 402–3, cited with approval in *Calder et al. v. Attorney-General of British Columbia*, [1973] S.C.R. 313, where the Privy Council stated, 'Their Lordships make the preliminary observation that in interpreting the native title to land, not only in Southern Nigeria, but other parts of the British Empire, much caution is essential. There is a tendency, operating at times unconsciously, to gender that title conceptually in terms which are appropriate only to systems which have grown up under English law. But this tendency has to be held in check closely.' The problem of describing Indigenous peoples in Western terms was discussed in great detail in Edward Said, *Orientalism* (New York: Vintage Books, 1978).

19 *R. v. Van der Peet*, [1996] at para. 46.

20 *Delgamuukw v. British Columbia*, [1997] 3 S.C.R. 1010 at para. 144; *Tsilhqot'in Nation v. British Columbia*, 2014 S.C.C. 44 at paras. 12, 14, 25, 28, 29, 32, 45–8, 50, 57–9, 69, and 75.

21 *R. v. Marshall*, [1999] 3 S.C.R. 456 at para. 14.

22 *R. v. Van der Peet*, [1996] at para. 28.

23 *Delgamuukw v. British Columbia*, [1997] at para. 145. For a critique of the crystallization theory of Aboriginal title, see John Borrows, 'Sovereignty's Alchemy: An Analysis of *Delgamuukw v. British Columbia*' (1999) 37 *Osgoode Hall Law Journal* 537 at 558.

24 *R. v. Marshall*, [1999] at paras. 58 and 60.
25 A living-tree approach is appropriately attentive to a law's roots but is more forward-looking in its approach.
26 *Edwards v. Attorney-General for Canada*, [1930] A.C. 124 at 136 (J.C.P.C.). For a comparative analysis of this metaphor in other constitutional contexts, see Vicki Jackson, 'Constitutions as "Living Trees"? Comparative Constitutional Law and Interpretive Metaphors' (2006) 75 *Fordham Law Review* 921.
27 *British North America Act, 1867*, 30–31 Vict., c. 3 (U.K.).
28 The Supreme Court wrote, in *Edwards v. Canada (Attorney General)*, [1928] S.C.R. 276 at 288, 'Passed in the year 1867, the various provisions of the B.N.A. Act … bear to-day the same construction which courts would, if then required to pass upon them, have given to them when they were first enacted. If the phrase "qualified persons" in s. 24 includes women to-day, it has so included them since 1867.'
29 *Edwards v. Attorney-General for Canada*, [1930] at 136.
30 The Privy Council gave the government the burden of proving that the word 'person' did not include women: 'The word "person" … may include members of both sexes, and to those who ask why the word ["person"] should include females the obvious answer is why should it not? In these circumstances the burden is upon those who deny that the word includes women to make out their case.' *Edwards v. Attorney-General for Canada*, [1930] at 138.
31 *Reference re Same-Sex Marriage*, [2004] 3 S.C.R. 698 at para. 22; *Attorney General of British Columbia v. Canada Trust Co. et al.*, [1980] 2 S.C.R. 466 at 478–9; *Canada (Attorney General) v. Hislop*, [2007] 1 S.C.R. 429 at para. 94; *Re Residential Tenancies Act, 1979*, [1981] 1 S.C.R. 714 at 723; *Re B.C. Motor Vehicle Act*, [1985] 2 S.C.R. 486 at para. 53; *Reference re Employment Insurance Act* (Can.), ss. 22 and 23, [2005] 2 S.C.R. 669 at para. 9; *Reference Re Provincial Electoral Boundaries (Sask.)*, [1991] 2 S.C.R. 158, at 180; *R. v. Demers*, [2004] 2 S.C.R. 489 at para. 78; *Canadian Western Bank v. Alberta*, [2007] 2 S.C.R. 3 at para. 23; *Ontario Home Builders' Association v. York Region Board of Education*, [1996] 2 S.C.R. 929 at para. 145.
32 For a series of essays on this topic, see Ian Peach, Graeme Mitchell, David Smith, and John White, eds., *A Living Tree: The Legacy of 1982 in Canada's Political Evolution* (Markham, ON: LexisNexis, 2007).
33 *Reference re Securities Act*, 2011 S.C.C. 66 at para. 56, also citing *Reference re Employment Insurance Act (Can.), ss. 22 and 23*, 2005 S.C.C. 56, [2005] 2 S.C.R. 669, at para. 9, *per* Deschamps J.
34 *Reference re Same-Sex Marriage*, [2004] at para. 22.

35 Ibid. at para. 25.
36 *Attorney General of British Columbia v. Canada Trust Co. et al.*, [1980] at 478–9.
37 Ibid. at 479 (emphasis in original).
38 *Reference Re Provincial Electoral Boundaries (Sask.)*, [1991] at 180.
39 Ibid.
40 *Hunter v. Southam Inc.*, [1984] 2 S.C.R. 145, at 155.
41 For an excellent discussion of this point as its relates to the balance of power between the prime minister and Parliament, see Peter Aucoin, Mark D. Jarvis, and Lori Turnbull, *Democratizing the Constitution: Reforming Responsible Government* (Toronto: Emond Montgomery, 2011).
42 Balkin, *Living Originalism* at chap. 13.
43 Robert C. Post and Reva B. Siegel, 'Democratic Constitutionalism,' in *The Constitution in 2020*, ed. Jack M. Balkin and Reva B. Siegel (New York: Oxford University Press, 2009) at 25.
44 *Reference re Secession of Quebec*, [1998] 2 S.C.R. 217 at para. 78.
45 Hogg, *Constitutuional Law of Canada* at 1–2. The significance of Canada's evolutionary constitution for Indigenous peoples is developed in Borrows, *Canada's Indigenous Constitution*.
46 *Reference re Secession of Quebec*, [1998] at paras. 33 and 46.
47 *Constitution Act, 1982*, being Schedule B to the *Canada Act 1982* (U.K.), 1982, c 11; see the schedule to this act, which non-exhaustively references thirty such constitutional acts.
48 *Constitution Act, 1867 (British North American Act, 1867)* 30 & 31 Victoria, c. 3 (U.K.).
49 In the *Reference re Sucession of Quebec*, [1998], at para. 150, the Supreme Court observed, 'The Constitution is not a straitjacket. Even a brief review of our constitutional history demonstrates periods of momentous and dramatic change. Our democratic institutions necessarily accommodate a continuous process of discussion and evolution …'
50 *Ontario Home Builders' Association v. York Region Board of Education*, [1996] at para. 145. For a discussion of the organic nature of Canada's constitution, see Brian Slattery, 'The Organic Constitution: Aboriginal Peoples and the Evolution of Canada' (1996) *Osgoode Hall Law Journal* 101.
51 For a discussion of the differences between Canadian and U.S. approaches to constitutional interpretations, see Peter W. Hogg, 'The Charter of Rights and American Theories of Interpretation' (1987) 25 *Osgoode Hall Law Journal* 87. For a discussion of the development and ratification of the U.S. constitution, see Pauline Maier, *Ratification: The People Debate the Constitution, 1787–1788* (New York: Simon and Schuster, 2010).
52 *Reference re Succession of Quebec*, [1998] at para. 52.

53 *R. v. Blais*, [2003] 2 S.C.R. 236. For a history of the Natural Resources Transfer Agreement, see Frank Tough, 'Metis and Treaty Rights: The Forgotten Constitution: The Natural Resources Transfer Agreements and Indian Livelihood Rights, ca. 1925–1930' (2004) 41 *Alberta Law Review* 999.

54 *R. v. Blais*, [2003] at paras. 19–34.

55 Ibid. at paras. 39–40.

56 *R. v. Marshall*, [1999] at para. 14.

57 The Supreme Court held that there is a 'boundary that must not be crossed' when interpreting Aboriginal rights; see *Mitchell v. M.N.R.*, [2001] 1 S.C.R. 911 at para. 39. This boundary line is set by originalism.

58 *Reference Re Provincial Electoral Boundaries (Sask.)*, [1991] at 180: 'The doctrine of the constitution as a living tree mandates that narrow technical approaches are to be eschewed ... It also suggests that the past plays a critical but non-exclusive role in determining the content of the rights and freedoms granted by the *Charter*. The tree is rooted in past and present institutions, but must be capable of growth to meet the future.'

59 Government of Canada, Statement of Apology, 11 June 2008, at http://www.aadnc-aandc.gc.ca/eng/1100100015644.

60 See 'section D' of this chapter, where it should become clear that the extension of a living-tree approach into section 35(1) jurisprudence and beyond would lead to a greater scrutinize of originalism's colonial roots and enhance the role of Indigenous peoples' own role in the constitution's ongoing formation.

61 *Canada (Attorney General) v. Hislop*, [2007] at para. 94.

62 *Edwards v. Attorney-General for Canada*, [1930] at 136.

63 See Leonard Rotman, 'Taking Aim at the Canons of Treaty Interpretation in Canadian Aboriginal Rights Jurisprudence' (1997) 46 *University of New Brunswick Law Journal* 1.

64 *Worcester v. Georgia*, 31 U.S. (6 Pet.) 515, 8 L. Ed. 483. For further discussion of the development of Indians' canons of construction in the United States, see Charles Wilkinson and John Volkman, 'Judicial Review of Indian Treaty Abrogation: "As Long as the Water Flows or Grass Grows Upon the Earth – How Long a Time is That?"' (1975) 63 *California Law Review* 601.

65 *Worcester v. Georgia* at 553–4.

66 *Jones v. Meehan*, 175 U.S. 1 (1899) at 10–11:

> In construing any treaty between the United States and an Indian tribe, it must always ... be borne in mind that the negotiations for the treaty are conducted, on the part of the United States, an enlightened and powerful nation, by representatives skilled in diplomacy, masters of a

written language, understanding the modes and forms of creating the various technical estates known to their law, and assisted by an interpreter employed by themselves; that the treaty is drawn up by them and in their own language; that the Indians, on the other hand, are a weak and dependent people, who have no written language and are wholly unfamiliar with all the forms of legal expression, and whose only knowledge of the terms in which the treaty is framed is that imparted to them by the interpreter employed by the United States; and that the treaty must therefore be construed, not according to the technical meaning of its words to learned lawyers, but in the sense in which they would naturally be understood by the Indians.

67 The canons of Indian treaty constructed have been applied in leading U.S. Supreme Court cases, such as *United States v. Winans*, (1905) 198 U.S. 971, 25 S.Ct. 662, 49 L. Ed. 1089; *Winters v. United States*, (1908) 207 U.S. 564 at 576–7; *Choate v. Trapp*, (1912) 224 U.S. 665 at 675; *Carpenter v. Shaw*, (1930) 280 U.S. 363 at 367; *Choctaw Nation v. United States*, (1943) 318 U.S. at 423 at 431–2; *McClanahan v. Arizona State Tax Commission*, (1973) 411 U.S. 164 at 174; *Minnesota v. Mille Lacs Band of Chippewa Indians*, (1999) 526 U.S. 172 at 195–8.

68 *R. v. Sioui*, [1990] 1 S.C.R. 1025:

Our courts and those of our neighbours to the south have already considered what distinguishes a treaty with the Indians from other agreements affecting them. The task is not an easy one. In *Simon v. The Queen*, [1985] 2 S.C.R. 387, this Court adopted the comment of Norris J.A. in *R. v. White and Bob* (1964), 50 D.L.R. (2d) 613 (B.C.C.A.) (affirmed in the Supreme Court (1965), 52 D.L.R. (2d) 481), that the courts should show flexibility in determining the legal nature of a document recording a transaction with the Indians. In particular, they must take into account the historical context and perception each party might have as to the nature of the undertaking contained in the document under consideration. In my opinion, this liberal and generous attitude, heedful of historical fact, should also guide us in examining the preliminary question of the capacity to sign a treaty ...

69 *R. v. White and Bob*, (1964) 50 D.L.R. (2d) 613 (B.C.C.A.); affd. (1965) 52 D.L.R. (2d) 481n.

70 *R. v. Taylor and Williams*, (1981) 34 O.R. (2d) 360 (Ont. C.A.).

71 *R. v. Simon*, (1985) 24 D.L.R. (4th) 390.

72 *R. v. Horseman*, [1990] 1 S.C.R. 901 at 907.

73 *R. v. Badger*, [1996] 1 S.C.R. 771 at paras. 4 and 41.

74 *R. v. Sundown*, [1999] 1 S.C.R. 393 (S.C.C.) at paras. 24–5.

75 *R. v. Marshall*, [1999] 3 S.C.R. 456 at paras. 9–14.

76 *R. v. Marshall*, [1999] 3 S.C.R. 533 at paras. 19.

77 *R. v. Marshall; R. v. Bernard*, [2005] at para. 26.

78 *R. v. Morris*, [2006] 2 S.C.R. 915 at para. 19.

79 *R. v. White and Bob* (B.C.C.A.) at 648–9 cited in *R. v. Sioui*, [1990] at para. 16.

80 *R. v. Taylor and Williams*, [1981] at 367.

81 *R. v. Simon*, (1985) at para. 24.

82 *R. v. Horseman*, [1990] at 907.

83 Ibid.

84 *R. v. Badger*, [1996] at paras. 4 and 41.

85 *R. v. Sundown*, [1999] at para. 25.

86 *R. v. Marshall*, [1999] at para. 43.

87 Ibid. at 14 (emphasis in original).

88 *R. v. Marshall*, [1999] at para. 20.

89 Ibid. at para. 19.

90 *R. v. Marshall; R. v. Bernard*, [2005] at para. 25.

91 *R. v. Morris*, [2006] at para. 18.

92 By way of contrast, treaty jurisprudence in the United States does not regard treaties as exhaustive statements of law. Issues not discussed during treaty negotiations continue to be vested in Indigenous communities; see *United States v. Winans*, (1905). In this case, the Court held that treaties are 'not a grant of rights to the Indians, but a grant of rights from them – a reservation of those not granted.' Thus, anything not discussed in a treaty is retained by the tribe. This is known as the reserved rights doctrine: the tribes retain everything within their territory unless they affirmatively give it up; *Menominee Tribe v. United States*, (1968) 391 U.S. 404 (U.S.S.C.).

93 *Ontario Home Builders' Association v. York Region Board of Education*, [1996] at para. 145; *Reference re Same-Sex Marriage*, [2004] at para. 23.

94 *Manitoba Metis Federation Inc. v. Canada (Attorney General)*, 2013 S.C.C. 14, [2013] 1 S.C.R. 623 para. 76.

95 *R. v. Gladstone*, [1996] 2 S.C.R. 723 at para. 9.

96 *R. v. Van der Peet*, [1996].

97 *Delgamuukw v. British Columbia*, [1997].

98 *R. v. Sappier; R. v. Gray*, [2006] 2 S.C.R. 686.

99 *R. v. Marshall; R. v. Bernard*, [2005].

100 The Court held that the test for proving Aboriginal rights would be linked to 'an element of a practice, custom or tradition integral to the distinctive

culture of the aboriginal group claiming the right' (*R. v. Van der Peet*, [1996] at para. 46).

101 Ibid. at para. 32.

102 Justice Lamer distinguished Aboriginal rights from other 'liberal' rights and wrote that 'aboriginal rights must be viewed differently from *Charter* rights because they are rights held only by aboriginal members of Canadian society.' He then went on the say that Aboriginal rights 'arise from the fact that aboriginal people are aboriginal; ... aboriginal rights inhere in the very meaning of aboriginality' (*R. v. Van der Peet*, [1996] at para. 19).

103 *R. v. Van der Peet*, [1996] at para. 62. For a critique of this view, see Russell Barsh and Sakej Henderson, 'The Supreme Court's Van der Peet Trilogy: Native Imperialism and Ropes of Sand' (1997) 42 *McGill Law Journal* 993; John Borrows, 'Frozen Rights in Canada: Constitutional Interpretation and the Trickster' (1997) 22 *American Indian Law Review* 37.

104 *Delgamuukw v. British Columbia*, [1997] at para. 144.

105 For a critique of crystallization of title more broadly, see Borrows, *Recovering Canada* at 93–4.

106 The Supreme Court noted that Aboriginal rights were diminished at contact in *Guerin v. The Queen*, [1984] 2 S.C.R. 335 at 377–8, as follows: 'The rights of Indians in the lands they traditionally occupied prior to European colonization both predated and survived the claims to sovereignty made by various European nations in the territories of the North American continent. The principle of discovery which justified these claims gave the ultimate title in the land in a particular area to the nation which had discovered and claimed it. *In that respect at least the Indians' rights in the land were obviously diminished*; but their rights of occupancy and possession remained unaffected ...' (emphasis mine).

107 Justice McLachlin used this language in dissent in *R. v. Van der Peet*, [1996] at para. 247.

108 *R. v. Sappier; R. v. Gray*, [2006] at para. 22.

109 Ibid. at para. 23.

110 Barsh and Henderson, 'The Supreme Court's Van der Peet Trilogy'; John Borrows, 'The Trickster: Integral to a Distinctive Culture' (1997) *Constitutional Forum* 29–38.

111 *R. v. Sappier; R. v. Gray*, [2006] at para. 48.

112 Ibid. at paras. 60–7.

113 *Tsilhqot'in Nation v. British Columbia* 2014 at para. 32.

114 Ibid. at para. 25.

115 Ibid. at para. 69.

116 Ibid.

117 John Borrows, 'The Durability of Terra Nullius' (2015) *University of British Columbia Law Review* (forthcoming).

118 See Robert J. Miller, Jacinta Ruru, Larissa Behrendt, and Tracey Lindberg, *Discovering Indigenous Lands: The Doctrine of Discovery in the English Colonies* (Oxford: Oxford University Press, 2010); Lindsay G. Robertson, *Conquest by Law How the Discovery of America Dispossessed Indigenous Peoples of Their Lands* (New York: Oxford University Press, 2007); Robert Williams Jr., *The American Indian in Western Legal Thought: The Discourses of Conquest* (New York: Oxford University Press, 1990).

119 Sidney Harring, *White Man's Law: Native People in Nineteenth-Century Canadian Jurisprudence* (Toronto: University of Toronto Press, 1998) at 8–10.

120 *Tsilhqot'in Nation v. British Columbia* [2014] at para. 69

121 'Because it does not make sense to speak of a burden on the underlying title before that title existed, aboriginal title crystallized at the time sovereignty was asserted' (*Delgamuukw v. British Columbia*, [1997] at para. 145). For a critique of this reasoning, see Borrows, 'Sovereignty's Alchemy.'

122 *R. v. Van der Peet*, [1996] at para. 19.

123 There are many sources of constitutional authority in Canada that are not based in European thought, such as the role the Universal Declaration of Human Rights played in the drafting of the Charter; see *Reference Re Public Service Employee Relations Act (Alta.)*, [1987] 1 S.C.R. 313 at paras. 57–74; *Suresh v. Canada (Minister of Citizenship and Immigration)*, 2002 S.C.C. 1, [2002] 1 S.C.R. 3. The Supreme Court has also recognized that Aboriginal rights partially flow from Indigenous peoples' own laws; *Delgamuukw v. British Columbia*, [1997] at para. 147; *R. v. Van der Peet*, [1996] at paras. 38–42; *R. v. Marshall; R. v. Bernard*, [2005] at paras. 45–54. The Indigenous sources of Canada's constitution are discussed in Borrows, *Canada's Indigenous Constitution*.

124 *R. v. Van der Peet*, [1996] at para. 19: 'Although equal in importance and significance to the rights enshrined in the *Charter*, aboriginal rights must be viewed differently from *Charter* rights because they are rights held only by aboriginal members of Canadian society.'

125 *R. v. Sparrow*, [1990] 1 S.C.R. 1075 at para. 62: 'The best way to achieve that reconciliation is to demand the justification of any government regulation that infringes upon or denies aboriginal rights.' For a discussion of the place of similarity and difference in Aboriginal and treaty rights see Patrick Macklem, *Indigenous Difference and the Constitution of Canada* (Toronto: University of Toronto Press, 2001).

126 For a critique of the prevalence of rights discourse in Canadian law, see Andrew Petter, *The Politics of the Charter: The Illusive Promise of Constitutional*

Rights (Toronto: University of Toronto Press, 2010). For a discussion of the limitations of rights discourse in an Indigenous context, see Christopher Manfredi, 'Fear, Hope and Misunderstanding: Unintended Consequences and the Marshall Decision,' in *Advancing Aboriginal Claims: Visions/Strategies/Direction*, ed. Kerry Wilkins (Saskatoon: Purich Publishing, 2004).

127 *R. v. Sparrow*, [1990] at para. 65.

128 See John Borrows, 'Let Obligations be Done,' in *Let Right Be Done: Aboriginal Title, the Calder Case, and the Future of Aboriginal Rights*, ed. Hamar Foster, Heather Raven, and Jeremy Webber (Vancouver: UBC Press, 2007) 201 at 212, from which the argument in this paragraph is drawn.

129 *R. v. Van der Peet*, [1996] at para. 18.

130 *R. v. Sparrow*, [1990] at para. 53.

131 Ibid. at para. 54: 'The approach to be taken with respect to interpreting the meaning of s. 35(1) is derived from general principles of constitutional interpretation, principles relating to aboriginal rights, and the purposes behind the constitutional provision itself. Here, we will sketch the framework for an interpretation of "recognized and affirmed" that, in our opinion, gives appropriate weight to the constitutional nature of these words.'

132 *Reference re Secession of Quebec*, [1998] at para. 63: 'The evolution of our democratic tradition can be traced back to the Magna Carta (1215) and before, through the long struggle for parliamentary supremacy which culminated in the English *Bill of Rights* of 1689, the emergence of representative political institutions in the colonial era, the development of responsible government in the nineteenth century, and eventually, the achievement of Confederation itself in 1867 … [T]he Canadian tradition … is one of evolutionary democracy moving in uneven steps toward the goal of universal suffrage and more effective representation.'

133 See *R. v. Rahey*, [1987] 1 S.C.R. 588 at para. 98: 'The great defect of Magna Carta, however, lay in its failure to provide adequate mechanisms for the enforcement of the rights it purported to guarantee.'

134 See Kent McNeil, 'Aboriginal Title as a Constitutionally Protected Aboriginal Right,' in *Beyond the Nass Valley: National Implications of the Supreme Court's Delgamuukw Decision*, ed. Owen Lippert (Vancouver: Fraser Institute, 2000): '*Magna Carta* would have been received as part of the applicable statute law in all the common law provinces.' As a fundamental part of the British constitution, no doubt it applies in Quebec as well, despite the reintroduction of French civil law by the *Quebec Act*, 14 Geo. III (1774), c. 83 (U.K.). The preamble to the *Constitution Act, 1867*, provides that Canada shall have 'a Constitution similar in Principle to that of the United Kingdom.'

135 For a general discussion of this history, see Edward Vallance, *The Glorious Revolution: 1688, Britain's Fight for Liberty* (London: Little Brown, 2006); L.G. Schwoerer, ed., *The Revolution of 1688–89: Changing Perspectives* (Cambridge: Cambridge University Pres, 2004).

136 *An Act Declaring the Rights and Liberties of the Subject and Settling the Succession of the Crown,* 1689, 16 December 1689, at pages 67 to 73 of Dandy Pickering, ed., *The Statutes at Large,* vol. 9 (Cambridge: Bentham, 1762–1804); *English Historical Documents, 1660–1714,* ed. Andrew Browning (London: Eyre and Spottiswoode, 1953) at 122–8.

137 Vallance, *The Glorious Revolution* at 164, 177.

138 Jonathon I. Israel, ed., *The Anglo-Dutch Moment: Essays on the Glorious Revolution and Its World Impact* (Cambridge: Cambridge University Press, 2003).

139 Patrick Malcolmson and Richard Meyers, *The Canadian Regime: An Introduction to Parliamentary Government in Canada* (Toronto: University of Toronto Press, 2009) at 37–54.

140 The Charter constrains the Crown relative to individual citizens and obligates it to respect enumerated rights in the document.

141 For a significant period of time, assimilation guided the Crown's actions towards Aboriginal peoples, as illustrated by the following statement: 'Our object is to continue until there is not a single Indian in Canada that has not been absorbed into the body politic' [Duncan Campbell Scott, testimony before the Special Committee of the House of Commons examining the Indian Act amendments of 1920, National Archives of Canada, Record Group 10, volume 6810, file 470–2-3, volume 7, pp. 55 (L-3) and 63 (N-3), quoted in John Leslie, *The Historical Development of the Indian Act,* 2nd ed. (Ottawa: Department of Indian Affairs and Northern Development, Treaties and Historical Research Branch, 1978) at 114].

142 Royal Commission on Aboriginal Peoples, *Looking Forward and Looking Back,* vol. 1 of *The Report of the Royal Commission on Aboriginal Peoples* (Ottawa: Supply and Services Canada, 1996) at 137–200 and 245–592; *R. v. Sparrow* 70 D.L.R. (4th) 385 at 412 (S.C.C.).

143 See *R. v. Côté,* [1996] 3 S.C.R. 139 at para. 59, citing *Mabo v. Queensland* [No. 2] (1992), 175 C.L.R. 1 (H.C.), at 42. Whatever the justification advanced in earlier days for refusing to recognize the rights and interests in land of the Indigenous inhabitants of settled colonies, an unjust and discriminatory doctrine of that kind can no longer be accepted.

144 For a seemingly lone exception to this practice, see *Grassy Narrows First Nation v. Ontario (Natural Resources),* 2014 S.C.C. 48. In this case, the Court chose a living-tree federalist argument that favoured the province over an

originalist Ojibwe argument that would have secured victory for the First Nations.

145 In fact, this is what occurred in the *Grassy Narrows* case: the Supreme Court did not effectively consider the historic or contemporary perspectives of Aboriginal peoples regarding Crown unilateralism.

146 For a historical overview of these views in the Canadian legal context, see Sidney Harring, *White Man's Law: Native People in Nineteenth Century Canadian Jurisprudence* (Toronto: University of Toronto Press, 1998) at 8–10; Paul Tennant, *Aboriginal Peoples and Politics: The Indian Land Question in British Columbia, 1849–1989* (Vancouver: UBC Press, 1990); J.R. Miller, *Skyscrapers Hide the Heavens: A History of Indian-White Relations in Canada* (Toronto: University of Toronto Press, 2000) at 103–312. For an examination of how Aboriginal peoples can still be labelled as inferior in the present context, see Wayne Warry, *Ending Denial: Understanding Aboriginal Issues* (Toronto: University of Toronto Press, 2008).

147 The Supreme Court has indicated it is inappropriate to view Aboriginal peoples as being inferior; see *Calder v. A.G.B.C.*, [1973] S.C.R. 313 at 346–7: 'The assessment and interpretation of the historical documents and enactments tendered in evidence must be approached in the light of present day research and knowledge disregarding ancient concepts formulated when understanding of the customs and culture of our original people was rudimentary and incomplete and when they were thought to be wholly without cohesion, laws or cultures, in effect subhuman species.'

148 *Edwards v. Attorney-General for Canada*, [1930] at 134.

149 Ibid.

150 Justice Binnie, formerly of the Supreme Court of Canada, would seem to agree. In an article dismissing originalism and arguing for living-tree constitutionalism in Canada, he wrote the following:

> Canadians will remember that until the last 50 years or so Aboriginal peoples in Canada were effectively denied almost all civil rights on the basis, and I quote a Nova Scotia judge writing in 1929, that: 'The savages' rights of sovereignty even of ownership were never recognized … In my judgment the Treaty of 1752 is not a treaty at all and is not to be treated as such; it is at best a mere agreement made by the Governor and council with a handful of Indians.' Eventually our Supreme Court declared this approach to be 'unacceptable' and brought to bear a more contemporaneous view of aboriginal peoples and of federal responsibilities under section 91(24) of the Constitution Act, 1867. In 1984, I acted for the federal government in a case that decided that exercise by the

Crown of its power to accept a surrender of Indian lands creates a trust enforceable in the courts, a conclusion which would have been unthinkable in 1867. However, the evolving view of the courts toward Aboriginal rights, initially signalled in Calder v. Attorney General of British Columbia, in 1973, in effect was endorsed by the political leadership when they included a recognition of existing treaty and aboriginal rights in the Constitution Act, 1982. (Ian Binnie, 'Interpreting the Constitution: Living Tree vs. Original Meaning,' *Policy Options*, October 2007, http://www.irpp.org/en/po/free-trade-20/interpreting-the-constitution-the-living-tree-vs.-original-meaning/ 104 at 106–7)

151 See *R. v. Côté*, [1996] at para. 53:

A static and retrospective interpretation of s. 35(1) cannot be reconciled with the noble and prospective purpose of the constitutional entrenchment of aboriginal and treaty rights in the *Constitution Act, 1982*. Indeed, the respondent's proposed interpretation risks undermining the very purpose of s. 35(1) by perpetuating the historical injustice suffered by aboriginal peoples at the hands of colonizers who failed to respect the distinctive cultures of pre-existing aboriginal societies. To quote the words of Brennan J. in *Mabo v. Queensland [No. 2]* (1992), 175 C.L.R. 1 (H.C.), at p. 42: 'Whatever the justification advanced in earlier days for refusing to recognize the rights and interests in land of the indigenous inhabitants of settled colonies, an unjust and discriminatory doctrine of that kind can no longer be accepted.'

152 Borrows, 'Sovereignty's Alchemy' at 558–67.
153 For further critiques concerning discrimination in *Johnson. v. McIntosh* and other cases relying on the doctrine of discovery, see Robert J. Miller, Jacinta Ruru, Larissa Behrendt, and Tracey Lindberg, *Discovering Indigenous Lands: The Doctrine of Discovery in the English Colonies* (Oxford: Oxford University Press, 2010); Lindsay G. Robertson, *Conquest by Law: How the Discovery of America Dispossessed Indigenous Peoples of Their Lands* (New York: Oxford University Press, 2007); Stuart Banner, *How the Indians Lost Their Land: Law and Power on the Frontier* (Cambridge, MA: Harvard University Press, 2007); Robert Williams Jr., *The American Indian in Western Legal Thought: The Discourses of Conquest* (Oxford: Oxford University Press, 1990).
154 *Johnson v. M'Intosh*, 21 U.S. (8 Wheat.) 543 at 573–4 (1823): 'On the discovery of this immense continent, the great nations of Europe were eager to appropriate to themselves as much of it as they could respectively acquire.

Its vast extent offered an ample field to the ambition and enterprise of all; and the character and religion of its inhabitants offered an apology for considering them as a people over whom the superior genius of Europe might claim an ascendancy.'

155 *Guerin v. The Queen*, [1984] at 378.

156 *R. v. Sparrow*, [1990] at 1103: 'There was from the outset never any doubt that sovereignty and legislative power, and indeed the underlying title, to such lands vested in the Crown'; *Delgamuukw v. British Columbia*, [1997] at para. 145: 'Crown did not gain this title until it asserted sovereignty over the land in question. Because it does not make sense to speak of a burden on the underlying title before that title existed, aboriginal title crystallized at the time sovereignty was asserted.'

157 Paraphrasing *Edwards v. Attorney-General for Canada*, [1930] at 134.

158 Richard Lillich, Hurst Hannum, S. James Anaya, and Dinah Shelton, *International Human Rights: Problems of Law, Policy and Practice*, 4th ed. (New York: Aspen, 2006) at 31–4; Paul Keal, *European Conquest and the Rights of Indigenous Peoples* (Cambridge: Cambridge University Press, 2003).

159 *R. v. Marshall; R. v. Bernard*, [2005] at para. 132. Unfortunately, despite critiquing *res nullius*, the doctrine of discovery applied in this case because the Aboriginal peoples were regarded as being nomadic at the time that the Crown asserted sovereignty, such that they could not claim exclusive possession of the land they used.

160 *Tsilhqot'in Nation v. British Columbia,* [2014] at para. 69.

161 See Royal Commission on Aboriginal Peoples, *Looking Forward and Looking Back* at recommendation 1.16.2 at page 696: 'Federal, provincial and territorial government further the process of renewal by: (a) acknowledging that concepts such as *terra nullius* and the doctrine of discovery are factually, legally and morally wrong.'

162 *Edwards v. Attorney-General for Canada*, [1930] at 136.

163 The Supreme Court wrote that a living-tree approach would allow confederation to change with new social realities in *Reference Re Provincial Electoral Boundaries (Sask.)*, [1991] at 180 citing *Reference re Employment Insurance Act (Can.), ss. 22 and 23*, [2005] at para. 9, *per* Deschamps J.

164 See John Borrows and Len Rotman, 'The Sui Generis Nature of Aboriginal Rights: Does it Make a Difference?' (1997) 35 *University of Alberta Law Review* 9; Borrows, *Canada's Indigenous Constitution*.

165 Some of these alternative sources might be Indigenous peoples' own laws, human rights law, international indigenous law, as well as laws based on textual, structural, doctrinal, prudential, and ethical modes of constitutional interpretation.

166 John Borrows, 'Ground Rules: Indigenous Treaties in Canada and New Zealand' (2006) 22 *New Zealand Universities Law Journal* 188.
167 *Reference Re Provincial Electoral Boundaries (Sask.)*, [1991] at 180.
168 *R. v. Sparrow*, [1990] at 1107.
169 Ibid. at 1016.
170 *Reference re Manitoba Language Rights*, [1985] 1 S.C.R. 721 at 745 in *R. v. Sparrow*, [1990] at 1107.
171 *Edwards v. Attorney-General for Canada*, [1930] at 136.
172 *R. v. Sparrow*, [1990] at 1109.
173 Ibid.
174 Ibid. at 1106.
175 Ibid. at 1108.
176 In *R. v. Sparrow*, [1990] at 1112, the Court wrote, 'While it is impossible to give an easy definition of fishing rights, it is possible, and, indeed, crucial, to be sensitive to the aboriginal perspective itself on the meaning of the rights at stake.'
177 *Mitchell v. M.N.R.*, [2001].
178 For a critique of the *Mitchell* case, see Gordon Christie, 'The Court's Exercise of Plenary Power: Rewriting the Two-Row Wampum' (2002) 16 *Supreme Court Law Review* (2d) 285–301.
179 This is most consistent with the approach that dominated U.S. Federal Indian case law before the U.S. Supreme Court between 1959 and the early 1980s; see Charles Wilkinson, *American Indians, Time and The Law* (New Haven, CT: Yale University Press, 1987). Felix Cohen was the most prominent proponent of this approach; see Felix Cohen, *Handbook of Federal Indian Law* (Washington, DC: Department of Interior, 1941) at 122–3. During the Rehnquist court era, federal Indian case law became more preoccupied with originalism. For a critique of the U.S. Supreme Court's approach, see Frank Pommershein, *Broken Landscapes: Indians, Indian Tribes, and the Constitution* (New York: Oxford University Press, 2009); Walter Echo-Hawk, *In the Courts of the Conqueror: The 10 Worst Indian Law Cases Ever Decided* (Golden, CO: Fulcrum Publishing, 2010); Robert Williams Jr., *Like a Loaded Weapon: The Rehnquist Court, Indian Rights, and the Legal History of Racism in America* (Minneapolis: University of Minnesota Press, 2005).
180 In discussing the nature of Aboriginal rights, the Court observed that English law 'accepted that the aboriginal peoples possessed pre-existing laws and interests' while recognizing that 'the Crown asserted that sovereignty over the land, and ownership of its underlying title' (*Mitchell v. M.N.R.*, [2001] at para. 9).
181 (Emphasis in original.) Justice McLachlin wrote:

Stripped to essentials, an aboriginal claimant must prove a modern practice, tradition or custom that has a reasonable degree of continuity with the practices, traditions or customs that existed prior to contact. The practice, custom or tradition must have been 'integral to the distinctive culture' of the aboriginal peoples, in the sense that it distinguished or characterized their traditional culture and lay at the core of the peoples' identity. It must be a 'defining feature' of the aboriginal society, such that the culture would be 'fundamentally altered' without it. It must be a feature of 'central significance' to the peoples' culture, one that 'truly made the society what it was.' (*Mitchell v. M.N.R.*, [2001] at para. 10, quoting *R. v. Van der Peet*, [1996] at paras. 54–9 [emphasis in original])

182 *Mitchell v. M.N.R.*, [2001] at para. 10.
183 Gordon Christie, 'Aboriginal Citizenship: Sections 35, 25 and 15 of Canada's *Constitution Act, 1982'* (2003) *Citizenship Studies* 481–95.
184 Borrows, *Canada's Indigenous Constitution* at 136.
185 See, generally, Neal McLeod, *Cree Narrative Memory: From Treaties to Contemporary Times* (Saskatoon: Purich Publishing, 2007); Daniel Paul, *We Were Not the Savages: A Mi'kmaq Perspective on the Collision between European and Native American Civilizations*, 21st century ed. (Halifax, NS: Fernwood, 2000); Boyce Richardson, ed., *Drum Beat: Anger and Renewal in Indian Country* (Toronto: Summerhill Press, 1989); Kiera Ladner and Leanne Simpson, eds., *This Is an Honour Song: Twenty Years Since the Blockades* (Winnipeg: Arbeiter Ring, 2010).
186 See *R. v. Van der Peet*, [1996] at para. 31. More specifically, what section 35(1) does is provide the constitutional framework through which the fact that Aboriginals lived on the land in distinctive societies, with their own practices, traditions and cultures, is acknowledged and reconciled with the sovereignty of the Crown. The substantive rights which fall within the provision must be defined in light of this purpose; the Aboriginal rights recognized and affirmed by section 35(1) must be directed towards the reconciliation of the pre-existence of Aboriginal societies with the sovereignty of the Crown. For a wide-ranging discussion of reconciliation, see Paulette Regan, *Unsettling the Settler Within: Indian Residential Schools, Truth Telling, and Reconciliation in Canada* (Vancouver: UBC Press, 2010).
187 Sakej Henderson, *First Nations Jurisprudence and Aboriginal Rights: Defining the Just Society* (Saskatoon: University of Saskatchewan, Native Law Centre, 2006).
188 *Attorney General of British Columbia v. Canada Trust Co. et al.*, [1980] at 478–9.

189 *Haida Nation v. British Columbia (Minister of Forests)*, [2004] 3 S.C.R. 511.
190 Ibid. at para. 17.
191 Ibid. at para. 32.
192 Ibid. at para. 25. Even where reconciliation has taken place, the accommo-dation of Aboriginal and treaty rights is an ongoing process; see *Mikisew Cree First Nation v. Canada (Minister of Canadian Heritage)*, [2005] 3 S.C.R. 388 at paras. 51–8.
193 *Haida Nation v. British Columbia (Minister of Forests)*, [2004] at para. 35.
194 Ibid. at para. 38.
195 *Edwards v. Attorney-General for Canada*, [1930] at 136.
196 Indigenous perspectives on the law are relevant to constitutional interpre-tation. As the Supreme Court of Canada wrote in *R. v. Sparrow*, [1990] at 1112, 'It is possible, and, indeed, crucial, to be sensitive to the aboriginal perspective itself on the meaning of the rights at stake.'
197 Indigenous law based on environmental sources is discussed in greater depth in Borrows, *Canada's Indigenous Constitution* at 28–35, and Borrows, *Recovering Canada* at 29–55.
198 An interesting example of how environmental law might develop and be operative within Indigenous communities is found in the writings of Julie Cruikshank. See Julie Cruikshank, *Do Glaciers Listen? Local Knowledge, Colonial Encounters, and Social Imagination* (Vancouver: UBC Press, 2005). See also William Robinson as told by Walter Wright, *Men of Medeek*, 2nd ed. (Kitimat, BC: Northern Sentinel Press, 1962); Jo-Anne Fiske and Betty Patrick, *Cis Dideen Kat (When the Plumes Rise): The Way of the Lake Babine Nation* (Vancouver: UBC Press, 2000); Kiera L. Ladner, 'Governing Within an Ecological Context: Creating an AlterNative Understanding of Black-foot Governance' (2003) 70 *Studies in Political Economy* 125 at 150; James [Sákéj] Youngblood Henderson, 'Mi'kmaq Tenure in Atlantic Canada' (1995) 18 *Dalhousie Law Journal* 196 at 218; John Borrows, 'Living Law on a Living Earth: Aboriginal Religion, Law, and the Constitution,' in *Law and Religious Pluralism in Canada*, ed. Richard Moon (Vancouver: UBC Press, 2008) at 161.
199 Analogies to law and the natural world are found in many treaty speeches; see Robert Williams Jr., *Linking Arms Together: American Indian Treaty Visions of Law and Peace, 1600–1800* (New York: Oxford University Press, 1997). For a more general discussion of analogical reasoning, see Cass R. Sunstein, commentary on 'On Analogical Reasoning' (1993) 106 *Harvard Law Review* 741.
200 For a discussion of this concept in law, see Wilkinson and Volkman, 'Judi-cial Review of Indian Treaty Abrogation.' An early use of a similar phrase

is found in a treaty made by William Penn with the Conestoga in 1701; see Kevin Kenny, *Peaceable Kingdom Lost: The Paxton Boys and the Destruction of William Penn's Holy Experiment* (New York: Oxford University Press, 2009) at 15: 'As long as the Sun and Moon shall endure.' Benjamin Franklin reported this treaty as saying, 'as long as the sun shall shine, or the waters run in the rivers,' in part II of *The Works of Benjamin Franklin: Autobiography*, ed. Jared Sparks (T. MacCoun, 1882). Other associations between treaties and the phrase are found in Harold Cardinal and Walter Hildebrandt, *Treaty Elders of Saskatchewan: Our Dream Is That Our Peoples Will One Day Be Clearly Recognized as Nations* (Calgary: University of Calgary Press, 2000) at 20; Treaty 7 Elders and Tribal Council with Walter Hildebrandt, Sarah Carter, and Dorothy First Rider, *The True Spirit and Original Intent of Treaty 7* (Montreal: McGill-Queen's University Press, 1996) at 133; Rene Fumoleau, *As Long as This Land Shall Last: A History of Treaty 8 and 11* (Toronto: McClelland and Stewart, 1976) at 74, 133, 240, 257, 314, 340, and 502; Arthur Ray, J.R. Miller, and Frank Tough, *Bounty and Benevolence: A History of Saskatchewan Treaties* (Montreal: McGill-Queen's University Press, 2000) at 116–17. For a contrary view about questioning this relationship of this phrase to treaties, see Sharon Venne, 'Understanding Treaty Six: An Indigenous Perspective,' in *Aboriginal and Treaty Rights in Canada: Essays on Law, Equality, and Respect for Difference*, ed. Michael Asch (Vancouver: UBC Press, 1997) 173 at 194.

201 For example, for a brief discussion of laws related to the sun, waters, and earth, see Deanna Christensen, *Atahkakoop: The Epic Account of a Plains Cree Head Chief, His People, and Their Struggle for Survival, 1816–1896* (Shell Lake, SK: Ahtahkakoop, 2000) at 5–14. For an ingenious literary treatment of this idea, see Thomas King, *Green Grass, Running Water* (Toronto: HarperCollins, 1993).

202 For example, when Alexander Morris proposed Treaty 6, he said, 'What I trust and hope we will do is not for today or tomorrow only; what I promise and what I believe and hope you will take, is to last as long as that sun shines and yonder river flows' [Alexander Morris, *The Treaties of Canada with the Indians of Manitoba and the North-West Territories, Including the Negotiations on Which They Were Based, and other Information Relating Thereto* (Saskatoon: Fifth House, 1991) at 202; see similar words in relation to Treaty 3 at p. 51]. This phrase was also used in an 1818 treaty with the Ojibway; see J.R. Miller, *Compact, Contract, Covenant: Aboriginal Treaty-Making in Canada* (Toronto: University of Toronto Press, 2009) at 101.

203 Francis Jennings, *The Ambiguous Iroquois Empire* (New York: W.W. Norton and Company, 1990).

204 Taiaiake Alfred, *Peace, Power, Righteousness: An Indigenous Manifesto* (Toronto: Oxford University Press, 1999). Some commentators have made 'originalist-type' arguments linking the Great Law of Peace to the U.S. Constitution; see Donald A. Grinde Jr. and Bruce E. Johansen, *Exemplar of Liberty: Native America and the Evolution of Democracy* (Los Angeles: American Indian Studies Center 1991); Bruce E. Johanesen, *Forgotten Founders: How the American Indian Helped Shape Democracy* (Boston: Harvard Common Press, 1982); Elizabeth Tooker, 'The United States Constitution and the Iroquois League,' in *The Imaginary Indian: Cultural Fictions and Government Policy*, ed. James Clifton (New Brunswick, NJ: Transactions Publishers, 1996) at 108.

205 The Haudenosaunee have in times past invited others to seek shelter in their Confederacy and Great Law; see William Fenton, *The Great Law and the Longhouse: A Political History of the Iroquois Confederacy* (Norman: University of Oklahoma Press, 1998) at 73.

206 Ibid. at 103.

207 Anishinaabe people at times also formulated law based on living trees. One such example comes in a council at Detroit in 1773. In this case, a Shawane chief named Tshwabame was speaking on behalf of Anishinaabe people who were accused of murdering several fur traders. In the course of his speech, he recalled that when their British Father replaced their French Father at Detroit, he 'planted a Tree' so that whenever 'any bad thing' should happen they could 'assemble at s[aid] tree & talk together' and 'try to moderate any difficulties' ('Speech of Tshwabame Shawanese & Minitowabe Chiefs, with Sixteen Sawinan Indians who brot in ye three Murderers of Pond &c.,' Detroit, 9–10 May 1773, Haldimand Add. 21,670: 42–5). I thank Mark Walters for bringing this reference to my attention.

208 For a discussion of First Nations' use of trees and poles in communicating their laws and political relationships, see Marius Barbeau, *Totem Poles* (Ottawa: Queen's Printer, 1950); Michael D. Blackstock. *Faces in the Forest: First Nations Art Created on Living Trees* (Montreal: McGill-Queen's University Press, 2001).

209 Johnny Mack has observed that the Nuu-chah-nuulth Nation

> cannot rely on a reified constitutional order because they are living in a constant state of renewal, where history is brought to the present by carvers/weavers whose hand is greatly inspired by contemporary, lived experience as well as the past that, of course, constitutes the present … The phrase 'dead tree constitutionalism' [seems] to capture the corporeal character of the indigenous constitutional order. That is to

say, the constitutions, much like ourselves, have a physicality and life expectancy. Thus, we are charged with the responsibility of knowing the histories reflected in the totems and, having lived within the world normativised by them, go about the task of carving/weaving new ones. (Personal communication, 11 April 2012)

He has written about this issue more generally in Johnny Mack, 'Thickening Totems and Thinning Imperialism' (LL.M. thesis, University of Victoria, 2009) [unpublished] at 128–36.

210 Paul, *We Were Not The Savages* at 156 (comparing political authority to the light of the moon); Jean-Guy Goulet, *Ways of Knowing: Experience, Knowledge and Power Among the Dene Tha* (Vancouver: UBC Press, 1998) at 61–107; Andie Diane Palmer, *Maps of Experience: The Anchoring of Land to Story in Secwepmec Discourse* (Toronto: University of Toronto Press, 2005) at 118–35; Royal Commission on Aboriginal Peoples, *Looking Forward and Looking Back* at chap. 4; Fikret Berkes, *Sacred Ecology: Traditional Ecological Knowledge and Resource Management* (Philadelphia: Taylor and Francis, 1999); Robert Brighton, *Grateful Prey: Rock Cree Human-Animal Relations* (Berkeley: University of California Press, 1993); Antonia Mills, *Eagle Down Is Our Law: Witsuwit'en Feasts and Land Claims* (Vancouver: UBC Press, 1994) at 122; Mariano Aupilaarjuk, Marie Tulimaaq, Emile Imaruittuq, Lucassie Nutaraaluk, and Akisu Joamie, *Perspectives on Traditional Law*, vol. 2 of *Interviewing Inuit Elders*, ed. Jarich Oosten, Frédéric Laugrand, and Wim Rasing (Iqaluit: Nunavut Arctic College, 1999).

211 This is contrary to the claim of some scholars in the United States that the U.S. constitution was partially inspired by Indigenous legal traditions; see Donald A. Grinde Jr. and Bruce E. Johansen, *Exemplar of Liberty*; Johanesen, *Forgotten Founders*; Tooker, 'The United States Constitution and the Iroquois League' at 108.

212 For a discussion of the similarities and differences of originalism and biblical literalism, see Peter Smith and Robert Tuttle, 'Biblical Literalism and Constitutional Interpretation' (2011) 86 *Notre Dame Law Review* 693; Jaroslav Pelikan, *Interpreting the Bible and the Constitution* (New Haven, CT: Yale University Press, 2004); Karen Armstrong, *The Bible: A Biography* (New York: Atlantic Monthly Press, 2007). For arguments about literalism and dynamic interpretation under the Koran, see Anver Emon, *Islamic Natural Law Theories* (Oxford: Oxford University Press, 2010); Anver Emon, 'Techniques and Limits of Legal Reasoning in Shari'a Today' (2009) 2 *Berkeley Journal of Middle Eastern & Islamic Law* 101–24; Mohammad Hashim Kamali, 'Law and Society: The Interplay of Revelation and

Reason in the Shariah,' in *The Oxford History of Islam*, ed. John L. Esposito (Oxford: Oxford University Press, 1999) at 107–10.

213 Bruce Corley and Steve W. Lemke, *Biblical Hermeneutics: A Comprehensive Introduction to Interpreting Scripture*, 2nd ed. (Nashville: Broadman and Holman: 2009); Michael Fishbane, *The Garments of Torah: Essays in Biblical Hermeneutics* (Bloomington: Indiana University Press, 1992); Henry Virkler, *Hermeneutics: Principles and Processes of Biblical Interpretation* (Grand Rapids, MI: Baker House Books, 1991). For a philosophical application of hermeneutics, see Hans Georg Gadamer, J. Weinsheimer, and D.G. Marshall, trans., *Truth and Method*, 2nd rev. ed. (New York: Crossroad, 2004); Charles Stewart, *Syncretism/Anti-Syncretism: The Politics of Religious Synthesis* (New York: Routledge, 1994).

214 Sanford Levinson, *Constitutional Faith* (Princeton, NJ: Princeton University Press, 1988).

215 *Sawridge Band v. Canada*, [1996] 1 F.C. 3 (F.C.T.D.). The Federal Court of Appeal determined that the trial judges' decision raised a reasonable apprehension of bias; see *Sawridge Band v. Canada*, [1997] F.C.J. No. 794, [1997] 3 F.C. 580 (Fed. C.A.). The subsequent history of this case eventually led to its dismissal; see *Sawridge First Nation v. Canada*, 2008 F.C. 322 (CanLII); *Sawridge First Nation v. Canada*, 2009 F.C.A. 123 (CanLII). A leave to appeal was denied in *Sawridge Band v. Her Majesty the Queen, Congress of Aboriginal Peoples, Native Council of Canada (Alberta), Non-Status Indian Association of Alberta and Native Women's Association of Canada AND BETWEEN Tsuu T'ina First Nation (formerly the Sarcee Indian Band) v. Her Majesty the Queen, Congress of Aboriginal Peoples, Native Council of Canada (Alberta), Non-Status Indian Association of Alberta and Native Women's Association of Canada*, 2009 CanLII 69744 (S.C.C.).

216 For commentary on this case, see Joyce Green, 'Constitutionalizing the Patriarchy: Aboriginal Women and Aboriginal Government' (1993) 4 *Constitutional Forum* 4; Joyce Green, 'Exploring Identity and Citizenship: Aboriginal Women, Bill C-31 and the Sawridge Case' (PhD diss., University of Alberta, 1997) [unpublished]; Joyce Green, 'Canaries in the Mines of Citizenship: Indian Women in Canada' (2001) 34 *Canadian Journal of Political Science* 4; Thomas Isaac, 'Case Commentary: Self-Government, Indian Women and Their Rights of Reinstatement under the Indian Act: A Comment on *Sawridge Band v. Canada*' (1995) 4 *Canadian Native Law Reporter* at 1.

217 For a review of this history, see Royal Commission on Aboriginal Peoples, *Perspectives and Realities*, vol. 4 of *The Report of the Royal Commission on Aboriginal Peoples* (Ottawa: Ministry of Supply and Services, 1996) at 24–36. Important cases challenging the *Indian Act*'s discrimination against

Indian women are as follows: *Canada (Attorney General) v. Lavell*, [1973] S.C.J. No. 128, [1974] S.C.R. 1349, 38 D.L.R. (3d) 481 (S.C.C.); *Lovelace v. Canada*, 36 U.N. GOAR Supp. (No. 40) Annex XVIII; U.N. Doc. A/36/40 (1981); *McIvor v. The Registrar, Indian and Northern Affairs Canada*, 2007 B.C.S.C. 827 (CanLII), [2007] 3 C.N.L.R. 72 (B.C.S.C.); *McIvor v. Canada* (2009), 306 D.L.R. (4th) 193; 190 C.R.R. (2d) 249; [2009] 2 C.N.L.R. 236; 91 B.C.L.R. (4th) 1 (B.C.C.A.); *Sharon Donna McIvor and Charles Jacob Grismer v. Registrar, Indian and Northern Affairs Canada and Attorney General of Canada*, 2009 CanLII 61383 (S.C.C.). To partially remedy sex-based discrimination in the *Indian Act*, Parliament passed two amendments to the *Indian Act*: *An Act to amend the Indian Act*, R.S.C. 1985, c. 32 (Bill C-31) and *Gender Equity and the Indian Registration Act*, R.S.C. 2010, c-18 (Bill C-3).

218 *Sawridge Band v. Canada*, [1996] at 46, 116.

219 Ibid. at 92–3.

220 Wayne Roan testified at trial: 'The supreme being that gave me the language to identify these things. That's the way he said it. That's the way I believe it, that's the way I recognize it, and nothing you're going to say is going to change that. It is part of my way of life. It is not yours, it is my way. All I'm doing here is for you to try and understand I put into place, that's the way things worked' (*Sawridge Band v. Canada*, [1996] at 100).

221 Elders in the *Sawridge* case regarded the idea of 'woman-follows-man' as being foundational to Cree organization. They argued that Cree ways would be threatened if women with non-Native husbands did not follow them off the reserve when they married. These values are clearly discriminatory and cannot be excused by reference to original Cree teachings and law. Nevertheless, Elder Sophie Mackinaw testified at trial: 'I want to talk specifically about the white husband in this instance. It is not clear that the white husband is going to be able to accept our ways and live the way we are. It may be that the white man who comes to live on our reserve will want to impose his own values, his ways which he is familiar with on us, on our communities' (*Sawridge Band v. Canada*, [1996] at 29).

222 For an excellent discussion of the rich diversity of Indigenous legal thought, see Val Napoleon, 'Ayook: Gitksan Legal Order, Law and Legal Theory' (PhD diss., University of Victoria, 2009), http://dspace.library. uvic.ca:8080/bitstream/handle/1828/1392/napoleon%20dissertation%20April%2026-09.pdf?sequence=1.

223 For internal Indigenous opposition to discrimination on the basis of sex within Indigenous communities, see the work of the Native Women's Association of Canada, at http://www.nwac.ca/ [accessed 1 April 2014]. Indigenous women have developed important critiques of discrimination

from within many Indigenous traditions; see Val Napoleon, 'Aboriginal Discourse: Gender, Identity and Community,' in *Indigenous Peoples and the Law: Comparative and Critical Perspectives*, ed. Benjamin J. Richardson, Shin Imai, and Kent McNeil (Oxford: Hart Publishing, 2009); Sarah Deer, B. Clairmont, and C.A. Martell, eds., *Sharing Our Stories of Survival: Native Women Surviving Violence* (Lantham, MD: Altamira Press, 2008).

224 Arguments made by Indigenous peoples that appear to be originalist in the U.S. context are found in *Santa Clara Pueblo v. Martinez*, 436 U.S. 49 (1978) (U.S.S.C.); *In the Matter of Village Authority to Remove Tribal Council Representative (Bacavi Certified Question)* (February 11, 2010) No. 2008-AP-0001 (Hopi Appellate Court); *In Re Menefee*, (May 5, 204) No. 97–12–092-CV, 2004 WL 5714978 (Grand Traverse Band of Ottawa and Chippewa Indians Tribal Court); *Kavena v. Hopi Indian Tribal Court*, (March 21, 1989) NAHT 0000002 (Hopi Appellate Court); *Allen v. Cherokee Nation Tribal Council*, (2006) 6 Am. Tribal Law 18 (Cherokee Nation Judicial Appeals Tribunal).

225 Indigenous peoples are traditional, modern, and postmodern and their constituting laws should constantly be cross-referenced to ensure that rights are not frozen in the past; see Borrows, *Recovering Canada* at 75–6.

226 See 'Constitution of the Little River Band of Indians of Manistee, Michigan,' at http://www.lrboi-nsn.gov/images/docs/council/docs/Constitution%20-%202004%20Amendments.pdf [accessed 1 April 2014]. The Preamble reads as follows:

> We, the Little River Ottawa people have asserted our sovereignty throughout history including in the Treaty of Chicago [August 29, 1821; 7 Stat 218], the Treaty of Washington [March 28, 1836; 7 Stat 491], and the Treaty of Detroit [July 31, 1855; 11 Stat 621].
>
> Between the last treaty and the present day, the Grand River Ottawa people who became the Little River Band of Ottawa Indians were known and organized under several names, including members of 'Indian Village' on the Manistee River, residents of the Pere Marquette Village or 'Indian Town,' Unit No. 7 of the Northern Michigan Ottawa Association, the Thornapple River Band, and finally the Little River Band of Ottawa Indians.
>
> On September 21, 1994, Public Law 103–324 (108 Stat 2156) was enacted, reaffirming federal recognition of and confirming the sovereignty of the Grand River Bands comprising the Little River Band of Ottawa Indians (referred to as the Tribe or Little River Band).
>
> As an exercise of our sovereign powers, in order to organize for our common good, to govern ourselves under our own laws, to maintain

and foster our tribal culture, provide for the welfare and prosperity of our people, and to protect our homeland we adopt this constitution, in accordance with the Indian Reorganization Act of June 18, 1934, as amended, as the Little River Band of Ottawa Indians.

The Band also has a bureaucracy consisting of twenty-eight different departments administering programs and processes necessary to running a modern government.

227 The varied interpretive approaches within tribal courts can be studied in Matthew Fletcher, *American Indian Tribal Law* (New York: Aspen, 2011); Justin Richland and Sarah Deer, eds., *Introduction to Tribal Legal Studies*, 2nd ed. (Lanham, MD: Altamira Press, 2010); Carrie Garrow and Sarah Deer, eds., *Tribal Criminal Law and Procedure* (Lanham, MD: Altamira Press, 2004); Raymond Austin, *Navajo Courts and Navajo Common Law: A Tradition of Tribal Self-Governance* (Minneapolis: University of Minnesota Press, 2009); Justin Richland, *Arguing with Tradition: The Language of Law in Hopi Tribal Court* (Chicago: University of Chicago Press, 2008).

228 Case No. 06–178-AP, June 2007 (Little River Band of Indians Court of Appeal); see also Fletcher, *American Indian Tribal Law* at 405–12.

229 Fletcher, *American Indian Tribal Law* at 409–10.

230 Ibid. at 410.

231 Ibid.

232 There is a vast literature discussing the indeterminacy of originalism in the U.S. context; see Thomas McAfee, 'Originalism and Indeterminacy' (1996) 19 *Harvard Journal of Law and Public Policy* 429; Reva B. Siegel, 'Dead or Alive: Originalism as Popular Constitutionalism in Heller' (2008) 122 *Harvard Law Review* 191; Erwin Chemerinsky, *Intepreting the Constitution* (New York: Praeger Publishers, 1987) at 75–80; Brest, 'The Misconceived Quest.' The Supreme Court of Canada also discussed originalism in relation to the Charter; see *Re B.C. Motor Vehicle Act*, [1985] 2 S.C.R. 486 at paras. 51–3.

233 Fletcher, *American Indian Tribal Law* at 410.

234 *R. v. Van der Peet*, [1996] at para. 46, and *Delgamuukw v. British Columbia*, [1997] at para. 144.

235 *R. v. Marshall*, [1999] at para. 14.

236 The importance of a non-exclusivist use of history in constitutional law is found in *Reference Re Provincial Electoral Boundaries (Sask.)*, [1991] at 180: 'The doctrine of the constitution as a living tree mandates that narrow technical approaches are to be eschewed,' which means that 'the past plays a critical but non-exclusive role in determining the content of the rights and freedoms granted by the *Charter*.'

237 Case No. 06–178-AP, June 2007 (Little River Band of Indians Court of Appeal); see also Fletcher, *American Indian Tribal Law* at 405–12.
238 For a discussion of the trickster, see John Borrows, 'With or Without You: First Nations' Law (in Canada)' (1996) *McGill Law Journal* 630–65; Barbara Babcock Adams, 'A Tolerated Margin of Mess: The Trickster and His Tales Reconsidered' (1975) 11 *Journal of Folklore Institute* 147; Henry Rowe Schoolcraft, 'Historical and Methodological Perspectives,' in *Critical Essays on Native American Literature*, ed. Andrew Wiget (Boston: G.K. Hall, 1985) at 21; John Borrows, 'Constitutional Law From a First Nations Perspective' (1994) 28 *University of British Columbia Law Review* 1–48 at 6–10; Gerald Vizenor, *The Trickster of Liberty: Tribal Heirs to a Wild Baronage* (Minneapolis: University of Minnesota Press, 1988).
239 *People v. Champagne*, Opinion and Judgment at 6, No. 06-131-TM (Little River Band Tribal Court, Dec. 1, 2006) (*Champagne III*).
240 Elsewhere, I have argued that

> Nanabush roams from place to place and fulfills his goals by using ostensibly contradictory behaviors such as charm and cunning, honesty and deception, kindness and mean tricks. The trickster also displays transformative power as he takes on new personae in the manipulation of these behaviors and in the achievement of his objectives. Lessons are learned as the trickster engages in actions which in some particulars are representative of the listener's behavior, and on other points are uncharacteristic of their comportment. The trickster encourages an awakening of understanding because listeners are compelled to confront and reconcile the notion that their ideas may be partial and their viewpoints limited. Nanabush can kindle these understandings because his actions take place in a perplexing realm that partially escapes the structures of society and the cultural order of things. (Borrows, 'Frozen Rights in Canada' at 37)

241 For a discussion of the use of Anishinaabe law as a source of Canadian Law, see Borrows, *Recovering Canada* at 15–20, 47–54.
242 For an in-depth discussion of the place of Indigenous law in Canada's constitution, see Borrows, *Canada's Indigenous Constitution*.
243 *The Ojibwe Peoples Dictionary* (University of Minnesota) at http://ojibwe. lib.umn.edu/main-entry/inaakonige-vai [accessed 1 April 2014].
244 *Reference re Secession of Quebec*, [1998] at para. 148.
245 *Ocean Port Hotel Ltd. v. British Columbia (General Manager, Liquor Control and Licensing Branch)*, [2001] 2 S.C.R. 781 at para. 33: 'The Constitution is an organic instrument, and must be interpreted flexibly to reflect changing circumstances: *Attorney-General for Ontario v. Attorney-General for Canada,*

[1947] A.C. 127 (P.C.).' There are times when the U.S. constitution has also been called organic; see *Missouri v. Holland*, (1920) 252 U.S. 416 at 433. For an excellent article on this subject, see Slattery, 'The Organic Constitution.'

246   *The Queen v. Beauregard*, [1986] 2 S.C.R. 56 at para. 46: 'The Canadian Constitution is not locked forever in a 119-year old casket. It lives and breathes and is capable of growing to keep pace with the growth of the country and its people.'

247   The leading case on the constitution as a living tree is *Edwards v. Canada (Attorney General)* [1930]. An excellent history of the case is Robert Sharpe and Patricia McMahon, *The Persons Case: The Origins and Legacy of the Fight for Legal Personhood* (Toronto: University of Toronto Press, 2007). An example of contemporary references to the living tree are found in *Reference re Same-Sex Marriage*, [2004] at para. 22.

248   For further discussions of these six modes of constitutional interpretation, see Robin Elliot, 'References, Structural Argumentation and the Organizing Principles of Canada's Constitution' (2001) 80 *Canadian Bar Review* 67 at 72–4; Philip Bobbit, *Constitutional Fate: Theory of the Constitution* (New York: Oxford University Press, 1982).

249   *Reference re Securities Act*, 2011 at para. 56, also citing *Reference re Employment Insurance Act (Can.), ss. 22 and 23*, 2005 S.C.C. 56, [2005] 2 S.C.R. 669 at para. 9, *per* Deschamps J.

250   *Reference re Same-Sex Marriage*, [2004] at para. 22.

251   *Attorney General of British Columbia v. Canada Trust Co. et al.*, [1980] at 478–9.

252   Ibid. at 479 (emphasis in original).

253   *Reference Re Provincial Electoral Boundaries (Sask.)*, [1991] at 180.

254   Ibid.

255   Ibid.

256   John Saywell, *The Lawmakers: Judicial Power and the Shaping of Canadian Federalism* (Toronto: Osgoode Society for Canadian Legal History and University of Toronto Press, 2004).

257   William Kaplan, *The Jehovah's Witnesses and Their Fight for Civil Rights* (Toronto: University of Toronto Press, 1989); *Roncarelli v. Duplessis*, [1959] S.C.R. 121; *Reference Re Alberta Statutes*, [1938] S.C.R. 100; *Saumer v. City of Quebec*, [1953] 2 S.C.R. 299; *Switzman v. Ebling*, [1957] S.C.R. 285.

258   *Hunter v. Southam Inc.*, [1984] at 155.

Chapter Five

1   For excellent critiques about the perils of working with Canadian governments for Indigenous peoples, see Taiaiake Alfred, *Peace, Power, Righteousness: An Indigenous Manifesto* (Toronto: Oxford University Press, 1999);

Taiaiake Alfred, *Wasase: Indigenous Pathways to Action* (Peterborough, ON: Broadview Press, 2005); Glen Coulthard, 'Resisting Culture: Seyla Benhabib's Deliberative Approach to the Politics of Recognition in Colonial Contexts,' in *Realizing Deliberative Democracy*, ed. David Kahane, Dominique Leydet, Daniel Weinstock, and Melissa Williams (Vancouver: UBC Press, 2009); Glen Coulthard, 'Beyond Recognition: Indigenous Self-Determination as Prefigurative Practice,' in *Lighting the Eighth Fire: The Liberation, Resurgence, and Protection of Indigenous Nations*, ed. Leanne Simpson (Winnipeg: Arbeiter Ring, 2008).

2 Johnny Mack, 'Thickening Totems and Thinning Imperialism' (LL.M. thesis, University of Victoria, 2009) [upublished].

3 Ellen Laconte, *Life Rules: Nature's Blueprint for Surviving Economic and Environmental Collapse* (Gabriola Island, BC: New Society Publishers, 2011).

4 One could effectively critique any action designed to support Indigenous peoples within the nation state. See Frantz Fanon, *The Wretched of the Earth* (New York: Grove Press, 2004).

5 John Borrows, *Recovering Canada: The Resurgence of Indigenous Law* (Toronto: University of Toronto Press, 2002) at 138–58; John Borrows, *Canada's Indigenous Constitution* (Toronto: University of Toronto Press, 2010) at 271–82.

6 For early commentary on God's putative role in Indigenous affairs on both sides of the ledger, see Chester Eisinger, 'The Puritan's Justification for Taking the Land' (1948) 84 *Essex Historical Institute Historical Collections* 131.

7 Gary Nash, *The Unknown American Revolution: The Unruly Birth of Democracy and the Struggle to Create America* (New York: Penguin Books, 2006); John Foran, *Taking Power: On the Origins of Third World Revolutions* (Cambridge: Cambridge University Press, 2007); Robert Service, *Stalin: A Biography* (Cambridge, MA: Harvard University Press, 2004).

8 Jim Tully, *Democracy and Civic Freedom*, vol. 1 of *Public Philosophy in a New Key* (Cambridge: Cambridge University Press, 2008) at 240: our political lives are 'shot through with relations of inequality, force and fraud, broken promises, failed accords, degrading stereotypes, misrecognition, paternalism, enmity and distrust.'

9 Glen Coulthard, *Red Skin, White Masks: Rejecting the Colonial Politics of Recognition* (Minneapolis: University of Minnesota Press, 2014) at 23–4.

10 In this regard, I accept and support the practices of righteous resentment discussed in Coulthard, *Red Skin, White Masks* at 120–6, as long as they build through non-essentialized ideas and associations.

11 For a philosophical discussion related to pursuing legal action despite indeterminacy and power imbalances, see Robert Williams Jr., 'Taking Rights Aggressively: The Perils and Promise of Critical Legal Theory

for Peoples of Color' (1987–1988) 5 *Law and Inequality* 103 at 121–7. For arguments that law is never built on rational certainties and absolutes, see Joseph Singer, 'The Player and the Cards: Nihilism and Legal Theory' (1984–1985) 94 *Yale Law Journal* 1; Drucilla Cornell, 'Toward a Modern/Post-Modern Reconstruction of Ethics' (1985) 133 *University of Pennsylvania Law Review* 291; David Kennedy, 'The Turn to Interpretation' (1985) 58 *Southern California Law Review* 251.

12 The practice of not foreclosing or automatically shutting down avenues of action is the flaw, or strength, of the anti-structuralist approach developed in this book. If there really are *a priori*, essentialist, or universal structures and superstructures of power that shape and discipline our political actions and thoughts (which I have argued against), then the prescriptions developed in this book must be calibrated to these forces. However, in my view, the insights of Foucault, Tully, Nanaboozhoo, Basil Johnston, and Anishinaabe linguistic practices, coupled with my own experience and arguments developed in this and my other books, leads me to submit that each so-called structure and superstructure is a fictional, misleading invention to manufacture certainty out of ambiguity.

13 Communities could be strengthened and lives could be improved through legislation aimed at implementing international and domestic commitments and obligations regarding Aboriginal peoples. For a general discussion of where improvement is needed in the lives of Indigenous peoples in Canada as well as the United States, see Angela Mashford-Pringle, 'How'd We Get Here from There? American Indians and Aboriginal Peoples of Canada Health Policy' (2011) 9(1) *Pimatisiwin: A Journal of Aboriginal and Indigenous Community Health* 153. For a general discussion of improving Aboriginal socio-demographic circumstances for Aboriginal peoples in Canada, see J.B. Waldram, D.A. Herring, and T.K. Young, *Aboriginal Health in Canada: Historical, Cultural, and Epidemiological Perspectives*, 2nd ed. (Toronto: University of Toronto Press, 2006).

14 Article 3, United Nations Declaration on the Rights of Indigenous Peoples, 13 September 2007, Official Records of the General Assembly, Sixty-first Session, Supplement No. 53 (A/61/53), part one, chap. 2, sect. A.

15 A discussion of the development and implications of this fact is found in Erica I.A. Diaz, 'Equality of Indigenous Peoples Under the Auspices of the United Nations: Draft Declaration on the Rights of Indigenous Peoples' (1995) 7 *St. Thomas Law Review* 493; James Anaya, *Indigenous Peoples in International Law* (New York: Oxford University Press, 1996) at 151–82; Sharon Venne, *Our Elders Understand Our Rights: Evolving International Law Regarding Indigenous Rights* (Princeton, NJ: Theytus Books, 1998) 107–71.

16 Article 4, United Nations Declaration on the Rights of Indigenous Peoples.

17 Article 5, United Nations Declaration on the Rights of Indigenous Peoples.

18 Taiaiake Alfred, *Peace, Power, Righteousness* at 25–6.

19 While I have stressed that legislation involving Indigenous peoples raises distinctive issues, drafting effective law is challenging in any policy field. For a discussion critically questioning the value of legislation, see John Griffiths, 'Is Law Important?' (1979) 54 *New York University Law Review* 339. For a discussion of the positive possibilities of statutory interpretation more generally, see William Eskridge, *Dynamic Statutory Interpretation* (Cambridge, MA: Harvard University Press, 1994).

20 For a comparison of Canadian and U.S. Indian policy, see Roger L. Nichols, *Indians in the United States and Canada: A Comparative History* (Lincoln: University of Nebraska Press, 1999); Jill St. Germain, *Indian Treaty-Making Policy in the United States and Canada, 1867–1877* (Lincoln: University of Nebraska Press, 2001).

21 A similar conclusion can be found in Dan Russell, *A People's Dream: Aboriginal Self-Government in Canada* (Vancouver: UBC Press, 2000) at 14–40.

22 *Constitution Act, 1982*, being Schedule B to the *Canada Act, 1982* (U.K.), 1982, c 11.

23 For an argument that the United States constitution should formally recognize Native American rights, see Frank Pommersheim, *Broken Landscape: Indians, Indian Tribes, and the Constitution* (New York: Oxford University Press, 2009) at 309–11. Arguments have also been offered that would allow tribes to consensually incorporate themselves with the United States through compacts; see Alex Tallchief Skibine, 'Redefining the State of Indian Tribes within "Our Federalism": Beyond the Dependency Paradigm' (2006) 38 *Connecticut Law Review* 667.

24 Section 91(24) of the *Constitution Act, 1867* declares that exclusive legislative authority of the Parliament of Canada extends to 'Indians, and Lands reserved for the Indians' [*British North America Act, 1867*, 30–31 Vict., c. 3 (U.K.)]. The 'Indian trade and commerce clause,' located in Article 1, section 8, clause 3 of the United States constitution, states that the federal congress shall have power 'to regulate commerce with foreign Nations, and among the several States, and with the Indian Tribes.' For a critique of the United States Supreme Court's treatment of the Indian commerce clause about power, see Nell Jessup Newton, 'Plenary Power Over Indians: It's Scope, Sources and Limitations' (1984) 132 *University of Pennsylvania Law Review* 195; Philip Frickey, 'Domesticating Federal Indian Law' (1996) 81 *Minnesota Law Review* 31; Robert Clinton, 'There Is No Federal Supremacy Clause for Indian Tribes' (2002) 34 *Arizona State Law Journal* 113.

25 The words of Roger Gibbons, written in 1984, are prophetic:

> While the search for a new constitution appeared at first to be an important opportunity for Indians, it has turned out to be a policy trap. The constitutional debate has brought a new set of environmental factors to bear on Indian affairs which are largely beyond the control of Indian political organizations, and which threaten to constrain severely Indian policy options in the years ahead. Because Indian affairs have become entangled in broader constitutional issues, Indian control over those public policies which shape their very lives and futures may be further weakened. (Roger Gibbons, 'Canadian Indian Policy: The Constitutional Trap' [1984] IV *Canadian Journal of Native Studies* 1 at 2)

26 'The social, political and legal activism of Indian leaders and their advocates in the 1950's, 60's and 70's resulted in an unprecedented volume of Indian legislation, most of it favorable to Indian interests, and all of it enacted at the behest of the tribes or at least with their participation' (David Getches, Charles Wilkinson, Robert Williams Jr., and L.M. Fletcher, eds., *Cases and Materials on Federal Indian Law* [St. Paul, MN: West Publishing, 2011] at 220).

27 For an insightful film chronicling the challenge of constitutional negotiations among Canadian federal, provincial, and Aboriginal leaders, see the films by Maurice Bulbulian, *Dancing Around the Table, Part One* and *Dancing Around the Table, Part Two* (National Film Board of Canada, 1987). For a general discussion of these conferences, see Michael Asch, *Home and Native Land: Aboriginal Rights and the Canadian Constitution* (Vancouver: UBC Press, 1993). For a view that these conferences did produce benefits, see Kathy Brock, 'The Politics of Aboriginal Self-Government: A Canadian Paradox' (2001) 34 *Canadian Public Administration* 272.

28 For a discussion of the pre-emption power in federal Indian law, see *Williams v. Lee*, (1959) 358 U.S. 277, 79 S. Ct. 269 (U.S.S.C.); *Warren Trading Post v. Arizona Tax Commission*, (1965) 380 U.S. 685 (U.S.S.C.); *McClanahan v. Arizona State Tax Commission*, (1973) 411 U.S. 164 (U.S.S.C.); Robert Clinton, 'Isolated in Their Own Country: A Defense of Federal Protection of Indian Autonomy and Self-Governance' (1981) 33 *Stanford Law Review* 979; Jackie Gardina, 'Federal Preemption: A Roadmap for the Application of Tribal Law in State Courts' (2010–2011) 35 *American Indian Law Review* 1.

29 See, generally, J. Anthony Long and Menno Boldt, eds., *Governments in Conflict? Provinces and Indian Nations in Canada* (Toronto: University of Toronto Press, 1988).

30 The paradigmatic legislation in Canada is the *Indian Act*, which was designed to undermine Indigenous self-determination; see John Tobias, 'Protection, Civilization, Assimilation: An Outline History of Canada's Indian Policy,' in *As Long As the Sun Shines and Water Flows: A Reader in Canadian Native Studies*, ed. Ian Getty and Antoine Lussier (Vancouver: UBC Press, 1990) at 29.

31 Charles Wilkinson, *Blood Struggle: The Rise of Modern Indian Nations* (New York: W.W. Norton and Company, 2005) at 248.

32 Nell Jessup Newton et al., eds., *Cohen's Handbook of Federal Indian Law* (Newark, NJ: LexisNexis, 2005) at 99.

33 For an excellent critique of federal legislative initiatives over the last forty years, see Jeff Corntassel and Richard Witmer II, *Forced Federalism: Contemporary Challenges to Indigenous Nationhood* (Norman: University of Oklahoma Press, 2008). The authors argue that tribes are compelled to negotiate with states under many of the federal laws outlined in this paper, and that this results in a dilution of the tribe's nationhood and self-determination.

34 For a critique of the United States Supreme Court's approach, see Walter Echo-Hawk, *In the Courts of the Conqueror: The 10 Worst Indian Law Cases Ever Decided* (Golden, CO: Fulcrum Publishing, 2010); Robert Williams Jr., *Like a Loaded Weapon: The Rehnquist Court, Indian Rights, and the Legal History of Racism in America* (Minneapolis: University of Minnesota Press, 2005); David Wilkins, *American Indian Sovereignty and the U.S. Supreme Court: The Masking of Justice* (Austin: University of Texas Press, 1997).

35 See, generally, John Wunder, ed., *Native American Sovereignty* (New York: Taylor and Francis, 1999).

36 Charles Wilkinson, *American Indians, Time and the Law* (New Haven, CT: Yale University Press, 1987) at 83. The issue of Indian 'consent' in other areas of U.S. law is much more troubling; see Matthew Fletcher, 'Tribal Consent' (2012) 8 *Stanford Journal of Civil Rights and Civil Liberties* 45.

37 Robert Anderson, Bethany Berger, Philip Frickey, and Sarah Krakoff, eds., *American Indian Law, Cases and Commentary* (St. Paul, MN: West Publishing, 2010) at 155.

38 There are well over forty significant pieces of legislation addressing Indigenous self-determination in the United States; see United States Code (U.S.C.) Title 25 – Indians. Again, the words of Roger Gibbons, written in 1984, still ring true: 'Unlike the situation in the United States where over 4,000 separate unsystematized statutory enactments relating to Indian policy exist ... Canadian public policy in the field of Indian Affairs is concentrated within a ... single piece of legislation, last subjected to any comprehensive revision in 1951' (Roger Gibbons, 'Canadian Indian Policy: The Constitutional Trap' [1984] 4 *Canadian Journal of Native Studies* 1 at 2).

39 Robert J. Miller, Jacinta Ruru, Larissa Behrendt, and Tracey Lindberg, *Discovering Indigenous Lands: The Doctrine of Discovery in the English Colonies* (Oxford: Oxford University Press, 2010); Lindsay G. Robertson, *Conquest by Law: How the Discovery of America Dispossessed Indigenous Peoples of Their Lands* (New York: Oxford University Press, 2007); Stuart Banner, *How the Indians Lost Their Land: Law and Power on the Frontier* (Cambridge, MA: Harvard University Press, 2007); *The American Indian in Western Legal Thought: The Discourses of Conquest* (Oxford: Oxford University Press, 1990).

40 Unfortunately, the United States Supreme Court, which had been somewhat supportive of Native claims in the previous decades, became increasingly unreceptive to Indigenous arguments from the late 1970s through to the present day; see Sarah Krakoff, 'Undoing Indian Law One Case at a Time: Judicial Minimalism and Tribal Sovereignty' (2001) 50 *American University Law Review* 1178; Philip P. Frickey, 'A Common Law for Our Age of Colonialism: The Judicial Divestiture of Indian Tribal Authority over Nonmembers' (1999) 109 *Yale Law Journal* 1.

41 Unfortunately, termination can still occur through judicial disestablishment; see Judith V. Royster, 'The Legacy of Allotment' (1995) 27 *Arizona State Law Journal* 1; Charlene Koski, 'The Legacy of *Solemn v. Bartlett*: How Courts Have Used Demographics to By Congress and Erode the Basic Principles of Indian Law' (2009) 84 *Washington Law Review* 723.

42 Richard Nixon, 'Message from the President of the United States Transmitting Recommendations for Indian Policy' (8 July 1970) *H.R. Doc. No. 91-363*, 91st Congress, 2nd Session.

43 In Canada, during this period, Prime Minister Pierre Elliott Trudeau proposed the assimilation of First Nations in Canada. For an influential critique of this policy, see Harold Cardinal, *The Unjust Society* (Vancouver: Douglas and McIntyre, 1969).

44 *Indian Self-Determination and Educational Assistance Act*, 25 U.S.C. 450; David H. Getches, 'Conquering the Cultural Frontier: The New Subjectivism of the Supreme Court in Indian Law' (1996) 84 *California Law Review* 1573.

45 *Indian Self-Determination and Educational Assistance Act.*

46 *Tribal Self-Governance Act*, 25 U.S.C. 450n, 458aa to 458gg. This act also builds on the same base as the *Indian Self-Determination and Educational Assistance Act* by proclaiming that 'the Tribal right of self-governance flows from the inherent sovereignty of Indian Tribes and nations.' The Office of Self-Governance, which administers the *Tribal Governance Act*, oversees a budget of close to $500 million to ensure that tribes continue to develop their governance capacity. For general commentary, see Tadd Johnson and James Hamilton, 'Self-Governance for Indian Tribes: From

Paternalism to Empowerment' (1994–1995) 27 *Connecticut Law Review* 1251. For an examination of the act's operation in one field, see Mary Ann King, 'Co-Management or Contracting – Agreements between Native American Tribes and the U.S. National Park Service Pursuant to the 1994 Tribal Self-Governance Act' (2007) 31 *Harvard Environmental Law Review* 475.

47 *Tribally Controlled Colleges and Universities Assistance Act*, 25 U.S.C. 1801.

48 *Indian Education Act*, 25 U.S.C. 2601–2651.

49 *Native American Housing Assistance Self-Determination Act*, 25 U.S.C. 4101.

50 Programs administered by the tribes include the Temporary Assistance for Needy Families program, food stamps, child support enforcement, etc. See Newton et al., eds., *Cohen's Handbook of Federal Indian Law* at 1400–2.

51 *Indian Law Enforcement Reform Act*, 25 U.S.C. 2801–9.

52 *Indian Health Care Act*, U.S.C. 1613–1682; *Indian Alcoholism and Substance Abuse Prevention and Treatment Act*, 25 U.S.C. 2401–78.

53 For a discussion of the transformation of federal Indian law and policy in the years after Nixon, see George Pierre Castile, *To Show Heart: Native American Self-Determination and Federal Indian Policy, 1960–1975* (Tucson: University of Arizona Press, 1998).

54 George Pierre Castile, *Taking Charge: Native American Self-Determination And Federal Indian Policy, 1975–1993* (Tucson: University of Arizona Press, 2006).

55 Anderson, Berger, Frickey, and Krakoff, eds., *American Indian Law, Cases and Commentary* at 155.

56 Miriam Jorgensen, ed., *Rebuilding Native Nations: Strategies for Governance and Development* (Tucson: University of Arizona Press, 2007) at 146–74, 223–45.

57 Emmanuel Brunet-Jailly, 'The Governance and Fiscal Environment of First Nations' Fiscal Intergovernmental Relations in Comparative Perspectives,' document prepared for National Centre for First Nation Governance, March 2008, at 9–15. Available at http://fngovernance.org/ncfng_research/emmanual_brunet-jailley.pdf.

58 One small step away from the *Indian Act* is the *First Nations Land Management Act*, S.C. 1999, c. 24, which allows First Nations to opt out of certain sections of the *Indian Act* 'to create their own system for making reserve land allotments to individual First Nation members. They also have authority to deal with matrimonial real property interests or rights.' See http://laws-lois.justice.gc.ca/eng/acts/F-11.8/ (accessed 1 April 2014). For commentary, see Tom Flanagan, Christopher Alcantara, and André Le Dressay, *Beyond the Indian Act: Restoring Aboriginal Property Rights* (Montreal: McGill-Queen's University Press, 2010).

59 John Tobias, 'Protection, Civilization and Assimilation: An Outline History of Canada's Indian Policy,' in *Sweet Promises: A Reader on Indian-White Relations in Canada*, ed. James Miller (Toronto: University of Toronto Press, 1991) at 127; Brian E. Titley, *A Narrow Vision: Duncan Campbell Scott and the Administration of Indian Affairs in Canada* (Vancouver: UBC Press, 1986), particularly the chapter entitled 'General Aspects of Policy and Administration' at 37–59.

60 Larry Gilbert, *Entitlement to Indian Status and Membership Codes in Canada* (Toronto: Carswell, 1996); Bonita Lawrence, *'Real' Indians and Others: Mixed Blood Urban Native Peoples and Indigenous Nationhood* (Vancouver: UBC Press, 2004).

61 The reserve system is described in Richard Bartlett, *Indian Reserves and Aboriginal Lands in Canada: A Homeland* (Saskatoon: University of Saskatchewan Native Law Centre, 1990); broader land issues are discussed in Kerry Wilkin, ed., *Advancing Aboriginal Claims: Visions/Strategies/Directions* (Saskatoon: Purich, 2004).

62 Shin Imai, *Aboriginal Law Handbook*, 2nd ed. (Toronto: Carswell, 1999) 240–4.

63 Brian Crane, Robert Mainville, and Martin Mason, *First Nations Governance Law* (Markham, ON: LexisNexis, Butterworth's, 2006) at 101–29; Robert A. Reiter, *The Law of First Nations* (Edmonton, AB: Juris Analytica, 1996).

64 *Sharing the Harvest: The Road to Self-Reliance*, ed. Royal Commission on Aboriginal Peoples (Ottawa: Supply and Services, 1993).

65 Skeena Native Development Society, *Masters in Our Own House: The Path to Prosperity* (Terrace, BC: Skeena Development Society, 2003) at 59–74.

66 For an annotated description of the *Indian Act*, see Shin Imai, *Indian Act and Constitutional Provisions* (Toronto: Carswell, 2006).

67 Darlene Johnston, *The Taking of Indian Lands in Canada: Consent or Coercion* (Saskatoon: University of Saskatchewan, Native Law Centre, 1989).

68 For a history and legal analysis of section 88 of the *Indian Act*, see Kerry Wilkins, 'Still Crazy After All These Years: Section 88 at Fifty' (2000) 38 *Alberta Law Review* 458.

69 See *R. v. Dick*, [1985] 2 S.C.R. 309; *Kitkatla Band v. British Columbia (Minister of Small Business, Tourism and Culture)*, [2002] 2 S.C.R. 146.

70 For arguments questioning the constitutionality of section 88 of the *Indian Act*, see Leroy Little Bear, 'Section 88 of the Indian Act and the Application of Provincial Laws to Indians,' in Long and Boldt, eds., *Governments in Conflict?*; Kent McNeil, 'Aboriginal Title and Section 88 of the Indian Act' (2000) 34 *University of British Columbia Law Review* 157.

71 See *R. v. Dick*, [1985]; *Kitkatla Band v. British Columbia (Minister of Small Business, Tourism and Culture)*, [2002].

72 An innovative argument that develops First Nations autonomy in Canada along familiar constitutional lines is found in Bruce Ryder, 'The Demise and Rise of the Classical Paradigm in Canadian Federalism: Promoting Autonomy for the Provinces and the First Nations' (1991) 36 *McGill Law Journal* 308.

73 Office of the Auditor General of Canada, *2011 June Status Report of the Auditor General of Canada* at chap. 4, http://www.oag-bvg.gc.ca/internet/English/parl_oag_201106_e_35354.html. Metis people are even further disenfranchised because governments in Canada do not recognize Metis governance even in the limited ways found in the *Indian Act*.

74 For challenges in the area of child welfare, see *Canada (Attorney General) v. First Nations Child and Family Caring Society of Canada*, 2010 F.C. 343 (CanLII). For challenges in the area of education, see First Nations Child and Family Caring Society, *Information Sheet #2: First Nations Education*, July 2013, http://www.fncaringsociety.com/sites/default/files/Information%20Sheet%202_First%20Nations%20Education_1.pdf. First Nations children on reserve are underfunded $2,000 to $3,000 per child. Unlike provincial schools, the federal government provides $0 for libraries, $0 for computers, software, and teacher training, $0 for extracurricular activities, $0 for First Nations data management systems, $0 for second- and third-level services (including core funding for special education, school boards, governance, and education research), $0 for endangered languages, and $0 for principals, directors, pedagogical support, and the development of culturally appropriate curricula. In 2010/2011, Aboriginal Affairs and Northern Development Canada provided $1.5 billion in funding for First Nations education on reserve and $304 million for building construction and maintenance. The Parliamentary Budget Officer (PBO) released a report in 2009 with an analysis of actual costs for the delivery of education, finding that schools on reserves are systematically underfunded by less than half (58 per cent) of the actual costs needed to provide equal and equitable access to safe schools and education (A. Rajekar and R. Mathilakath, *The Funding Requirement for First Nations Schools in Canada* [Ottawa: Office of Parliamentary Budget Officer, 2009]).

75 The *Indian Act* is designed to assimilate First Nations; see 'The Indian Act' in *Report of the Royal Commission on Aboriginal Peoples*, vol. 1 at 255–332; John Tobias, 'Protection, Civilization and Assimilation' at 127; Titley, *A Narrow Vision*. In the late 1960s, the Trudeau government proposed completing the process of assimilation through the White Paper; see Sally Weaver, *Making Canadian Indian Policy: The Hidden Agenda 1968–1970* (Toronto: University of Toronto Press, 1981). After the constitution was

patriated, First Nations suspected the White Paper was still government policy that was being pursued by devolution of federal services to the provinces; see Long and Boldt, eds., *Governments in Conflict?*

76 Office of the Auditor General of Canada, *2011 June Status Report of the Auditor General of Canada* at chap. 4.

77 John Borrows, 'Stewardship and the First Nations Governance Act' (2003–2004) 29 *Queen's Law Journal* 103.

78 More generally, the United States Supreme Court has recognized general congressional trust responsibilities in *United States v. Sioux Nation*, (1980) 448 U.S. 371 (U.S.S.C.). For executive trust responsibilities to tribes see *Seminole Nation v. United States*, (1942) 316 U.S. 286 (U.S.S.C.); *Morton v. Ruiz*, (1974) 415 U.S. 199 (U.S.C.C.). However, the Supreme Court has loosened these standards in recent years; see *Lincoln v. Vigil*, (1993) 508 U.S. 182 (U.S.S.C.); *United States v. Navajo Nation*, (2003) 537 U.S. 488 (U.S.S.C.).

79 For a discussion of the importance of effective bureaucracies in First Nations, see Stephen Cornell and Joseph Kalt, *What Can Tribes Do? Strategies and Institutions in American Indian Economic Development* (Los Angeles: UCLA American Indian Studies Center, 1994).

80 *Indian Child Welfare Act*, 25 U.S.C. 1901–1931. The ICWA states: 'The Congress hereby declares that it is the policy of this Nation to protect the best interests of Indian children and to promote the stability and security of Indian tribes and families by the establishment of minimum Federal standards for the removal of Indian children from their families and the placement of such children in foster or adoptive homes which will reflect the unique values of Indian culture, and by providing for assistance to Indian tribes in the operation of child and family service programs.'

81 Prior to the enactment of the ICWA, state government agencies removed between 25 per cent and 35 per cent of all Indian children from their families nationwide; see Matthew Fletcher, 'The Origins of the Indian Child Welfare Act: A Survey of the Legislative History' (paper presented for the Occasional Paper Series, Indigenous Law and Policy Center, Michigan State University College of Law, 10 April 2009), available at http://www.law.msu.edu/indigenous/papers/2009-04.pdf; for further context, see Matthew Fletcher, Wenona T. Singel, and Kathryn E. Fort, eds., *Facing the Future: The Indian Child Welfare Act at 30* (Lansing: Michigan State University Press, 2009).

82 After the ICWA, Indian children now only represent approximately 3 per cent of children in care; see General Accounting Office, GAO-05–290, *Indian Child Welfare Act, Existing Information on Implementation Issues Could Be Used to Target Guidance and Assistance to States* 4 (2005) at 1. The leading

case concerning the ICWA is *Mississippi Band of Choctaw Indians v. Holyfield*, (1989) 490 U.S. 30, 109 S.Ct. 1597, 104 L.Ed. 2nd 29 (U.S.S.C.). However, see *Adoptive Couple v. Baby Girl*, (2013) 398 S. C. 625, 731 S.E. 2d 550, where the Supreme Court reads the ICWA to apply only to 'intact' Indian families, which opens room for undermining the statute when Indian families are in disarray.

83 *American Indian Religious Freedom Act*, 42 U.S.C.A. 1996. Section 1 of the act states that 'it shall be the policy of the United States to protect and preserve for American Indians their inherent right of freedom to believe, express, and exercise the traditional religions of the American Indian, Eskimo, Aleut, and Native Hawaiians, including but not limited to access to sites, use and possession of sacred objects, and the freedom to worship through ceremonials and traditional rites.' The act accomplishes its purposes by creating policy space for tribes to work with federal agencies to identify and protect sacred places. For leading cases related to this act, see *Employment Division v. Smith*, 494 U.S. 872 (1990); *Lyng v. Northwest Indian Cemetery Protective Assn.*, 485 U.S. 439 (1988). For commentary, see John Celichowski, 'A Rough and Narrow Path: Preserving Native American Religious Freedom' (2000) 25 *American Indian Law Review* 1.

84 *Native American Graves Protection and Repatriation Act* (NAGPRA), Pub. L. 101–601, 25 U.S.C. 3001 et seq., 104 Stat. 3048.

85 *Native American Languages Act*, 1990, 25 U.S.C. 2901–2906. The act begins by reciting the following provisions:

The Congress finds that –

(1) the status of the cultures and languages of Native Americans is unique and the United States has the responsibility to act together with Native Americans to ensure the survival of these unique cultures and languages;

(2) special status is accorded Native Americans in the United States, a status that recognizes distinct cultural and political rights, including the right to continue separate identities;

(3) the traditional languages of Native Americans are an integral part of their cultures and identities and form the basic medium for the transmission, and thus survival, of Native American cultures, literatures, histories, religions, political institutions, and values ...

(8) acts of suppression and extermination directed against Native American languages and cultures are in conflict with the United States policy of self-determination for Native Americans ...

86 *Indian Arts and Crafts Enforcement Act*, 2000, Pub. L. No. 105–497, 25 U.S.C.A. 305–305(e). The act prohibits misrepresentation in marketing of

Indian arts and crafts and authorizes the recovery of damages for all gross profits accrued by the seller of fake Indians arts and crafts.

87 *National Museum of the Indian Act Amendments* of 1996, Pub.L. No. 104–278, 20 U.S.C.A. 80q.

88 Sonia Harris Short, *Aboriginal Child Welfare, Self-Government and the Rights of Indigenous Children: Protecting the Vulnerable Under International Law* (Burlington, VT: Ashgate, 2012).

89 *Child, Family and Community Service Act* [R.S.B.C. 1996] c. 46, see sections 2 (*e*) & (*f*), 4(1), 35(1)(*b*), 70 (1)(*j*), 71(3); *Child and Family Services Act*, 1990 c-11 ss. 1(2)4, 1(2)5, 13(3), 34(2)(*d*), 34(10)(*f*), 35(1)(*e*), 36(4)(*c*), 37(3)3, 37(4), 39(1)4, 47(2)(*c*), 54(3)(*f*), 57(5), 58(2)(*b*), 58(4), 61(2)(*d*), 64(4)(*d*), 64(6)(*e*), 69(1)(*e*), 80(4)(*f*), Part X, 223 (Ontario); *Youth Protection Act*, 2002, P-34.1, ss. 2.4(5)(*c*), 37.5 (Quebec); *Child and Family Services Act*, c-7.2 1989–90, ss. 4(*c*), 23, 37(4)(*c*), 37(10), 37(11), 53, 61 (Saskatchewan); *Child, Youth and Family Enhancement Act*, RSA 2000, c C-12(Alberta); *Children and Family Services Act* c. 5, 1990, Preamble, ss. 2(*g*), 7(2), 6(1), 9(*i*), 20(*d*), 36(3), 39(8)(*c*), 42(3), 44(3)(*c*), 47(5), 88(1)(*e*) (Nova Scotia); *Children's Act* c. 22, ss. 107, 109, 131(*k*) (Yukon); *Family Services Act* c. F-2.2 1980 ss. 1(*g*), 3(1), 45(1)(*a*), 45(3)(*a*) (New Brunswick); *Child, Youth and Family Services Act*, c-12.1 1998, ss. 7(*f*), 7(*g*), 9(*c*), 75(2)(*e*) (Newfoundland); *Child and Family Services Act*, S.N.W.T. 1997, c. 13, Preamble, ss. 2(*f*), 2(*i*), 2(*l*), 3, 7(*l*), 7(*m*), 7(*n*), 15, 25 (*b*.1), 25 (*c*), 54 (3), 56, 57, 58, 58.1, 58.2, 59, 91(*i*) (North West Territories); *Consolidated Child and Family Services Act (Nunavut)*, S.N.W.T. 1997, c. 13, Preamble, ss. 2(*f*), 2(*i*), 2(*l*), 3, 7(*l*), 7(*m*), 7(*n*), 15, 25 (*b*.1), 25 (*c*), 54 (3), 56, 57, 58, 58.1, 58.2, 59, 91(i) (Nunavut).

90 In February 2007, the Assembly of First Nations (AFN) estimated that there were approximately 27,000 First Nations children in care in First Nations and provincial agencies, on and off reserve. They made the point that this number is three times the number of children that were in residential schools at the height of their operation; see Assembly of First Nations, First Nations Child and Family Services, Questions and Answers, nationtallk. ca/story/first-nations-child-and-family-services-questions-and-answers.

91 Justice Ted Hughes, *BC Children and Youth Review: An Independent Review of BC's Child Protection System*, 7 April 2006 at 48; Manitoba Aboriginal Affairs Secretariat, *Aboriginal People in Manitoba, Winnipeg*, 2006 at 42; Saskatchewan Institute of Public Policy, 'A Profile of Aboriginal Children in Regina,' January 2004, in *Commission on First Nations and Metis Peoples and Justice Reform*, Saskatoon, 2004 at 10–7.

92 *2011 June Status Report of the Auditor General of Canada*, chapter 4, at pages 23–5; see http://www.oag-bvg.gc.ca/internet/docs/parl_oag_201106_04_e.pdf.

93 The FNCFCS and the AFN have filed a human rights complaint alleging that the inequitable funding of child welfare services on First Nations reserves amounts to discrimination on the basis of race and national ethnic origin, contrary to section 5 of the *Canadian Human Rights Act*, RCS 1985, c. H-6. They have also filed a claim of retaliation alleging that the Canadian government's National Aboriginal Council (NAC) and Department of Justice officials monitored Cindy Blacstock's personal and private Facebook page; See *First Nations Child and Family Caring Society of Canada et al. v. Attorney General of Canada (for the Minister of Indian Affairs and Northern Development Canada)*, 2013 C.H.R.T. 16 (CanLII); *First Nations Child and Family Caring Society of Canada et al. v. Attorney General of Canada (for the Minister of Indian and Northern Affairs Canada)*, 2012 C.H.R.T. 24 (CanLII).

94 In fact, the ICWA recognized that state jurisdiction was a significant problem for native families. The ICWA's congressional finding 5 reads 'that the States, exercising their recognized jurisdiction over Indian child custody proceedings through administrative and judicial bodies, have often failed to recognize the essential tribal relations of Indian people and the cultural and social standards prevailing in Indian communities and families' (*Indian Child Welfare Act*, 25 U.S.C. 1901–1931).

95 For example, Ontario's Human Rights Code provides for 'a right to equal treatment with respect to services, goods and facilities, without discrimination because of race, ancestry, place of origin, colour, ethnic origin, citizenship, creed, sex, sexual orientation, age, marital status, family status or disability' [R.S.O. 1990, c. H.19, s. 1; 1999, c. 6, s. 28 (1); 2001, c. 32, s. 27 (1); 2005, c. 5, s. 32 (1)].

96 *An Act to amend the Canadian Human Rights Act* S.C. 2008, c. 30; section 67 the act reads:

-1. Section 67 of the *Canadian Human Rights Act* is repealed.

-1.1 For greater certainty, the repeal of section 67 of the *Canadian Human Rights Act* shall not be construed so as to abrogate or derogate from the protection provided for existing aboriginal or treaty rights of the aboriginal peoples of Canada by the recognition and affirmation of those rights in section 35 of the *Constitution Act*, 1982. -1.2 In relation to a complaint made under the *Canadian Human Rights Act* against a First Nation government, including a band council, tribal council or governing authority operating or administering programs and services under the *Indian Act*, this Act shall be interpreted and applied in a manner that gives due regard to First Nations legal traditions and customary laws, particularly the balancing of individual rights and interests against collective rights and interests, to the extent that they are consistent with the principle of gender equality ...

As a result of this legislation, First Nations will be challenged by their own members to comply with human rights law in the coming years.

97 Moreover, though not legislatively based, First Nations have access to the Canadian Charter of Rights and Freedoms, which, in section 2(a), reads: 'Everyone has the following fundamental freedoms: (a) freedom of conscience and religion.' First Nations could also make claims to religious freedoms under section 35(1) of the *Constitution Act, 1982*. For a discussion of the challenges in constitutional recognition of First Nations religious freedoms, see John Borrows, 'Living Law on a Living Earth: Aboriginal Religion, Law and the Constitution,' in *Constitutional Law, Religion and Citizenship in Canada*, ed. Richard Moon (Vancouver: UBC Press, 2008).

98 There are only a handful of Human Rights Board decisions dealing with the issue of Aboriginal religions, and they have not found discrimination of the basis of religion; see *Blais v. Canadian Union of Public Employees Local 3902*, 2011 H.R.T.O. 2113 (CanLII); *MacDonald v. Anishnawbe Health Toronto*, 2010 H.R.T.O. 329 (CanLII); *Kelly v. B.C. (Ministry of Public Safety and Solicitor General) (No. 2)*, 2009 B.C.H.R.T. 363 (CanLII); *George v. Jamin and others*, 2009 B.C.H.R.T. 19 (CanLII); *Smith v. B.C. (Ministry of Public Safety and Solicitor General) and another*, 2008 B.C.H.R.T. 36 (CanLII).

99 J.R. Miller, *Shingwauk's Vision: A History of Native Residential Schools* (Toronto: University of Toronto Press, 1996); John S. Milloy, *A National Crime: The Canadian Government and the Residential School System, 1879–1986* (Winnipeg: University of Manitoba Press, 1999).

100 Douglas Cole and Ira Chaikin, *An Iron Hand Upon the People: The Law against the Potlatch on the Northwest Coast* (Vancouver: Douglas and McIntyre, 1990); Constance Backhouse, *Colour-Coded: A Legal History of Racism in Canada, 1900–1950* (Toronto: University of Toronto Press, 1999) at 56–102; Sidney L. Harring, *White Man's Law: Native People in Nineteenth-Century Canadian Jurisprudence* (Toronto: University of Toronto Press, 1998) at 268–70.

101 Michael Lee Ross, *First Nations Sacred Sites in Canada's Courts* (Vancouver: UBC Press, 2005).

102 While environmental assessment legislation and planning laws might have some role to play in this regard, such legislation is generally ineffective in preventing negative impacts on First Nations spiritual practices; see Heather Dorries, 'Rejecting the "False Choice": Foregrounding Indigenous Sovereignty in Planning Theory and Practice' (PhD diss., University of Toronto, 2012) [unpublished].

103 Royal Commission on Aboriginal Peoples, *Gathering Strength*, vol. 3 of *The Report of the Royal Commission on Aboriginal Peoples* (Ottawa: Queen's Printer, 1996) at chap. 6, 'Arts and Heritage' (585–651). For a discussion of the limited ways in which Indigenous cultural heritage is protected in national legislation, see Catherine Bell and Robert Patterson, eds., *Protection of First Nations Cultural Heritage: Laws, Policy, and Reform* (Vancouver: UBC Press, 2009) at 35–7; Catherine Bell and Val Napoleon, eds., *First Nations Cultural Heritage and Law: Case Studies, Voices, and Perspectives* (Vancouver: UBC Press, 2009) at 367–414. However, it is important to note that the *Cultural Property Export and Import Act*, R.S.C., 1985, c. C-51, does provide a way to secure the return of cultural items taken from First Nations.

104 *Native American Graves Protection and Repatriation Act* (NAGPRA).

105 Julia A. Cryne, 'NAGPRA Revisited: A Twenty-Year Review of Repatriation Efforts' (2010) 34 *American Indian Law Review* 99; Steven J. Gunn, 'The Native American Graves Protection and Repatriation Act at Twenty: Reaching the Limits of Our National Consensus' (2010) 36 *William Mitchell Law Review* 503.

106 For examples of the impact of this failure, see Jennifer Kramer, *Switchbacks: Art, Ownership and Nuxalk National Identity* (Vancouver: UBC Press, 2006); Susan Roy, *These Mysterious People: Shaping History and Archaeology in a Northwest Coast Community* (Montreal: McGill-Queen's University Press, 2010); Barry Steven Mandelker, 'Indigenous People and Cultural Property Appropriation: Intellectual Property Problems and Solutions' (2000) 16 *Canadian Intellectual Property Review* 367.

107 For example, British Columbia's *Heritage Conservation Act* has not protected First Nations burial sites or culturally modified trees; see *Heritage Conservation Act*, R.S.B.C. 1996, c. 187, s. 13(b); *Nanoose Indian Band v. R.*, 1994 CanLII 1806 (B.C.S.C.); *Kitkatla Band v. British Columbia (Minister of Small Business, Tourism and Culture)*, [2002]; *Ontario's Cemeteries Act*, R.S.O. 1990 c. C.4 has also not provided significant protection for Aboriginal burial sites; see Peggy Blair, 'The Non-Protection Of Canadian Aboriginal Heritage (Burial Sites And Artifacts),' October 2005, *Scow Institute*, pages 6–7, available at http://scow-archive.libraries.coop/library/documents/RPHeritageSites.pdf.

108 Royal Commission on Aboriginal Peoples, *Gathering Strength* at 602–21.

109 Darcy Hallett, Michael J. Chandler, and Christopher E. Lalonde, 'Aboriginal Language Knowledge and Youth Suicide' (2007) 22 *Cognitive Development* 392–9; UNESCO, *Why Language Matters for the Millennium Development Goals* (Bangkok: United Nations Education Social Cultural Organization, 2012).

110 James Fife, 'The Legal Framework for Indigenous Language Rights in the United States' (2005) *Willamette Law Review* 325 at 328–9.

111 Mary Jane Morris, 'Aboriginal Languages in Canada: Emerging Trends and Perspectives on Second Language Acquisition' (2007) *Canadian Social Trends* (Ottawa: Statistics Canada), http://www.statcan.gc.ca/pub/11-008-x/2007001/9628-eng.htm.

112 Ibid.

113 Ibid.

114 J.A. Fishman, ed., *Can Threatened Languages Be Saved? Reversing Language Shift, Revisited: A Twenty-first-Century Perspective* (Clevedon, UK: Multilingual Matters, 2001); Summer Kupau, 'Judicial Enforcement of "Official" Indigenous Languages: A Comparative Analysis of Maori and Hawaiian Struggles for Cultural Language Rights' (2004) 26 *University of Hawaii Law Review* 495–535.

115 'In 2001, more people speak an Aboriginal language than had an Aboriginal mother tongue (239,600 versus 203,300). This suggests that some speakers must have learned their Aboriginal language as a second language. It appears that this is especially the case for young people. Learning an Aboriginal language as a second language cannot be considered a substitute for learning it as a first language.Nevertheless, increasing the number of second language speakers is part of the process of language revitalization, and may go some way towards preventing, or at least slowing, the rapid erosion and possible extinction of endangered languages' (Morris, 'Aboriginal Languages in Canada').

116 Joshua Fishman has discussed the strengths and limits of legislative intervention in revitalizing endangered languages in Fishman, ed., *Can Threatened Languages be Saved?* at 1–23; Nancy H. Hornberger and Martin Pütz, eds., *Language Loyalty, Language Planning, and Language Revitalization: Recent Writings and Reflections from Joshua A. Fishman* (Clevedon, UK: Multilingual Matters, 2006).

117 Section 104 of the U.S. *Native American Languages Act* states,

> It is the policy of the United States to – (1) preserve, protect, and promote the rights and freedom of Native Americans to use, practice, and develop Native American languages; (2) allow exceptions to teacher certification requirements for Federal programs, and programs funded in whole or in part by the Federal Government, for instruction in Native American languages when such teacher certification requirements hinder the employment of qualified teachers who teach in Native American languages, and to encourage State and territorial governments to make similar exceptions; (3) encourage and support the use of Native Ameri-

can languages as a medium of instruction in order to encourage and support – (A) Native American language survival, (B) educational opportunity, (C) increased student success and performance, (D) increased student awareness and knowledge of their culture and history, and (E) increased student and community pride; (4) encourage State and local education programs to work with Native American parents, educator, Indian tribes, and other Native American governing bodies in the implementation of programs to put this policy into effect; (5) recognize the right of Indian tribes and other Native American governing bodies to use the Native American languages as a medium of instruction in all schools funded by the Secretary of the Interior; (6) fully recognize the inherent right of Indian tribes and other Native American governing bodies, States, territories, and possessions of the United States to take action on, and give official status to, their Native American languages for the purpose of conducting their own business; (7) support the granting of comparable proficiency achieved through course work in a Native American language the same academic credit as comparable proficiency achieved through course work in a foreign language, with recognition of such Native American language proficiency by institutions of higher education as fulfilling foreign language entrance or degree requirements; and (8) encourage all institutions of elementary, secondary and higher education, where appropriate, to include Native American languages in the curriculum in the same manner as foreign languages and to grant proficiency in Native American languages the same full academic credit as proficiency in foreign languages. (*Native American Languages Act*, 1990)

118 Allison Dussias, 'Indigenous Languages Under Siege: The Native American Experience' (2008) 3 *Intercultural Human Rights Law Review* 5; Allison Dussias, 'Waging War with Words: Native Americans' Continuing Struggle against the Suppression of Their Languages' (1999) 60 *Ohio State Law Journal* 901; James Fife, 'The Legal Framework for Indigenous Language Rights in the United States' (2005) *Willamette Law Review* 325 at 355–7.
119 Brock Pitawanakwat, 'Anishinaabemodaa Pane Oodenang – A Qualitative Study of Anishinaabe Language Revitalization as Self-Determination in Manitoba and Ontario' (PhD diss., University of Victoria, 2009).
120 For two excellent detailed examples of Indigenous self-determination and the practice of tribal law, see Raymond Austin, *Navajo Courts and Navajo Common Law: A Tradition of Tribal Self-Governance* (Minneapolis: University of Minnesota Press, 2009); Justin Richland, *Arguing with Tradition: The*

Language of Law in Hopi Tribal Court (Chicago: University of Chicago Press, 2008).

121 Tom Tso, 'The Process of Decision Making in Tribal Courts' (1989) 31 *Arizona Law Review* 225; Frank Pommersheim, *Braid of Feathers: American Indian Law and Contemporary Tribal Life* (Berkeley: University of California Press, 1995); Gloria Valencia-Weber, 'Tribal Courts: Custom and Innovative Law' (1994) 24 *New Mexico Law Review* 225; Elizabeth E. Joh, 'Custom, Tribal Court Practice, and Popular Justice' (2000/2001) 25 *American Indian Law Review* 117–32.

122 For discussion and examples, see Justin Richland and Sarah Deer, eds., *Introduction to Tribal Legal Studies*, 2nd ed. (Lanham, MD: Altamira Press, 2010) at 312–26.

123 Parliament's failure to more formally recognize Indigenous legal orders is inconsistent with provisions in the UN Declaration on the Rights of Indigenous Peoples, available at http://www.un.org/esa/socdev/unp fii/documents/DRIPS_en.pdfhttp://www.unhcr.org/refworld/doc id/471355a82.html. Article 9 asserts that 'Indigenous peoples have the right to belong to indigenous communities or nations *according to their own traditions and customs*' (emphasis mine). Article 19 provides that 'Indigenous peoples have the right … to maintain and develop their own decision making institutions.' Article 33 recognizes that Indigenous peoples have the 'right to maintain a justice system in accordance with their legal traditions.'

124 Limited exceptions to the Canadian resistance to tribal courts is found in the Metis Settlement Appeals Tribunal – see Cathy Bell, *Contemporary Métis Justice* (Saskatoon: University of Saskatchewan, Native Law Centre, 1999) – and treaty settlements such as the Nisga'a Agreement – see R.S.C. 2000, c. 7; S.B.C. 1999 c. 2.

125 Vine Deloria and Clifford Lytle, *American Indians and American Justice* (Austin: University of Texas Press, 2003) at 111–16.

126 Christine Zuni, 'Strengthening What Remains' (1997) 7 *Kansas Journal of Law and Public Policy* 18. For a discussion of how tribal court power can continue to grow by pushing back jurisdictional intrusions by Federal Courts, see Matthew Fletcher, 'Indian Courts and Fundamental Fairness: "Indian Courts and the Future" Revisited' (2010) 81 *University of Colorado Law Review* 973.

127 Matthew Fletcher, 'Rethinking Customary Law in Tribal Court Jurisprudence' (2007) 13 *Michigan Journal of Race & Law* 57.

128 Joseph Singer, 'The Indian States of America: Parallel Universes and Overlapping Sovereignty' (2014) 38 *American Indian Law Review* 1.

129 Joseph Singer, 'Canons of Conquest: The Supreme Court's Attack on Tribal Sovereignty' (2002–2003) 37 *New England Law Review* 641.

130 However, congress has not usually provided sufficient resources for tribal courts to ensure their most effective operation; see Nell Jessup Newton, 'Tribal Court Praxis: One Year in the Life of Twenty Indian Tribal Courts' (1997–1998) 22 *American Indian Law Review* 285–353.

131 *Michigan v. Bay Mills Indian Community*, No. 12–515, 2014 WL 2178337 (May 27, 2014) United States Supreme Court: 'Although Congress has plenary authority over tribes, Courts will not lightly assume that Congress in fact intends to undermine Indian self-government.'

132 *Tribal Law and Order Act*, 25 U.S.C. 1302 (3)(a)-(f). For commentary, see David Patton, 'Tribal Law and Order Act of 2010: Breathing Life into the Miner's Canary' (2012) 47 *Gonzaga Law Review* 767–800. See also *Indian Tribal Justice Technical and Legal Assistance Act*, 25 U.S.C. 3651–81; *Indian Child Protection and Family Violence Act*, 25 U.S.C. 3201–11.

133 An excellent compilation of materials and cases from tribal courts in the United States is found in Matthew Fletcher, *American Indian Tribal Law* (New York: Aspen Publishers, 2011).

134 For further discussion, see Borrows, *Canada's Indigenous Constitution* at 206–18.

135 For a discussion of First Nations development in Canada, see Robert Anderson, *Aboriginal Entrepreneurship and Business Development* (North York, ON: Captus Press, 2002); Wanda Wuttenee, *Living Rhythms: Lessons in Aboriginal Economic Resilience and Vision* (Montreal: McGill-Queen's University Press, 2004); Dwight Dorey and Joseph Magnet, *Legal Aspects of Business Development* (Markham, ON: LexisNexis, Butterworth's, 2005); Harold Bherer, Sylive Gagnon, and Jancinte Roberge, *Wampum and Letters Patent: Exploratory Study of Native Entrepreneurship* (Montreal: Institute of Research on Public Policy, 1990); Rosalyn Kunin, *Prospering Together: The Economic Impact of Aboriginal Title Settlements in BC* (Vancouver: Laurier Institution, 2001); Skeena Native Development Society, *Masters in Our Own House*.

136 For a discussion of development as it relates to capabilities, see Amartya Sen, *The Idea of Justice* (Cambridge, MA: Belnap Press, 2009).

137 It should be noted that success in the United States related to tribal economic development only started about forty years ago, during the Nixon administration. Before this time, as the Cohen Handbook observes, 'For much of the past two centuries, federal Indian policies inhibited tribal economic development' (see Felix Cohen, *Cohen's Handbook of Federal Indian Law*, ed. Nell Jessup Newton [Newark, NJ: LexisNexis, 2005] at 21.01).

Furthermore, Indian tribes in the United States still suffer from higher rates of socio-economic dislocation than other groups; see Jonathan B. Taylor and Joseph P. Kalt, *American Indians on Reservations: A Databook of Socioeconomic Change Between the 1990 and 2000 Censuses*, January 2005 (Harvard Project on American Indian Economic Development), http://hpaied.org/publications/american-indians-reservations-databook-socioeconomic-change-between-1990-and-2000http://hpaied.org/images/resources/publibrary/AmericanIndiansonReservationsADatabookofSocioeconomicChange.pdf. However, at times there have been significant exceptions to these patterns; see Alexander Harmon, *Rich Indians: Native People and the Problem of Wealth in American History* (Chapel Hill: University of North Carolina Press, 2010).

138 *Indian Gaming Regulatory Act*, 25 U.S.C. 2701–21.
139 *Indian Financing Act*, 25 U.S.C. 1451–1544.
140 *Indian Tribal Regulatory Reform and Business Development Act*, 1999, Pub.L.No. 106–447.
141 *Indian Tribal Economic Development and Encouragement Act*, 25 U.S.C. 4301–7.
142 *Native American Business Development, Trade Promotion* and *Tourism Act*, 25 U.S.C. 4301–7.
143 *National Indian Forest Resources Management Act*, 25 U.S.C. 3101–20.
144 *Clean Air Act*, 42 U.S.C. 7474(c).
145 *Clean Water Act*, 33 U.S.C. 1377(e).
146 *American Indian Agricultural Resource Management Act*, 25 U.S.C. 3701–13.
147 *Indian Mineral Development Act*, 25 U.S.C. 2101–8.
148 Taylor and Kalt, *American Indians on Reservations*; Lorie Graham, 'An interdisciplinary Approach to American Indian Economic Development' (2004) 80 *North Dakota Law Review* 597–655; Steven Andrew Light, Alan P. Meister, and Kathryn R.L. Rand, 'Indian Gaming and Beyond: Tribal Economic Development and Diversification' (2009) 54 *South Dakota Law Review* 375.
149 Douglas Brockman, 'Congressional Delegation of Environmental Regulatory Jurisdiction: Native American Control of the Reservation Environment' (1992) 41 *Washington University Journal of Urban and Contemporary Law* 133–61; Dean Suagee, 'Tribal Environmental Policy Acts and the Landscape of Environmental Law' (2009) 23 *Natural Resources & Environment* 56.
150 Thaddieus Conner and William A. Taggart, 'Indian Gaming and Tribal Revenue Allocation Plans: A Case of "Play to Pay"' (2011) 15 *Gaming Law Review and Economics* 355.

151   Alan Meister, *Casino City's Indian Gaming Industry Report* (Newton, MA: Casino City Press, 2008) at 10–11, 14.

152   Ibid. at 10.

153   Stephen Cornell, 'The Political Economy of American Indian Gaming' (2008) 4 *Annual Review of Law and Social Science* 63; Matthew Fletcher, 'Bringing Balance to Indian Gaming' (2007) 44 *Harvard Journal on Legislation* 39.

154   For a discussion of backlash against this expansion, see Matthew Fletcher, 'Indian Tribal Businesses and the Off-Reservation Market' (2008) 12 *Lewis and Clark Law Review* 1047.

155   For a Canadian discussion of the benefits to non-Aboriginal peoples resulting from Indigenous economic development, see Andre LeDrassay, 'A Brief Tax (On A Me) of First Nations Taxation and Economic Development,' in *Sharing the Harvest: The Road to Self-Reliance* at 215.

156   William V. Ackerman and Rick L. Bunch, 'A Comparative Analysis of Indian Gaming in the United States' (2012) 36 *American Indian Quarterly* 36. For a discussion of the wider context of Aboriginal gaming in Canada, see Yale Belanger, *Gambling with the Future: The Evolution of Aboriginal Gaming in Canada* (Saskatoon: Purich Publishing, 2006).

157   *Criminal Code*, R.S.C. 1985, c. C-46 ss. 206–7.

158   *R. v. Pamajewon*, [1996] 2 S.C.R. 821. For commentary on this case, see Bradford W. Morse, 'Permafrost Rights: Aboriginal Self-Government and the Supreme Court in *R. v. Pamajewon*' (1997) 42 *McGill Law Journal* 1011; John Borrows, 'Frozen Rights in Canada: Constitutional Interpretation and the Trickster' (1997) 22 *American Indian Law Review* 37.

159   *R. v. Bear Claw Casino Ltd.*, [1994] S.J. No. 485, [1994] 4 CNLR 81 (Sask. Prov. Ct.); *Saskatchewan Indian Gaming Authority (SIGA) v. National Automobile, Aerospace, Transportation and General Workers Union of Canada*, [2000] S.J. No. 266 (Sask. Q.B.) (SIGA) at para. 11.

160   David Potter, Brenda Pritchard, and Paul Seaman, 'Betting on Reconciliation: Law, Self-governance, and First Nations Economic Development in Canada' (2011) 15 *Gaming Law Review and Economics* 207 at 208; Yale Belanger, Robert Williams, and Jennifer Archer, 'Casinos and Economic Well-Being: Evaluating the Alberta First Nations' Experience' (2011) 5 *Journal of Gambling Business and Economics* 23.

161   See Minister of Indian Affairs and Northern Development and Federal Interlocutor for Métis and Non-Status Indians, 'Federal Framework for Aboriginal Economic Development,' 2009, available at http://www.aadnc-aandc.gc.ca/eng/1100100033498/100100034499.

162   For a contextual treatment of these laws, see Robert Miller, *Reservation 'Capitalism': Economic Development in Indian Country: Native America: Yesterday and Today* (Santa Barbara, CA: AFL-CLIO, 2012).

163 *Indian Reorganization Act*, 25 U.S.C. 477.
164 *Financing Economic Development of Indians and Indian Organizations*, 25 U.S.C. 1451–1544.
165 *Indian Tribal Regulatory Reform and Business Development Act*, 1999, Pub.L.No. 106–447.
166 *Indian Tribal Economic Development and Encouragement Act*. For commentary on this act, see Anna-Emily C. Gaupp, 'The Indian Tribal Economic Development and Contracts Encouragement Act of 2000: Smoke Signals of a New Era in Federal Indian Policy?' (2001) 33 *Connecticut Law Review* 667.
167 In particular, the statute insists the tribes give notice of their sovereign immunity when making contracts. For a discussion of tribal sovereign immunity as it relates to contracts in Indian country, see Chloe Thompson, 'Exercising and Protecting Tribal Sovereignty in Day-to-Day Business Operations: What the Key Players Need to Know' (2010) 49 *Washburn Law Journal* 661.
168 *Native American Business Development, Trade Promotion* and *Tourism Act*.
169 Moreover, the act creates the Office of Native American Business Development in the Department of Commerce to provide resources to tribes. Furthermore, as one avenue of development, it requires the secretary of the interior to establish projects to enhance tourism opportunities for tribal entities; see 25 U.S.C. § 4305.
170 Legislation facilitating economic development in Canada is largely limited to enhancing taxation powers under the *Indian Act*. For example, First Nations can also implement property taxation under the *First Nations Fiscal and Statistical Management Act*, S.C. 2005, c. 9. The FSMA created four First Nations institutions to facilitate development: First Nations Tax Commission; First Nations Financial Management Board; First Nations Finance Authority; and First Nations Statistical Institute. These institutions are still fragile and, except for the First Nations Tax Commission, are still being established. Unfortunately, in 2012 the federal government withdrew financial support for the First Nations Fiscal Institute, which will make it more difficult for the First Nations Financial Management Board and First Nations Finance authority to do their work; see Shari Narine, 'Ottawa Kicks a Peg out from Foundational Organizations' (2012) 30 *Windspeaker* at http://www.ammsa.com/publications/windspeaker/ottawa-kicks-peg-out-foundational-organizations. For a discussion of the operation of these boards, see Aboriginal Affairs and Northern Development Canada, *A Report to Parliament on the Legislative Review of the First Nations Fiscal and Statistical Management Act* (March 2012) at http://www.aadnc-aandc.gc.ca/eng/1334169647868/1334169697578. Parliament also passed the *First Nations Commercial and Industrial Development Act*, S.C.

2005, c. 53, to provide for the adoption of provincial regulations on reserve, compatible with those off reserve. Unlike U.S. models, which work from a self-determination framework, this act seeks to assimilate reserve-based activities into provincial law. In 2010, this act was amended by Bill C-24, the *First Nations Certainty of Land Title Act*, S.C. 2010, c. 6.

171 *Indian Oil and Gas Act*, R.S.C., 1985, c. I-7. This act is complemented by the *First Nations Oil and Gas and Moneys Management Act*, S.C. 2005, c. 48, which allows First Nations to opt out of the *Indian Oil and Gas Act* and manage their own exploration activities' revenues from oil and gas. Furthermore, the *Indian Oil and Gas Regulations*, SOR/94–753, provides for the manner in which oil resources on reserve are developed. For commentary on this act and regulations, see Andrew Black, 'Devolution of Oil and Gas Jurisdiction to First Nations in Canada' (2008) 45 *Alberta Law Review* 537.

172 *Indian Mineral Development Act*, 25 U.S.C. 2101–8. For complementary legislation, see the *Indian Energy Act*, 25 U.S.C. 37 3501–6, which assists tribes in energy development through grants, loans, technical assistance, and streamlined approval procedures.

173 *National Indian Forest Resources Management Act*, 25 U.S.C. 3101–20; *Clean Air Act*, 42 U.S.C. 7474 (c); *Clean Water Act*, 33 U.S.C. 1377(e); *American Indian Agricultural Resource Management Act*, 25 U.S.C. 3701–13.

174 For commentary on this act, see Daria Mondon, 'Our Land is What Makes Us Who We Are: Timber Harvesting on Tribal Reservations after NIFRMA' (1997) 21 *American Indian Law Review* 259.

175 Anderson, Berger, Frickey, and Krakoff, eds., *American Indian Law, Cases and Commentary* at 157. For commentary, see James Grivala, 'The Origins of EPA's Indian Program' (2006) 15 *Kansas Journal of Law and Public Policy* 191; Regina Cutler 'To Clear the Muddy Waters: Tribal Regulatory Authority under Section 518 of the Clean Water Act' (1999) 29 *Environmental Law* 721; Judith V. Royster, 'Practical sovereignty, political sovereignty, and the Indian Tribal Energy Development and Self-Determination Act' (2008) 12 *Lewis & Clark Law Review* 1065–1101.

176 See *Jobs, Growth and Long-term Prosperity Act*, S.C., c.19, 29TH JUNE, 2012 (BILL C-38) and *Jobs and Growth Act, 2012*. S.C., c.31, 14TH DECEMBER, 2012, (BILL C-45).

177 *R. v. Sparrow*, [1990] 1 S.C.R. 1075, at 1112; *R. v. Marshall*, [1999] 3 S.C.R. 456 at para. 48; *Haida Nation v. British Columbia (Minister of Forests)*, [2004] 3 S.C.R. 511 at para. 53.

178 For a more general discussion of the necessity of legislative action in constitutional development, see Aharon Barak, *Proportionality: Constitutional Rights and Their Limitations* (Cambridge: Cambridge University Press, 2012).

179 *Indian Self-Determination and Educational Assistance Act.*

180 Former prime minister Stephen Harper recently recognized that legislative reform should occur in Canada, related to Indigenous peoples. However, self-determination was given as a justification for such change. He said:

> Why would we wish to change the rules?
>
> Because, 'from the rules you set, come the results you get,' and the incentives buried in the *Indian Act* self-evidently lead to outcomes that we all deplore.
>
> To be sure, our Government has no grand scheme to repeal or to unilaterally re-write the *Indian Act*: After 136 years, that tree has deep roots – blowing up the stump would just leave a big hole. However, there are ways, creative ways, collaborative ways, ways that involve consultation between our Government, the provinces, and First Nations leadership and communities, ways that provide options within the Act, or outside of it, for practical, incremental and real change.
>
> So that will be our approach, to replace elements of the *Indian Act* with more modern legislation and procedures, in partnership with provinces and First Nations. It is an approach that has already shown promise. With inspired leadership, energy and enterprise, some bands have already shown that First Nations people are as quick to prosper, as capable of excellence and as able to enjoy all that Canada's vibrant economy has to offer. ('PM addresses the Crown,' First Nations Gathering, 24 January 2012, Ottawa, Ontario, www.afn.ca./uploads/files/cfng/pm/cfng.pdy)

Chapter Six

* This chapter is a revised version of an article published under the title, John Borrows, 'Aboriginal and Treaty Rights and Violence against Women' (2013) 50 *Osgoode Hall Law Journal* 699.

1 Thomas Peacock, *The Four Hills of Life: Ojibwe Wisdom* (Afton, MN: Afton Historical Press, 2006) at 105. 'People who live a good life, or bimaadiziwaad, can be called "those who have power"' (Michael D. McNally, *Honoring Elders: Aging, Authority, and Ojibwe Religion* [New York: Columbia University Press, 2009] at 50).

2 *R. v. Sappier; R. v. Gray*, [2006] S.C.J. No. 54, [2006] 2 S.C.R. 686 at para. 38: 'I can therefore find no jurisprudential authority to support the proposition that a practice undertaken merely for survival purposes cannot be considered integral to the distinctive culture of an aboriginal people. I find that the jurisprudence weighs in favour of protecting the traditional means of survival of an aboriginal community.'

3 In a related context, the political nature of constitutional discourse is dis-
cussed in Joel Bakan, *Just Words: Constitutional Rights and Social Wrongs*
(Toronto: University of Toronto Press, 1997); Alan Hutchinson, *Waiting for
Coraf: A Critique of Laws and Rights* (Toronto: University of Toronto Press,
1995); Ted Morton and Rainer Knopf, *The Charter Revolution and the Court
Party* (Toronto: University of Toronto Press, 2000); Michael Mandel, *The
Charter of Rights and the Legalization of Politics in Canada* (Toronto: Thompson, 1989); Christopher Manfredi, *Judicial Power and the Charter: Canada and
the Paradox of Liberal Constitutionalism* (Toronto: Oxford University Press,
2001); Andrew Petter, *The Politics of the Charter: The Illusive Promise of Constitutional Rights* (Toronto: University of Toronto Press, 2010).

4 'For Indigenous women, the systematic violation of their collective rights
as Indigenous People is the single greatest risk factor for gender based
violence – including violence perpetrated within their communities.'
See Mairin Iwanka Raya, 'Indigenous Women Stand against Violence: A
Companion Report to the United Nations Secretary-General's Study on
Violence against Women' (New York: International Indigenous Women's
Forum, 2006) at 7, http://www.un.org/esa/socdev/unpfii/documents/
vaiwreport06.pdf .

5 Glen Coulthard, *Red Skin, White Masks: Rejecting the Colonial Politics of Recognition* (Minneapolis: University of Minnesota Press, 2014) 79–103.

6 In my view there is no external measure for determining whether our
actions are liberating or oppressive across varied situations. We must be
continually attentive to the physical philosophies in play that attend to
material, grounded realities of the parties in conflict.

7 'In 2009, close to 67,000 Aboriginal women aged 15 or older living in the
Canadian provinces reported being the victim of violence in the previous
12 months. Overall, the rate of self-reported violent victimization among
Aboriginal women was almost three times higher than the rate of violent
victimization reported by non-Aboriginal women. Close to two-thirds
(63%) of Aboriginal female victims were aged 15 to 34. This age group
accounted for just under half (47%) of the female Aboriginal population
(aged 15 or older) living in the ten provinces.' See Shannon Brennan, 'Violent Victimization of Aboriginal Women in the Canadian Provinces, 2009'
(2011, 17 May) *Juristat* (Ottawa: Statistics Canada) at 5, http://www.
statcan.gc.ca/pub/85-002-x/2011001/article/11439-eng.pdf. For further
commentary, see also Anita Olsen Harper, 'Is Canada Peaceful and Safe
for Aboriginal Women?' (2006) 25(1–2) *Canadian Woman Studies* 33 at 33,
36–7.

8 Brennan, 'Violent Victimization' at 7. For a more general discussion of
Aboriginal women and the law, see Patricia Monture, 'Standing against

Canadian Law: Naming Omissions of Race, Culture, and Gender' (1998) 2
YBNZ Juris 7.

9 See generally Manitoba, Aboriginal Justice Inquiry of Manitoba, *The Jus-
tice System and Aboriginal People*, vol. 1 of *Report of the Aboriginal Justice
Inquiry of Manitoba* (Winnipeg: Queen's Printer, 1991) at 475–87. (Chairs:
A.C. Hamilton and C.M. Sinclair).

10 Amnesty International, 'No More Stolen Sisters: The Need for a Comprehensive Response to Discrimination and Violence against Indigenous Women in
Canada' (London: Amnesty International, 2009) at 1, https://www.amnesty.
org/en/documents/AMR20/012/2009/en.

11 Jodi-Anne Brzozowski, Andrea Taylor-Butts, and Sara Johnson, 'Victimization and Offending among the Aboriginal Population in Canada,' (2006)
26(3) *Juristat* (Ottawa: Statistics Canada), http://publications.gc.ca/
collections/Collection-R/Statcan/85-002-XIE-002-XIE2006003.pdf.

12 Patricia Monture-Angus, 'Women and Risk: Aboriginal Women, Colonialism, and Correctional Practice' (1999) 19(1–2) *Canadian Woman Studies* 24;
Fran Sugar and Lana Fox, 'Nistum Peyako Seht'wawin Iskwewak: Breaking Chains' (1989–90) 3(2) *Canadian Journal of Women and the Law* 465.

13 *R. v. Gladue*, 1999 S.C.C. 679 at para. 64, [1999] 1 S.C.R. 688.

14 See Nova Scotia, Royal Commission on the Donald Marshall Jr., Prosecution, *Digest of Findings and Recommendations* (Halifax, NS: The Commission,
1989) (Chair: T Alexander Hickman); Ontario, The Osnaburgh-Windigo
Tribal Council Justice Review Committee, *Report of the Osnaburgh-Windigo
Tribal Council Review Committee* (Toronto: Government of Ontario, 1990)
(Chair: Alan Grant); Canada, Law Reform Commission of Canada, *Report
on Aboriginal Peoples and Criminal Justice: Equality, Respect and the Search
for Justice* (Ottawa: The Commission, 1991); Manitoba, Aboriginal Justice
Inquiry of Manitoba, *The Justice System and Aboriginal People*; Alberta, Task
Force on the Criminal Justice System and Its Impact on the Indian and
Metis People of Alberta, *Main Report*, vol. 1 of *Justice on Trial: Report of the
Task Force on the Criminal Justice System and its Impact on the Indian and Metis
People of Alberta* (Edmonton: The Task Force, 1991); Saskatchewan, Indian
Justice Review Committee, *Report of the Saskatchewan Indian Justice Review
Committee* (Regina, SK: The Committee, 1992) (Chair: Patricia Linn); Brit-
ish Columbia, Cariboo-Chilcotin Justice Inquiry, *Report on the Cariboo-
Chilcotin Justice Inquiry* (Victoria: Cariboo-Chilcotin Justice Inquiry, 1993)
(Commissioner: Anthony Sarich); Canada, Royal Commission on Aborigi-
nal Peoples, *Bridging the Cultural Divide: Report on Aboriginal People and
Criminal Justice in Canada* (Ottawa: Canada Communication Group, 1996);
Canada, Royal Commission on Aboriginal Peoples, *Gathering Strength*,
vol. 3 of *Report of the Royal Commission on Aboriginal Peoples* (Ottawa:

Canada Communication Group, 1996) at 54; Saskatchewan, Commission on First Nations and Metis Peoples and Justice, *Legacy of Hope: An Agenda for Change* (Saskatoon: The Commission, 2004); Ontario, Ministry of the Attorney General, *Report of the Ipperwash Inquiry* (Toronto: Queen's Printer for Ontario, 2007).

15 See *Criminal Code*, R.S.C. 1985, c. C-46 s. 718.2(e). For further discussion of this issue, see Elizabeth Adjin-Tettey, 'Sentencing Aboriginal Offenders: Balancing Offenders' Needs, the Interests of Victims and Society, and the Decolonization of Aboriginal Peoples' (2007) 19(1) *Canadian Journal of Women and the Law* 179.

16 There is a 'near fatal lack of resources' available for dealing with violence on reserves. See Anne McGillivray and Brenda Comaskey, *Black Eyes All of the Time: Intimate Violence, Aboriginal Women, and the Justice System* (Toronto: University of Toronto Press, 1999) at 79–80. See also Angela Cameron, '*R. v. Gladue*: Sentencing and the Gendered Impacts of Colonialism,' in *Moving Toward Justice*, ed. John D. Whyte (Saskatoon: Purich Publishing, 2008) at 160; Angela Cameron, 'Sentencing Circles and Intimate Violence: A Canadian Feminist Perspective' (2006) 18 *Canadian Journal of Women and the Law* 479.

17 Neil Andersson, Beverley Shea, Carol Amaratunga, Patricia McGuire, and Georges Sioui, 'Rebuilding from Resilience: Research Framework for a Randomized Controlled Trial of Community-led Interventions to Prevent Domestic Violence in Aboriginal Communities' (2010) 8(2) *Pimatisiwin* 61.

18 For example, see Native Women's Association of Canada, online at www. nwac.ca, for information about the broad array of activities undertaken by Indigenous women to deal with the violence against women. See also National Aboriginal Circle Against Family Violence, 'Ending Violence in Aboriginal Communities: Best Practices' (Ottawa: National Aboriginal Circle Against Family Violence, 30 November 2005).

19 Recently, the Assembly of First Nations has also become more active in addressing violence against women. See 'Demanding Justice and Fulfilling Rights: A Strategy to End Violence against Indigenous Women & Girls,' retrieved on 25 November 2015 from http://www.afn.ca/uploads/files/misssing_and_murdered_indigenous_women/afn_draft_strategy_to_ensure_rights_of_indigenous_women_&_girls_e.pdf.

20 The work of the Native Women's Association of Canada was very significant in securing Indian status for hundreds of thousands of people who were disenfranchised on a sexually discriminatory basis. See Janet Silman, *Enough is Enough: Aboriginal Women Speak Out* (Toronto: Women's Press, 1987). Loss of status made Aboriginal women more vulnerable to

violence because of the precarious position in which they were placed relative to Indian men. Indian women's inability to reside or own property on reserve, participate in the political life of the community, and access the support of extended family and kin exposed them to greater challenges in confronting and fleeing abuse. The work of the Native Women's Association of Canada and their allies helped address some of these challenges. See *McIvor v. Canada (Registrar, Indian and Northern Affairs)*, 2009 B.C.C.A. 153, 306 D.L.R. (4th) 193.

21 For examples of advocacy, see Native Women's Association of Canada, 'What Their Stories Tell Us: Research Findings from the Sisters in Spirit Initiative' (Ottawa: NWAC, 2010), http://www.nwac.ca/sites/default/files/imce/2010_NWAC_SIS_Report_EN_Lite.pdf; Jeannette Corbiere Lavell, 'Combating Violence against Indigenous Women and Girls' (statement of the Native Women's Association of Canada, delivered at the Eleventh Session of the Permanent Forum on Indigenous Issues, New York, 7–18 May 2012), http://www.afn.ca/en/news-media/latest-news/eleventh-session-of-the-permanent-forum-on-indigenous-issues-combating. For protocols dealing with sexual violence in Aboriginal communities, see Jarem Sawatsky, *The Ethic of Traditional Communities and the Spirit of Healing Justice: Studies from Hollow Water, the Iona Community, and Plum Village* (London: Jessica Kingsley Publishers, 2009).

22 Sharon McIvor, 'Aboriginal Women's Rights as "Existing Rights"' (1995) 15(2–3) *Canadian Woman Studies* 34–8.

23 For commentary on Native women's advocacy related to violence against women, see Native Women's Association of Canada, 'Arrest the Legacy: From Residential Schools to Prisons,' in *Gender Matters: Building Strength in Reconciliation* (Ottawa, 2012), http://www.nwac.ca/wp-content/uploads/2015/05/Gender-Matters-Introduction.pdf; Wendee Kubik, Carrie Bourassa, and Mary Hampton, 'Stolen Sisters, Second-Class Citizens, Poor Health: The Legacy of Colonization in Canada' (2009) 33(1–2) *Humanity & Society* 18.

24 Robert A. Williams Jr., 'Vampires Anonymous and Critical Race Practice' (1997) 95(4) *Michigan Law Review* 741; Robert A. Williams Jr., 'Taking Rights Aggressively: The Perils and Promise of Critical Legal Theory for Peoples of Color' (1987) 5(1) *Law & Inequality* 103.

25 See, for example, Teressa Nahanee, '"Dancing with a Gorilla": Aboriginal Women, Justice and the Charter' (NWAC submission for the Round Table on Justice Issues, 25–27 November 1992), http://www.rapereliefshelter.bc.ca/sites/default/files/imce/DancingwithaGorilla.pdf; Thomas Flanagan, *First Nations? Second Thoughts* (Montreal: McGill-Queen's University

Press, 2000); Frances Widdowson and Albert Howard, *Disrobing the Aboriginal Industry: The Deception Behind Indigenous Cultural Preservation* (Montreal: McGill-Queen's University Press, 2008).

26 Emily Snyder, 'Indigenous Feminist Legal Theory' (2014) 26(2) *Canadian Journal of Women and the Law* 365.

27 Val Napoleon discusses the need for a broader political and gendered analysis of Indigenous issues. See 'Aboriginal Feminism in a Wider Frame' (2007) 41(3) *Canadian Dimension* 44.

28 The S.C.C. has held that Aboriginal and treaty rights should be construed in broad ways that favour Aboriginal interpretations. See *R. v. Gladstone*, [1996] 2 S.C.R. 723 at para. 9, 137 D.L.R. (4th) 648; *R. v. Van der Peet*, [1996] 2 S.C.R. 507, 137 D.L.R. (4th) 289; *Delgamuukw v. British Columbia*, [1997] 3 S.C.R. 1010, 153 D.L.R. (4th) 193; *R. v. Sappier; R. v. Gray*, 2006 S.C.C. 54, 274 D.L.R. (4th) 75; *R. v. Taylor and Williams*, 34 O.R. (2d) 360, [1981] 3 C.N.L.R. 114 (CA); *R. v. Simon*, [1985] 2 S.C.R. 387, 24 D.L.R. (4th) 390; *R. v. Horseman*, [1990] 1 SCR 901 at paras. 2–4, 4 W.W.R. 97; *R. v. Badger*, [1996] 1 S.C.R. 771 at paras. 4, 41, 133 D.L.R. (4th) 324; *R. v. Sundown*, [1999] 1 S.C.R. 393 at paras. 24–5; *R. v. Marshall*, [1999] 3 S.C.R. 456 at paras. 9–14, 177 D.L.R. (4th) 513; *R. v. Marshall*, [1999] 3 S.C.R. 533 at para. 19, 179 D.L.R. (4th) 193; *R. v. Marshall; R. v. Bernard*, 2005 S.C.C. 43, [2005] 2 S.C.R. 220 at para. 26; *R. v. Morris*, 2006 S.C.C. 59, [2006], 2 S.C.R. 915 at para. 19. The leading cases in the United States applying similar canons of construction are *United States v. Winans*, 198 U.S. 371 (1905); *Winters v. United States*, 207 U.S. 564 at 576–7 (1908); *Choate v. Trapp*, 224 U.S. 665 at 675 (1912); *Carpenter v. Shaw*, 280 U.S. 363 at 367 (1930); *Choctaw Nation v. United States*, 318 U.S. 423 at 431–2 (1943); *McClanahan v. Arizona State Tax Commission*, 411 U.S. 164 at 174 (1973); *Minnesota v. Mille Lacs Band of Chippewa Indians* 526 U.S. 172 at 195–8 (1999).

29 *R. v. Pamajewon*, [1996] 2 S.C.R. 821 at para. 27, 138 D.L.R. (4th) 204.

30 See Brian Slattery, 'The Generative Structure of Aboriginal Rights' (2007) 38 *Supreme Court Law Review* (2d) 595; Kent McNeil, 'Self-Government and the Inalienability of Aboriginal Title' (2002) 47(3) *McGill Law Journal* 473; Russell L. Barsh and James Y. Henderson, 'The Supreme Court's Van der Peet Trilogy: Naive Imperialism and Ropes of Sand' (1997) 42(4) *McGill Law Journal* 993; Bradford Morse, 'Permafrost Rights: Aboriginal Self-Government and the Supreme Court in *R. v. Pamajewon*' (1997) 42(4) *McGill Law Journal* 1011; John Borrows, 'Frozen Rights in Canada: Constitutional Interpretation and the Trickster' (1998) 22 *American Indian Law Review* 37.

31 *R. v. Ignace* (1998), 156 D.L.R. (4th) 713 at para. 11, 103 B.C.A.C. 273; *Mississaugas of Scugog Island First Nation v. National Automobile, Aerospace,*

Transportation and General Workers Union of Canada (CAW-Canada), Local 444, 2007 O.N.C.A. 814, 287 D.L.R. (4th) 452 [*Mississaugas of Scugog Island First Nation* cited to ONCA]; *Sawridge Band v. Canada*, [2006] 4 C.N.L.R. 279 at para. 42; *Mitchell v. Minister of National Revenue*, 2001 S.C.C. 33 at paras. 125–6, [2001] 1 S.C.R. 911; *NIL/TU,O Child and Family Services Society v. BC Government and Service Employees' Union* (23 March 2006), B72/2006 at paras. 54–66, http://www.lrb.bc.ca/decisions/B072$2006.pdf; *NIL/TU,O Child and Family Services Society v. BC Government and Service Employees' Union*, 2010 S.C.C. 45 at para. 80, [2010] 2 S.C.R. 696. Note how the claim to Indigenous governance virtually disappeared by the time *NIL/TU,O v. BC Government* got to the S.C.C. because of the narrow reading of *Pamajewon* in the lower court.

32 *Delgamuukw v. British Columbia*, [1997] at paras. 170–1.
33 For an excellent discussion of this issue, see Felix Hoehn, *Reconciling Sovereignties: Aboriginal Nations and Canada* (Saskatoon: University of Saskatchewan, Native Law Centre, 2012).
34 For the first case dealing with tribal criminal jurisdiction, see *Ex Parte Crow Dog*, 109 U.S. 556 (1883). For commentary on this case, see Sidney Harring, *Crow Dog's Case: American Indian Sovereignty, Tribal Law, and United States Law in the Nineteenth Century* (Cambridge: Cambridge University Press, 1994). For the leading case dealing with tribal civil jurisdiction, see *Williams v. Lee*, 358 U.S. 277 (1959).
35 *Johnson v. McIntosh*, 21 U.S. 543 (1823); *Cherokee Nation v. State of Georgia*, 30 U.S. 1 (1831). These principles were reaffirmed in *United States v. Lara*, 541 U.S. 193, 124 S Ct 1628 (2004).
36 For critical discussions of the plenary power, see Nell Jessup Newton, 'Federal Power Over Indians: Its Scope, Sources and Limitations' (1984) 132(2) *University of Pennsylvania Law Review* 195; Philip P. Frickey, 'Domesticating Federal Indian Law' (1996) 81 *Minnesota Law Review* 31; Robert N. Clinton, 'There Is No Federal Supremacy Clause for Indian Tribes' (2002) 34(1) *Arizona State Law Journal* 113; David H. Getches, 'Conquering the Cultural Frontier: The New Subjectivism of the Supreme Court in Indian Law' (1996) 84(6) *California Law Review* 1573.
37 *The Major Crimes Act*, 18 U.S.C. § 1153 (1885) (outlining some of these limits).
38 *United States v. Wheeler*, 435 U.S. 313, 98 S Ct 1079 (1978).
39 U.S. constitutional amendment I–XXVII.
40 *Talton v. Mayes*, 163 U.S. 376 (1896).
41 *Indian Civil Rights Act*, 25 U.S.C. § 1302(8) (1968).
42 *Santa Clara Pueblo v. Martinez*, 436 U.S. 49, 98 S Ct 1670 (1978).

43 For a general overview of the issue of violence against women on Indian reservations, see *Sharing Our Stories of Survival: Native Women Surviving Violence*, ed. Sarah Deer, Bonnie, Clairmont, Carrie A. Martell, and Maureen L. White Eagle (Lanham, MD: Altamira, 2008).

44 Gloria Valencia-Weber and Christine P. Zuni, 'Domestic Violence and Tribal Protection of Indigenous Women in the United States' (1995) 69 *St. John's Law Review* 69.

45 Royal Commission on Aboriginal Peoples, *Partners in Confederation: Aboriginal Peoples, Self-Government and the Constitution* (Ottawa: Supply and Services, 1993).

46 Resources are also greatly needed to deal with violence against women. For an in-depth study of poverty and federal policy on reserves, see Hugh Shewell, *'Enough to Keep them Alive': Indian Welfare in Canada, 1873–1965* (Toronto: University of Toronto Press, 2004).

47 Foundational flaws resting at the base of constitutional law must be exposed, nullified, and repaired to effectively address this issue. See Gordon Christie, 'Judicial Justification of a Recent Development in Aboriginal Law?' (2002) 17(2) *Canadian Journal of Law and Society* 41.

48 See Hilary N. Weaver, 'The Colonial Context of Violence: Reflections on Violence in the Lives of Native American Women' (2009) 24(9) *Journal of Interpersonal Violence* 1552; Kiera L. Ladner, 'Gendering Decolonisation, Decolonising Gender' (2009) 13(1) *Australian Indigenous Law Review* 62.

49 For a discussion of how colonization is linked with violence against women, see Andrea Smith, *Conquest: Sexual Violence and American Indian Genocide* (Cambridge, MA: South End Press, 2005); Mary Ellen Turpel, 'Patriarchy and Paternalism: The Legacy of the Canadian State for Women' (1993) 6(1) *Canadian Journal of Women and the Law* 174. For a discussion of how s. 35(1) is designed to address colonialism, see *R. v. Sparrow*, [1997] 1 S.C.R. 1075 at 412, 70 D.L.R. (4th) 385; *Delgamuukw v. British Columbia*, [1997]; *R. v. Côté*, [1996] 3 S.C.R. 139 at para. 59, 177 D.L.R. (4th) 513.

50 The connection was made in at page one of the Executive Summary of a 2006 Report prepared for the General Assembly, detailing global violence against women, (UN Docs A/61/122/Add.1); Sally Engle Merry, *Gender Violence: A Cultural Perspective* (Oxford: Wiley Blackwell, 2009).

51 For extended scholarship on this issue, see Patricia A. Monture, 'Women's Words: Power, Identity, and Indigenous Sovereignty' (2008) 26(3) *Canadian Woman Studies* 154; Particia A. Monture, 'Ka-Nin-Geh-Heh-Gah-E-Sa-Nonh-Yah-Gah' (1986) 2(1) *Canadian Journal of Women and the Law* 159; Paticia Monture-Angus, *Thunder My Soul: A Mohawk Woman Speaks*

(Halifax, NS: Fernwood Publishing, 1995); Patricia Monture-Angus, 'Standing against Canadian Law: Naming Omissions of Race, Culture and Gender'(1998) 2 *YBNZ Juris* 7; Patricia Monture-Angus, 'Women and Risk: Aboriginal Women, Colonialism, and Correctional Practice' (1999) 19(1–2) *Canadian Woman Studies* 24; Patricia A. Monture-Okanee, 'The Violence We Women Do: A First Nations View,' in *Challenging Times: The Women's Movement in Canada and the United States*, ed. Constance Backhouse and David H Flaherty (Montreal: McGill-Queen's University Press, 1992) at 193; Patricia A. Monture-Okanee, 'The Roles and Responsibilities of Aboriginal Women: Reclaiming Justice' (1992) 56(2) *Saskatchewan Law Review* 237.

52 For a discussion of the care required in asking and addressing this question, see Maneesha Deckha, 'Gender, Difference, and Anti-Essentialism: Towards a Feminist Response to Cultural Claims in Law,' in *Diversity and Equality: The Changing Framework of Freedom in Canada*, ed. Avigail Eisenberg (Vancouver: UBC Press, 2006) at 114; Emma LaRocque, 'Re-examining Culturally Appropriate Models in Criminal Justice Applications,' in *Aboriginal and Treaty Rights in Canada: Essays on Law, Equality, and Respect for Difference*, ed. Michael Asch (Vancouver: UBC Press, 1997) at 75; Kim Anderson, 'Affirmations of an Indigenous Feminist,' in *Indigenous Women and Feminism: Politics, Activism, Culture*, ed. Cheryl Suzack, Shari Huhndorf, Jeanne Perreault, and Jean Barman (Vancouver: UBC Press, 2010) at 81.

53 This was particularly the case during the early 1990s when constitutional discussions excluded Aboriginal women's groups. See John Borrows, 'Contemporary Traditional Equality: The Effect of the Charter on First Nations Politics' (1994) 43(1) *University of New Brunswick Law Journal* 19; Sharon Donna McIver, 'Self-Government and Aboriginal Women,' in *Scratching the Surface: Canadian Anti-Racist Feminist Thought*, ed. Enakshi Dua and Angela Robertson (Toronto: Women's Press, 1999) at 167; Lilianne Ernestine Krosenbrink-Gelissen, *Sexual Equality as an Aboriginal Right: The Native Women's Association of Canada and the Constitutional Process on Aboriginal Matters, 1982–1987* (Saarbrücken, Germany: Verlag Breitenbach, 1991).

54 Carol Gilligan and David A.J. Richards, *The Deepening Darkness: Patriarchy, Resistance, and Democracy's Future* (Cambridge: Cambridge University Press, 2009).

55 For a good overview of the struggle faced by Indigenous women in the face of male dominance, see Sharon McIvor, 'Aboriginal Women Unmasked: Using Equality Litigation to Advance Women's Rights,' in *Poverty: Rights, Social Citizenship, and Legal Activism*, ed. Margot Young, Susan B.Boyd, Gwen Brodsky, and Shelagh Day (Vancouver: UBC Press, 2007) at 96. For

another viewpoint, see Kim Anderson, 'Leading by Action: Female Chiefs and the Political Landscape in Restoring the Balance,' in *Restoring the Balance: First Nations Women, Community, and Culture*, ed. Gail Guthrie Valaskakis, Madeleine Dion Stout, and Eric Guimond (Winnipeg: University of Manitoba Press, 2009) at 99.

56 Emily Snyder, Val Napoleon, and John Borrows, 'Gender and Violence: Drawing on Indigenous Legal Resources' (2014) 47 *University of British Columbia Law Review* 593.

57 For an example of the failure of some First Nations leaders in Manitoba to deal with sexual violence in the child welfare context, see Ruth Teichroeb, *Flowers on My Grave: How an Ojibwa Boy's Death Helped Break the Silence on Child Abuse* (Toronto: HarperCollins, 1997).

58 Aboriginal Justice Inquiry of Manitoba, *The Justice System and Aboriginal People* at 487.

59 Aboriginal organizations have called for inquiries and action to deal with violence against women, particularly in relation to murdered and missing Aboriginal women. See Native Women's Association of Canada, 'Collaboration to End Violence: National Aboriginal Women's Forum' (27 July 2011), http://www.afn.ca/en/news-media/latest-news/assembly-of-first-nations-responds-to-cedaw-report-stating-canada-has-.

60 Emma LaRocque, 'Violence in Aboriginal Communities,' in *Violence against Women: New Canadian Perspectives*, ed. Katherine M.J. McKenna and June Larkin (Toronto: Inanna, 2002) at 147.

61 Douglas A. Brownridge, 'Understanding the Elevated Risk of Partner Violence against Aboriginal Women: A Comparison of Two Nationally Representative Surveys of Canada' (2008) 23 *Journal of Family Violence* 353; Douglas A. Brownridge, 'Male Partner Violence against Aboriginal Women in Canada: An Empirical Analysis' (2003) 18(1) *Journal of Interpersonal Violence* 65.

62 Wayne Warry, *Unfinished Dreams: Community Healing and the Reality of Aboriginal Self-Government* (Toronto: University of Toronto Press, 1998) at 160–2.

63 For example, in past constitutional debates the concerns of Aboriginal women were not adequately taken into account. See Joyce Green, 'Constitutionalizing the Patriarchy: Aboriginal Women and Aboriginal Government' (1992) 4(1) *Constitutional Forum* 110.

64 Judith Lewis Herman, *Trauma and Recovery* (New York: Basic Books, 1992) at 155–74.

65 A tragically poignant example of the failure to recognize this fact is recorded in *Jane Doe v. Awasis Agency of Northern Manitoba*, (1990), 67 Man R (2d) 260, 72 D.L.R. (4th) 738 (CA).

66 Those who have experienced violence usually have a good of idea of which actions are effective and which are not in this field. See, more generally, Francine Pickup, Suzanne Williams, and Caroline Sweetman, *Ending Violence against Women: A Challenge for Development and Humanitarian Work* (Oxford: Oxfam, 2001).

67 Boyce Richardson, ed., *Drum Beat: Anger and Renewal in Indian Country* (Ottawa: Summerhill Press, 1989) at 137–66; Leanne Simpson, *Dancing on Our Turtle's Back: Stories of Nishnaabeg Re-creation, Resurgence, and a New Emergence* (Winnipeg: Arbeiter Ring, 2011). For a discussion of how Aboriginal communities actually contribute positively to Canadian society, see *Hidden in Plain Sight: Contributions of Aboriginal Peoples to Canadian Identity and Culture*, ed. Cora Voyageur, David Newhouse, and Daniel Beavon (Toronto: University of Toronto Press, 2005).

68 Some communities have taken positive steps to address violence against women. See Sawatsky, *The Ethic of Traditional Communities and the Spirit of Healing Justice*. Furthermore, the complexities of membership in multiple communities must be considered in dealing with violence against Aboriginal women. See Rauna Kuokkanen, 'Self-Determination and Indigenous Rights at the Intersectionn of International Human Rights' (2012) 34 *Human Rights Quarterly* 225.

69 I have addressed this issue in John Borrows, 'Seven Generations, Seven Teachings: Ending the Indian Act' (research paper for the National Centre for First Nations Governance, May 2008), http://fngovernance.org/resources_docs/7_Generations_7_Teachings.pdf.

70 For a discussion of the ability of traumatized communities to positively respond amidst violence, see *Strategies of Community Intervention*, 5th ed., ed. Jack Rothman, John E. Tropman, and John L. Erlich (Itasca, IL: Peacock, 1995); John Rothman, *Reflections on Community Organization: Enduring Themes and Critical Issues* (Itasca, IL: Peacock, 1999); Barbara Levy Simon, *The Empowerment Tradition in American Social Work: A History* (New York: Columbia University Press, 1994).

71 See, generally, Monica McGoldrick, ed., *Re-Visioning Family Therapy: Race, Culture and Gender in Clinical Practice* (New York: Guilford Press, 1998).

72 For examples and a discussion of this issue, see Taiaiake Alfred, *Peace, Power, Righteousness: An Indigenous Manifesto* (Toronto: Oxford University Press, 1999); Gerald R. Alfred, *Heeding the Voices of Our Ancestors: Kahnawake Mohawk Politics and the Rise of Native Nationalism* (Toronto: Oxford University Press, 1995); Taiaiake Alfred, *Wasáse: Indigenous Pathways of Action and Freedom* (Peterborough, ON: Broadview Press, 2005).

73 Rupert Ross, 'Traumatization in Remote First Nations: An Expression of Concern' (2006) [unpublished, on file with author].

74 For a list of women's and Indigenous organizations that have had their funding cut by the federal government in recent years, see Gina Starblanket, *Beyond Culture in the Courts: Re-inspiring Approaches to Aboriginal and Treaty Rights in Canadian Jurisprudence* (master's thesis, University of Victoria, 2012) [unpublished] at 89–90:

> Aboriginal Healing Foundation (cuts affected several healing centres that focused on providing support to abused women, such as the Native Women's Shelter of Montreal)
> Action travail des femmes; Alberta Network of Immigrant Women
> Association féminine d'éducation et d'action sociale (AFEAS)
> Canadian Child Care Federation
> Canadian Research Institute for the Advancement of Women (CRIAW)
> Centre de documentation sur l'éducation des adultes et la condition feminine
> Child Care Advocacy Association of Canada
> Conseil d'intervention pour l'accès des femmes au travail (CIAFT)
> Elspeth Heyworth Centre for Women Toronto (funding cut by CIC in December 2010)
> Feminists for Just and Equitable Public Policy (FemJEPP) in Nova Scotia
> First Nations Child and Family Caring Society
> International Planned Parenthood Federation
> Kelowna Women's Resource Centre (KWRC)
> Marie Stopes International (a maternal health agency, has received only a promise of 'conditional' funding IF it avoids any & all connection with abortion)
> MATCH International
> National Association of Women and the Law (NAWL)
> Native Women's Association of Canada
> New Brunswick Coalition for Pay Equity
> Older Women's Network
> Ontario Association of Interval and Transition Houses (OAITH)
> Ontario Coalition for Better Child Care
> Réseau action femmes
> Réseau des Tables régionales de groupes de femmes du Québec
> Riverdale Immigrant Women's Centre, Toronto
> Sisters in Spirit
> South Asian Women's Centre

Status of Women Canada, (mandate also changed to exclude 'gender equality and political justice' and to ban all advocacy, policy research and lobbying)
Tri-Country Women's Centre Society
Womanspace Resource Centre (Lethbridge, Alberta)
Women and Health Protection
Women for Community Economic Development in Southwest Nova Scotia (WCEDSN)
Women's Innovative Justice Initiative –Nova Scotia
Workplace Equity/Employment Equity Program (http://dspace. library.uvic.ca:8080/bitstream/handle/1828/3914/Gina%20Starblan ket%20UVic%20MA%20Thesis%20DSpace.pdf?sequence=3)

75 See Pauktuutit Inuit Women of Canada, 'National Strategy to Prevent Abuse in Inuit Communities' (Ottawa: Pauktuutit Inuit Women of Canada, 2006), http://pauktuutit.ca/wp-content/blogs.dir/1/assets/Inuit Strategy_e.pdf.
76 British Columbia, Missing Women Commission of Inquiry, *Forsaken: The Report of the Missing Women Commission of Inquiry: Executive Summary* (Victoria, BC: The Inquiry, 2012), http://www.ag.gov.bc.ca/public_inquiries/docs/Forsaken-ES.pdf.
77 Manitoba has created an Integrated Task Force for Murdered and Missing Women as a joint effort between the Government of Manitoba, the RCMP, and the Winnipeg Police Services. See Government of Manitoba, 'Integrated Task Force Formed – Cases of Missing and Murdered Women to be Subject of Enhanced Scrutiny' (news release, 26 August 2009), http:// news.gov.mb.ca/news/index.html?item=6621.
78 Jennifer Koshan, 'Aboriginal Women, Justice and the Charter: Bridging the Divide?' (1998) 32(1) *University of British Columbia Law Review* 23 at 1.
79 Diane Majury, 'The Charter, Equality Rights, and Women: Equivocation and Celebration' (2002) 40(3) *Osgoode Hall Law Journal* 297 at 320. Majury observes: 'Violence against women is probably the area in which section 15 has been most frequently argued before the Supreme Court of Canada.' Despite this attention, Aboriginal women, as Aboriginals and women, have not received sustained attention from the courts under the Charter.
80 'The root causes and major sites of violence against Aboriginal women have been theorized too narrowly, and solutions proposed and implemented … have not been responsive to the needs of Aboriginal women.' Jennifer Koshan, 'Sounds of Silence: The Public/Private Dichotomy, Violence and Aboriginal Women,' in *Challenging the Public/Private Divide:*

Feminism, Law, and Public Policy, ed. Susan Boyd (Toronto: University of Toronto Press, 1997) at 88–9. For a broader analysis of Canada's failure to address issues facing Aboriginal women, see Mary Ellen Turpel, 'Patriarchy and Paternalism: The Legacy of the Canadian State for First Nations Women' (1993) 6(1) *Canadian Journal of Women and the Law* 174.

81 See also Sherene H. Razack, 'Gendered Racial Violence and Spatialized Justice: The Murder of Pamela George' (2000) 15(2) *Canadian Journal of Law and Society* 91.

82 *R. v. Sparrow*, [1997] at para. 64.

83 John Borrows, 'Let Obligations Be Done,' in *Let Right Be Done*, ed. Hamar Foster, Heather Raven, and Jeremy Webber (Vancouver: UBC Press, 2007) at 130.

84 *R. v. Sparrow*, [1997] at para. 65.

85 Governments in Canada do not function as watertight compartments within Canada's constitutional scheme. See *AG Canada v. AG Ontario (The Labour Conventions Case)*, [1937] A.C. 326 at 354, [1937] 1 D.L.R. 673.

86 If the constitution does not equalize the Crown's power to infringe Indigenous jurisdiction with Indigenous peoples' power to infringe Crown jurisdiction in a coordinated, harmonized manner, then critiques regarding the unilateral, coercive nature of Crown sovereignty made by the following scholars could be further strengthened. See Gordon Christie, 'Judicial Justification of a Recent Development in Aboriginal Law?' (2002) 17(2) *Canadian Journal of Law and Society* 41; Kent McNeil, 'Extinguishment of Aboriginal Title in Canada: Treaties, Legislation, and Judicial Discretion' (2001–2) 33(2) *Ottawa Law Review* 301; Ardith Walkem and Halie Bruce, eds., *Box of Treasures or Empty Box? Twenty Years of Section 35* (Penticton, BC: Theytus Books, 2003).

87 The dominant judicial approach to Indigenous governance in Canada regards jurisdiction as being exercised through overlapping spheres. See *Starr v. Houlden*, [1990] 1 S.C.R. 1366, 68 D.L.R. (4th) 641. Indigenous governance under section 35(1) should be treated as also operating in ways that overlap with federal and provincial governments.

88 *Constitution Act*, s 35(4). For a discussion of s 35(4)'s place in the constitution, see Maurice Bulbulian, *Dancing Around the Table, Part 1*, Film, and *Dancing Around the Table, Part 2*, Film (Ottawa: National Film Board of Canada, 1987), https://www.nfb.ca/film/dancing_around_the_table_1 & https://www.nfb.ca/film/dancing_around_the_table_part_two.

89 In applying section 35(4), it must be recognized that equality does not always mean identical treatment. Thus, section 35(4) would allow differential treatment in gender relations if such distinctions did not constitute adverse discrimination. This could permit healthy gendered traditions

within Indigenous communities and these would be reinforced by section 25 of the Charter, which prevents important collective rights from being eroded. As Justice Iacobucci observed: 'True equality does not necessarily result from identical treatment.' See *Law v. Canada (Minister of Employment and Immigration)*, [1999] 1 S.C.R. 497 at para. 25, 170 D.L.R. (4th) 1.

90 Some of the contours of section 35(4) could be drawn from Indigenous feminist scholarship. In *R. v. Sparrow*, the Court wrote, 'While it is impossible to give an easy definition of ... rights, it is possible, and, indeed, crucial, to be sensitive to the aboriginal perspective itself on the meaning of the rights at stake' (para. 69). For some examples of Aboriginal women's perspectives related to Aboriginal rights, see Joyce Green, ed., *Making Space for Indigenous Feminism* (Halifax, NS: Fernwood Publishing, 2007); Bonita Lawrence and Kim Anderson, *Strong Women Stories: Native Vision and Community Survival* (Toronto: Sumach Press, 2003).

91 Formal distinctions in treatment will sometimes be necessary to accommodate differences between individuals and thereby produce equal treatment in a substantive sense. See *Andrews v. Law Society of British Columbia*, [1989] 1 S.C.R. 143; *Minority Schools in Albania* (1935), P.C.I.J. (Ser A/B) No 64 at 17; *South West Africa Cases (Ethiopia v South Africa; Liberia v South Africa)*, [1966] I.C.J. Rep 6 at 248. For an excellent discussion of Indigenous women and international human rights, see Rebecca Tsosie, 'Indigenous Women and International Human Rights Law: The Challenges of Colonialism, Cultural Survival, and Self-Determination' (2010) 15(1) *UCLA Journal of International Law and Foreign Affairs* 187.

92 Kathie Dobie, 'Tiny Little Laws: A Plague of Sexual Violence in Indian Country,' *Harper's Magazine* (February 2011), 55, http://harpers.org/archive/2011/02/tiny-little-laws/4/.

93 Michael Penn and Rachel Nardos, *Overcoming Violence against Women and Girls: The International Campaign to Eradicate a Worldwide Problem* (Lanham, MD: Rowan Littlefield, 2003) at 1–13.

94 Some of this pressure is intensified by the inadequacy of federal law in this field. See Kevin Washburn, 'American Indians, Crime and the Law' (2006) 104(4) *Michigan Law Review* 709 at 738.

95 For a discussion of the politics of violence against women, see Jacqui True, *The Political Economy of Violence against Women* (New York: Oxford University Press, 2012).

96 Sarah Deer, Carrie A. Martell, Hallie Bongar White, and Maureen White Eagle, *Tribal Legal Code Resource: Domestic Violence Laws Guide for Drafting or Revising Victim-Centered Tribal Laws against Domestic Violence* (West Hollywood: Tribal Law and Policy Institute, 2012), http://www.tribal-institute.

org/download/Amended%20Domestic_Violence_Code_Resource_2012. pdf.

97 Sarah Deer and Maureen White Eagle, *A Victim-Centered Approach to Sexual Violence and Stalking against Native Women: Resource Guide for Drafting or Revising Tribal Criminal Laws against Sexual Assault and Stalking* (West Hollywood: Tribal Law and Policy Institute, 2012) at 29.

98 See *Hannahville Indian Community Criminal Sexual Conduct Code*, § 1.2084; *Nez Perce Tribal Code*, § 4–1-48; *Little Traverse Bay Band of Odawa Indians*, § 4; *Blackfeet Tribal Law*, c 5, § 9; *Skokomish Tribal Code*, § 9.02A.020; *Fort Peck Comprehensive Code of Justice*, c 2(C), § 224.

99 For examples of provisions outlining concurrent criminal law jurisdiction with the federal government, see *White Mountain Apache Criminal Code*, § 1.2; *White Earth Band of Chippewa Judicial Code* title 1, c 2, § 1.

100 See *Salt River Pima-Maricopa Indian Community Domestic Violence Code*, art I, § B; *Sault Ste Marie Tribal Code*, § 34.102; *Turtle Mountain Band of Chippewa Indians Domestic Violence Code*, § 5000; *Ninilchik Village Ordinance No 99-01*, § 3.

101 For examples of domestic violence provisions, see *Makah Tribal Law and Order Code*, title 11, c 1, § 11.1.04; *Colville Law and Order Code*, c 5–5; *Confederated Tribes of Siletz Indians Domestic and Family Violence Ordinance*, § 12.505; *Kickapoo Tribe in Kansas Domestic Violence Code*, §§ 205(3), (7); *Saginaw Chippewa Domestic Abuse Protection Code*, c 1.241. For examples of tribal court procedures, see *Oglala Sioux Tribal Code*, § 218; *Oglala Sioux Tribe Domestic Violence Code*, § 99.2, c 1, § 214; *Yakama Nation Domestic Violence Code*, c 2, § 2.8. For examples of sanctions and victims' rights, see *Sault Ste Marie Tribal Code*, § 75.103; *Jicarilla Apache Tribe*, c 5, § 3; *White Mountain Apache*, c 6, § 6.3; *Makah Tribal Code*, § 11.4.09(h); *Saginaw Chippewa Domestic Abuse Protection Code*, § 1.2404; *Omaha Tribe of Nebraska, Domestic Violence Code*, § 3.08; *Muscogee (Creek) Nation Code, Domestic and Family Violence*, c 4, §3–401. For examples of protection orders, see *Hopi Family Relations Ordinance*, c 2, § 6.01; *Salt River Pima-Maricopa Indian Community*, § 1; *Nez Perce Tribal Code*, c 7, § 7–3-4; *Muscogee (Creek) Nation*, tit 6, § 3–407(c); *Confederated Tribes of Siletz Tribal Code*, § 12.504; *Ninilchik Village Ordinance No. 99-01*, § 11; *Oglala Sioux Tribe*, § 315; *Turtle Mountain Band of Chippewa Indians, Domestic Violence*, § 3060. For example of prevention and intervention programs, see *Oglala Sioux Tribe Domestic Violence Code*, c 5, §506.

102 *Fort Mojave Indian Reservation Law and Order Code*, art XIII, c A § 1301:

The Fort Mojave Tribal Council finds that:
      a) All persons have the right to live free from domestic violence;
      b) Domestic violence in all its forms poses a major health and law enforcement problem on the Fort Mojave Indian Reservation;

c) Domestic violence can be reduced and deterred through the intervention of law; and

d) There is a need to provide the victims of domestic violence with the protection which the law can provide.

103 *Hopi Family Relations Ordinance*, c 1, § 3.01:

The Hopi Tribal Council finds that:

a) Many persons are subjected to abuse and violence within the family and clan setting;

b) Family members are at risk to be killed or suffer serious physical injury as a result of abuse and violence within the family and clan setting;

c) Children suffer lasting emotional damage as direct targets of abuse and violence, and by witnessing the infliction of abuse and violence on other family and clan members;

d) The elderly Hopi residents are at risk for abuse and violence, the lack of services available for these citizens and the changing family structure indicates that laws are necessary to insure the protection of elders within the family and clan setting, and in their caretaking settings;

e) All persons have the right to live free from violence, abuse, or harassment;

f) Abuse and violence in all its forms poses a major health and law enforcement problem to the Hopi Tribe;

g) Abuse and violence can be prevented, reduced, and deterred through the intervention of law;

h) The legal system's efforts to prevent abuse and violence in the family and clan setting will result in a reduction of negative behaviour outside the family and clan setting;

i) Abuse and violence among family and clan members is not just a 'family matter,' which justified inaction by law enforcement personnel, prosecutors, or courts, but an illegal encounter which requires full application of protective laws and remedies;

j) An increased awareness of abuse and violence, and a need for its prevention, gives rise to the legislative intent to provide maximum protection to victims of abuse and violence in the family and clan setting; and

k) The integrity of the family and clan. Hopi culture and society can be maintained by legislative efforts to remedy abuse and violence.

104 *Northern Cheyenne Indian Reservation*, title VII, §§ 1, 5–10.

105 *Oglala Sioux Tribe Domestic Violence Code*, title 99.2, c 1, § 101: The Oglala
    Sioux Tribe Domestic Violence Code is construed to promote the following:

    1. That violence against family members is not in keeping with tradi-
tional Lakota values. It is the expectation that the criminal justice system respond to victims of domestic violence with fairness, compassion,
and in a prompt and effective manner. The goal of this code is to provide victims of domestic violence with safety and protection.

    2. It is also the goal to utilize the criminal justice system in setting
standards of behaviour within the family that are consistent with traditional Lakota values and, as such, the criminal justice system will be
used to impose consequences upon offenders for behaviours that vio-
late traditional Lakota values that hold women and children as sacred.
These consequences are meant as responses that will allow offenders
the opportunity to make positive changes in their behaviour and understand 'wolakota.'

    3. The prevention of future violence in all families through preven-
tion and public education programs that promote cultural teachings
and traditional Lakota values so as to nurture nonviolence within Lakota families and respect for Lakota women.

106 Donna Coker, 'Enhancing Autonomy for Battered Women: Lessons from
    Navajo Peacemaking' (1999) 47(1) *UCLA Law Review* 1.
107 See, for example, 'Collaboration to End Violence: National Aboriginal Wom-
    en's Forum,' http://www.afn.ca/en/news-media/latest-news/assembly-
    of-first-nations-responds-to-cedaw-report-stating-canada-has-.
108 The United States Department of Justice, Office on Violence Against
    Women, *Tribal Communities* (Washington: U.S. Department of Justice,
    2013), www.ovw.usdoj.gov/tribal.html.
109 United Nations, 'Convention on the Elimination of All Forms of Dis-
    crimination Against Women,' 18 December 1979, Can TS 1982 No 31. See
    also United Nations, Declaration on the Elimination of Violence Against
    Women, GA Res. 48/104, UNGAOR, 48 Sess, UN Doc/A/Res/48/104
    (1993).
110 The United States Department of Justice, Office on Violence Against
    Women, *Tribal Communities*.
111 The United States Department of Justice, Tribal Justice and Safety, *Indian
    Country Accomplishments of the Justice Department* (Washington: U.S.
    Department of Justice, 2013), www.justice.gov/tribal/accomplishments.
    html.
112 The failure to recognize and harmonize Indigenous jurisdiction with
    state and federal jurisdiction is one of the most serious challenges in

dealing with violence against Indigenous women. See Sumayyah Waheed, 'Domestic Violence on the Reservation: Imperfect Laws, Imperfect Solution' (2004) 19(1) *Berkeley Women's Law Journal* 287.

113 If passed, the *SAVE Native Women Act* is designed to 'decrease the incidence of violent crimes against Indian women, to strengthen the capacity of Indian tribes to exercise the sovereign authority of Indian tribes to respond to violent crimes committed against Indian women, and to ensure that perpetrators of violent crimes committed against Indian women are held accountable for that criminal behavior, and for other purposes.' U.S., Bill HR, *Stand Against Violence and Empower Native Women Act* (*SAVE Native Women Act*), 112th Congress, 2011, s. 1763, http://www.indian.senate.gov/news/press-release/senator-daniel-k-akaka-introduces-bill-protect-native-women-against-domestic.

114 See Virginia H. Murray, 'A Comparative Study of the Historic Civil, Common and American Indian Tribal Law Responses to Domestic Violence' (1998) 23 *Oklahoma City University Law Review* 433. Professor Sarah Deer has also written extensively on the issue of tribal law in relation to violence against women; see 'Decolonizing Rape Law: A Native Feminist Synthesis of Safety and Sovereignty' (2009) 24(2) *Wičazo Ša Review* 149; Carrie A. Martell and Sarah Deer, 'Heeding the Voice of Native Women: Toward an Ethic of Decolonization' (2005) 81(4) *North Dakota Law Review* 807; Sarah Deer, 'Sovereignty of the Soul: Exploring the Intersection of Rape Law Reform and Federal Indian Law' (2005) 38(2) *Suffolk University Law Review* 455; Sarah Deer, 'Expanding the Network of Safety: Tribal Protection Orders for Survivors of Sexual Assault' (2004) 4(3) *Tribal Law Journal*; Sarah Deer, 'Toward an Indigenous Jurisprudence of Rape' (2004) 14(1) *Kansas Journal of Law and Public Policy* 121.

115 U.S., Bill HR, *Stand Against Violence and Empower Native Women Act* (*SAVE Native Women Act*), s 1763, http://www.indian.senate.gov/news/press-release/senator-daniel-k-akaka-introduces-bill-protect-native-women-against-domestic at s 201. This provision is designed to redress the U.S. Supreme Court's conclusions that tribal criminal and civil jurisdiction over non-Indians were limited. See, respectively, *Oliphant v. Suquamish Indian Tribe et al.*, 435 U.S. 191 at 196, 98 S Ct 1011 (1978); *Montana et al. v. United States*, 450 U.S. 544 at 564, 101 S Ct 1245 (1981); *Nevada v. Hicks*, 533 U.S. 353 at 359–60, 121 S Ct 2304 (2001).

116 U.S., Bill HR, *Stand Against Violence and Empower Native Women Act* (*SAVE Native Women Act*), s. 1763, http://www.indian.senate.gov/news/press-release/senator-daniel-k-akaka-introduces-bill-protect-native-women-against-domestic at s. 201, amending *Indian Civil Rights Act of 1968*, 25 U.S.C. § 1301–3. For further analysis of the problem of non-Indians and

violence against women, see Amy Radon, 'Tribal Jurisdiction and Domestic Violence: The Need for Non-Indian Accountability on the Reservation' (2004) 37(4) *University of Michigan Journal of Law Reform* 1275.

117 *Violence Against Women Act*, 42 U.S.C. § 13925 (1994).

118 U.S., Bill HR, *Stand Against Violence and Empower Native Women Act* (*SAVE Native Women Act*), s. 1763, http://www.indian.senate.gov/news/press-release/senator-daniel-k-akaka-introduces-bill-protect-native-women-against-domestic at s. 207. See also, Sarah Deer, 'Relocation Revisited: Sex Trafficking of Native Women in the United States' (2010) 36(2) *William Mitchell Law Review* 621.

119 Native Women's Association of Canada, 'What Their Stories Tell Us'; Lavell, 'Combating Violence against Indigenous Women and Girls.'

120 Judith Herman, *Trauma and Recovery* (New York: Basic Books, 1992) at 175–94.

121 Martha Minow, *Between Vengeance and Forgiveness: Facing History after Genocide and Mass Violence* (Boston: Beacon Press, 1998) at 121. However, for a critique of the potential hollowness of acknowledgment without action, see Lee Taft, 'Apology Subverted: The Commodification of Apology' (2000) 109(5) *Yale Law Journal* 1135 at 1158–9.

122 Daniel K. Akaka, *Chairman Akaka Introduces the SAVE Native Women Act* (YouTube, at 1:00), http://www.youtube.com/watch?v=VrXzcXynOd0.

123 U.S., Bill HR, *Stand Against Violence and Empower Native Women Act* (*SAVE Native Women Act*), s. 1763.

124 I have written elsewhere about the grassroots development of Indigenous institutions, norms, and legal traditions. See John Borrows, *Drawing Out Law: A Spirit's Guide* (Toronto: University of Toronto Press, 2010); John Borrows, *Canada's Indigenous Constitution* (Toronto: University of Toronto Press, 2010).

125 The distinction between Aboriginal rights and title was first identified in *R. v. Adams* [1996] 3 S.C.R. 101 at para. 26, 138 D.L.R. (4th) 657. The test for Aboriginal title was first articulated in *Delgamuukw v. British Columbia*, [1997] at para. 143.

126 *R. v. Van der Peet*, [1996].

127 Ibid. at para. 53; *R. v. Pamajewon*, [1996] at para. 25; *Lax Kw'alaams Indian Band v. Canada (Attorney General)*, 2011 S.C.C. 56 at para. 46, 338 D.L.R. (4th) 193.

128 *R. v. Pamajewon*, [1996] at para. 27. For a discussion of this principle in relation to Aboriginal governance, see John Borrows, 'Tracking Trajectories: Aboriginal Governance as an Aboriginal Right' (2005) 38:2 *University of British Columbia Law Review* 285.

129 *R. v. Pamajewon*, [1996] at para. 27.
130 For a discussion of the precise identification of practices upon which rights can be claimed, see *R. v. Sappier; R. v. Gray*, 2006 at paras. 20–4.
131 The characterization of Aboriginal rights often seems to be out of the hands of Aboriginal people, as courts routinely recharacterize claims in order to suit their view of the issue. For a historian's perspective on this process, see Arthur Ray, *Telling It to the Judge: Taking Native History to Court* (Montreal: McGill-Queen's University Press, 2011).
132 *R. v. Van der Peet*, [1996] at para. 46.
133 Ibid. at para. 4; *R. v. Sappier; R. v. Gray*, 2006 at para. 38.
134 Ibid. at para. 39.
135 Aboriginal claims that failed due to lack of precise evidence include *R. v. Van der Peet*, [1996]; *Delgamuukw v. British Columbia*, [1997]; *Mitchell v. Minister of National Revenue*, 2001; *Lax Kw'alaams Indian Band v. Canada (Attorney General)*, 2011.
136 *Lax Kw'alaams Indian Band v. Canada (Attorney General)*, 2011 at para. 46.
137 Aboriginal peoples should not have to publicly shame themselves with detailed proof of violence and effective response to take legislative and judicial action within their communities, particularly when this is an issue that poisons every society. See Charlotte Watts and Catherine Zimmerman, 'Violence against Women: Global Scope and Magnitude' (2002) 359 *Lancet* 1232; UN Study of the Secretary-General, *Ending Violence against Women: From Words to Action* (New York: United Nations Publication, 2006); Andrea Parrot and Nina Cummings, *Forsaken Females: The Global Brutalization of Women* (Oxford: Rowman and Littlefield, 2006).
138 *R. v. Van der Peet*, [1996] at para. 55. See also *Lax Kw'alaams Indian Band v. Canada (Attorney General)*, 2011 at para. 46.
139 Parrot and Cummings, *Forsaken Females*.
140 For a discussion of these stereotypes in law, policy, and the media, see Robert F. Berkhofer, *The White Man's Indian: Images of the American Indian from Columbus to the Present* (New York: Random House, 1978).
141 What if Aboriginal communities somehow failed to produce sufficient evidence of pre-contact violence against women or their associated protections? It seems absurd even to contemplate the implications of such an argument. And even if the Crown managed to prove that Indigenous peoples were free of violence or lacked meaningful protections or sanctions against it, would this mean that such communities could not respond to the current crisis on any meaningful jurisdictional basis today?
142 For a discussion of these stereotypes in law, policy, and the media, see Berkhofer, *The White Man's Indian*.

143 Reconciliation as a constitutional goal within s 35(1) is discussed in *R. v. Van der Peet*, [1996] at paras. 48–9; decolonization as a constitutional goal is expressed in *R. v. Côté*, [1996] at paras. 53, 59; *R. v. Sparrow*, [1997] at para. 65. For a wide-ranging discussion of reconciliation and decolonization, see Paulette Regan, *Unsettling the Settler Within: Indian Residential Schools, Truth Telling, and Reconciliation in Canada* (Vancouver: UBC Press, 2010).

144 For an alternative view, see McIvor, 'Aboriginal Women's Rights as "Existing Rights."'

145 *R. v. Marshall*, [1999] at para. 14.

146 Ibid. at para. 13.

147 Ibid. at para. 78.

148 *R. v. Marshall; R. v. Bernard*, 2005 at paras. 13, 16, 25; *R. v. Morris*, 2006 at paras. 16–32.

149 *R. v. Marshall*, [1999] at para. 19.

150 *R. v. Taylor and Williams*, [1981]; *R. v. Simon*, [1985]; *R. v. Horseman*, [1990] at 907; *R. v. Badger*, [1996] at paras. 4, 41; *R. v. Sundown*, [1999] at paras. 24–5; *R. v. Marshall*, [1999] at paras. 9–14; *R. v. Marshall; R. v. Bernard*, 2005 at para. 26; *R. v. Morris*, 2006 at para. 19.

151 *R. v. Sioui*, [1990] 1 S.C.R. 1025, 70 D.L.R. (4th) 427.

152 Ibid.

153 John J. Borrows, 'A Genealogy of Law: Inherent Sovereignty and First Nations Self-Government' (1992) 30(2) *Osgoode Hall Law Journal* 291; John Borrows, 'Wampum at Niagara: The Royal Proclamation, Canadian Legal History, and Self-Government,' in *Aboriginal and Treaty Rights in Canada: Essays on Law, Equity, and Respect for Difference*, ed. Michael Asch (Vancouver: UBC Press, 1997).

154 For general treaty histories, see Harold Cardinal and Walter Hildebrandt, *Treaty Elders of Saskatchewan: Our Dream is That Our Peoples Will One Day Be Clearly Recognized as Nations* (Calgary: University of Calgary Press, 2000); Treaty 7 Tribal Council, Walter Hildebrandt, Sarah Carter, and Dorothy First Rider, *The True Spirit and Original Intent of Treaty 7* (Montreal: McGill-Queen's University Press, 1996) at 133; René Fumoleau, *As Long as This Land Shall Last: A History of Treaty 8 and Treaty 11* (Calgary: University of Calgary Press, 2004) at 74, 133, 240, 257, 314, 340, 502; Arthur J. Ray, J.R. Miller, and Frank Tough, *Bounty and Benevolence: A History of Saskatchewan Treaties* (Montreal: McGill-Queen's University Press, 2000) at 116–17; William C. Wicken, *Mi'kmaq Treaties on Trial: History, Land and Donald Marshall Junior* (Toronto: University of Toronto Press, 2002).

155 See, generally, J.R. Miller, *Compact, Contract, Covenant: Aboriginal Treaty-Making in Canada* (Toronto: University of Toronto Press, 2009).

156 Silence in treaties is not to be construed against Indians. See *R. v. Marshall; R. v. Bernard* 2005 at para. 104; *R. v. Sioui,* [1990]. Courts require 'strict proof of the fact of extinguishment.' *R. v. Badger,* [1996] at para. 41. The Crown has the onus of proving that it clearly and plainly intended to extinguish an Aboriginal or treaty right and the 'clear and plain' hurdle for extinguishment is quite high. See *R. v. Van der Peet,* [1996] at para. 133. For further discussion of the development of Indian canons of construction, see Leonard Rotman, 'Taking Aim at the Canons of Treaty Interpretation in Canadian Aboriginal Rights Jurisprudence' (1997) 46 *University of New Brunswick Law Journal* 1.

157 *United States v. Winans,* (1905), 198 U.S. 371 at 381, 25 S Ct 662. The U.S. Supreme Court stated, 'In other words, the treaty was not a grant of rights to the Indians, but a grant of rights from them – a reservation of those not granted.'

158 For instance, the legal right for a man to 'beat' his wife was removed from English law only in 1891. See *R. v. Jackson,* [1891] 1 QB 671 at 682, 7 TLR 382 (CA). For a discussion of women's rights under the common law during this period, see Lori Chambers, '"So Entirely Under His Power and Control": The Status of Wives before Reform,' in *Married Women and Property Law in Victorian Ontario,* ed. Lori Chambers (Toronto: The Osgoode Society for Canadian Legal History, 1997) at 14; Sarah Carter, 'Categories and Terrains of Exclusion: Constructing the "Indian Woman" in the Early Settlement Era in Western Canada,' in *Telling Tales: Essays in Western Women's History,* ed. Catherine Cavanaugh and Randi Warne (Vancouver: UBC Press, 2000) at 60; Constance Backhouse, *Carnal Crimes: Sexual Assault Law in Canada, 1900–1975* (Toronto: The Osgoode Society for Canadian Legal History, 2008); Constance Backhouse, *Petticoats & Prejudice: Women and Law in Nineteenth-Century Canada* (Toronto: The Osgoode Society, 1991).

159 For insight into eyewitness interpretations of these agreements, see Peter Erasmus, *Buffalo Days and Nights* (Calgary: Glenbow-Alberta Institute, 1976) at 248–9; Alexander Morris, *The Treaties of Canada with the Indians of Manitoba and the North-West Territories Including the Negotiations on Which they are Based, and Other Information Relating Thereto* (Toronto: Willing and Williamson, 1880) at 101–2.

160 *R. v. Marshall,* [1999].

161 *Beattie v. Canada (Minister of Indian Affairs and Northern Development),* 1998 1 FC 104, [1997] FCJ 745; *Mississaugas of Scugog Island First Nation, supra; Conseil des Innus de Pessamit v. Assoc des policiers et policières de Pessamit,* 2010 FCA 306, [2010] FCJ No 1377; *R. v. Pamajewon,* [1996].

162 Treaties 'cannot be wholly transformed' by engaging in an 'extended interpretation' of their original meaning. See *R. v. Marshall,* [1999] at para. 19.

This view was reinforced in *R. v. Bernard*, 2005where the S.C.C. observed that an Aboriginal group's historic 'activity must be essentially the same' as that occurring the in past in order for it to receive recognition. See 2005 S.C.C. 43 at para. 25, [2005] 2 S.C.R. 220.

163 See John Borrows, '(Ab)Originalism and Canada's Constitution' (2012) 58 *Supreme Court Law Review 351* (for a discussion of the ideas developed in this section). The argument in the next three paragraphs, including reproduction of selected arguments in the text and footnotes, is derived from the same source.

164 At significant points in history, Indigenous peoples have also understood their constitutional relations in living-tree terms. See William N. Fenton, *The Great Law and the Longhouse: A Political History of the Iroquois Confederacy* (Norman: University of Oklahoma Press, 1998) at 73, 103.

165 As Justice McLachlin wrote in *Mitchell v. Minister of National Revenue*, 2001, 'European settlement did not terminate the interests of aboriginal peoples arising from their historical occupation and use of the land. To the contrary, aboriginal interests and customary laws were presumed to survive the assertion of sovereignty, and were absorbed into the common law as rights' (*Mitchell v. Minister of National Revenue*, 2001 at para. 10).

166 Chief Justice Lamer observed that imperial powers treated Indians as independent nations. *R. v. Sioui*, [1990] at para. 69.

167 *Haida Nation v. British Columbia (Minister of Forests)*, 2004 S.C.C. 73, [2004] 3 S.C.R. 511 at para. 32.

168 Felix S. Cohen, *Handbook of Federal Indian Law* (Washington: U.S. Department of the Interior, 1942) at 122–3; Charles Wilkinson, *American Indians, Time and the Law* (New Haven: Yale University Press, 1987) at 60.

169 For example, these powers were evident in *Calder v. AGBC*, wherein Justice Judson wrote, 'The fact is that when the settlers came, the Indians were there, organized in societies and occupying the land as their forefathers had done for centuries.' Organization is essential to governance; see John Borrows, 'Tracking Trajectories: Aboriginal Governance as an Aboriginal Right' (2005) 38(2) *University of British Columbia Law Review* 285 at 292–3.

170 Robert A. Williams Jr., 'Gendered Checks and Balances: Understanding the Legacy of White Patriarchy in an American Indian Cultural Context' (1990) 24(4) *Georgia Law Review* 1019.

171 The reserved rights theory of Aboriginal governance is also consistent with the proposition articulated by the S.C.C. in *R. v. Van der Peet*, [1996] at para. 30.

172 However, it has been held that 'discovery' diminished Indian rights to land. See *Guerin v. Canada* [1984] 2 S.C.R. 335 at para. 88, 13 D.L.R. (4th) 321.

173 Chief Justice Lamer expressed hesitation in applying the 'integral to a distinctive culture' test to the claim of self-government. See *Delgamuukw v. British Columbia*, [1997] at paras. 170–1.

174 Slattery, 'The Generative Structure of Aboriginal Rights,' at 20–48.

175 Carrie Menkel-Meadow, 'Unsettling the Lawyers: Other Forms of Justice in Indigenous Claims of Expropriation, Abuse, and Injustice' (2014) 64(3) *University of Toronto Law Journal* 620–40.

176 Val Napoleon, *Ayook: Gitksan Legal Order, Law and Legal Theory* (PhD diss., University of Victoria, 2009), https://dspace.library.uvic.ca:8443/bitstre am/handle/1828/1392/napoleon%20dissertation%20April%2026-09. pdf?sequence=1.

177 Indigenous law exists alongside the common law and the civil law in Canada in regulating behaviour and resolving disputes; John Borrows, *Canada's Indigenous Constitution* (Toronto: University of Toronto Press, 2010).

178 Andrea Smith, 'Not an Indian Tradition: The Sexual Colonization of Native Peoples' (2003) 18(2) *Hypatia* 70.

179 Val Napoleon, Hadley Friedland, and Emily Snyder, eds., *Thinking About and Practicing with Indigenous Legal Traditions: One Approach: A Community Handbook* [on file with author].

180 The teaching of Indigenous legal traditions in Canadian law schools must also draw on the insights developed in this chapter. Traditions can be liberating if they are seen as living frameworks for action that place at their heart the elimination of violence against women in all its forms. Problems arise when traditions are essentialized and not analysed in light of Aboriginal peoples' experiences of intersectionality, subjectivity, and unequal social positioning – particularly as they relate to women. Traditions are also troubling when people are excluded from participating in their ongoing reconstruction based on stereotypes and misunderstandings arising out of the system's larger structures. This chapter has critiqued Canada's misinterpretation and misuse of its traditions in marginalizing Aboriginal women on both of these points. As a result, it has shown how Canada's own legal traditions related to violence against women are discriminatory in the extreme. The same critique could be applied in teaching and practising Indigenous legal traditions that do not take account of these points. Gender and the elimination of violence against women is a necessary site of inquiry and action for working with Indigenous peoples' own laws. Tradition, whether Aboriginal or Canadian, must not be essentialized or regarded as being homogeneous, objective, neutral, or necessarily equality enhancing just because it is 'tradition.' We must constantly subject all our laws to these inquiries in order to ensure that all to whom they apply are safe from violence in any form.

Conclusion

1 Basil Johnston, *Ojibway Heritage* (Toronto: McClelland and Stewart, 1976) at 128–31. The story is also found in William Jones, *Ojibwa Texts*, vol. 12, part 2 (New York: E.J. Brill, 1917) at 307–8. The story was dictated by John Pinesi (Gaagige-pinesi) of Fort William to Fox anthropologist William Jones, who spoke Mesquakie, a language related to Anishinaabemowin. The story was written down in 1907 or 1908. Another version of the story is written by Henry Schoolcraft, *The Myth of Hiawatha and Other Oral Legends* (Philadelphia: J.P. Lippincott and Co., 1856) at 109–12.

2 For a description of the expectations that arose in the history between generations of my family, see John Borrows, 'A Genealogy of Law: Inherent Sovereignty and First Nations Self-Government' (1992) 30 *Osgoode Hall Law Journal* 29.

3 She had spent her lifetime learning different traditions through family and friends. As she prepared to attend college, I was happy to know that she would discover new dimensions of life. While I was very excited for her, I was also concerned about the pressures she might encounter along the way. False horizons, including the ones she picked up at home, can be thrust upon us, causing us to question our identities and limit our growth. While I was very confident in her abilities, I wanted to ensure she knew she had the power to live freely and live well. Fortunately, there was nothing to worry about. Through years of moving with her family, and listening to hundreds of stories, she had internalized many important lessons surrounding these issues. She had learned she could excel, be happy, and be her best self no matter where she lived.

4 Jennifer Borrows, 'Generative Fathering Among the Canadian Chippewa: Narrative Accounts of the Circle of Life' (master's thesis, Brigham Young University, 1996) [unpublished]:

> This research concerns how successful Chippewa fathers care for and connect with their children. This research assists therapists, educators and researchers in gaining knowledge regarding culturally appropriate indicators through the symbols found within Chippewa culture. The research flows from interviews with 14 participants. The interviews demonstrated how Chippewa fathers participated in generative fathering with their children, in line with a model developed by Dr. Dollahite and others. It explains that father's work carries with it the following responsibilities: commit, choose, create, consecrate, care, change, connect, and communicate. The Chippewa fathers interviewed were helping to nurture the next generation through

developing relationships with nature, teaching wisdom traditions and being agents of change.

See also Jennifer Borrows, 'The Chippewa Experience with the Therapy Process: Stepping Stones to Healing' (PhD diss., Kansas State University, 2000) [unpublished]. The abstract of the dissertation states,

> The treatment of the Canadian Anishinabe people, commonly referred to as Chippewa, presents unique challenges to mental health service providers and researchers. There has been a need to understand the First Nations peoples' perception of therapies and the healing process to ensure that services providers will help, not harm, this population. This study employed a hybrid of ethnographical and phenomenological methods to collect experiences of therapy/healing from ten Chippewa participants from a band in Southern Ontario. Information was collected by interviews and field observations. Many Chippewa people sought services as a result of oppression and both present and historical trauma. Common healing experiences, which were identified, included requiring the service provider to heal him or herself, be trustworthy, be non-judgmental, know the bands historical trauma, use silence, and listen. Many left or returned to the reservation to begin the healing process. They attended traditional ceremonies with the goal of being in harmony with nature. Follow-up services were important. A wide variety of mental health services were accessed. Both mainstream methods and Chippewa 'traditional' means have been utilized by all the participants. Different modes of services had specific functions at different stages in their healing journeys. Healing integrated holistic (i.e. spiritual) elements. Substance abuse had been used to deal with grief. The reasons for attending therapy/healing were to connect with self, connect with the band/community and to connect to the Chippewa culture. Participants felt the duty to assist others in the healing process, as they started to heal themselves. Participants, who had used family therapy services, were more likely to access them during times of crisis and did not expect to attend more than four sessions. Implications included marriage and family therapists' networking with multiple services providers, evaluating the trajectory of healing frequently, and being available for follow-up services. Implications and ideas for future research were outlined.

5 When telling a story using this methodology, a hearer must 'sit with' the concepts in the narrative for a while before re-engaging with the storyteller. At some later point, after a period of reflection, it might be appropriate to

seek the storyteller's reasons for their narrative – but it must not be done too soon. There is no *a priori* way of knowing when it is 'too soon' for hearer and listener to re-engage after a story has been told. In exceptional cases, it might be a few minutes or many years; in most cases, it will be sooner to ensure that the lesson does not get lost.

6 The story is meant to illustrate the book's themes by encouraging the reader to compare and contrast it with their own experiences, and those discussed elsewhere in these pages, to determine what freedom might be enhanced in their own and others' lives. For a discussion of how perspicuous contrast and vocabularies of comparison can be an important learning method, see Charles Taylor, *Philosophy and the Human Sciences* (Cambridge: Cambridge University Press, 1985) at 116–33; Charles Taylor, 'The Politics of Recognition,' in *Multiculturalism and the Politics of Recognition*, ed. Amy Gutman and Charles Taylor (Princeton, NJ: Princeton University Press, 1992); John Borrows, 'Constitutional Law From a First Nations Perspective' (1994) *University of British Columbia Law Review* 1 at 1–10.

Index